FIRST BOSTON'S
DESKTOP GUIDE TO THE
FIXED INCOME SECURITIES
M·A·R·K·E·T

HARRY KAVROS

PROBUS PUBLISHING COMPANY
CHICAGO, ILLINOIS

This publication is designed to provide accurate and authoritative information in regard to the subject matter covered. It is sold with the understanding that the publisher is not engaged in rendering legal, accounting or other professional service. If legal advice or other expert assistance is required, the services of a competent professional person should be sought.

FROM A DECLARATION OF PRINCIPLES JOINTLY ADOPTED BY A COMMITTEE OF THE AMERICAN BAR ASSOCIATION AND A COMMITTEE OF PUBLISHERS.

Library of Congress Cataloging-in-Publication Data Available

ISBN 1-55738-046-5

Printed in the United States of America

1   2   3   4   5   6   7   8   9   0

Contents

Introduction

Often in the course of human events words become so varied and complex that no single person, whether layman or expert, can hope to understand them all. These are the times that demand dictionaries. In the third century B.C. a Greek named Philotas was the earliest known scholar to feel the pressure to collect and define words for easy retrieval. The result was the first dictionary—*Miscellaneous Difficult Words*. His student Zenodotus had the then brilliant idea of alphabetizing the entries. His dictionary, *Difficult Words*, was one of the prizes of the great library at Alexandria. Zenodotus' student Aristophanes of Byzantium greatly expanded the entries. His dictionary had the simplest title of them all—*Words*.

Two thousand years later in this great tradition came Samuel Johnson, who did for an expanding English language in the eighteenth century what his lexicographical ancestors did for Greek. For his nine years of hard work in a dingy room he received high praise, in person, from King George III. In the next century Noah Webster, reacting to English affectations and vulgarity, compiled the American dictionary many of us still use.

More recently, the bond market community has been treated to an increasingly vast array of vivid, colorful, idiomatic, and often puzzling terms. Much of this terminology has flourished primarily in an oral tradition, shouted from trader to trader or heard on the street. *The First Boston Bond Market Reference Guide* defines a wide range of these terms, both common and uncommon. Of course, new words are coined every day, and they are often hoarded by specialists. We cannot hope to have included them all. Also, glossary entries are by definition concise. We do not try to provide the volumes of background material that exist elsewhere. We cross reference extensively because readers are likely to encounter financial terms in a variety of forms.

Appendix 1 provides an overview of U.S. government and agency securities. Appendix 2 is a guide to money market securities. Appendix 3, which lists terms by category, is designed to help those readers who specialize or want to master an area of the market. Appendix 4 contains common abbreviations and acronyms. Those still undaunted will want to peruse Appendix 5, which explains the origins of over 150 bond market terms.

The editor would like to thank his colleagues at First Boston, too numerous to mention here, whose patience he tried while tapping their expertise. The Fixed Income Research Department contributed Appendix 1. Appendix 2, written by the Economist Department, originally appeared in First Boston's 1988 publication, *Handbook of Securities of the United States Government and Federal Agencies and Related Money Market Instruments.* Dexter Senft improved most of the entries.

A

Abandon—To allow an option contract to expire unexercised.

Abatement—The cancellation, in whole or in part, of a government tax.

A-B-C Agreement—Agreement between an employee of a brokerage firm and the firm outlining the terms of the purchase of a seat on the New York Stock Exchange for the employee. Only an individual can be a member of the NYSE.

Ability-to-Pay—The principle that tax levels should be determined by those who can pay rather by those who can benefit. *See* Benefit Received.

Aboriginal Cost—The cost of an asset to the first entity putting it to public use. Public utility accounting is based on aboriginal cost, lest one utility raise its rate base after acquiring an asset from another utility.

Above Par—Refers to a security that is selling for more than its face value.

Above the Market—Refers to a security or to a sell order with a price greater than the market offering price.

Above Water—Refers to a security whose market value is greater than its book or acquisition value. *See* Below Water.

Absolute Prepayment Rate (ABS)—Prepayment rate expressed as a percentage of the original collateral amount, as opposed to the outstanding collateral amount. ABS is used for automobile receivables.

Absolute Rate—In the context of Euronotes, a bid made that is not expressed in relation to a particular funding base (e.g., LIBOR). For example, 10.05% as opposed to LIBOR + 0.05% (if LIBOR equals 10%) is an absolute rate.

Absorbed—New issue securities that have been distributed. *See* Undigested.

Abstinence Theory—Theory that interest is the compensation to lenders for refraining from current spending. Also called *Agio Theory*.

A/B Structure—*See* Senior/Subordinated Pass-Through.

Accelerated Depreciation—Any method to calculate depreciation, such as double declining balance and sum-of-the-years' digits methods, in which the charges progressively decrease. *See* Double Declining Balance and Sum-of-the-Years' Digits.

Accelerated Remittance Cycle (ARC)—FHLMC agreement to decrease the management and guarantee fee in return for remitting principal and interest payments early.

Acceleration Clause—A mortgage clause requiring payment in full when a covenant is broken.

Acceleration Feature—*See* Acceleration Clause.

Accelerationist Theory—Economic theory that the inverse relationship between unemployment and inflation holds only in the short term, because unemployment in the long term is controlled by non-fiscal factors such as labor supply, labor unions, and demand. *See* Phillips Curve, Fiscal Policy, and Say's Law.

Acceleration Principle—Economic principle that a rise in demand causes a corresponding rise in investment.

Accelerator—A macroeconomic constant equal to change in investment divided by change in demand.

Acceptance—A written promise to pay a debt. *See* Bankers' Acceptance.

Acceptance Ratio—*See* Placement Ratio.

Accommodative—Refers to Federal Reserve monetary policy intended to increase the money supply.

Account—1) Any retail customer. 2) The entire group of underwriters in any one offering.

Accountancy—British term for accounting.

Account Executive—*See* Registered Representative.

Accounting—A system of financial information about economic entities.

Accounting Current Yield—Yield on a mortgage-related security that takes prepayments into consideration, calculated as the coupon minus the product of the prepayment rate and the premium, divided by the price.

Accounting Cycle—The series of accounting procedures from journal entry to financial statements.

Accounting Equation—Assets equal liabilities plus owners' equity. Also called *Balance Sheet Equation.*

Accounting Period—The interval covered by the income statement and the statement of changes in financial position.

Accounting Rate of Return—Income (rather than discounted cash flows) divided by average investment for a period.

Account Payable—A liability, typically a current liability representing a purchase.

Account Receivable—A claim against a debtor, typically a current asset representing a sale. Also called *Receivable.*

Accounts Receivable Turnover—The number of times in each accounting period that credits are converted into cash, calculated as annual credit sales divided by average amount of receivables.

Accredited Investor—As defined by Regulation D of the Securities Act of 1933, accredited investors are 1) financial institutions, large tax-exempt plans, and private business development companies, 2) directors, executive officers, or general partners of the issuer, or 3) investors with a minimum net worth of $1 million, or an annual income of $200,000, or who use no more than 20% of their net worth to buy at least $150,000 of an investment. Regulation D allows an unlimited number of accredited investors, but only 35 non-accredited investors, to purchase securities through a private placement.

Accretion—The addition of value over a period of time. Accretion results in an increase of accounting worth, while amortization results in a decrease. In portfolio accounting, discount bonds are accreted to par while premium bonds are amortized to par.

Accretion Bond—*See* Accrual Bond.

Accretion Termination Date—The first principal payment date for accrual bonds.

Accrual—An accounting method that reports costs as expenses in the period in which the associated revenues are recognized. The accrual method of accounting is often considered more accurate and useful than the cash basis method because revenues more accurately reflect sales activity and because expenses are associated with the appropriate revenues. With the accrual method, bond interest may accrue on a corporation's books each month even though it is paid semiannually. *See* Cash Basis.

Accrual Accounting—*See* Normalized Accounting.

Accrual Bond—Deferred coupon tranche of a CMO. An accrual bond receives payments of neither principal nor interest until all tranches preceding it are retired. In effect, an accrual bond is a deferred interest obligation, resembling a zero coupon bond prior to the time that the preceding tranches are retired, except that accrual bonds carry an explicit coupon rate. The accrual bond then receives cash payments representing interest and principal on the accrued amount outstanding. Accrual bonds are purchased most frequently by investors who require the greatest degree of protection against reinvestment and call risk, or who seek the greater price leverage afforded by these classes. Also called *Accretion Bond* and *Z Bond.*

Accrual Date—Date on which the accrued rate on an adjustable or variable rate mortgage is reset.

Accrual Factor—*See* Z Factor.

Accrual Rate—Interest rate used to compute interest accrued on an adjustable rate mortgage; when borrower's monthly payment is less than interest accrued, negative amortization will occur. *See* Negative Amortization.

Accrued Depreciation—*See* Accumulated Depreciation.

Accrued Interest—Interest earned from the last interest payment to the present, but not yet due and payable. The buyer of a bond pays the seller accrued interest.

Accumulated Depreciation—The sum of an asset's depreciation charges. Also called *Allowance for Depreciation.* Incorrectly called Accrued Depreciation and Reserve for Depreciation.

Accrued Dividend—A dividend of cumulative preferred stock that is due but not yet paid.

Accumulated Interest—Past due interest payments.

Accumulation—Investment of a fixed amount at regular intervals in a mutual fund.

Accumulation Account—An account in which a unit investment trust places securities until they are deposited into the trust. *See* Bond Fund and Unit Investment Trust.

Accumulation Area—A price range in which buyers accumulate. *See* Distribution Area.

Accumulator—An investor whose goal is to acquire as much of a specific issue as possible in order to control the floating supply of the issue and thereby affect its market value. Typically associated with sinking fund securities.

Acid Test Ratio—A measure of liquidity, defined as the sum of cash, marketable securities, and accounts receivable divided by current liabilities. Also called *Quick-Asset Ratio.*

Acquisition—Taking control of a corporation.

Acquisition Date—Date of purchasing an asset. Also called *Trade Date*. *See* Settlement Date.

Across the Board—A market trend that affects almost all securities in the same way.

Acting in Concert—More than one investor trying to affect the market for the same purpose.

Active—1) Refers to a market with frequent transactions. 2) In reference to sinking funds, those that are currently operating. 3) Owning more than 20% of a corporation's stock, thus having a controlling interest. *See* Passive.

Active Account—An account in which securities are frequently traded.

Active Bond Crowd—Traders whose transactions are usually in actively traded bonds. Also called *Free Crowd*. *See* Cabinet Crowd.

Active Box—Vault of a broker-dealer containing securities used as collateral for broker or customer account financing.

Active Management—A portfolio strategy of aggressively managing assets to take advantage of market opportunities. *See* Passive Management.

Actual Cost—Historical cost. Also called *Basis*.

Actual Delay—*See* Payment Delay.

Actual Reserves—Liquid assets that a bank has in its vaults and in its reserve account in its Federal Reserve Bank. *See* Excess Reserves.

Actual Return—A holding period return that is not annualized, defined as the sum of all proceeds received from an investment (including any reinvestment income) divided by the cost of the investment.

Actuals—The commodities or securities that underlie futures, forwards, or options contracts. Also called *Cash, Spot*, or *Physicals*.

Actuarial—Referring to calculations involving compound interest and/or probabilities.

Actuarial Interest as Scheduled—*See* Effective Interest.

Actuarial Rate—The rate of return, as specified by an actuary, that allows a pension plan's assets to cover its liabilities.

Actuarial Yield—In the case of serial bonds, the redemption yield on a bond assuming it is held until redemption and that all coupon and principal repayments will occur as provided in the terms and conditions of the issue. *See* Serial Security.

Actuary—A mathematician who calculates data for insurance companies, such as premiums, dividends, and annuity rates. Calculations are based on statistics in experience tables.

Additional Bonds Test—A provision of a revenue bond covenant in which an additional issue can be approved only if past revenues and, in some cases, estimated revenues exceed projected debt service requirements by a specified amount.

Additional Paid-In Capital—*See* Paid-In Surplus.

Add-Ons—Treasury securities added on to the announced size of public auctions and sold to official foreign institutions.

Adequate Consideration—A requirement of valid contracts according to which all parties must provide something of value (quid pro quo).

Adequate Disclosure—Auditing standard of stating all material information on financial statements.

Adjustable Rate Convertible Note (ARCN)—Floating rate debt security issued at a premium and exchangeable for common stock equal in value to the issue price of the note.

Adjustable Rate Index—Benchmark for computing interest on adjustable rate mortgages.

Adjustable Rate Mortgage (ARM)—A mortgage whose interest rate is periodically readjusted to reflect movements in market interest rates. ARMs are usually tied to a government index, with limitations on the rate change within a period and a rate cap for the life of the loan. *See* Variable Rate Mortgage (VRM).

Adjustable Rate Preferred Stock (ARP)—A type of floating rate preferred stock whose dividend rate is reset quarterly at a given spread to an "applicable rate." Since March 1984, the applicable rate has been the highest yield of three Treasury rates: the 3-month Treasury bill discount rate and the yield levels of the 10-year and 20-year constant maturity issues. The determination of the applicable rate is based on a 2-week average of each of these rates prior to the reset date. The first ARP was issued in May 1982.

Adjusted Aggregate Exercise Value—The exercise price of GNMA options, taking into consideration the different coupon rates on all GNMA mortgages and the fact that the delivering party may submit a par amount ranging from $97,500 to $102,500. One purpose of the Adjusted Aggregate Exercise Value was to remove the incentive to over- or under-deliver. The GNMA CDR contract no longer exists.

Adjusted Basis—The price of a security used to calculate capital gains or losses, taking into consideration commission costs and stock splits.

Adjusted Debit Balance (ADB)—The amount a client owes a broker plus any special miscellaneous account adjusted for paper gains on short accounts.

Adjusted Duration—*See* Modified Duration.

Adjusted Trade—A violation of SEC and MSRB rules in which a dealer and an investor purchase securities from each other at above market prices.

Adjustment Bond—*See* Income Bond.

Adjustment Frequency—*See* Reset Frequency.

Ad Valorem Tax—A tax levied according to the value of the taxed item.

Advance/Decline Index—Any measure of advancing issues versus declining issues, typically the number of advancing issues divided by the number of declining issues, used as a measure of market sentiment.

Advance Refunding—A financing technique that permits an issuer to replace outstanding debt with new debt. To do so, an issuer sells new debt and invests the proceeds in U.S. government securities, the principal and interest from which will be sufficient to pay the entire debt service on the outstanding debt. Such securities may provide funds until maturity, in which case they are said to be escrowed to maturity, or until the first call date. It is referred to as "advance" refunding because an issuer is able to realize the advantages of refunding before the outstanding bonds are callable. For almost all tax-exempt advance refundings, the outstanding debt is legally defeased.

Advances Option—An option given to underwriters who are required to purchase notes at a predetermined rate, or maximum margin, to make a short-term advance instead of purchasing the note.

Adverse Opinion—Auditor's report claiming that a corporation's financial statements do not include all material information or do not follow generally accepted accounting principles.

Advertisement—In securities law, any material used in any public media. Letters are considered advertisements if more than ten similar letters are sent to clients.

Affiliated Corporation—A corporation that controls or is controlled by another corporation.

Affiliated Person—*See* Insider.

Affirmation—An institutional investor's acknowledgment that the dealer's confirmation of a trade is correct. *See* Dealer's Confirmation and National Institutional Delivery System.

African Development Bank—*See* Development Bank.

After Acquired Clause—Clause in the indenture of a mortgage bond stating that any property acquired after the bond is issued will become additional security for the bond, unless the bondholders agree to waive this provision.

After Hours Trading—Trading over-the-counter securities when the exchanges are closed.

After Market—The secondary market immediately after an issue is free to trade. *See* Secondary Market.

After-Tax Yield—The net return a bond earns after income taxes are paid on interest income and capital gains taxes are assessed on changes in book value. It is common practice to disregard any long-term capital losses in calculating after-tax yield.

Against Actuals—*See* Exchange for Physicals.

Against the Box—Selling short a security an investor owns.

Aged Fail—A trade that has failed for 30 days or more.

Agency—1) An agency chartered by the U.S. government to serve public purposes specified by the Congress. *See* Government National Mortgage Association (GNMA), Federal National Mortgage Association (FNMA), Federal Home Loan Mortgage Corporation (FHLMC), the Federal Farm Credit System, the Federal Home Loan Bank System, the Export-Import Bank, the Small Business Administration (SBA), the Student Loan Marketing Association (SLMA), Washington Metropolitan Transit Authority (WMTA), and the Tennessee Valley Authority (TVA). 2) The debt of such an agency. Payment of principal and interest may or may not be guaranteed by the full faith and credit of the U.S. government itself.

Agency Cross—A clean trade for a municipal securities broker. *See* Clean.

Agency for International Development (AID)—U.S. government agency that helps developing countries finance low-cost housing. AID securities are backed by the full faith and credit of the U.S. government.

Agency Trade—A transaction in which the trader acts as an agent for the seller or buyer and is paid a commission that is specifically identified on the customer's confirmation.

Agent—A person who acts on behalf of another (the principal) and is subject to his control and authority.

Agent Bank—1) In the context of floating rate securities, an agent bank determines the interest rate on such securities at each fixing. 2) In the context of short-term Euronote and CD facilities, an agent bank may be responsible for the issuing and paying agent functions as well as for the normal functions of an agent bank-to-bank loan.

Aggregate Demand—Total amount of goods and services demanded in the economy, given current prices and incomes. Also called *Total Spending.*

Aggregate Exercise Price—An option's strike price times the number of options in the contract. For GNMA, Treasury bill, Treasury note, and Treasury bond options, the aggregate exercise price is the strike price times the face value of the underlying contract.

Aggregate Indebtedness—A broker-dealer's total debt to customers.

Aggregate Supply—Total amount of goods and services supplied to the market at prevailing prices. Also called *Total Output.*

Aggressive Portfolio—A portfolio whose goal is price appreciation.

Agio Theory—*See* Abstinence Theory.

Agreement Among Managers—In the context of a Eurobond issue, an agreement to which all the managers are parties, which both stipulates the rights and obligations of each manager with respect to the joint and several rights and obligations of the management group as a whole and delegates certain powers to the lead manager.

Agreement Among Underwriters (AAU)—The legal document that binds underwriters together into a syndicate and grants the managing underwriters the power to act on behalf of the group.

AIBD Yield—Yield of a bond calculated using the AIBD method (non-annual payments of interest are compounded so as to give annual equivalent). Thus, a 10% bond with semiannual payments traded at 100% has an AIBD yield of 10.25%.

AID Call—*See* Any-Interest-Date Call.

Air Pocket—Refers to a security whose price falls suddenly.

Aladdin Bond—A new issue that a corporation exchanges for an existing issue.

Alien Corporation—A corporation incorporated under the laws of a country other than that in which it operates.

All-Capital Earnings Rate—Rate of return on assets.

All Financial Resources—Total assets minus total liabilities.

Alligator Spread—An option spread rendered unprofitable by commission costs.

All-In Cost—Percentage cost of debt to an issuer after underwriting expenses.

Allocate—To spread costs among several accounts, products, or periods.

Allonge—A blank piece of paper added to a certificate for signatures.

All or Any Part (AOAP)—Trade order instruction to execute as bids or offers become available until the order is filled.

All or None (AON)—1) Underwriting agreement stating that no securities will be issued unless all are purchased. 2) An order to be executed only in its entirety.

Allotment—Distribution of securities by the lead manager among members of a syndicate.

Allowance for Funds Used During Construction (AFUDC)—Capitalized interest for construction costs.

Alpha—1) The premium a portfolio earns if the market rate of return is equal to that of the Treasury bill. Positive alpha means that the portfolio has outperformed Treasuries. 2) The value added by a portfolio manager, calculated as (Portfolio Return—Risk Free Rate) - Beta × (Market Return - Risk Free Rate). *See* Beta.

Alternative Cost—*See* Opportunity Cost.

Alternative Mortgage Instrument (AMI)—A non-traditional mortgage. A mortgage is considered to be an AMI if it has one or more of the following characteristics:

- A variable interest rate.
- Graduating payments.
- Non-monthly payments (e.g., biweekly).
- A buydown or other payment subsidy.
- A shared appreciation feature.
- Any option other than the option to prepay.

Alternative Order—A simultaneous limit and stop order for the same security. Because alternative orders may not combine buy and sell orders, the execution of the limit (or stop order) requires the cancellation of the stop order (or limit). Also called *Either-Or Order* or *One Cancels Other (OCO)*. *See* Stop Order.

Ambulance Stock—Stock sold by a Japanese brokerage firm to a client in financial distress. The term refers to the common practice in Japan of brokerage firms rescuing troubled clients by then promoting the stock to encourage a significant rise in price.

American Depository Receipt (ADR)—A negotiable certificate receipt issued by an American depository stating that a certain number of foreign securities have been deposited with an overseas branch of the depository or with a custodian. ADRs are denominated in U.S. dollars and trade on the New York and other stock exchanges. Dividends are paid to the depository bank, which deducts foreign withholding taxes, converts them into dollars, and distributes the balance to the security owners.

American Municipal Bond Assurance Corporation (AMBAC)—Corporation that guarantees principal and interest payments on municipal securities.

American Option—A contract that gives the holder the right to buy from or sell to the writer of the option a specified amount of securities or commodities at a specific price, good for a specified period of time. An American Option may be exercised at any time prior to its maturity, whereas a European Option is exercisable only on its maturity date.

American Stock Exchange (AMEX)—The second largest stock exchange in the United States by trading volume. Located in New York City's financial district, the AMEX is often referred to as the Curb due to its origin in a Manhattan street. Most stocks and bonds traded on the AMEX are those of medium-size companies. *See* Exchange.

Americus Trust—A unit investment trust authorized to issue units in exchange for validly tendered shares of eligible securities. The units are divisible into two parts: the prime component, which entitles holders to the income from the underlying shares; and the score component, which entitles holders to the appreciation from the underlying shares. *See* Unit Investment Trust.

Amortization—1) The gradual extinguishment of any amount over a period of time, as in the periodic writedown of a bond premium to par, or of a mortgage balance to zero. *See* Depreciation and Accretion. 2) The scheduled principal portion of a mortgage payment.

Announcement Date—*See* Launch Date.

And Interest—Term signifying that accrued interest is included in a security's price.

Annual Equivalent—The yield of a bond that pays more frequently than once per year expressed in annual terms. Used to compare the yields of semiannual bonds, such as U.S. Treasuries, with annual bonds, such as Eurodollar bonds.

Annualize—To express a rate of return as a yearly percentage.

Annually Compounded Yield—Yield calculated under the assumption that interest is reinvested annually. *See* Yield to Maturity.

Annual Percentage Rate (APR)—The effective cost of funds for a loan, taking into consideration not only the stated interest rate but also points, payment frequency, and term to maturity.

Annual Report—Annual corporate financial statement that shows assets, liabilities, revenues, and expenses as of year end. Also gives yearly earnings and profits as well as other information of interest to stockholders.

Annual Return—A holding period return that has been annualized. It is computed by expressing the actual return on a per annum basis, adjusting for the desired compounding frequency.

Annuitant—Person receiving annuity payments.

Annuity—A series of periodic payments, often in equal amounts at regular intervals (e.g., a bond's interest payments).

Annuity Bond—A bond in which the principal and interest payments are amortized over the life of the bond to produce a series of equal payments.

Anomaly Switch—British term for the simultaneous sale of one security and purchase of another similar security to take advantage of temporary aberrations in relative value.

Anticipatory Hedge—The purchase (or sale) of futures contracts or other securities in anticipation of or to protect against a change in market prices.

Antidilution—Refers to measures that prevent the devaluation of equity-related securities that occurs when the number of common shares increases but the company's assets do not. Any action or covenant that protects against such dilution is considered antidilutive. *See* Antidilution Clause and Dilution.

Antidilution Clause—A provision in a warrant agreement providing for an adjustment in the warrant terms in the event of stock splits, stock dividends, or the sale of new stock. As a result, the warrant value is not impacted by any of the above events and the warrant holder's proportionate claim to equity in the issuing company remains unchanged.

Any-Interest-Date Call—Call feature stipulating that an issuer may redeem a security on any interest payment date after a specified call protection period.

Applicable Percentage—The adjustment factor for Price Adjusted Rate Preferred Stock, calculated as the market price adjustment ratio (par divided by the average issue price) multiplied by the applicable percentage of the prior period.

Applied Proceeds Swap—Using the proceeds or monies from the sale of one block of securities to purchase as large a block of another security as possible.

Apportioned Tax—A tax derived from districts that may not receive all of its redistributions.

Appreciation—A rise in price.

Appropriation—Government expenditure. A continuing appropriation is renewed automatically until it is revoked.

Arbitrage—1) Technically, the purchase of a security in one market and the simultaneous sale of it or its equivalent in other markets, for the differential or spread prevailing, at least temporarily, because of conditions peculiar to each market. 2) Commonly refers to a swap done between two similar issues based upon an anticipated change in price spreads.

Arbitrage Bond—A municipal bond whose proceeds are invested in higher yielding bonds. Interest is taxable on arbitrage bonds.

Arbitrage Short Sale—Sales made by investors who own bonds or warrants convertible into the stock sold short.

Arbitrage Pricing Theory (APT)—A capital asset pricing theory that the expected return on an investment is the risk-free rate plus a risk premium (for systematic risk). *See* Capital Asset Pricing Model.

Arbitration—A system of resolving conflicts in securities transactions in which both parties agree to accept the resolution of an impartial panel.

Arithmetic Mean—The arithmetic average of a series of numbers.

Arithmetic Return—The average of successive returns.

Arm's Length—Refers to a transaction negotiated by a disinterested third party.

Arrearage—Unpaid dividends on cumulative preferred stock.

Arrears—An unpaid, overdue debt.

Articles of Incorporation—*See* Charter.

Ascending Rate Bond—A CMO tranche with a predetermined schedule of increasing coupon rates.

Ascending Yield Curve—*See* Yield Curve.

Asked—The price at which securities are offered to a potential buyer; the price sellers offer to take.

Assay—To determine the purity of a precious metal deliverable in a futures contract.

Assessed Valuation—A municipality's assessment of the dollar value of a property for tax purposes.

Asset—Anything of value, whether tangible (e.g., machinery, stock) or intangible (e.g., a popular brand name, good will). In accounting, an asset is an entry on a balance sheet showing property or a claim to cover liabilities.

Asset Backed Preferred Stock—Preferred stock issued by a special purpose subsidiary whose assets are comprised almost entirely of financial instruments such as trade or consumer receivables or intercompany notes. Credit support in the form of an irrevocable direct-pay letter of credit and the bankruptcy-proof nature of the subsidiary enable the issue to obtain a triple-A or double-A rating.

Asset Backed Security (ABS)—Publicly traded notes backed by loans, leases, or instalment contracts on personal property such as computers and automobiles.

Asset Depreciation Range—The range of depreciable lives the IRS allows for an asset.

Asset/Liability Management—The process of controlling or matching the cash flows, durations, or maturities of assets and liabilities to maximize return and/or minimize interest rate risk.

Asset Turnover Ratio—A measure of revenue generated by each dollar of assets, calculated as sales revenue divided by average assets.

Assign—To designate an option writer for fulfillment of his obligation to sell a security (call option writer) or buy a security (put option writer). The writer receives an assignment notice from the Options Clearing Corporation.

Assignee—*See* Assignment.

Assignment—1) A form printed on a registered security certificate authorizing the transfer of that security to another owner, the assignee. *See* Bond Power. 2) In the swap market, the sale of a swap contract by one party to another, usually for a lump-sum payment. Assignments require the approval of the remaining original party.

Assimilation—Distribution of a new security.

Associated Person—Registered Commodity Representative.

Association of International Bond Dealers (AIBD)—An association of presently over 800 members from 30 countries whose primary objectives are to provide a basis for examination and discussion of questions relating to the practices in the Eurosecurities secondary market, to issue rules governing their functions, and to maintain a close liaison between the primary and secondary markets.

Assumable—A mortgage that a homebuyer is permitted to take over from the seller.

Assumed Bond—A bond issued by one corporation and guaranteed by another. Also called *Guaranteed Bond* and *Indorsed Bond*.

Assumed Rate of Return—For a pension fund, the interest rate used by a company to calculate the actuarial present value of accumulated plan benefits.

Assumption—In the mortgage market, refers to the takeover of a seller's mortgage loan by the buyer of the home. The buyer assumes responsibility for making the mortgage payments.

Astronomical Theory of Business Cycles—Theory that sunspots affect agricultural output, and therefore business cycles.

At Best—An instruction to a dealer to buy or sell securities at the best available rate or price.

At or Better—In connection with a buy order, to purchase at the price specified or under; in a sell order, to sell at the price specified or above. Also called *Or Better*.

At Risk—1) Refers to an investment whose value is subject to change. Securities are at risk, but bank deposits generally are not. Deductions for depreciation are allowed only for capital that is at risk. 2) An unhedged position.

At-Risk Rule—Rule limiting tax write-offs to the amount of money invested in an asset.

Attached—A description of warrants that have not been separated from the securities with which they were originally issued.

At the Close Order—Order to buy or sell at the close of the market. Execution is not guaranteed.

At the Market—At the current market price, typically used in trade orders.

At the Money—When the underlying security of an option is selling at the exercise price of the option.

At the Open Order—Order to buy or sell at the price in effect at the opening of the market. If the order is not executed at this price, it is canceled.

Auction—*See* Competitive Auction, Dutch Auction, English Auction, and Non-Competitive Auction.

Auction Market—A two-sided market, or one in which there are many buyers and many sellers. Prices are determined by competitive bidding among brokers who represent buyers and sellers.

Auslandobligation(en)—German for foreign security. The term is applied in Switzerland to foreign bonds (8 to 15 years maturity) or notes (3 to 8 years). Foreign bonds are normally public issues managed by a consortium of Swiss-based banks, with minimum denominations of Sfr. 5,000 with optional redemption features. Foreign notes are normally private placements handled by a single Swiss bank, with minimum denominations of Sfr. 50,000.

Aussie Bond—An Australian dollar-denominated Eurobond.

Authentication—The process carried out by the issuing and paying agent to give securities legal effect. This usually involves both the issuing and paying agent's signature and the issuer's facsimile signature on the face of the note.

Authorized Capital Stock—The number of common shares that can be issued by a corporation, as specified in the articles of incorporation.

Automated Execution System (Auto Ex)—Automated system for executing orders used on the American Stock Exchange. *See* Automated Order Entry System.

Automated Order Entry System—Computerized system used to execute orders efficiently. The size of an order executed using such a system may be limited. *See* Automated Execution System, Designated Order Turnaround, Order Support System, Philadelphia Automated Communication and Execution, Small Order Execution System, and Special Order Routing and Execution System.

Automatic Exercise—A procedure whereby the Options Clearing Corporation attempts to protect the holder of an expiring in-the-money option by automatically exercising the option on behalf of the holder.

Available Information—Market information that is widely known and understood (information that cannot be used to earn excess return).

Average Down—To buy or sell a large volume of a security in stages as the security is falling in the market. In this fashion the average cost of the block of securities falls with each incremental purchase.

Average Equity—Average daily balance in a margin account.

Average Life—The weighted average retirement date of a bond or block of bonds; the average amount of time each dollar of principal amount will be outstanding. Average life is computed by multiplying each principal repayment by the time of payment (months or years from the evaluation date), summing these products, and dividing the sum by the total amount of principal repaid. *See* Duration.

Average Up—To buy or sell a large volume of a security in stages as the security is rising in the market. In this fashion, the average cost of the block of securities rises with each incremental sale.

Award—An issuer's acceptance of an underwriter's bid to purchase a new issue. The sale date of the issue is the date the award is given.

Away—Refers to a trade, quote, or market made by a competitor. "99 1/2 away" means that another dealer quoted 99 1/2.

Away from the Market—Pertaining to a limit order when the bid is lower or the offer price is higher than the current market price. *See* Limit Order.

Axe—Refers to a trading position or preference.

B

Babson Break—The sharp market decline of September 5, 1929, predicted by Roger Babson, which was the first significant decline in the bull market of the late 1920s. Sometimes the Babson Break refers to the crash itself.

Baby Bond—A bond with a denomination lower than $1,000, typically $100 or $500.

Back Bond—A bond received upon exercise of a warrant or option. Also called *Virgin Bond*.

Back Contract—Futures contract farthest from expiration. Also called *Deferred Contract*.

Back-End Load—Mutual fund sales charge paid at time of withdrawal. Also called *Redemption Fee*.

Backing Away—When a trader fails to honor a firm bid for the minimum quantity of a security.

Back Month—Refers to any futures contract due to expire after the next expiration date.

Back Office—Departments or functions in a brokerage house not directly involved with trading, such as accounting, trade orders, and maintaining margin accounts.

Backspread—Purchase of one call option and sale of two calls with a lower strike price. *See* Ratio Spread.

Backstop—Commitment by the underwriters in a Euro-note facility to purchase notes at a predetermined margin, usually expressed in relation to LIBOR, if notes cannot otherwise be placed at or under this rate.

Back-to-Back Loan—Loans of equal value made by two parties in different countries. Each loan is denominated in the currency of the lender and matures on the same date. The payment flows are identical to those of spot and forward currency transactions. Currency swaps have a similar structure except that there may not be a loan on the balance sheet.

19

Back Up—1) When yields rise and prices fall. 2) When an investor swaps securities to shorten maturity.

Backup Withholding—A provision incorporated under the Tax Equity and Fixed Responsibility Act of 1982 (TEFRA), whereby a payer must withhold tax at a 15 percent rate if the taxpayer fails to supply a tax-payer identification number (TIN) or supplies a false TIN. This requirement applies to rents, salaries, wages, fees, interest, and dividends.

Backwardation—An abnormal relationship in the cash-futures market. Futures prices are usually higher than cash due to the cost of carry. If cash becomes more expensive than futures, the market is in a state of backwardation. Also called *Inverted Market. See* Contango.

Backward-Bending Supply Curve—Labor supply curve suggesting that higher wages produce not more work but less.

Bad Delivery—The presentation of physical securities that are not acceptable to the purchaser.

Balance—Debits minus credits in an account. If debits are greater than credits, the sum is called a debit balance; if credits are greater than debits, the sum is called a credit balance.

Balance Sheet Equation—*See* Accounting Equation.

Balanced Company—An investment company that tries to minimize risk and ensure moderate current income. This strategy results in less downside and upside potential.

Balanced Fund—A mutual fund that invests in stocks and bonds, in an attempt to reduce the risk of a pure equity fund.

Balanced Manager—A manager whose portfolio includes a variety of investments (e.g., stocks, bonds, etc.).

Balance of Payments—Record of transactions between one nation and all other nations. The current account, capital account, and official reserve account make up the balance of payments. *See* Current Account, Capital Account, and Official Reserve Account.

Balance of Trade—*See* Trade Balance.

Balance Order—The netting of orders among dealers by a registered clearing agency. The balance order may be a Deliver Balance Order (DBO), stating that securities must be delivered to other dealers, or a Receive Balance Order (RBO), stating that securities are owed by other dealers.

Balance Sheet—A financial accounting statement that lists corporate assets on the left side and liabilities, capital, and surplus on the right (the columns are reversed in England). For credit analysis purposes, the balance sheet shows how much capital is invested in the business, the capital structure (amounts of senior issues and common stock), the working capital position, the amount earned on invested capital, and data for other key financial ratios.

Balance Sheet Equation—*See* Accounting Equation.

Balloon—A principal amount retired at maturity on a sinking fund issue that is substantially larger than any previous sinking fund payment. For example, an issue might have 12 payments of 5 percent of the issue followed by a balloon of 40 percent at maturity.

Balloon Interest—Interest on serial bonds, whose early coupons are lower than later ones.

Balloon Maturity—Maturity of serial bonds, whose early maturities have smaller dollar amounts than later ones.

Balloon Payment—The final payment on a loan when it is larger than the regular payments. Also called *Pick-Up Payment.*

Bancor—International monetary unit proposed by Keynes to provide international liquidity. The Keynes Clearing Arrangement, which proposed an international central bank as well as the bancor, was rejected at the Bretton Woods conference in 1944. *See* Bretton Woods.

Bank—A financial intermediary that takes deposits and makes loans. Bank deposits are insured by the Federal Deposit Insurance Corporation.

Bank Basis—Refers to the method used to calculate accrued interest on CDs, FRCDs, and FRNs. The rate of interest is multiplied by the number of days in the accounting year. *See* Money Market Basis.

Bank Call—A request from a bank regulatory agency for a financial statement.

Bank Check—Draft drawn by a bank upon itself (not on its account with the Fed). A bank check is considered good settlement.

Bank Deposit Note—A bank liability that has the same credit risk and FDIC protection as CDs but pays interest on a corporate basis (every 30 days over a 360-day year).

Bankers' Acceptance (BA)—A short-term negotiable discount note. BAs are drawn on and accepted by banks, which are obliged to pay the face value amount at maturity. As borrowers are importers and exporters, BAs finance international trade.

Bankers' Acceptance Tender Facility—A facility that allows for tender panel bids on a borrower's bankers' acceptances.

Bank for Cooperatives—A government-sponsored corporation, supervised by the Farm Credit Administration, that makes loans to agricultural cooperative associations.

Bank Grade—Investment grade.

Bank Guarantee Letter—Letter from a commercial bank to a broker/dealer concerning a customer's funds on deposit, which can serve as collateral for writing a put option.

Banking Act—Congressional act of 1933 that separated commercial and investment banking and created the Federal Deposit Insurance Corporation. Also called *Glass-Steagall Act.*

Bank Note—Debt of the National Bank paid, usually in gold, upon demand of the bearer. Bank notes were replaced by Treasury money and Federal Reserve notes as legal tender in 1935.

Bank of England (B of E)—Central bank of the United Kingdom, which controls and regulates the domestic money and bond markets.

Bank of Japan (BOJ)—Central bank of Japan, which controls and regulates the domestic money and bond markets.

Bank Quality—Investment grade.

Bank Rate—British for discount rate.

Bank Reserves—*See* Reserves.

Bank Risk—1) The risk of default on a bond due to the collapse of the bank guaranteeing that bond. 2) The risk in a Euronote facility when a borrower carries the guarantee of more than one bank.

Bankruptcy—Legal state of insolvency in which an individual or corporation is unable to pay debts. May be voluntary bankruptcy, in which the debtor petitions the courts for protection, or involuntary bankruptcy, in which one or more creditors petition the courts to have the debtor declared insolvent. Bankruptcy may result in the invocation of Chapter 11 of the Bankruptcy Reform Act, which provides for the reorganization of the bankrupt entity.

Bank Wire—A computer message system linking major banks. It is used not for effecting payments, but as a mechanism to advise the receiving bank of some action that has occurred, e.g., the payment by a customer of funds into that bank's account. *See* Fed Wire.

Barbell—*See* Dumbbell.

Barometer—Economic data used for market forecasting. Barometers include market indices and economic indicators. *See* Market Index and Leading Indicator.

Barrel—Unit of oil equal to 42 U.S. gallons at 60 degrees Farenheit, the price of which is a component of the consumer price index.

Base Market Value—Average price of a group of securities.

Base Period—Interval to which economic statistics refer.

Base Rate—British for prime rate.

Basic Accounting Equation—*See* Accounting Equation.

Basis—1) Yield to maturity. 2) Discount basis. 3) The difference in price or yield between a futures position and the financial instrument being hedged. 4) The standard grade of a commodity that must be delivered in a futures contract. 5) With respect to preferred stock, the spread between the dividend rate and the reference rate. 6) In accounting, the acquisition, or historical, cost of an item.

Basis Book—Book containing tables used to convert yield percentages to equivalent dollar prices and vice versa.

Basis Net of Carry (BNOC)—Discount of futures to cash.

Basis Order—An order to buy or sell a futures contract if a specified event occurs in another commodity or in another delivery month. Also called *Contingent Order* and *Net Order*.

Basis Point—One one-hundredth of a percent (.01%), used to express yield differentials.

Basis Price—1) Price expressed in terms of yield or return on investment. 2) Purchase price of a security, used to calculate capital gain or loss.

Basis Risk—The risk of an unfavorable basis change resulting in a futures gain less than a cash market loss or a futures loss greater than a cash market gain.

Basis Swap—An interest rate swap in which each party makes payments based on floating rate indices.

Basis Trading—Trading activity that seeks to take advantage of the differences in relative value between the cash bond and the Treasury bond futures contract. Also called *Relationship Trading* and *Yield Trading*.

Basket—1) A portfolio that tends to track an index. Trading the portfolio to make it resemble the index more closely is called Basket Trading. 2) A composite (e.g., the European Currency Unit is a composite, or basket, currency, consisting of specified amounts of other currencies).

Basket Delivery—The delivery mechanism for some futures contracts, such as Treasury bond or note futures, that have several deliverable cash instruments.

Basket Option—An option for which more than one security may be delivered when the option is exercised.

Basket Trading—*See* Basket.

BD Form—Document that a brokerage house files with the SEC, concerning the firm's financial position and its officers.

Beamer (BMIR)—A low-coupon mortgage-backed annuity.

Bear—A person who expects prices to fall and sells securities hoping to make a profit by subsequently repurchasing them at a lower price. *See* Bull.

Bear and Bull Bond—*See* Bull and Bear Bond.

Bearding—Having several broker/dealers execute portions of one large order, in order to disguise one's market strategy. *See* Sunshine Trading.

Bearer Bond—A bond whose owner is not identified on the bond. Also called *Coupon Bond*. *See* Registered Security.

Bearer Depository Receipt (BDR)—A depository receipt made out in bearer form, used to facilitate trading in shares of foreign companies. For example, in the U.K., General Motors has issued bearer depository receipts representing units equivalent to one-twentieth of a fully-paid share of General Motors common stock. The BDR permits trading in relatively small amounts in foreign countries without U.S. paperwork. *See* American Depository Receipt.

Bearer Participation Certificate (BPC)—Non-voting se-curity issued in bearer form and incorporating the right to participate in net profits, dividends, and liquidation proceeds, and to subscribe to new shares when the entity increases its equity.

Bearer Security—A negotiable security owned by its holder. Title to bearer securities is transferred by delivery. *See* Registered Security.

Bear Hug—Takeover attempt.

Bearish—Pessimistic about the market; anticipating a decline in prices.

Bear Market—A market characterized by a trend of falling prices.

Bear Raid—Illegal practice of selling short at prices lower than that of the previous trade in order to manipulate the price downward.

Bear Spread—1) An option transaction in which a put option is purchased and a second put option with the same expiration but a lower strike price is sold, in anticipation of moderately falling prices. 2) A futures transaction consisting of the simultaneous sale of a nearby delivery month and the purchase of a deferred delivery month, in anticipation of a rise in short-term interest rates, thereby increasing the relative attractiveness of the back month contract. The reverse is true for precious metals. Also called *Selling the Spread*.

Bear Squeeze—*See* Short Squeeze.

Bear Trap—When the market goes up after giving technical sell signals.

Bed and Breakfast—Selling a security late in a trading session and repurchasing it early the next day.

Bedbug—SEC deficiency letter in response to an inadequate preliminary registration statement.

Beggar-Thy-Neighbor—*See* Protectionism.

Beige Book—A Federal Reserve Board publication consisting of a summary of reports made by each of the twelve Federal Reserve Banks on the condition of the economy in their districts, compiled before every Federal Open Market Committee Meeting. Formerly a private publication called the Red Book, it is now available to Congress and the public.

Belgian Dentist—European slang for individual investors.

Bells and Whistles—Additional features to an issue designed to attract investors and/or reduce borrower costs. *See* Plain Vanilla.

Bellwether—Standard. Commonly refers to bonds against which others are compared (e.g., IBM, AT&T).

Belly Up—Bankrupt.

Below Water—Refers to a security whose market value is less than its book or acquisition value. Also called *Under Water*.

Benchmark Bond—A bond whose terms are used for comparison with other issues. *See* Bellwether.

Beneficial Owner—Legal owner of securities, as opposed to the broker who keeps them in a custody account. *See* Nominal Owner.

Benefit Received—Principle that tax levels should be determined by those who can benefit rather than those who can pay. Also called *Cost of Service Principle*. *See* Ability to Pay.

Best Effort—1) When dealers or syndicates do not underwrite an issue but agree to sell as much of it as possible at a given price. *See* Firm Commitment. 2) In the money market, usually refers to a firm order to buy or sell a given amount of securities or currency at the best price available over a given period of time.

Beta—A measure of a security's sensitivity to changes in the overall market. A beta of 0.9 means that a 1% change in the market in the short run implies a 0.9 percent change in the value of the security. Securities with a beta greater than one are more volatile than the market.

Bid—1) The price that someone will pay for a given security. 2) To submit a price one is willing to pay for a security.

Bid-Asked Spread—1) The offered price minus the bid price. 2) The bid yield minus the offered yield, usually expressed in basis points.

Bid Deadline—In a tender panel Euronote facility, the time by which a member of the tender panel must submit a bid to the tender panel agent.

Bid Form—Form used to bid on a municipal bond underwriting.

Bidding Syndicate—Two or more underwriters that submit a joint proposal to an issuer.

Bidding Up—Raising the bid for a security in a rising market.

Bid Only—Describes a security that a dealer will not offer to sell. Also called *Bid Without.*

Bid Wanted (BW)—A request for bids for a security that is being offered. The inference is that the security will be sold to the highest bidder.

Bid Will Improve (BWI)—Phrase signifying that a trader can pay more than a recent bid.

Bid Without—*See* Bid Only.

Big Board—New York Stock Exchange.

Big Figure—The whole number part of a price. For example, 98 of the price 98.5. *See* Handle.

Big Four—1) Major Japanese brokerage firms: Daiwa, Nikko, Nomura, and Yamaichi. 2) Major European economic powers: the United Kingdom, Germany, France, and Italy.

Bill—U.S. Treasury short-term discount security.

Bill of Exchange—Claim for payment made by a seller of foreign goods on the buyer. *See* Draft.

Bill Pass—Federal Reserve open market operation in which the Fed buys Treasury bills outright, instead of on repo. The added reserves remain in the financial system longer than those added through system repo. *See* Coupon Pass and System Repo.

Bill Squeeze—*See* Short Squeeze.

Bill Strip—Treasury bill auction with bills of different maturities offered at one average price.

Binomial Option Pricing—A numerical method for pricing options that assumes that the price of the security moves up or down by a fixed percentage over each time increment from the present to expiration. The option's value for each time increment is computed by arbitraging the change in the option price against the change in the underlying security price. As the time increments become very small, the option value given by the method approaches the value given by the Black-Scholes model. *See* Black-Scholes.

Biweekly Mortgage—A mortgage whose payments are due every other week as opposed to every month. The biweekly payments are determined by calculating the monthly principal and interest amount and dividing by two. Because of the frequency of payments, a biweekly mortgage is paid off before thirty years (typically in seventeen to twenty-four years).

Black Friday—Financial catastrophe. The original Black Friday was September 24, 1869, when Jay Gould caused a depression by trying to corner the gold market.

Black Knight—Hostile corporate raider. *See* White Knight.

Black Market Bond—Bond sold by a dealer not in the offering syndicate, between the effective date and the removal of pricing restrictions.

Black Monday—October 19, 1987, when the Dow Jones Industrial Average fell 508 points.

Black-Scholes—A mathematical formula that calculates the value of a European option based on the price of the underlying asset, the strike price and time to expiration of the option, the price volatility of the asset, and the current risk-free interest rate.

Black Thursday—October 24, 1929, the beginning of the stock market crash. Also refers to May 9, 1901, when traders could not cover their short positions in Northern Pacific because Harriman and Schiff were competing with Hill and Morgan to buy enough shares to control the company.

Blanket Bills—Paper currency issued before July 1929, whose dimensions were larger than those of subsequent paper currency.

Blanket Bond—*See* Fidelity Bond.

Blast Furnace Barometer—Rule of thumb during the 1920s and 1930s that if at least 60 percent of the nation's blast furnaces were operating, the stock market would rise. The measure was remarkably accurate because of the high correlation between opening or closing a blast furnace (at vast expense) and the long-term demand for steel.

Blind Broker—Broker who does not reveal names to either side of a trade.

Blind Pool—A group of investors that gives a representative discretionary trading powers.

Block—An amount of bonds, usually substantially larger than what would be considered a normal round lot of a given issue.

Block Positioner—A dealer who will take the opposite side of a trade to give liquidity to a buyer or seller.

Block Trade—1) Generally, a secondary market trade that is larger than a typical trade. *See* Program Trading. 2) Specifically, refers to a new issue of CDs or FRCDs in which the sponsoring manager purchases the entire issue and distributes it.

Blotter—Daily record of trading activity, often handwritten. Placement of orders, receipt or delivery of securities, and other such activities are recorded in a blotter.

Blowout—An offering that sells out immediately.

Blue Chip—The stock of a company known nationwide for its quality products or services, the reputation of its management, and a long record of profit growth and dividend payments.

Blue List—Generally refers to a daily list of dealer offerings of municipal bonds. Also includes corporate bond offerings, job advertisements, etc.

Blue Monday—Refers to the tendency of stock prices to decline on Mondays. The term was coined after the tendency was observed during the period from 1953 to 1977. Also called *Weekend Effect.*

Blue Sky—Laws designed to protect the public from securities fraud. Each state has its own securities distribution restrictions and guidelines that must be met by each issue offered therein. Blue Sky rules relate to state approval or disapproval of distribution within each state. The term came from a reported statement by a Kansas legislator on the enactment day of the first state securities law in the early 1900s: "Now Kansas citizens will have more of a basis for making investment decisions than merely by the shade of blue sky."

Blue-Skying—1) Qualification of a security for sale. 2) Registration of a broker-dealer.

Board Broker (BB)—1) A U.S. exchange member in charge of keeping the book of public orders on the U.S. exchanges using the market-maker system, as opposed to the specialist system, of executing orders. *See* Market-Maker and Specialist. 2) Employee of Chicago Board Option Exchange who lists out-of-the-money option orders.

Board of Governors of the Federal Reserve System—Board consisting of seven members appointed by the President of the U.S. for 14-year terms. The Board controls the operations of the Federal Reserve System, including formulating monetary policy, setting reserve requirements (within Congressional limits), establishing maximum interest rates member banks may pay on deposits, and establishing the discount rate.

Board of Trade Clearing Corporation—A separate corporation that acts as the clearing house for the Chicago Board of Trade. *See* International Commodities Clearing House.

Board Order—*See* Market if Touched.

Bo Derek—U.S. Treasury bond 10s of 2010.

Body—1) The first $1 million in principal. 2) The first $100,000 in equivalent principal amount of a single GNMA Certificate delivered against a GNMA option contract.

Bond—1) An interest-bearing certificate of debt; a written contract by an issuer to pay to the lender a fixed principal amount on a stated future date, and a series of interest payments on the principal amount until it is paid. 2) Colloquially, any debt instrument.

Bond Administration Agreement—An agreement between an issuer and the manager of a bond issue requiring the manager to perform daily functions in the management of the issue.

Bond Anticipation Note (BAN)—Notes issued by states and municipalities for interim financing.

Bond Authority—Congressional authority to issue a specified amount of Treasury bonds, defined as Treasury securities with a maturity of at least ten years with a coupon of greater than 4 1/4%.

Bond Basis—Refers to the method used to calculate accrued interest on some bonds and money market instruments in the U.S. corporate market that use the 30-day month and 360-day year convention. *See* Money Market Basis and Bond Days.

Bond Broker—New York Stock Exchange member who executes orders in the bondroom.

Bond Buyer Municipal Bond Index—The price index of 40 tax-exempt bonds on which the municipal bond futures contract is based.

Bond Counsel—*See* Legal Opinion.

Bond Days—The number of days between two dates, calculated for bonds using a 30-day month and 360-day year.

Bonded Debt—*See* Direct Debt.

Bond Equivalent Yield (BEY)—*See* Equivalent Bond Yield.

Bond House—A firm primarily engaged in underwriting, distributing, and dealing in bonds.

Bond Investors Guaranty Insurance Company (BIGI)—A corporation that guarantees timely payment of principal and interest of municipal securities.

Bond Pool—*See* Pooled Financings.

Bond Power—A separate form attached to a registered security authorizing transfer of ownership. *See* Assignment.

Bond Price Quotation—Bond prices are quoted as a percentage of par. Thus, 90 means 90% of a $1,000 bond ($900), and 110 means 110% of par ($1,100).

Bond Ratio—The par value of a corporation's bonds with maturities greater than one year divided by the value of those bonds plus equity. Bond ratios greater than 1/3 (33%) are considered highly leveraged (except for utilities, which typically have high bond ratios).

Bond Reinvestment Equivalent (BRE)—A method for analyzing the value of discount or premium bonds and reinvestment potential in yield to maturity terms. BRE yield allows the investor to compare relative values under uniform reinvestment assumptions.

Bond Value—Refers to the principal amount of CMO bonds that the underlying mortgage collateral can support. Mortgages with coupons below the current coupon have a lower bond value than the same par amount of mortgages with coupons above the current coupon.

Bond Years—For a block of bonds, the sum of the products of the years to maturity and the number of bonds retired on each maturity date. Bond years divided by total bonds equals average life.

Book—1) Used as a verb, to record a transaction. 2) Used as a noun, the preliminary indications of interest in a new issue deal.

Book Entry—A system that records ownership of shares at the Depository Trust Company. A master certificate held by the DTC supports book entry registration.

Book Entry Securities—Securities recorded at the Federal Reserve Bank.

Book Gain—The difference between the original cost or book value and the proceeds from the sale of a security if sold for a profit.

Book Loss—The difference between the original cost or book value and the proceeds from the sale of a security if sold at a loss.

Book Price—*See* Book Value.

Book-Running—To have responsibility for the documentation, syndication, distribution, and payment and delivery of a new primary market issue of securities. Although there have been a few instances of joint book-runners, usually only one manager runs the books. *See* Lead-Manager and Co-Lead Manager.

Book Value—1) For an investor, the value of a security for accounting purposes. Frequently, this may be the acquisition cost or another figure different from market value. Also called Book Price. 2) For a corporation, the net worth or stockholders' equity.

Book Yield—1) The yield (current or to maturity) of a security calculated using book value as the price. 2) The yield at which a security was acquired.

Boom—Rapid economic expansion.

Bootstrap—Refers to a takeover defense strategy in which a target company sells assets to buy back some of its own common stock and sells the rest of the corporation to a friendly investor.

Borrowed Reserves—Bank reserves borrowed from the Federal Reserve System. Borrowed reserves subtracted from excess reserves equals free reserves. When the amount of free reserves is negative, it is called net borrowed reserves.

Borrower—An entity that raises funds against a contractual obligation to repay those funds (except in the case of perpetuals) together with payment of interest either as capital appreciation or coupon payments.

Borrower Limit—Many banks and investors have limits to the portion of a fund that may consist of securities of a particular borrower. This is considered prudent management of the fund's assets, as it restricts the potential losses due to adverse changes in the circumstances of a particular borrower. More global limits usually exist for types of borrowers, such as banks, utilities, and supranationals, and the country of the borrower.

Borrower's Option—Lender's Option—An issue in which the issuer has the option, at a specified future date, to choose a new coupon rate. The holder may then choose to have the bond redeemed or to accept the new coupon rate. *See* Retractable and Lender's Option—Borrower's Option.

Bottleneck Inflation—Inflation resulting from a shortage in one sector of the economy. Also called *Sectoral Inflation*.

Bottom Fisher—Investor who buys securities whose prices have fallen and are believed to be about to rise.

Bottom Line—Any result, especially the net profit of a period.

Bottom-Up Manager—Portfolio manager whose decisions are based on individual corporations rather than on the economy. *See* Top-Down Manager.

Borse—A stock market.

Bought Deal—A firm commitment on the part of an underwriting syndicate to buy an entire issue from the issuer. *See* Best Effort, Syndicate, and Stand-By Commitment.

Box—Where physical securities are kept.

Box Spread—A type of option arbitrage in which both a bull spread and a bear spread are established for a riskless profit. One spread is established using put options and the other is established using calls. The spreads may both be debit spreads (call bull spread vs. put bear spread) or credit spreads (call bear spread vs. put bull spread). *See* Bull

Spread and Bear Spread. Using different terminology, a box spread consists of a put calendar spread and a call calendar spread, or a vertical put spread and a vertical call spread. *See* Calendar Spread and Vertical Spread.

Bracket—A grouping determined by the dollar amount of securities underwritten by various firms in a syndicate. Tombstone advertising is normally in bracket order, with each firm appearing alphabetically within a given bracket.

Brassage—Cost of minting coins from bullion. Mintage is the amount charged.

Break—1) Sudden price decline. 2) The term used to indicate that the price and trading restrictions of the Agreement Among Underwriters contract have been terminated and that the security is trading or is expected to trade at a discount from its initial offering price. 3) To terminate an underwriting syndicate.

Breakeven Analysis—A method of analyzing investments to determine under what circumstances the returns of different securities would be equal.

Breakeven Exchange Rate—The exchange rate at which the returns in two bond markets would be equal, allowing for currency movements. For example, if the U.S. Treasury market were predicted to outperform the U.K. gilt market by 5 percent, the breakeven exchange rate would produce a sterling appreciation of 5 percent above the U.S. dollar.

Breakeven Point—The point in time at which the returns of two securities are equal.

Breakeven Reinvestment Rate—Reinvestment rate that equates the returns of two securities.

Breakeven Time—For convertible stock, the time it would take for the premium over conversion value to be erased by the stock's yield advantage. Expressed mathematically, it is the conversion premium divided by the convertible income advantage. *See* Conversion Premium and Convertible.

Breakeven Yield—The yield at which the returns of two securities are equal. Also called *Rollover Yield*.

Breaking the Syndicate—Terminating the restrictions of an agreement among underwriters.

Breakout—When a security's price movement deviates from its previous trading pattern.

Breakout Level—The price of a security at which it deviates from its trading pattern. *See* Break and Bulge.

Breakpoint—The dollar investment in a mutual fund needed to make an investor eligible for a reduction in sales charge.

Breakpoint Sales—The unethical soliciting of mutual fund purchases at levels too low to be eligible for a reduced sales charge.

Breakup Value—British for book value (net asset value per share).

Bretton Woods—Conference of 44 nations in June 1944 at Bretton Woods, New Hampshire, to discuss post-war economic strategy. Keynes' objective was to avoid consequences of the strategies that followed World War I, namely a harsh peace and a strict gold standard. The conference resulted in the formation of the International Bank for Reconstruction and Development and the International Monetary Fund. *See* Development Bank, International Monetary Fund, and Bancor.

Bridge Financing—*See* Interim Financing.

British Clearer—One of the large clearing banks that dominate deposit taking and short-term lending in the U.K. domestic sterling market. *See* Clearing Bank.

Broad Market—A market with large trading volume in several sectors.

Broken—Refers to a convertible security that has the same yield as a comparable non-convertible security (i.e., the market is unwilling to pay for the conversion feature).

Broker—1) A person or firm acting as an agent for buyers and sellers, charging a commission for services rendered. 2) To act as a broker.

Broker-Dealer—An individual or firm that acts as an intermediary between buyers and sellers (i.e., as a broker) as well as a principal in securities transactions (i.e., as a dealer). Principals trade for their own account, and must disclose to customers when they sell securities from their inventory.

Broker's Broker—*See* Two-Dollar Broker.

Broker's Loan—*See* Call Loan.

Broker's Transaction—A transaction made on an agency basis only and that does not involve solicitations, except in certain limited circumstances. Limited circumstances include making an inquiry either of a customer who has indicated unsolicited interest in the securities within the preceding 10 days or of another broker within the preceding 60 days.

Bubble—A highly speculative and usually disastrous venture. Famous bubbles include the Tulip Bulb Mania in Holland in the seventeenth century, the South Sea Bubble in England in the eighteenth century, and the Mississippi Company in France in the eighteenth century.

Bucketing—Holding a firm customer order that can be executed immediately at market levels while attempting to get execution away at a better price (i.e., "holding the order in a bucket").

Bucket Shop—Brokerage house that takes orders and does not execute them, or executes them later and confirms them at the earlier price. The Securities Exchange Act of 1934 made this practice illegal.

Budget Deficit—Government spending (on goods, services, transfers, etc.) minus government receipts. The precise definition varies from country to country, and several measures are usually available. In the U.S. and Germany, the federal government deficit is usually of most interest to the financial markets, while in the U.K. the entire Public Sector deficit (which includes local government and state corporations as well as central government) is of most interest. The definition of spending also varies. The deficit must be financed by the sale of government securities, by intervention in the foreign exchange markets, and by direct sale of savings instruments to the general public.

Budget Sequester—Budget cuts made by Congress to conform to the Gramm Rudman Amendment, which requires that cuts be made equally between defense and other non-exempt budget items.

Builder Bond—1) A CMO issued by a home builder, usually to reap tax benefits of instalment sales accounting. 2) A builder buydown loan.

Builder Buydown Loan—A mortgage loan in which the home builder deposits cash into an escrow account, which is used to supplement the monthly payments from the homeowner for some period of time. *See* Buydown.

Builder Operative Loan—A loan that is made to a home builder and insured by the FHA pursuant to Section 203 of the Housing and Urban Development Act. Such a loan may be assumed by the eventual home buyer. If not assumed, the loan is repaid by the builder with the proceeds of the sale of the home.

Building Society—In the United Kingdom, an organization that takes in savings deposits, principally from the retail market, and originates mortgages. *See* Savings and Loan.

Bulge—A rapid and sharp price advance. *See* Break.

Bulk Segregation—When a broker-dealer keeps non-registered customer securities separate from the firm's securities.

Bull—A person who believes prices will rise. *See* Bear.

Bull and Bear Bond—A bond structured to allow half the investors to benefit from rising prices and half the investors to benefit from falling prices.

Bulldog Bond—A sterling-denominated bond issued in the United Kingdom by a foreign issuer. *See* Foreign Bond.

Bullet—1) A security or loan with only one payment. 2) A security with no amortization features.

Bullet Loan—A bank loan with no amortization.

Bull Floating Rate Note—*See* Reverse Floater.

Bullish—Optimistic about the market; anticipating a rise in prices.

Bull Market—A market characterized by a trend of rising prices.

Bull Spread—1) An option transaction in which a call option is purchased and a second call option with the same expiration date but a higher strike price is sold, in anticipation of moderately rising prices. 2) A futures transaction consisting of the simultaneous purchase of a nearby delivery month and sale of a deferred delivery month in expectation of a decline in short-term interest rates, thereby increasing the relative attractiveness of the front month contract. The reverse is true for precious metals. Also called *Buying the Spread*.

Bunching—Combining orders for convenience of execution.

Bundbahnpost Bonds—Bonds issued by the German Federal Republic (Bundesrepublik), the Federal Railways (Bundesbahn), and the Federal Post Office (Bundespost).

Bundeskassenobligation(en)—Medium-term notes issued by the Federal German Republic, with maturities of between two and six years.

Bundesobligation(en)—A German savings bond with a maturity of about five years, issued on a standing basis with the issue price adjusted to market conditions. Bundesobligationen cannot be purchased by foreign investors.

Bunny Bond—An issue in which the holder has the option to receive the interest payments either in cash or as more bonds of the same issuer.

Burden—Amount of taxes due. On a national scale, the tax burden is the cost of government, estimated as goods and services not privately produced.

Burnout—The decline in prepayments that normally follows a surge in prepayments created by falling interest rates.

Business Conduct Committee (BCC)—Court that hears complaints made under NASD's Code of Procedure.

Business Cycle—Regularly recurring cycle of economic prosperity, recession, depression, and recovery.

Business Day—(1) In the Euromarkets, a day in which related markets are open for banking business (e.g., in the Eurodollar market, a day when both London and New York banks are open for business). 2) In the U.S. market, any day excluding Saturdays, Sundays, and legal holidays on which business can be conducted. *See* Clearing Day.

Business Sector—One of the three sectors of the economy, the other two being consumer and government. Also called *Industrial Sector*. Consumer and business sectors together are called the Private Sector.

Bust—1) Rapid economic decline. 2) To cancel an order that has been filled.

Busted Convertible—A convertible issue whose conversion privilege has no value because the underlying conversion price on the equity is significantly above the market level for the stock.

Butterfly Spread—1) When an investor sells positions in two bonds and buys one bond with a maturity between those of the two bonds sold. 2) An options strategy of selling two calls then buying two calls with one strike price higher and one lower than the short calls. The investor is thus partially hedged in both directions.

Buy—To pay to acquire an asset.

Buy Back—*See* Repurchase Agreement.

Buy Bullish News—A trading strategy of buying a security upon hearing a favorable piece of news about that security and selling it when the news becomes fact.

Buyer's Market—Market in which supply far exceeds demand.

Buydown—A mortgage loan in which the seller places funds in a segregated account to augment the buyer's mortgage payments. Those funds are gradually drawn down, effectively creating a graduated payment mortgage (GPM) for the borrower.

Buy-In—A procedure, detailed in the Uniform Practice Code, for the closing of a contract by the buyer purchasing securities if the seller does not complete the contract according to its terms.

Buying Ahead—Refers to the purchasing of bonds in the open market to satisfy a sinking fund, either in excess of its current requirements or before the sinking fund due date. The purchasing of excess bonds because of an option to double is not considered buying ahead.

Buying Climax—Rapid price increase, followed by a price decline.

Buying Hedge—*See* Long Hedge.

Buying Power—The potential to use excess loan value in a margin account to buy additional securities.

Buying the Basis—Buying a cash bond and selling a delivery-weighted number of futures contracts.

Buying the Spread—Anticipating rising prices in financial instruments by going long the front contract month and selling the deferred contract month. The reverse is true for precious metals. Also called *Bull Spread*. The reverse situation is called Selling the Spread or Bear Spread.

Buying the Yield Curve—A duration-weighted spread trade consisting of selling a short maturity and buying a longer maturity security to take advantage of an anticipated flattening of the yield curve. *See* Selling the Yield Curve.

Buy on Close—To purchase a security at the end of a trading session at a price within the closing range. *See* Buy on Opening.

Buy on Opening—To purchase a security at the start of a trading session at a price within the opening range. *See* Buy on Close.

Buyout—Purchase of a controlling interest in a corporation.

Buy Stop—An order to buy a security at the best available price after a specified market price is touched.

Buy the Book—An order to buy all the securities available from a specialist.

Buywrite—An options strategy of writing call options in conjunction with a long bond or futures position. Also called *Covered Write* and *Covered Call*. *See* Standstill Return, Yield Standstill Return, and Overwrite.

Bylaws—The rules of a corporation adopted by its shareholders.

C

Cabinet Crowd—Traders whose transactions are often in inactive bonds. Also called *Can Crowd*. *See* Active Bond Crowd.

Cabinet Security—An inactively traded security.

Calamity Call—Provision in a CMO indenture stating that bonds may be called if a specified level of prepayments is reached. *See* Special Redemption.

Calendar—The list of new issues scheduled to come to market in the near future, usually within 30 days. Also called the *Visible Supply*.

Calendar Spread—An option position created by selling one call/put option and buying another with a longer expiration date at the same strike price. Also called *Horizontal Spread* and *Time Spread*.

California VRM—*See* Variable Rate Mortgage.

Call—1) The exercise of the right of a corporation to prepay its debt and demand surrender of its bonds for redemption (cash call), refunding, or sinking fund purposes on a specific date at a specified price. 2) An option contract that gives the holder the right to purchase from the writer of the call a specified amount of securities at a specific price, good for a specified period of time. 3) *See* Bank Call.

Callable—Securities whose indenture contains a provision giving the issuer the right to retire the issue prior to its maturity date. *See* Redemption and Putable.

Callable Bond—A bond that the issuer can redeem prior to maturity.

Callable Preferred Stock—Preferred stock that a corporation may call. The corporation typically pays a premium if it redeems the stock soon after issuance.

Call Deferment—Period during which a bond cannot be called, typically a period of five years from issuance for utilities and ten years from issuance for industrials.

Called Away—Refers to a bond redeemed before maturity.

Call Loan—Loan a broker gets from a bank to finance a customer's purchases (when a customer buys on margin). Also called *Broker's Loan*.

Call Loan Rate—The interest rate charged by a bank on a collateralized loan to a brokerage firm used to cover client positions in a margin account. The call loan rate usually tracks slightly above short-term interest rates such as the Treasury bill rate.

Call Market—A futures market procedure in which trading occurs in rotation for each contract, usually at the opening of trading. After trading in all contracts has been opened, all contracts trade simultaneously.

Call Money—1) Money that can be withdrawn from a bank on 24 hours' notice. 2) Money lent to brokers by bankers for one day.

Call Option Deutsche Marks (CODM)—European option allowing the holder to buy a specified amount of Deutsche marks at a specified amount of U.S. dollars.

Call Price—The price an issuer pays to redeem a bond. Typically, the call price is above par in the early years that a bond is outstanding. *See* Redemption Price.

Call Protection—Guarantee not to call a security for a specified time. *See* Refunding Protection.

Call Protection Warrant—Long maturity harmless warrant that, during the initial part of its life, can be exercised only by surrendering a host bond, thereby avoiding an immediate call on the host bond. *See* Harmless Warrant.

Call Rate—Bank interest rate on a call loan.

Call Schedule—For a callable issue, a schedule of call prices that decreases toward par as the issue reaches its maturity date.

Call Yield Premium—An extra yield on a callable bond paid by an issuer over the yield on a similar noncallable bond to compensate investors for the risk of the bond being called.

Canadian Interest Cost (CIC)—*See* True Interest Cost.

Canadian Rollover—*See* Rollover Mortgage.

Canadian Sinking Fund—A sinking fund that obligates the issuer to set aside in cash a specified percentage of the principal amount outstanding of an issue. This cash may be used to purchase either the given issue or another approved security, as defined in the original indenture.

Cancel—To withdraw an order before execution or to withdraw a new issue before it is officially brought to market.

Can Crowd—*See* Cabinet Crowd.

Cap—1) An upper limit on the interest rate that may be paid on a floating rate security. 2) A contract in which the seller pays the buyer if and when an agreed upon floating interest rate exceeds a certain level. *See* Rate Cap. 3) The highest interest rate an issuer is willing to pay on a new issue.

Capability Margin—*See* Reserve Margin.

Capacity—The number of products that can be produced in a specified period of time.

Capacity Utilization Rate—The ratio of physical output to full industrial production capacity or potential.

Capillarity—Economic law stating that individuals will limit family size to maximize standard of living. The opposite is the iron law of wages, which states that family size will increase with wages. *See* Iron Law of Wages.

Capital—1) One of the three productive inputs of classical economic theory, the other two being land and labor. Capital consists of relatively permanent assets, such as machinery, buildings, and products. Also called *Real Capital.* 2) The dollar amount of stock issues on the balance sheet.

Capital Account—Part of the balance of payments, defined as transactions (either real estate or loans) between Americans and foreigners. *See* Balance of Payments.

Capital Appreciation Bond (CAB)—A CAB in the tax-exempt market is similar to a zero coupon security in the taxable market. Unlike zero coupon securities, however, which are always issued at a deep discount with the maturity value at par, CABs are always issued at par and appreciate to a premium. The investor receives a return through the accretion of principal or through the compounding to maturity of unpaid interest. CABs are also variously known as zeros, deferred interest bonds, or deferred coupon bonds, and are usually issued with maturities in excess of twenty years.

Capital Asset—Debt or equity security that can generate capital gains or losses. Money market securities, with the exception of Treasury bills, are not capital assets.

Capital Asset Pricing Model (CAPM)—A market model that describes the way prices of individual assets are determined. The model makes two assumptions: the market is efficient, because it consists of many rational, risk-averse investors; and the market behaves in no regular pattern (the random walk hypothesis). According to the model, return should be directly related to systematic risk. The basic formula for the model is that a security's rate of return is equal to beta times market return, minus the risk-free rate. Beta is the relationship of the price volatility of a security to that of the market. The model measures the

the risk and return of a security in relation to the risk and return of the market. The return of a risk-free asset is called the alpha. *See* Arbitrage Pricing Theory, Modern Portfolio Theory, Classical Security Analysis, Efficient, Risk, Random Walk, Beta, and Alpha.

Capital Consumption Allowance—The amount of depreciation included in the gross national product (GNP). GNP minus the capital consumption allowance equals the net national product (NNP). NNP adjusted for indirect taxes equals national income. *See* Depreciation.

Capital Debenture—In the Netherlands, a subordinated bond, usually issued by a bank.

Capital Flight—The transfer of funds out of a country to avoid risks such as currency depreciation and confiscation.

Capital Gain/Loss—A profit/loss realized from buying a security or commodity at one price and selling it at another. If the purchase and sale occur within a one-year period, the capital gain/loss is considered short term; if the holding period is longer than one year, it is considered long term.

Capitalism—Economic system based on private ownership and laissez-faire government. *See* Laissez-Faire.

Capitalization—1) All of a corporation's securities (stocks and bonds) held by the public. 2) A corporation's outstanding debt and equity, earned surplus, and capital surplus.

Capitalization Rate—*See* Discount Rate.

Capitalization Ratio—Ratio of long-term sources of funds (bonds, preferred stock, or common stock) to total long-term debt.

Capitalize—1) In accounting, to record a capital outlay as an asset rather than an expense. 2) In an economic sense, to take advantage of an opportunity.

Capitalized Interest—That part of the proceeds of an issue used to pay interest on the securities for a specified period. In revenue bonds, interest is typically capitalized for the construction period. Also called *Funded Interest.*

Capital Levy—Non-cash tax.

Capital Market Line—A graph of the average rate of return for various risk levels.

Capital Markets—Markets in which debt and equity are traded.

Capital-Output Ratio—Change in capital investment divided by change in output. Also called *Incremental Capital-Output Ratio.*

Capital Spending—Non-residential fixed investment in the GNP. Capital spending consists of business outlays on long-lived productive facilities (plant and equipment) including office building and shopping center construction, as well as purchases of such long-lived items as trucks, office, and farm equipment.

Capital Stock—Common and preferred stock.

Capital Structure—The division of a company's capitalization among bonds, debentures, preferred and common stock, earned surplus, and retained earnings.

Capital Surplus—*See* Paid-In Surplus.

Capital Turnover—*See* Turnover.

Cap Order—A large buy or sell order authorizing the specialist to use market judgment in execution. Also called *Hook* or *On the Hook Order*. *See* Discretionary Order.

Capped Floating Rate Note—A type of floating rate note that sets an upper limit on the borrower's interest rate. The lender foregoes the possibility of obtaining a return above the cap rate should the market interest rates exceed the cap rate. *See* Cap, Floating Rate Note, Floor, and Delayed Cap Floating Rate Note.

Capping—Illegal practice of selling a security to lower prices, thus keeping previously sold call options on that security out of the money.

Carry—The cost or benefit of financing positions; the rate of interest earned from the securities held less the cost of funds borrowed to purchase them. When the interest earned is greater than the cost of funds, there is positive carry; when the cost of funds is greater than the interest earned, there is negative carry.

Carrying Charge Market—*See* Normal Market.

Carryover—Refers to economic statistics of a prior period accounted for in a later period.

Cartel—A group of countries or corporations that tries to control the price of a commodity.

Carter Bonds—Series of ten nonmarketable U.S. Treasury securities, denominated in Deutsche marks and Swiss francs, issued to residents of West Germany and Switzerland as private placements.

Cascade Tax—Tax levied at several stages of the manufacturing process, with each tax becoming part of the base for the next tax. *Also called* Turnover Tax.

Cash—The physical commodity or security underlying futures and option contracts. *See* Actuals.

Cash Account—An account at a brokerage firm in which transactions are settled in cash. *See* Margin Account.

Cash and Carry—A transaction in which an investor or arbitrager purchases a cash market security, simultaneously sells one or more futures contracts, and holds or finances (carries) the cash instrument until the delivery date of the futures contract. A cash and carry analysis is based on the assumption that the cash security can be delivered into the futures position.

Cash Basis—Accounting method that recognizes revenues and expenses only after cash transactions. *See* Modified Cash Basis and Accrual.

Cash Call—*See* Redemption.

Cash Cow—Business or security that is a dependable source of income.

Cash Dividend—Dividend on a security paid in cash.

Cash Equivalents—Investments readily converted into cash (e.g., Treasury bills and CDs).

Cash Flow—1) The cash return generated by a security, made up of interest and principal payments. 2) New money contributions to a portfolio. 3) A business firm's reported net income plus depreciation, depletion, amortization, deferred taxes, and extraordinary charges to reserves (which are bookkeeping deductions and not actual dollar payouts), less undistributed earnings of nonconsolidated subsidiaries reported on an equity basis.

Cash Flow Bond—*See* Pay-Through Bond.

Cash Flow Buyer—Investor who trades to increase yield in order to match investment income against liabilities.

Cash Flow from Operations—Income from continuing operations plus expenses (less revenues) not affecting working capital. Also called *Funds from Operations*.

Cash Flow from Operations to Debt Ratio—A measure of long-term liquidity risk, calculated as cash flow from operations divided by average total liabilities.

Cash Flow Investment—Guaranteed investment contracts and short-term securities that enable an issuer to reinvest principal and interest receipts between payment dates.

Cash Flow Matching—The creation of a portfolio of assets designed to produce cash flows sufficient to pay off a given set of liabilities. *See* Dedication.

Cash Flow Uncertainty—Uncertainty concerning the payments of a mortgage security due to prepayments.

Cash Flow Yield—*See* Honest-to-God (HTG) Yield.

Cash Forward Contract—Purchase or sale of a financial instrument or other commodity in the cash market for future delivery.

Cash Immediate Market—Refers to settlement in the pass-through market, in which conventional pass-through securities must be settled within seven business days of the trade date and GNMA pass-throughs may be settled within the current month.

Cash Index—*See* Corporate Bond Index Futures.

Cash Management Bill—U.S. Treasury bills issued for short-term financing purposes.

Cash Market—Market in which trades have immediate delivery. Also called *Spot Market*.

Cash on Delivery—Term used with buy orders signifying that assets be delivered at time of payment. Also called *Delivery Against Cash*.

Cash Program—FHLMC securities for which principal is computed by estimating future principal payments rather than actual payments.

Cash Ratio—Cash and marketable securities divided by current liabilities. Cash ratio reflects a borrower's ability to meet short-term obligations. Also called *Cash Asset Ratio* and *Liquidity Ratio*.

Cash Sale—*See* Cash Settlement.

Cash Security—A security that is traded for immediate delivery and settlement.

Cash Settlement—A delivery made and settled on the day of the transaction for government securities. Also called *Cash Transaction* and *Cash Sale*.

Cash Sinking Fund—*See* Sinking Fund.

Cash Transaction—*See* Cash Settlement.

Catch-Up Floater—A floating rate CMO tranche containing a provision to recoup interest that was previously lost due to the floater reaching its cap. Any interest not recouped by the maturity of the floating rate tranche is forfeited.

Cats and Dogs—Slang for speculative securities.

Caveat Emptor—Let the buyer beware (i.e., of the value and risk of the security to be purchased).

Caveat Venditor—Let the seller beware (i.e., of the laws relating to security transactions).

C&D—Cease and desist. Refers to orders sought by the SEC and CFTC, which do not have civil or criminal jurisdiction, to stop an illegal or fraudulent practice.

CEDEL—*See* Centrale de Livraison de Valeurs Mobilieres.

Ceiling—Maximum interest rate or price, regardless of market forces.

Central Bank—*See* Federal Reserve System.

Centrale de Livraison de Valeurs Mobilieres (CEDEL)—A book-entry clearing facility for Eurocurrency and foreign securities, located in Luxembourg. It is jointly owned by a large number of European banks. CEDEL is one of two Eurobond clearing systems, the other being Euroclear. *See* Clearing System and Euroclear.

Certificate—The piece of paper evidencing ownership of a security.

Certificate Delivery—1) One of two methods of delivery for GNMA futures contracts. It calls for the delivery of actual GNMA certificates, whose total par amount is determined by a yield maintenance formula. *See* Collateralized Depository Receipt. 2) A futures contract traded on the CBOT, representing $100,000 face amount of 8% yield maintenance GNMAs.

Certificated Security—A security represented by a physical certificate, as opposed to a book entry security. Also called *Definitive Form.*

Certificated Stock—A daily report on the visible supply of commodities other than grains that are inspected and approved for delivery on futures.

Certificate of Beneficial Ownership (CBO)—*See* Farmers Home Administration.

Certificate of Deposit (CD)—An interest-bearing negotiable time deposit of fixed maturity at a commercial bank. CDs trade on a yield basis with interest computed for the actual number of days held, on the basis of a 360-day year.

Certificate of Incorporation—*See* Charter.

Certificate of Indebtedness—*See* Treasury Certificate.

Certificate of Necessity—Tax write-off for capital equipment needed for a national emergency, used during the Korean War.

Change of Control Bond—A bond with a put option exercisable upon the occurrence of a designated event, such as a merger or takeover of the issuing corporation. *See* Super Put.

Channel Sinking Fund—Funnel Sinking Fund. *See* Sinking Fund.

Chapter 11—Part of the Bankruptcy Reform Act, it provides for the reorganization of a bankrupt company, allowing it to stay in business and meet its obligations. May include such measures as management changes and the restructuring of debt and payment schedules.

Charge—1) Used as a noun, a debit to an account. 2) Used as a verb, to debit.

Charge Off—To convert an asset into a loss or expense.

Chart Analysis—The use of graphs and charts to analyze market trends. *See* Technical Analysis.

Charter—Two documents that together give a corporation its legal existence. The first document is called the Articles of Incorporation, which the founders of a corporation file with a state. The second document is called the Certificate of Incorporation, in which the state approves the Articles. The charter includes such information as the corporation's name, its purpose, the amount of authorized shares, and the identity of its directors. Also called *Certificate of Incorporation.*

Charting—Using graphs and charts to analyze market trends. *See* Technical Analysis.

Chartist—A technical analyst. *See* Technical Analysis.

Chattel Mortgage—Mortgage that places a lien on personal property pledged as collateral.

Cheap—Relatively inexpensive; having a price perceived to be undervalued. *See* Rich.

Chicago Board of Trade (CBOT)—Exchange on which futures and options are traded.

Chinese Arbitrage—*See* Reverse Hedge.

Chinese Wall—Ethical barrier between investment bankers and traders of the same broker/dealer, preventing trading profits from inside information.

Choice—When one market maker is offering bonds at the same price that another market maker is willing to bid. The price is termed a choice price. *See* Locked Market.

Chronic Deficit—Several consecutive negative balance of payments.

Churning—The process of frequently trading for a client's account, in order to generate commission. Also called *Twisting and Switching.*

Circle—An industry practice whereby an underwriter seeks commitments to buy a security at a specified price before it is issued. Circling helps establish the fair market price for an issue and reduce underwriting risk.

Circulating Capital—*See* Working Capital.

Circus—A combined interest rate and currency swap.

City—Refers to the financial center of London.

Class—1) A group of options, including all puts or calls, with the same underlying security. 2) A specific security in a new issue in which multiple securities are offered. *See* Tranche.

Classical School—Economic school of thought that replaced mercantilism in the mid-eighteenth century. Adam Smith is generally considered the founder of the classical school, whose tenets include laissez-faire and free competition. *See* Laissez-Faire.

Classical Security Analysis—Quantitative fundamental valuation techniques popularized by Benjamin Graham and David Dodd in the 1930s with their book *Security Analysis*. Instead of risk and reward analysis, Graham and Dodd focussed on corporate financial ratios. Classical security analysis advocates investing in undervalued companies. The classical security analyst accordingly recommends buying stock in companies selling at a substantial discount from its working capital, whose current assets are greater than all liabilities, whose stock has low price-earnings ratios, and whose stock is selling below liquidating value.

Classic Warrant—A warrant that is exercisable at any time with cash. Warrant life usually varies from one to five years.

Clean—1) A matched buy and sell order leaving the broker with no inventory. Also called *Natural*. *See* Agency Cross. 2) The total price of a bond less accrued interest. Also called *Flat*. *See* Dirty. 3) Noncallable.

Clean Float—Foreign exchange rates established without any government intervention.

Clean on the Print—Announcement that a broker/dealer executed a block trade among clients, without acting as principal.

Clean Opinion—*See* Qualified Opinion.

Clean Price—*See* Stripped Price.

Cleanup Call—A form of optional redemption provided in a CMO indenture allowing an issuer to call bonds when only a small amount remain outstanding. The call trigger mechanism is typically based on a percentage of original principal amount outstanding (e.g., 10 percent), thereby enabling an issuer to avoid excessive administrative expenses in servicing a small portion of remaining bonds outstanding. Also called *Nuisance Call*.

Clear—To consummate a trade by delivery of securities in a proper form to the buyer and by payment of funds to the seller. Trades that are not cleared by the settlement date are said to fail. *See* Settle and Fail.

Clearing Bank—Any commercial bank that settles corporate and government securities for customers and dealers. The clearing bank agrees to deliver and receive securities, taking cash against delivery. The bank is usually part of the Federal Reserve System, and therefore able to use the Federal Reserve Bank book entry system for government securities.

Clearing Day—Any business day.

Clearing House—A corporation connected with an exchange, through which all futures and options contracts are reconciled, guaranteed, and settled. By placing itself between the buyer and seller, the clearing house becomes the counterparty to every trade. Investors, therefore, do not have to concern themselves with the creditworthiness of the party taking the opposite side of the trade. The clearing house also oversees the margin requirements and the daily mark-to-market process.

Clearing House Bank—A member of a clearing house; usually one of the 11 members of the New York Clearing House.

Clearing House Funds—Funds represented by checks drawn on a clearing house bank, which if deposited on one day will be federal funds on the next day.

Clearing House Interbank Payments System (CHIPS)—A New York computerized system through which most Euro transactions are cleared.

Clearing Member Trade Agreement (CMTA)—Standard Options Clearing Corporation agreement allowing exchange members to execute, clear, and settle contracts through a clearing member.

Clearing System—A depositary/transaction system established to expedite physical delivery. The two Eurobond clearing systems are CEDEL and Euroclear. Transactions and deliveries between accounts are effected by way of book entry only.

Close—The period at the end of a trading session.

Closed—Refers to an underwriting pot in which there are no further securities available and through which no further bonds can be run. *See* Pot and Running Bonds Through the Pot.

Closed-End—1) A mutual fund in which the number of shares, representing an interest in the mutual fund's portfolio, are fixed. New shares are not issued regularly and old shares cannot be redeemed. Instead, shares are traded on the open market and may differ in value from the underlying net asset value per share. 2) Mortgage bonds that specify that no additional bonds of the same priority be issued on the same property.

Closely Held—Refers to a corporation whose stock is owned by relatively few shareholders.

Close Out—1) To eliminate a short position in stocks or bonds by delivering the identical securities to the lender. 2) To take an offsetting position in the same futures contract to eliminate the delivery obligation.

Closet Indexer—An active portfolio manager who tries to match the performance of a market index.

Close Up—To narrow the bid-asked spread.

Closing—1) The procedures relating to the completion of a primary market issue on the closing date. 2) Transfer of title in a real estate transaction. 3) In accounting, the transfer of balances in the revenue and expense accounts to the retained earnings account at the end of each period.

Closing a Market—*See* Narrowing the Spread.

Closing Date—The date on which a new issue's proceeds are paid to the borrower by the lead-manager and the securities, in temporary or definitive form, are delivered to the lead-manager by the borrower.

Closing Price—The price at which transactions are made just before the close on a given day. Frequently, there is not one price, but a range of prices at which transactions are made just before the close.

Closing Purchase—A transaction in which a short position in an option is reduced or eliminated.

Closing Range—The high and low prices at which transactions took place during the close.

Closing Sale—1) A transaction in which a long position in an option is reduced or eliminated. 2) The last transaction of the day in a security.

Closing Transaction—The termination of an open position by its corresponding offset. Closing buy transactions reduce short positions and closing sell transactions reduce long positions.

CMO Equity—*See* Residual.

Coincident Indicator—An economic indicator that has no predictive value because it changes simultaneously with the economy. *See* Indicator.

Co-Lead Manager—A manager who participates in some of the functions of the lead manager, usually takes a share of the praecipuum, but does not run the books of an issue. *See* Lead Manager and Praecipuum.

Collar—Upper and lower limits on the dividend rate or coupon on a floating rate security. These may be absolute rates or relative limits, such as a percentage of a reference rate. *See* Reference Rate.

Collar Swap—An interest rate swap of fixed rate against floating rate payments, with the latter having a maximum and minimum rate.

Collateral—1) Securities or other property pledged by a borrower to secure payment of a loan. 2) The mortgages underlying a mortgage-backed security.

Collateralized—Refers to securities that are secured by an asset, such as mortgages, leases, or receivables, of the issuer. *See* Asset Backed Security and Collateralized Mortgage Obligation.

Collateralized Depository Receipt (CDR)—1) A document signed by a depository bank evidencing a $100,000 minimum principal balance of GNMAs with an 8% coupon or their equivalent. 2) A method of delivery for GNMA futures contracts. It calls for the delivery of a receipt (the CDR) instead of actual GNMA certificates. *See* Certificate Delivery. 3) A futures contract traded on the CBOT representing $100,000 principal amount of 8% GNMA certificates or their equivalent.

Collateralized Floating Rate Note—A floating rate note whose credit is enhanced by collateral, such as Treasury, Agency, or mortgage securities, deposited in a trust account.

Collateralized Mortgage Obligation (CMO)—A corporate bond backed by a pool of mortgages in which the principal cash flows of the pool are channeled, usually sequentially, into two or more series of bonds (tranches). Interest payments are made on all tranches except, in some CMOs, accrual bonds or Z bonds.

Collateral Loan—A loan backed by a pledge of securities or other property.

Collateral Mortgage Bond (CMB)—Collateral trust bond secured by a deposit of mortgage bonds, and thus indirectly secured by the underlying mortgages. CMBs often pay interest semiannually instead of monthly.

Collateral Trust Certificate—A bond backed by securities placed with a trustee by the issuing corporation.

Collateral Value—The lesser of 1) the sum of the remaining scheduled principal and interest payments on a mortgage certificate and 2) the product of the outstanding principal balance and a collateral value cap.

Collateral Value Cap—A factor that when multiplied by the principal amount of mortgage certificates outstanding determines the principal amount of CMOs that may be supported in the event of total prepayment on the underlying collateral.

Collection Account—A separate account established by a CMO trustee to aggregate and record the receipts and disbursements relating to a particular CMO. Receipts include collateral principal and interest payments and reinvestment interest. Disbursements include bond principal and interest payments, bond administrative expenses, and residual cash flow to be released to the residual owner.

Color—Information that helps describe a security, such as facts about management, industry, and market trends. Also called *Story*. A bond described by color is called a Story Bond.

Co-Manager—A term used when there is more than one manager in a securities offering. Usually refers to a manager not running the books.

books. The manager running the books is known as the lead manager and is the only one who directly controls distribution of securities throughout the syndicate.

Combination—Variation of a straddle, with put and call having different terms; typically the strike prices differ.

Combination Matching—A portfolio strategy that combines immunization and dedication. A combination matched portfolio is one that is immunized (or duration matched) overall, but also cash flow matched for some initial time period. This method is appropriate when short-term liabilities are known but longer-term liabilities are not as certain. *See* Immunization, Dedication, and Cash Flow Matching.

Come Back—Return to former prices. In America the term implies a return to a former higher price; in Britain it implies a return to a former lower price.

Coming to Me (CTM)—Indicates that the market level quoted by the trader is not his own, but is being made by another trader.

Commercial Bank—An institution legally authorized to issue demand deposit accounts, as opposed to thrift institutions or investment banks, which are not so empowered. Thrift institutions offering demand deposit facsimile accounts in certain states are not considered to be commercial banks. Called *Clearing Bank* in Britain.

Commercial Paper (CP)—The market name for short-term, unsecured promissory notes that are exempt from registration with the SEC. The most common exemptions are Section 3(a)(3) of the Securities Act of 1933, which exempts securities with maturities of nine months or less that are used for financing current transactions, and Section 4(2), which exempts privately placed securities.

Commingled Real Estate Funds (CREF)—A pool of capital from pension funds invested in real estate.

Commingling—Combining a customer's fully paid or segregated securities with hypothecated securities to obtain a loan from a broker. Commingling is fraudulent and illegal under the Securities and Exchange Act of 1934.

Commission—1) A broker's fee for buying or selling securities as an agent. 2) A percentage of the profit or expected profit from a securities transaction that is paid to the sales person.

Commission Broker—A member of an exchange who executes orders for the sale or purchase of financial futures contracts.

Commission Give-Up—The practice of directing a portion of NYSE commissions, paid by the customer to an executing broker, to another firm not involved in the execution of the trade. This practice was largely limited to stock and was usually in payment for research. It is now prohibited by the SEC.

Committed Facility—A line of credit in which a bank is obliged to lend an amount of money subject to satisfaction of specified conditions. *See* Line of Credit.

Committee on Uniform Securities Identification Procedures—*See* CUSIP.

Commodity-Backed Bond—Bond whose interest payments are based on the price of an underlying commodity, such as gold or silver. *See* Oil Indexed Notes.

Commodity Future Contract—*See* Future.

Commodity Exchange (COMEX)—A New York exchange trading futures contracts on gold and silver, and option contracts in gold futures.

Commodity Futures Trading Commission (CFTC)—A commission created by an act of Congress in 1974 that is directly responsible to the federal government for supervisory and enforcement functions in the futures industry.

Commodity Paper—Commercial paper collateralized by commodities.

Commodity Pool Operator (CPO)—Any entity that solicits funds and pools them to trade in commodity futures.

Commodity Research Bureau (CRB) Index—The CRB's index of twenty-seven commodity futures prices.

Commodity Trading Advisor (CTA)—Futures investment advisor.

Common Stock—A share, usually represented by a certificate, representing participation in the ownership of an enterprise, generally with the right to participate in dividends and in most cases to vote on major matters affecting stockholder interests. Also called *Shares* and *Equity*. *See* Stock.

Common Stock Ratio—Common stock divided by total capital.

Common Stock Warrant—*See* Warrant.

Common Trust Fund—A trust fund incorporating the assets of several trusts.

Comparable—Refers to preferred stock that has a public market, call prices, protective features, and other characteristics substantially similar to those of non-publicly traded preferred stock of the same issuer.

Comparative Advantage—Situation in which a producer (individual, corporation, or nation) can produce a good more cheaply than another producer.

Comparison Ticket—A sheet containing details of a transaction for brokers to confirm before settlement.

Compensation Bid—A form of competitive bid for securities whereby the price to be paid by the underwriters equals the reoffer price to the public. Each bid specifies the dividend or coupon rate along with the amount to be paid by the issuer as compensation to the underwriters.

Compensatory Principle—*See* Benefit Received.

Competitive Auction—An auction, either English or Dutch, for securities, usually Treasury bonds. At an English auction, bidders buy securities at their bid price if they bid above the stop out price; if they bid below, they receive any unsold securities. At a Dutch auction, bidders buy securities at the stop out price if they bid above the stop out price. *See* Stop Out Price.

Competitive Bid—1) A method of selling securities of public utilities and railroads whereby the issuer invites bids from two or more syndicates. The syndicate bid that provides the lowest borrowing cost (in the case of a debt or preferred offering) or the highest price (in the case of a common stock offering) will be awarded the business. 2) An investor's bid in a Treasury or municipal auction. Noncompetitive bidders pay the average of all bid prices. 3) A process in which dealers submit prices that they are willing to pay for certain securities held by the requesting customer.

Competitive Options Trader (COT)—New York Stock Exchange options market maker.

Complete Inelasticity—*See* Perfect Inelasticity.

Complex Option—An option for which the exercise price and the amount of the underlying securities may vary over time. *See* Simple Option.

Compo—In competition.

Composite Demand—*See* Aggregate Demand.

Composite Supply—*See* Aggregate Supply.

Compound Accreted Value (CAV)—The nominal value of a zero coupon bond, printed in the official statement and on the certificate at six month intervals.

Compound Interest—Interest earned on principal as well as accrued interest.

Compound Interest Bond—Deep discount bond, including zero coupon bonds.

Comptroller—*See* Controller.

Concavity—Negative convexity. *See* Convexity.

Concession—The allowance an underwriter allows a non-member of the syndicate. Also called *Dealer's Reallowance*. *See* Reallowance.

Concurrent Pay—A CMO tranche that pays principal simultaneously with another tranche, rather than sequentially. Also called *Parallel Pay*.

Conditional Prepayment Rate (CPR)—The percentage of outstanding mortgages in a pool expected to prepay on average over a one-year period. *See* Single Monthly Mortality.

Condor—Selling two call options at different strike levels (usually at the money) and buying two calls with strike levels above and below those of the shorted calls. A condor looks like a short strangle, with the risk of large price moves reduced.

Conduit—A system that allows issuers with a limited amount of collateral to pledge collateral along with similar issuers to market a single large bond offering.

Conduit Financing—Uses municipal securities, such as Industrial Revenue Bonds, to finance a corporate project. Such securities are backed by the security of the corporation, not the municipality.

Conduit Theory—The IRS rule that avoids double taxation by allowing qualifying investment companies and REITs to pass income to investors without being taxed. Investors are then taxed as individuals.

Conduit-Type—Refers to a client whose broker/dealer does not disclose the principals of a transaction. Also called *Omnibus Account on an Undisclosed Basis*.

Confirmation—A formal memorandum given to a client detailing all data relevant to a trade made by the client. Confirmations must be sent on or before the first full business day following the trade date, except for cash transaction confirmations, which must be sent on the trade date. *See* Affirmation and National Institutional Delivery System.

Confirmation Note—A formal contract confirming and detailing all data relevant to a trade in the secondary market. Also called *Contract Note*.

Conforming Loan—Mortgage loan conforming to FNMA and FHLMC standards, including underwriting standards (LTV and income to total debt ratios), principal balances, and standardized documentation.

Congestion Area—A narrow trading range (i.e., when small price rises induce selling and small price declines induce buying).

Conglomerate—Holding company that owns companies with dissimilar businesses.

Connie Mac—Conventional mortgage pass-through security of an issuer other than GNMA, FNMA, or FHLMC.

Conservatism—A financial reporting convention that calls for anticipation of all losses and expenses but defers recognition of gains and profits until they are realized in an arm's-length transaction.

Consideration—Anything of value, typically cash or securities, exchanged for a promise, a contract, or title to securities.

Consistency—In reference to pass-through securities, refers to the historical regularity of prepayments. Low consistency means prepayments were infrequent and of irregular size; high consistency implies more frequent payments of relatively similar size.

Consol—1) Perpetual bond, such as those issued by England during the Napoleonic wars. *See* Perpetual. 2) Bond whose proceeds are used to retire other issues. Short for Consolidation Bond. Also called *Unifying Bond*.

Consolidated Balance Sheet—Financial statement, such as a balance sheet or annual report, listing the total assets, liabilities, and net worth of a parent corporation.

Consolidated Mortgage Bond—Bond whose proceeds are used to refund mortgage bonds.

Consolidated Tape—The combined ticker tapes reporting transactions in both NYSE-listed and AMEX-listed securities. Also identifies the originating market for NYSE-listed securities and reports on selected securities listed on regional exchanges.

Consolidation—1) A combination of companies to form a new one. *See* Merger. 2) A loan that combines and refinances other debt.

Consolidation Bond—*See* Consol.

Consortium—A partnership of financial institutions or individuals that raises capital, especially for international finance.

Consortium Bank—A merchant banking subsidiary set up by several banks that may or may not be of the same nationality. Consortia banks are common in the Euromarket and are active in loan syndication.

Constant Dollar (C$)—1) A hypothetical unit used to calculate general purchasing power. 2) An accounting method in which items are measured in constant dollars. 3) Investment plan in which a specified amount is invested in a security or fund at regular intervals. Also called *Dollar Cost Averaging*. 4) Investment plan in which the total dollar amount of a portfolio remains constant.

Constant Maturity Swap—An interest rate swap involving the exchange of floating rate payments between two counterparties. One party typically pays 3- or 6-month LIBOR while the other pays a rate equal to the yield of an on-the-run Treasury note minus a specified margin. Both rates reset periodically. Also called *Yield Curve Swap*.

Constant Maturity Treasury (CMT)—An index based on the average yield of a range of Treasury securities adjusted to a constant maturity of one year. The index is calculated by the Federal Reserve Board and published in its statistical release H-15. It moves closely, but not precisely, with the one-year Treasury bill auctions.

Constant Percent Prepayment (CPP)—A prepayment model in which the average monthly prepayment rate (SMM) is annualized by multiplying it by twelve. *See* Single Monthly Mortality and Conditional Prepayment Rate.

Constant Yield Method—Method used, for tax purposes, to accrete the cost paid for a bond purchased at an original issue discount. Zero coupon bonds and corporate discount bonds are two examples of bonds whose cost is accounted for using the constant yield method.

Construction Loan—Mortgage originated during the construction period of a multi-family project, which converts into a project loan upon completion. Construction loans are packaged under the GNMA program.

Construction Loan Note (CLN)—Notes issued to fund housing projects.

Constructive—Bullish.

Consumer Price Index (CPI)—Often called the cost of living, the CPI measures price changes at the retail level. It is based primarily on prices found in stores.

Consumer Spending—The sum of personal outlays on new (as opposed to used) goods and services other than housing.

Consumption—Consumer use of goods and services. The gross national product is the total of consumption plus government spending, net exports, and capital investment.

Contango—1) The normal relationship between prices in the cash-futures market, that is, when cash prices are below futures prices, and deferred futures are trading above near futures. *See* Backwardation. 2) The cost of deferring settlement on a security, usually added to the price of a security. 3) *See* Lombard Rate.

Contingency—A potential liability.

Contingent Asset—Asset whose value depends on a future event or condition.

Contingent Bargain—A simultaneous sale of one security and purchase of another security. The settlement of both transactions must take place simultaneously. *See* Free Delivery and Delivery Versus Payment.

Contingent Claim—Refers to an option or any security having the features of an option such as a warrant, convertible bond, or convertible preferred stock. The option writer has the liability to deliver stock in the case of calls (warrants) or to receive stock in the case of puts. These obligations are contingent upon the buyer paying the exercise price in the case of calls or delivering stock in the case of puts.

Contingent Immunization—A form of active management within an immunization framework that provides a minimum return by adding a safety net to the modern immunization theory approach. For example, if current rates are 8%, a contingent immunization plan might lock in a return of 7%. This 1% margin allows for active management in pursuit of a higher return if rates decline but triggers an immunization strategy once the potential return drops to 7% if rates rise. *See* Immunization.

Contingent Liability—A potential obligation; a circumstance or agreement that is not currently a liability but could become one if certain events occur.

Contingent Order—*See* Basis Order.

Contingent Swap—A swap that is activated by the action of a third party, such as the exercising of a warrant. Also called *Option Swap*.

Continued Bond—Bond that earns interest after maturity if not redeemed.

Continuing Appropriation—*See* Appropriation.

Continuity—When trade prices differ by an insignificant amount.

Continuity of Operations—An accounting assumption that the entity will be in business at least until current plans are fulfilled. Also called *Going Concern Assumption*.

Continuous Market—A market in which an investor can almost certainly find a buyer or seller, or one in which an investor can find a buyer or seller at a price close to that of the previous trade. A continuous market has frequent sales, narrow spreads, minimum price changes, prompt execution, and liquidity.

Continuous Settlement—Method of clearing and settling securities in which the National Securities Clearing Corporation keeps a daily balance record among dealers. *See* Contract Sheet and Window Settlement.

Contra Account—In accounting, an account that receives subtractions from another account. For example, allowance for uncollected receivables is the contra account for accounts receivable.

Contra Broker—Broker on the other side of a transaction.

Contra-Party—The party that buys a security.

Contract—1) Agreement between buyer and seller. 2) The unit of a traded commodity or security. 3) The unit of trade in a futures or forward market.

Contract Grade—The type of cash instruments listed in the rules of the exchange that can be used for delivery in futures transactions.

Contractionary—Refers to a slowing of economic activity.

Contract Market—A market that is eligible to trade in futures.

Contract Month—The month in which a futures contract is fulfilled by making or taking delivery.

Contract Note—*See* Confirmation Note.

Contract Sheet—Daily list of transactions prepared by the Securities Industry Automation Corporation, used by dealers to prepare for settlement. *See* Don't Know.

Contractual Plan—Plan to accumulate fixed dollar amounts of mutual fund shares at regular intervals over 10 to 15 years.

Contracyclical Trading—Taking a trading position opposed to current market expectations. *See* Contrarian.

Contrarian—An investor who deliberately takes positions that are opposed to market trends. Contrarians are technical analysts who follow sentiment indicators, such as opinion polls, short interest, the ratio of puts to calls, and other measurements of investment behavior. *See* Technical Analysis and Odd Lot Theory.

Contributed Capital—Corporate funds invested by shareholders. *See* Shareholders' Equity.

Controlled Account—*See* Discretionary Account.

Controlled Amortization Bond (CAB)—A CMO tranche that amortizes with a sinking fund that is predetermined as long as the prepayments on the underlying collateral remain at a constant level within a broad range of speeds. Also called *Planned Amortization Class (PAC)*.

Controlled-Growth Arbitrage—*See* Risk-Controlled Arbitrage.

Controlled Market—Regulated market in which supply, demand, and price may be artificially set. *See* Free and Open Market.

Controller—Chief corporate accountant. Also called *Comptroller*.

Control Person—*See* Insider.

Control Stock—Shares owned by an affiliated person, such as an officer or director.

Convenience Shelf—A form of registration statement that requires less information than shelf registration (e.g., pricing information and names of non-lead managers are not required). Also called *Phantom Shelf*. *See* Shelf Registration.

Conventional Loan—A mortgage loan usually granted by a bank or thrift institution. The loan is based solely on real estate as security rather than being insured or guaranteed by a government agency.

Conventional Mortgage-Backed Security (CMBS)—Mortgage-backed security that is not agency-guaranteed.

Convergence—The process by which the cash-futures basis narrows over time. Futures prices will move towards cash prices to reflect the lessening importance of net carry over time. In a cash-settled contract, such as the municipal futures, the future price will equal the cash price at settlement.

Conversion—Arbitrage strategy of buying a put and selling a call with the same expiration and strike price, and buying the underlying security. Conversion is considered a riskless alternative to money market instruments.

Conversion Date—The date on which conversion of a convertible bond can be exercised.

Conversion Discount—*See* Conversion Premium.

Conversion Factor—The number that must be multiplied by the price of the futures contract to arrive at the delivery price for a particular security.

Conversion Issue—A new issue of bonds timed to mature at the same time as another issue of the same borrower. The offering is normally structured in such a way that investors are given an incentive to exchange or convert the old issue into the new one.

Conversion Parity—A price at which a convertible must sell for it to equal the current market value of the common shares to be received upon conversion. If the convertible is trading at a premium to conversion parity, it is generally better to sell the convertible rather than convert.

Conversion Premium—The amount by which the price of a convertible security exceeds the price of the underlying stock.

Conversion Price—The price at which a convertible security can be converted into common stock.

Conversion Ratio—The number of shares of stock into which a convertible bond may be converted. *See* Parity.

Conversion Value—The conversion ratio multiplied by the current price of the underlying security.

Converted Put—*See* Synthetic Put.

Convertible—1) A security, usually a bond or preferred stock, that can be exchanged for other securities of the issuer (or, more rarely, for the stock of another entity), usually its common stock. For legal and/or fiscal reasons, convertibles are often issued by one corporation and are convertible into common stock of its parent. 2) Refers to adjustable rate mortgages that can be changed to fixed rate mortgages after a specified number of years.

Convertible Arbitrage—A simultaneous purchase and sale of related securities for an immediate profit upon conversion. This technique generally involves the purchase of a convertible bond or convertible preferred that is trading at a price below its conversion value, and the short sale of the related common stock. The stock received from the conversion offsets the short sale.

Convertible Bond—A bond that, at the option of the holder, is convertible into other securities of the corporation, usually into common equity. Occasionally, converti-bles have been issued by one corporation that are convertible into the equity of another. Some securities have been issued that are convertible into a specified amount of an underlying commodity.

Convertible Adjustable Preferred Stock—Corporate equity with two distinctive features: 1) the holder can convert the security into the common stock of the company at any time, at the price determined at the offering; and 2) the corporation can exchange the convertible preferred for convertible subordinated debentures after a specified period of time. In the event of an exchange, the coupon rate of the convertible subordinated debentures will be the equivalent of the dividend rate on the preferred stock. The convertible subordinated debentures will allow conversions into the same number of shares of common stock at an equivalent dollar amount of the convertible preferred stock.

Convertible Floating Rate Note—A floating rate note that is convertible, usually at the holder's option, into a fixed rate bond.

Convertible Preferred Stock—Preferred stock that, in addition to having preference over common stock, can also be converted into common stock according to a formula.

Convexity—A measure of the change in duration with respect to changes in interest rates. Convexity is the second derivative of a bond's price with respect to yield. The more convex a bond is, the more its duration will change given a change in interest rates. Modified duration assumes that prices change linearly with interest rates; it therefore becomes increasingly imprecise in estimating price changes as yield changes increase. If a bond is convex, its change in price given a specified change in yield will be of a different magnitude than that predicted by modified duration. If the change in price is greater than that predicted by modified duration, the bond has positive convexity. Conversely, if the change in price is less than that predicted by modified duration, the bond has negative convexity. *See* Modified Duration, Option-Adjusted Convexity, and Par Compression.

Cooked Books—Falsified financial information.

Cooling-Off Period—Period between filing the preliminary prospectus with the SEC and the public offering of securities, typically 20 days.

Core Holding—That portion of a portfolio that is regarded as a long-term holding.

Core Management—A relatively passive portfolio management strategy that tries to reduce transaction costs.

Corner—To control a market.

Corner the Market—To buy a large proportion of a security. An investor who has cornered the market can force a short seller to pay inflated prices to cover the short.

Corporate Bond—Debt issued by a corporation that pays interest and principal to the bondholders at specified times. The corporation may have the right to call the bond. The bondholder may have the right to convert the bond into the corporation's common stock. Bondholders have priority over stockholders in the case of bankruptcy.

Corporate Bond Equivalent (CBE) Yield—The yield that a given instrument must offer in order to produce the same rate of return as a corporate bond. Corporate bonds pay interest semiannually and their yields are assumed to be compounded semiannually; therefore, corporate bond equivalent yield is ordinarily computed for those instruments that pay interest other than semiannually, or for which compounding is assumed to be other than semiannually.

Corporate Bond Index Futures—Futures contract based on an index of one hundred corporate bonds chosen by the Chicago Board of Trade each quarter. The bonds must be issued by U.S. corporations, have a current maturity of at least fifteen years, have a credit rating of at least Baa3/BBB- and not be a likely downgrade candidate, have at least $100 million principal amount outstanding, and not be imminently callable. The index is also called the *Cash Index*. The spread between the bonds and the Index is called the CUB spread.

Corporate Resolution—A document authorizing an individual to act on behalf of a corporation.

Corporate Settlement—In the U.S., the settlement of a securities transaction five business days after the trade date.

Corporate Tax Equivalent (CTE) Yield—The rate of return required on a par bond to produce the same after-tax yield to maturity as a given bond.

Corporation—Legal, taxable entity chartered by a U.S. state or by the federal government, which is distinct from those who own it. Ownership is evidenced by the holding of the corporation's stock.

Corpus—1) Principal of a security. 2) The property in a trust fund.

Corpus TR—Custodial receipts are issued in respect of principal payments on specific Treasury securities. Holders of Corpus TRs receive principal payments at maturity of the underlying Treasury security and receive no payments prior to such time. Also called *Principal TR*.

Correction—A reverse price movement in a trend, usually a downward movement in a rising trend.

Correspondent Bank—Bank that performs banking functions for another bank.

Cost Accounting—*See* Managerial Accounting.

Costing—The British term for cost accounting. *See* Managerial Accounting.

Cost of Carry—*See* Carry.

Cost of Funds—A bank index. The 11th District Cost of Funds is the weighted average interest rate paid by the 11th FHLB District member savings institutions on their sources of funds. The Monthly Median National Cost of Funds is the median average interest rate paid by all FSLIC-insured institutions on their sources of funds.

Cost of Insurance and Freight (CIF)—Measurement of the value of merchandise imports inclusive of all shipping and insurance charges necessary to land the goods in the importing country.

Cost of Issuance—A borrower's costs, including legal, printing, and rating agency fees.

Cost of Service Principle—*See* Benefit Received.

Cost-Push Inflation—A rise in prices that results from increasing production costs. *See* Demand-Pull Inflation.

Cottage Industry—Manufacturing done by non-specialists, family members, or individuals at the workers' homes. Also called *Domestic Production, Home Industry,* and *Household Industry*.

Counter Cyclical—Refers to an economic force that tends to dampen business and economic cycles. *See* Wealth Effect and Pro-Cyclical.

Country Limit—*See* Borrower Limit.

Country Risk—*See* Sovereign Risk.

Coupon—1) The annual rate of interest that the borrower promises to pay the bondholder; the face interest rate of a security. 2) A certificate attached to a bond that must be surrendered in order to collect the interest due on a specified date. 3) With respect to mortgage securities, it is the mortgage rate less servicing, guarantee and/or securitization fees.

Coupon Bond—*See* Bearer Bond.

Coupon Issue—In the Treasury market, a bond or note (i.e., an issue paying semiannual coupons) as opposed to a Treasury bill. May be collectively referred to as simply coupons (e.g., "The Fed is buying all coupons").

Coupon Market—Market in which the federal government raises money through the sale of coupon bearing Treasury securities.

Coupon Pass—Federal Reserve open market operation in which the Fed buys Treasury notes or bonds outright, instead of on repo. This adds reserves to the financial system on a longer-term basis than system repo. *See* Bill Pass and System Repo.

Coupon Payment Period—The period of time between coupon payments of a bond.

Coupon Rate—1) *See* Nominal Yield. 2) For CMOs, the annual rate at which a tranche will pay interest while it is outstanding. On an accrual tranche, the rate at which interest accrues and is added to the principal amount outstanding to be paid when the bond begins to make payments.

Coupon Spread—*See* Margin.

Coupon Stripping—A process of producing single-payment (zero coupon) instruments from existing conventional bonds. It can be accomplished either by separating the coupons from the principal or by selling receipts representing the individual coupons and principal on a security held by a trustee. *See* Zero Coupon Bond, Corpus TR, and Coupon TR.

Coupon TR—Custodial receipt issued in respect of interest payments on specific Treasury securities.

Covariance—The correlation between the returns of two securities. Investors look for securities with little correlation, or negative correlation, of returns in order to diversify risk or hedge.

Covenant—A promise in an indenture, which protects the lender. Also called *Restrictive Covenant* and *Protective Covenant.*

Covenant of Equal Coverage—*See* Negative Pledge Clause.

Cover—1) To offset a transaction. For example, an investor buys a futures contract to offset a previous opposite futures transaction of equal size. In a short cover, an investor buys a security to offset a previous sale. 2) The bid or offer made to offset a transaction. 3) The difference between the best bid and the second best bid on a new issue.

Coverage—The margin of safety for payment of debt service calculated as the ratio of operating income plus interest expense to long- and short-term interest requirements over a period. May be calculated before or after taxes.

Cover Bid/Cover Offer—The second-best bid or offer, usually in a competitive bid-wanted or offer-wanted situation. Also called *Cover*.

Covered Call—A short position in a call option for which the writer owns sufficient deliverable securities or other eligible collateral to satisfy an exercise of that call by the holder. *See* Buywrite.

Covered Industry Investing—Choosing corporations to invest in (or boycotting corporations) for social reasons.

Covered Interest Arbitrage—When an investor buys a security denominated in a foreign currency and hedges the exchange risk either by selling the return on the investment forward for dollars or by selling the currency short in the futures market.

Covered Position—A position in one security that is hedged by a position in another security.

Covered Put—A short position in a put option for which the writer owns sufficient eligible collateral to ensure his ability to take delivery of the underlying security in the event the put is exercised.

Covered Write—*See* Buywrite.

Covered Writing—Selling a call option while owning the underlying security. This strategy is intended to increase overall returns by earning fee income from the options. *See* Naked.

Cram Down Paper—Bonds issued directly to shareholders in exchange for stock, typically as a defensive measure against a takeover attempt or in a recapitalization. *See* Pay-in-Kind.

Crash—A dramatic drop in market prices and activity.

Creative Destruction—Term describing economic cycles, because expansions create forces that cause contractions.

Credit—1) A liability. 2) To record a liability. 3) A rating given to a corporation signifying its ability to repay debt. *See* Standard & Poor's and Moody's. 4) A loan.

Credit Balance—Amount the investor has in a margin account that belongs to him.

Credit Card Asset Backed Security—Asset backed security backed by credit card receivables, which differs from other asset backed securities in that it does not amortize principal for a specified period. *See* Payout Event and Non-Amortization Period.

Credit Crunch—Economic situation in which demand for money exceeds supply.

Credit Department—1) Margin department. 2) Department that evaluates customer credit. 3) Department that evaluates creditworthiness of securities.

Credit Enhancement—When a third party guarantees the debt service payments of an issuer for a negotiated fee. Usually either banks supply letters of credit or lines of credit (typically for short-term debt) or guarantor agencies underwrite municipal bond insurance.

Credit Market—Refers to the debt market in general, including all bonds, short-term non-equity securities, and non-securitized debt obligations.

Credit Money—Money in circulation not fully backed by a precious metal, including all U.S. currency. Also called *Fiduciary Money*.

Creditor—A person who loans money. *See* Debtor.

Credit Risk—*See* Risk.

Credit Spread—1) The difference between the value of two options when one is sold at a higher price than the other is purchased. 2) A yield spread that is a function of the credit quality of one of the securities. For example, the spread between U.S. Treasury bills and LIBOR is a function of the credit of the banking industry.

Credit Theory—Economic theory that recessions are caused by debtors slowing their rate of consumption as they try to reduce their amount of debt outstanding.

Creeping Inflation—A constant inflation rate of 2 to 3 percent.

Creeping Tender Offer—SEC term to describe the purchase of a large percentage of a corporation's stock without public notification.

Crisis-at-Maturity—The situation in which a lesser quality borrower has greater difficulty procuring funds for the final maturity repayment in a debt issue than in finding the funds for interest payments during the issue's life. A sinking fund reduces the risk of crisis-at-maturity by requiring the final payment to be spread over a number of years.

Cross—1) A transaction in which there is one broker for both sides. The broker legally must offer the security at a price higher than the bid. Also called *Exchange Distribution*. 2) *See* Clean Trade.

Cross Default—A covenant by a borrower, referring to itself and any subsidiaries and guarantors, stating that the default in a payment of one of its borrowings will be considered a default of the issue to which the cross default covenant applies.

Cross-Margining—Using a position held at one exchange as margin for a position held at another exchange. For example, using a stock index futures account held at the Chicago Mercantile Exchange as margin for a position in put options held at the Chicago Board Options Exchange.

Crossed Market—When one broker's bid is higher than another's lowest offer, or vice versa.

Crossed Trade—An illegal practice whereby offsetting buy and sell orders are not recorded on the exchange.

Cross Hedge—A position created when a long or short position in one security or derivative is hedged by short or long position in a different security or derivative.

Crossrate—The rate of exchange of two foreign currencies determined by the rate of exchange of each currency in a third nation's currency.

Cross-Trading—Illegal commodity futures transaction in which two parties execute a private trade.

Crowding Out—Situation in which increased government spending reduces the private sector's ability to borrow. The crowding out effect is a monetarist argument against fiscal spending.

Crown Jewel—Defense against a hostile takeover in which a corporation sells valuable assets to a third party, making the corporation a less attractive target.

Crush Spread—The purchase of futures of a primary commodity (e.g., soybeans) and sale of futures of products derived from the primary commodity (e.g., soybean oil and meal). *See* Reverse Crush Spread.

Cuff Quote—Estimate.

Cum—With. A security cum dividend is one from which the buyer will receive the next dividend. *See* Ex.

Cumulative—A preferred dividend is cumulative if the dividend flows accrue when payments are not made as scheduled.

Cumulative Gap—*See* Gap.

Cumulative Preferred—A stock with the provision that if one or more dividends are omitted, the omitted dividends will be paid before any dividend can be paid on any junior security (e.g., common stock) of the issuing company.

Cumulative Prepayment Experience—The average prepayment rate since the issuance of a mortgage-related security.

Cumulative Sinking Fund—A sinking fund in which any unapplied monies for the sinking fund may be used in the following period.

Cumulative Voting—A method of voting for corporate board members in which shareholders may cast all their votes for one candidate rather than apportioning their votes equally among all candidates.

Cumulative voting is the most important type of proportional representation.

Cum Warrant—Warrant with a host bond. *See* Naked Warrant.

Curb Exchange—Original name of the American Stock Exchange.

Curb Stock—Issues traded at the American Stock Exchange.

Curing—Rental payments made by the lessor on behalf of a utility.

Currency—Coins and paper money. *See* Money.

Currency Basket—A unit reflecting the absolute composite value of specific amounts of several underlying currencies. *See* Special Drawing Rights.

Currency Devaluation—Reduction of the value of one currency in relation to others.

Currency-Linked Bond—A bond whose payments of interest and principal are valued by reference to one currency but made in another.

Currency of Denomination—Currency in which an issuer pledges to pay interest and principal amount.

Currency Risk—*See* Risk.

Currency Swap—An agreement between two parties to exchange future payments in one currency for payments in a second currency. These agreements are used by corporations, financial institutions, sovereign governments, government agencies, and supranational entities to transform the currency denomination of assets or liabilities. Unlike interest rate swaps, currency swaps include an exchange of principal at maturity.

Currency Warrant—A detachable option included in securities issues giving the holder the right to purchase from the issuer additional securities denominated in a currency different from that of the original issue. The coupon and price of the securities covered by the warrant are fixed at the time of the sale of the original issue.

Current Account—1) Demand deposit. 2) Part of the balance of payments, defined as one nation's record of transactions with another nation or nations. Transactions include exchanges and transfers of goods and services. *See* Balance of Payments.

Current Account Balance—The value of all exports (goods and services) less all imports, plus net receipts of interest, profits, and dividends from abroad. That is, the sum of the trade balance and the invisible trade balance.

Current Assets—Assets that can be easily liquidated.

Current Coupon—1) A security selling at or close to par. 2) In reference to pass-throughs, the nominal rate (coupon rate) at which most issuers sell securities currently. 3) The interest rate on a floating rate security in the current interest period.

Current Coupon Spread—Yield spread of a current coupon mortgage security over Treasury securities.

Current Delivery—A futures contract that will become deliverable during the coming month. *See* Deferred Futures.

Current Income Bonds—*See* Series HH.

Current Issue—The most recent issue of a short-term security.

Current Liabilities—Money owed within one year.

Current Maturity—The amount of time until a security matures. Also called *Remaining Term*.

Current Ratio—Current assets divided by current liabilities.

Current Yield—1) The ratio of the coupon to the market price of a bond, expressed as a percentage. For mutual funds, it is the dividend divided by the offering price plus capital gain. 2) For preferred stock, the dividend rate divided by the price, expressed as a percentage.

Cushion—The amount of time between bond issuance and the call date.

Cushion Bond—A high coupon bond selling above its call price. Because high coupon bonds have shorter durations and lower price volatility than low coupon bonds, they are cushioned against price decreases, and therefore against being called.

Cushion Theory—Theory that short sellers contribute to market liquidity and cushion the fall of a bear market.

CUSIP—Committee on Uniform Securities Identification Procedures. Standard alphanumeric system used throughout the financial community for identification of security issues. A nine character code is assigned to each issue and is printed on the face of the security. The first six digits identify the issuer in alphabetic sequence, the next two characters (alphabetic or numeric) identify the particular issue, and the ninth digit is a check digit that mathematically ensures the integrity of the entire code.

Custodian—An institution holding securities in safekeeping for a client.

Customer Agreement—An agreement an investor must sign when opening an account, which contains rules of the exchange, such as margin requirements. *See* Transfer Authorization.

Customer Man—*See* Registered Representative.

Customer Repo—Federal Reserve open market operation in which the Fed buys collateral on repo on behalf of customers (foreign central banks). While this adds cash to the financial system, it is considered technical rather than stimulative action.

Customer's Broker—*See* Registered Representative.

Custom Pool—Security issued under GNMA II program in which a single issuer packages the mortgages. Also called *Single Issuer Pool.*

Customs Value Basis (CVB)—Measurement of the value of merchandise imports at the point at which they are loaded in a carrier to be transported to the importing country.

Cut-Off Date—In reference to pass-through securities, the last day of the month on which a prepayment received by the issuer will be remitted to a security holder in the forthcoming payment.

Cutting a Melon—Declaring an extra large dividend.

Cycle—1) *See* Expiration Cycle. 2) *See* Business Cycle.

Cyclically Perverse—*See* Pro-Cyclical.

Cyclical Stock—Stock whose performance is strongly affected by changes in economic activity and the business cycle.

Cyclical Trend—Short-term movements in prices or interest rates, which reflect stages in the business cycle or other technical factors. *See* Secular Trend.

D

Daily Accretion—A method of portfolio accounting in which capital gains on discount bonds are accumulated daily in anticipation of receipt of par at maturity.

Daily Bond Buyer—Publication that contains fixed income market statistics and indexes. Published daily.

Daily Price Limit—The maximum price change permitted for a futures contract during a trading session, set by the exchange.

Daimyo—Bonds offered in the Japanese domestic market, listed in Luxembourg, and settled through Euroclear and CEDEL.

Daisy Chain—Trading among manipulators to give the appearance of an active, liquid market.

Dated Date—Date from which accrued interest is calculated on newly offered securities.

Date of Record—*See* Record Date.

Dawn Raid—Rapid purchase of a large percentage of a corporation's stock at above-market prices. Also called *Market Raid* and *Premium Raid*.

Daylight Overdraft—Bank loan to be repaid the same business day.

Daylight Risk—The risk of being unable to access a market in another time zone.

Day Order—A trade order that is cancelled if it is not filled that day.

Day Trading—Intraday trading as opposed to long-term investing or positioning.

Deal—*See* Trade.

Dealer—A person or institution that buys and sells securities continuously as principal. The difference between the buying price and the selling price is the dealer spread or bid-asked spread. *See* Broker and Broker-Dealer.

Dealer Loan—Collateralized loan made by a money market bank to a dealer to finance an overnight position.

Dealer Market—Market in which all trades are executed between broker/dealers.

Dealer Paper—Commercial paper initially sold to a broker/dealer.

Dealer Pot—*See* Pot.

Dealer Spread—*See* Bid-Asked Spread.

Dealer's Reallowance—*See* Concession.

Dear—Expensive.

Debenture—Debt secured only by unpledged assets and the general credit of the issuer (e.g., Treasuries and most corporate bonds). Also called *Unsecured Bond*.

Debenture Stock—British term for Preterred Stock.

Debenture with Warrants—A debt issue that has a fixed number of warrants attached. The warrants usually can be detached after a specified date, and separate trading markets develop for the bonds with warrants attached and for the bonds and warrants separately. The bonds frequently have the provision that they can be used at face value to exercise the warrants in lieu of cash.

Debit—1) Used as a noun, an asset. 2) Used as a verb, to record an asset.

Debit Balance—Amount the investor owes the broker.

Debit Spread—The difference between the value of two options, when one is purchased at a higher price than the other is sold. *See* Credit Spread.

Debt—Liabilities such as bonds and loans, as opposed to stock. Interest payments on debt are tax deductible; dividends are not.

Debt Capital—Noncurrent liabilities.

Debt Ceiling—*See* Debt Limit.

Debt/Equity Ratio—A measure of long-term liquidity risk, calculated as long-term debt divided by shareholders' equity. The higher the ratio, the more highly leveraged the company. From a bondholder's perspective, generally the lower the ratio the more secure the debt.

Debt/Equity Swap—A transaction in which a company retires a portion of its outstanding discounted debt by exchanging it for equity. The gain on the transaction is the difference between the market value of the equity exchanged and the book value of the debt.

Debt Financing—Raising money through bond, mortgage, or note issuance.

Debt Leverage—Investing borrowed money.

Debt Limit—The limit of a government, agency, or municipality's authority to incur debt. The U.S. government debt limit is the Congressional limit on the total face value of U.S. Treasury obligations. Also called *Debt Ceiling*.

Debtor—A person who owes money. *See* Creditor.

Debtor Nation—A nation that imports more than it exports.

Debt Retirement—Repayment of debt. *See* Refunding and Sinking Fund.

Debt Service—1) A series of payments comprised of principal and interest that are calculated to extinguish a debt over a specified period of time. For level debt service these payments would be equal. 2) The periodic payment of principal and interest on mortgage loans.

Debt Service Fund—A fund established to cover the initial shortfall of principal and interest on graduated payment mortgages. Also called *Reserve Fund*.

Debt Service Reserve Fund—Fund used to service municipal debt if revenues are insufficient to pay interest and principal.

Declaration Date—Date on which quarterly dividend payment amounts are declared.

Declare—To authorize a dividend payment on a specified date.

Decrement (DEC) Table—A table in the prospectus supplement or offering memorandum for a CMO issue with the projected percentage of principal balance that would be outstanding at various dates for each tranche, given various prepayment speeds. Also called *Prepayment Table*.

Dedicate—1) To cash-flow match a portfolio. *See* Dedication. 2) To transfer from private to public ownership.

Dedication—A pension plan strategy designed to minimize the funding risks for a portion of a plan's assets and, with the actuary's permission, help raise a plan's investment return assumption. With a dedicated strategy, a bond portfolio is structured so that the cash flow from the portfolio matches the specific stream of cash liabilities. Also called *Cash Flow Matching*.

Deed of Trust—*See* Indenture.

Deep Bid/Offer—Large bid or offer that is away from the market.

Deep Discount Bond—A bond issued (or currently in the market) at a large discount from par. Deep discount bonds have below-market interest rates and effective call protection. The ultimate form of deep discount bond is the zero coupon bond. *See* Zero Coupon Bond and Flower Bond.

Deep in the Money—An option that can be exercised at a relatively large profit.

Deep out of the Money—An option that if exercised would result in a relatively large loss.

Defalcation—Embezzlement.

Default—Failure to fulfill a contract. Specifically, failure to make timely payment of interest or principal on a bond or otherwise comply with any provision of the indenture.

Default Rate—The percentage of mortgages in a population whose payments are late by more than a specified period of time (e.g., there is a 30-day, a 60-day, and a 90-day default rate). Default rate may also refer to the percentage of mortgages in a population that are liquidated due to non-payment. In this context, mortgage payments are divided into two categories: voluntary (prepayments) and involuntary (default).

Default Risk—The risk that an issuer will be unable to meet timely interest and principal payments.

Defeasance—The process of rendering something null and void. In a fixed income context, it involves setting up a riskless portfolio of bonds designed to service the cash flows promised to creditors. The cash flows derived from this portfolio must be sufficient to pay principal and interest on the debt defeased, assuming a very low reinvestment rate. The stringency of this requirement makes it difficult or impossible to include callable Treasury bonds or GNMAs in the defeasance portfolio.

In Legal Defeasance, the bond issuer places cash or a portfolio of Treasuries in an irrevocable trust for the benefit of the bondholders. The relationship between the issuer and the creditor is at this point severed, and the issuer is released from the covenants in the indenture. Creditors must look solely to the portfolio in trust for the timely payment of principal and interest, and the trust becomes the primary obligor to the bondholders. Legal defeasance is an extinguishment of debt for both tax and accounting purposes and hence is a taxable event. Legal defeasance is well known in the tax-exempt area because tax-exempt obligations generally may be extinguished, or defeased, by the issuer.

Economic Defeasance also allows a corporation to remove debt from its balance sheet by depositing U.S. Treasury securities in an irrevocable grantor trust. The cash flow from these securities must at all times be sufficient to meet the obligation which is defeased. The issuer is generally not released from the terms of the indenture. Since there is no change in the legal relationship, the action is non-taxable.

Defensive Corporation—A corporation that feels the negative effects of a business downturn last (e.g., food, utilities).

Defensive Interval—A financial ratio used to predict bankruptcy, defined as quick assets divided by cash expenditure per day.

Defensive Portfolio—A portfolio of short-term securities (or bonds with low durations).

Defensive Security—A relatively stable security, or one that tends to decline less than most others in a weak market.

Deferred Annuity—Annuity whose payments begin after a specified period of time.

Deferred Contract—Futures contracts with distant delivery, that is, past the delivery of the nearby contract. Also called *Back Contract.*

Deferred Coupon Bond—*See* Deferred Interest Security.

Deferred Futures—The most distant delivery months in which futures trading is taking place. *See* Current Delivery.

Deferred Interest Security—Security that has no coupon payments for a specified interval, allowing the issuer to defer interest costs. Also called *Deferred Coupon Bond. See* Zero Coupon Bond, Stepped Coupon, and Zero-Fixed Coupon.

Deferred Purchase Note (DPN)—A new issue whose terms call for payment of a percentage (e.g., 25%) of the issue price on the normal closing date with the remaining percentage paid at a future date, usually six months to one year later. Failure to make the second payment results in forfeiture of the initial payment. Also called *Partly Paid Bond.*

Deficiency Judgment—A court order to pay the balance owed on a loan if the proceeds from the sale of the security are insufficient to pay off the loan.

Deficiency Letter—A statement the SEC sends to a corporation if there are omissions or misrepresentations in a registration statement. *See* Registration Statement.

Deficiency Payment—On an FHLMC issue, a principal amount guaranteed and paid to bondholders in excess of actual principal collections on the underlying mortgages. All deficiency payments on a given issue must be repaid to FHLMC before bondholders may receive any payments of principal in excess of the guaranteed amounts.

Deficit—The amount by which expenditures exceed revenues.

Deficit Financing—Raising money by issuing debt, usually government debt.

Deficit Reduction Act—Tax reform bill of 1984 that included the repeal of the 30 percent withholding tax on interest paid to foreign investors on debt issued after July 18, 1984.

Deficit Spending—Government spending in excess of revenues.

Defined Benefit Pension Plan—Tax-exempt plan that invests in securities in order to pay retirement benefits. Contributions are made by the employee and/or the employer. *See* Defined Contribution Pension Plan.

Defined Contribution Pension Plan—Retirement plan, profit-sharing plans being the most common. in which annual contributions depend on the profitability of the firm and retirement benefits are not known. Also called *Fixed Benefit Plan* and *Money Purchase Plan*. *See* Defined Benefit Pension Plan.

Definitive Form—*See* Certificated Security.

Deflation—Period during which consumer spending, bank loans, money in circulation and prices are reduced. *See* Inflation.

Degressive Tax—A progressive tax in which each rate increase is smaller than the previous one.

Delay—The time between the record date and the payment date. A bond that pays interest on the record date has zero delay.

Delayed Cap Floating Rate Note—A floating rate note with a maximum rate of interest effective after an initial period. *See* Cap, Capped Floating Rate Note, Collar, Floating Rate Note, and Floor.

Delayed Convertible—A warrant or other convertible security that can be converted only after a specified date.

Delayed Delivery—An arrangement that may be made with the underwriters of a new issue that permits certain persons or institutions to pay for and take delivery of certain amounts of the new securities on specified dates after the original offering.

Delayed Opening—Postponement of the opening of trading in a particular stock due to an unusual condition, such as a large imbalance in buy and sell orders. Such an imbalance often is associated with a particular event, such as a takeover offer, or pending corporate news.

Delinquent—Describes a borrower, typically a mortgagor, who fails to make a payment.

Delist—To remove a corporation's name from an exchange, because the corporation has either failed to meet financial ratio or sales requirements or violated an exchange regulation.

Deliverable—Securities that meet standards of futures contracts as to quality, maturity, principal amount, and coupon rate and that may be physically delivered to satisfy the contract. Not applicable to cash settlement contracts.

Deliver Balance Order (DBO)—*See* Balance Order.

Delivery—The tender and receipt of a financial instrument or cash in settlement of a futures contract. *See* Good Delivery.

Delivery Against Cash (DAC)—*See* Cash on Delivery.

Delivery Date—First day of the month during which delivery may be made on a futures contract.

Delivery Factor—The amount that when multiplied by the settlement price of a futures contract gives the delivered invoice price (i.e., the price that is received for delivered bonds). For GNMAs, the settlement price is divided by the delivery factor. Delivery factors for Treasury bonds and notes are based on the price for an issue that produces a yield of 8% to maturity (or call), and for GNMAs on a yield maintenance price for GNMA 8s at par.

Delivery Mechanism—The procedure used to fulfill futures contract obligations at the delivery date, including basket delivery, cash settlement, or simple delivery where only one specific instrument may be delivered.

Delivery Month—Month during which a futures contract can be fulfilled via the delivery mechanism.

Delivery Notice—A seller's notice of intention to make delivery against a short futures position.

Delivery Price—A price, fixed by the clearing house, at which deliveries on future contracts are invoiced.

Delivery Versus Payment (DVP)—Delivery of securities to a designated point (bank or broker) upon receipt of payment for the securities, in the form of a bank wire or check. *See* Receipt versus Payment and Free Delivery.

Delta—The theoretical change in the value of an option premium relative to a small change in the value of the underlying security. The inverse of the delta gives the theoretical hedge ratio. *See* Gamma and Hedge Ratio.

Delta Hedge—A strategy to hedge an options position, in which the investor dynamically trades a position in the underlying security. The amount of the position is determined by the option's delta.

Demand—1) In the context of a new issue, the amount of securities underwriters believe they can place. *See* Allotment. 2) The quantity of goods and services consumers are willing and able to consume.

Demand Bond—A bond, priced at par, which the investor has the option to redeem at specified intervals after giving the required notice. *See* Variable Rate Demand Note.

Demand Certificate—Delivery paper for iced broilers in a futures contract.

Demand Deposits—Checking accounts, which constitute about 3/4 of the money supply. Currency in circulation accounts for the remaining 1/4.

Demand Elasticity—A market environment in which a rise or decline in price causes a decline or rise in demand. *See* Supply Elasticity.

Demand Line of Credit—*See* Line of Credit.

Demand Loan—A loan on which the lender can demand payment in full at any time.

Demand-Pull Inflation—A rise in prices caused by too much money chasing too few goods. Also called *Buyers' Inflation*. *See* Cost-Push Inflation.

Demonitization—Removing a form of currency from circulation.

Denomination—1) Face, par, or dollar amount. Denominations are usually $1,000 for corporate bonds and $5,000 for municipal bonds. 2) The deliverable quantity (or quantities) of a security.

De Novo—New (e.g., a de novo bank).

Depletion—1) The allocation of costs of natural resources. *See* Depreciation. 2) Use of a wasting asset. *See* Wasting Asset.

Depository—A bank or other entity responsible for holding assets.

Deposit Note—*See* Bank Deposit Note.

Depository Preferred—Preferred shares evidencing fractional ownership in a preferred share (often having a greater par or stated value), held by a depository agent.

Depository Receipt—Delivery paper for gold in a futures contract.

Depository Trust Company (DTC)—A central securities certificate depository through which members effect security deliveries among one another via computerized bookkeeping entries, thereby reducing the physical movement of securities. The four depositories registered with the SEC are The Depository Trust Company (New York), Midwest Securities Trust Company (Chicago), Pacific Securities Trust Company (San Francisco), and Philadelphia Depository Trust Company.

Depreciation—The estimated decline in value of a capital asset, due to use, time, or improved technology. Amortization, by contrast, is associated with intangible assets, and depletion with natural resources.

See Capital Consumption Allowance, Straight Line, Double Declining Balance, and Sum-of-the-Years' Digits.

Depression—A severe recession. There have been eleven depressions in the U.S. since 1790, although the term usually refers to the Great Depression of the 1930s. *See* Recession.

Depth—Characteristic of a security for which it is possible to trade large amounts without affecting the price significantly. A security with large trading volume usually has depth.

Deregulation—The relaxation of regulations governing a market or industry.

Derivative—A market instrument that has an underlying security or is created from other securities. Derivatives include futures, options, and swaps.

Derived Book Value—Reported book value plus retained earnings, used to adjust the market-to-book ratio by taking into consideration restructurings and stock repurchases.

Descending Yield Curve—*See* Yield Curve.

Designated Order Turnaround (DOT)—Automated system for executing orders used on the New York Stock Exchange. *See* Automated Order Entry System.

Designation—The portion of an investor's order allocated to an underwriter by the manager of the offering.

Devaluation—Decreasing the value of one currency in relation to another.

Development Bank—There are three well-known Development Banks: The International Bank for Reconstruction and Development (IBRD or World Bank); The Inter-American Development Bank (IADB); and The Asian Development Bank (ADB). The African Development Bank differs from the others in that it has no U.S. Government participation. World Bank programs vastly exceed those of the other three entities combined.

Diagonal Spread—The purchase of an option with one expiration date and strike price and the offsetting sale of an option on the same security with a different expiration date and strike price. This creates a diagonal line through the "box" of options across expiration dates and strike prices.

Difference Check—A check issued when the same securities have been both bought and sold for delivery on the same date; the check is for an amount that equals the difference between the purchase and sale prices.

Differential—Extra commission for a dealer who executes a relatively small or odd lot trade.

Difficult Trade—Occurs when a security is relatively illiquid, forcing the broker-dealer to take time executing the trade, or when finding the exact amount of the security is difficult, forcing the broker-dealer to buy or sell some of the security for his own account.

Diffusion—Theory that all taxes cause price increases.

Dilution—When common shares increase and the company's assets do not. Convertible issues can be protected against dilution by a reduction in the conversion price. This contingency is stated in an antidilution clause.

Dime—Ten basis points.

Dip—A small decline in a variable such as prices or interest rates.

Direct Debt—A municipality's total outstanding debt. Also called *Bonded Debt.*

Direct Financing—Obtaining funds directly from investors, without the mediation of an underwriter.

Direct Hedge—A futures purchase or sale intended to reduce price risk for a deliverable financial instrument. *See* Cross Hedge.

Direct Paper—Commercial paper that a corporation sells directly to investors.

Direct Pay—*See* Letter of Credit Backed.

Direct Pay Letter of Credit—*See* Letter of Credit.

Direct Placement—*See* Private Placement.

Direct Placement Memorandum—*See* Private Placement Memorandum.

Dirt Bonds—Farmers Home Administration securities.

Dirty—1) Refers to the market price of a bond that includes accrued interest. *See* Clean. 2) Callable.

Dirty Float—System of floating currency exchange rates in which national central banks occasionally intervene.

Disclaimer—A statement made by the lead-manager as representative for the underwriting syndicate, and contained in offering documents, which asserts among other things that certain information provided in the prospectus was supplied by the borrower and is therefore not the responsibility of the managers or underwriters. A notice or statement intending to limit or avoid potential legal liability.

Disclosure—Showing financial information.

Disclosure Document—Document that outlines the risks of option trading. Distribution of the disclosure document to clients is required before or at the time their account is approved for option trading.

Discount—1) To compute the present value of a future cash flow. 2) The difference between par and the price of an issue for issues selling below par. 3) A discount bond.

Discount Basis—A method for quoting non-coupon securities (which always sell at a discount) in which the discount from par is annualized based on a 360-day year. Also called *Bank Discount Basis* and *Discount Yield*.

Discount Bond—Bond selling below par.

Discounted Cash Flows—The present value of future principal, interest, and reinvestment income. When referring to CMOs, the discount rate is usually the highest bond interest rate.

Discounted Information—When a security's price fully reflects a piece of information, the information is said to be discounted. In an efficient market, all information is discounted.

Discounted Investment in Negotiated Government Obligations (DINGO)—Australian Treasury securities whose principal is stripped of interest coupons.

Discounted Margin (DM)—Formula for valuing floating rate securities, representing the increment over the index rate (e.g., LIBOR) that is returned by the floater. DM is the standard formula for valuing European floaters, and has been refined by First Boston to account for variables in U.S. issues. *See* Yield to Maturity for Floating Rate Securities.

Discount House—British financial institution that trades money market instruments by borrowing overnight funds from banks.

Discounting—The mathematical process of calculating the present value of future income.

Discounting a Note—*See* Factoring.

Discount Market—Market in which prices for advanced months of futures contracts progressively decrease. *See* Normal Market.

Discount Paper—*See* Discount Securities.

Discount Rate—1) Interest rate the Fed charges member banks that borrow at the discount window. The discount rate used to be a true discount, or interest rate deducted from the amount loaned, but is now an add-on rate. Called *Bank Rate* in Britain. Also called *Capitalization Rate*. 2) German term for prime rate. 3) Rate used to discount cash flows in calculating present value. *See* Discounting.

Discount Securities—Money market instruments that are issued at a discount and redeemed at maturity at face value (e.g., Treasury bills).

Discount Window—Provision whereby Federal Reserve member banks can borrow against collateral in the form of government bonds or other acceptable paper.

Discount Yield—*See* Discount Basis.

Discretionary Account—Account in which the account executive, having been given permission, may trade without the customer's approval for each transaction. Also called *Controlled Account.*

Discretionary Consumer Spending—Consists of purchases deemed postponable rather than routine (i.e., luxuries vs. necessities).

Discretionary Order—An order giving the broker a specified amount of discretion.

Disinflation—A slowing of the rate of inflation. Deflation is when prices drop.

Disintermediation—1) When investors buy securities directly, without going through a bank or a broker. 2) Transfer of funds between investment vehicles.

Disinvest—To reduce capital investment.

Dismal Science—Economics, so called by Thomas Carlyle.

Dispersion—A measure of the variance in timing of a bond's cash flow. A relatively large dispersion number means that the cash flow (interest and principal) is spread out (dispersed) over time. A relatively small number means that most of the cash flow occurs at or near a single date. A mortgage typically has a large dispersion. A zero coupon bond has a dispersion of zero.

Duration assumes a flat yield curve environment, in which reinvestment income precisely balances capital gains or losses. When the curve is not flat, however, reinvestment income (short term) will not balance the capital gain or loss (long term). Dispersion takes non-flat yield curves into account. Using the timing of the cash flows on either side of the duration point, dispersion is a measure of the risk with respect to a change in the yield curve.

The dispersion of a particular bond is a useful figure in the context of portfolio management strategies such as immunization. For example, if a bond portfolio is immunized (duration matched) against multiple liabilities, the dispersion of the portfolio's assets should ideally be equal to or greater than that of its liabilities. The dispersion of a portfolio's cash flows may be regarded as a measure of the risk of not being able to meet a target rate of return due to potential twists in the shape of the yield curve. *See* Duration.

Disposable Income—After-tax income.

Dissolution—Termination of a business enterprise.

Distressed Exchange—An exchange of new debt or equity securities for existing debt, the terms of which a corporation makes attractive by providing only one, less attractive, alternative.

Distribute—*See* Place.

Distributer—Underwriter of mutual fund shares.

Distribution (DIST)—Sale of securities, whether in the primary or secondary market.

Distribution Area—A relatively narrow price range of a security, in which investors are willing to buy. *See* Accumulation Area.

District Business Conduct Committee (DBCC)—Committee empowered by the NASD to handle complaints brought against the NASD and misconduct by NASD members.

Diversifiable Risk—That part of a security's total risk that becomes negligible when that security is part of a diversified portfolio. *See* Systematic Risk.

Diversification—Reduction of risk by holding different securities in a portfolio. The more securities in a portfolio, and the less in common they have with each other, the more diversification the portfolio is likely to have.

Divest—To sell.

Divided Account—*See* Western Account.

Dividend—A cash or other distribution to preferred or common stockholders.

Dividend Capture—Buying stock in order to be the holder of record and receive the current dividend.

Dividend Discount Model—Equity valuation model that discounts a forecasted dividend stream to derive the intrinsic value of a stock.

Dividend Payout Ratio—A measure of dividend payments made by a company, calculated as dividends paid on common stock divided by net income available for dividend payments.

Dividend Period—The period from the business day after an auction date for STAR preferred stock through and including the next auction date.

Dividend Reinvestment—The reinvestment of an investor's dividend payment into more shares of a company's stock.

Dividend Scrip—Fractional shares of stock received as stock dividend. Dividend scrip is entitled to neither dividends nor voting rights until combined into full shares.

Dividends Received Deduction (DRD)—The reduction of intercorporate dividend income from taxable income, provided for in section 301 of the Internal Revenue Code (1954).

Dividend Yield—The percentage obtained by dividing the dividend by the market price of a stock.

Documented Discount Note—Commercial paper backed by a bank letter of credit. *Also called* Letter of Credit (LOC) Paper.

Documented Discount Note (DDN)—Commercial paper used by member banks as collateral at a Federal Reserve District Bank.

Dole—Pejorative term for government expenditure.

Dollar Bloc—A group of currencies tied to the U.S. dollar.

Dollar Bond—1) A municipal bond quoted and traded in price (or dollars) rather than yield. 2) Bond issued in amounts below $500. Also called *Baby Bond*.

Dollar Cost Averaging—*See* Constant Dollar.

Dollar Duration—Duration times price (including accrued interest) of a security; used to properly weight swaps for arbitrage purposes.

Dollar Price—Percentage of face value at which a security is quoted.

Dollar Price Repo—*See* Dollar Repo.

Dollar Repo—A method of borrowing versus securities owned. A dollar repo is similar to a repurchase agreement except in the following respects: 1) Unlike ordinary repo, in which the securities are used to collateralize a loan, the securities are actually sold and subsequently repurchased in the dollar repo. This means that the seller loses possession of the securities during the dollar repo period. 2) The sale and repurchase prices are agreed upon at the time of the dollar repo, and both confirmations are printed simultaneously. In each transaction, the buyer pays the seller accrued interest, and the buyer keeps any coupon income. 3) The securities repurchased need not be the same physical securities sold—an equal par amount of the same issue may be acceptable. Also known as *Dollar Repurchase Agreement* and *Dollar Price Repo*.

Dollar Repurchase Agreement—*See* Dollar Repo.

Dollar Return—The return on an asset in terms of dollars.

Dollar Roll—A simultaneous buy and sell transaction of a mortgage-backed security whereby a client sells the security for near month settlement and buys it back for forward month settlement. The price difference between the sale and repurchase of the security, along with the client's opportunity to put cash to work during the period of the dollar roll determines the additional income or cost of funds inherent in the transaction. This financial technique is frequently used by thrifts.

Domestic Production—*See* Cottage Industry.

Domicile—Place of residence, for tax and legal purposes.

Done—A binding term used to signify the completion of a transaction.

Do Not Reduce (DNR)—Instruction on buy limit orders, sell stop orders, and sell stop limit orders not to reduce the amount of the order by the amount of a cash dividend on the ex-dividend date.

Don't Know (DK)—A discrepancy between brokers, noted on contract sheets. Also called *QT* for questioned trade. *See* Contract Sheet.

Double-Barrelled Bond—Bond secured by more than one income source (usually revenues and taxes).

Double Dated—U.K. gilt-edged securities that have call features.

Doubled Average Life—Average life that results when sinking fund redemption amounts are doubled.

Double Declining Balance (DDB)—Method of depreciation that uses twice the percentage of the straight-line method. *See* Straight Line.

Double Drop-Lock Security—A variation on a drop-lock security, in which the index rate must lie below the trigger rate on two consecutive reset dates for the security to become fixed rate. *See* Drop Lock Security and Trigger Rate.

Double Entry—Accounting method in which each entry is recorded as an equal debit and credit, thus maintaining the accounting equation.

Double Exempt—Municipal bonds exempt from both federal and state taxes.

Double Taxation—Taxation of dividends first as corporate income then as personal income.

Double Taxation Agreement—An agreement between two countries intended to avoid double taxation of income under the terms of which an investor with tax liabilities in both countries can apply either for a reduction of taxes imposed by one country or for credit for taxes paid in that country against tax liabilities in the other.

Double-Up—*See* Option to Double.

Doubling Up—Buying a number of securities equal to the amount already held and about to be sold at a loss. This strategy enables the investor to generate a tax loss, avoid wash sale rules, and maintain the original position. *See* Wash Sale.

Dow Jones—A stock price average based on 65 stocks—30 industrial, 20 transportation, and 15 utility stocks.

Dow Jones Industrial Average (DJIA)—Stock price average determined by adding the prices of thirty specified NYSE stocks and dividing by a factor. The factor has been changed because of stock splits, stock dividends, and stock substitutions. No adjustment is made for the number of outstanding shares in each of the thirty component stocks.

Dow Jones Transportation Average—Stock price average using the prices of 20 transportation-related corporations.

Dow Jones Utility Average—Stock price average using the prices of 15 gas and electric utility companies.

Downgrade—1) Lowering of credit rating. 2) The sale of one block of bonds and the purchase of another with a lower rating.

Downside—Risk.

Downstream—Corporate activity from parent to subsidiary.

Downtick—*See* Minus Tick.

Downturn—A slowing of the economy.

Down Under—Refers to Australian or New Zealand securities.

Dow Theory—Theory that major stock market trends are not valid until reflected in a similar movement in the Dow Jones Industrial Average and the Dow Jones Transportation Average. Dow theory proponents do not believe that a real breakout has occurred until the level of both of these averages exceeds their previous high or low.

Draft—Claim for payment. A draft used in foreign transactions is called a Bill of Exchange. A draft payable on demand is called a Sight Draft. A draft payable at a specified time is called a Time Draft.

Draft Attached—The delivery of securities to another city through a corresponding bank. Securities are financed at the current rate of interest until paid for in the city of delivery.

Drain—To decrease banks' lending reserves. The Fed can drain reserves by raising reserve requirements, increasing the discount rate, and engaging in open market operations.

Draw—*See* Retire.

Drawdown—In connection with a banking facility, a request by an issuer to borrow money under the terms of the facility.

Drawer—*See* Maker.

Drawing—Lottery held to identify which bonds will be redeemed at a predetermined price, when bond issues are to be redeemed in more than one payment.

Dressed—1) A hedged position. 2) A covered option. *See* Naked.

Drop—1) The difference between a security's price from one month to the next. 2) The difference between the sale price and the repurchase price of a mortgage-backed security in a dollar roll. *See* Dollar Roll.

Drop Lock—A floating rate security that becomes a fixed rate security once the index drops below a specified level (trigger level).

Dual Banking System—A banking system, such as that in the U.S., in which banks can be chartered by either state or federal regulatory agencies.

Dual Currency Bond—Long-term security denominated in one currency with interest and/or principal payments in another.

Duality—1) Double entry accounting standard of recording each entry as an equal debit and credit. 2) For credit cards, the situation in which a member of either the Visa or MasterCard associations is not precluded from being a member of the other. This applies to both card issuers and acquirers.

Dual Listings—The listing of a security on more than one exchange, such as the New York Stock Exchange and a regional exchange. Securities can not be listed on both the New York Stock Exchange and the American Stock Exchange.

Dual Option (Du-Op)—1) A bond whose face value is expressed in two currencies. The bondholder may choose the currency in which to receive payment of principal and interest. 2) Warrant consisting of two options, allowing the holder to subscribe to either common or preferred stock.

Dual Purpose Fund—Closed-end investment company that has two classes of stock—growth (capital appreciation) and income (dividends from investments).

Dual Tranche—Two simultaneous issues of differing terms by the same borrower.

Due Bill—An assignment or other instrument used to evidence the transfer of title to any dividend, interest, or rights pertaining to securities contracted for, or evidencing the obligation of, a seller to deliver such dividend, interest, or rights to a subsequent owner. Also called *Letter of Confirmation*.

Due Bill Check—A due bill in the form of a check payable on the date of payment of a cash dividend or coupon.

Due Date—Maturity date.

Due Diligence—Under a 1983 Act, civil liabilities flow from material misstatements or omissions of fact in the registration statement and prospectus. The company directors and officers who sign the registration statement as well as the underwriters and experts involved in the issuance of securities are all subject to such liabilities. Each of these is jointly and severally liable; the potential civil liability is the full sales price of the security. All other persons and firms involved, however, are entitled to a due diligence defense against such liability. In general, this defense requires that each person, after conducting a reasonable investigation, must believe and have a reasonable basis to believe that the statements made in the registration statements are true and do not omit to state any material fact necessary.

Due Diligence Meeting—A meeting between corporate officers and the underwriting syndicate, before the effective date, to discuss the registration statement, to prepare a prospectus, and to negotiate an underwriting agreement.

Due on Sale—A mortgage clause requiring a mortgage to be prepaid upon transfer of ownership of the property. A due on sale clause is not enforceable in some states. It applies only to conventional mortgages; all government-backed loans are assumable.

Duesenberry Effect—Consumers' tendency not to cut consumption when income declines.

Duet Bond—An issue in which the coupon rate is expressed as the difference of amounts in two currencies.

Dumbbell—A fixed income portfolio strategy in which assets are concentrated only in very short and very long maturity issues. Also called *Barbell*.

Dump—To sell a security or product at below market prices in order to hurt the competition.

Durable Goods—Goods with a life expectancy of at least three years.

Duration—A measure of a bond's price sensitivity, expressed in years. As defined by Frederick Macaulay in 1938, it is a measure of the interest rate risk of a bond, taking into consideration that there may be cash flows before the maturity date and that the cash flows must be considered in terms of their present value. Duration is similar to, but much more precise than, average life. It is a measure of the number of years until the average dollar—in present value terms—is received from coupon and principal payments. As such, it is one measure of systematic risk. Average life, on the other hand, is a measure of the time to receive a dollar of principal only—it takes into consideration neither interest payments nor present value. Duration is computed by multiplying each principal and interest payment by its present value, summing these products, and dividing the sum by the full price of the bond. Also called *Macaulay Duration* and *Unmodified Duration*. *See* Effective Duration and Modified Duration.

Duration Date—The average date on which all cash flows from a bond or schedule of liabilities are received, when analyzed on a present value basis. If a bond has a duration of 5 years, the duration date is today plus 5 years.

Duration Matching—*See* Immunization.

Duration-Weighted Trade—A trade in which the weighted average duration of securities purchased is equal to that of the securities sold. Used when an investor wants the result of the swap to be independent of changes in interest rates.

Duration Weighting—*See* Trade Weighting.

Dutch Auction—A competitive bidding technique in which the seller gradually lowers the price, and the lowest price necessary to sell the entire amount of securities offered becomes the price at which all of the securities are sold.

Duty—Tax.

Dwarf—An FNMA security with a 15-year maturity.

Dynamic Hedging—Adjusting a hedge position frequently.

E

Early Exercise—When an option is exercised before expiration.

Early Ownership Mortgage (EOM)—Fixed rate mortgage whose payments increase after the sixth year, thereby paying down in less than 30 years.

Earned Income—Income received for goods or services. *See* Unearned Income.

Earned Surplus—Improper term for retained earnings. *See* Retained Earnings.

Earnings—*See* Net Income.

Earnings Before Interest and Taxes—Corporate earnings before bond interest and taxes have been paid.

Earnings per Share—A corporation's profits divided by the number of shares of common stock outstanding.

Earnings Report—*See* Income Statement.

Earnings Yield—The percentage calculated by dividing the earnings per share by the market price of a stock.

Easing—Falling in price.

Easement—The legal right to make limited use of another's property.

Eastern Account—A municipal syndicate in which members are responsible for selling the entire issue. Also called *Undivided Account, United Account,* and *Severally and Jointly.*

Easy—An economic condition of low interest rates and readily available credit. The Fed can create this condition by increasing the money supply. Also called *Loose Credit. See* Tight.

E Bond—*See* Extension Protected Floating Rate CMO.

Econometrics—Branch of economics that uses mathematical models to perform quantitative analyses.

Economic Defeasance—*See* Defeasance.

Economic Growth Rate—The rate of change in the gross national product, expressed as an annual percentage. The economic growth rate adjusted for inflation is called the Real Economic Growth Rate.

Economic Indicator—*See* Leading Indicator.

Economic Liberalism—*See* Classical School.

Economic Life—Time during which an asset can be depreciated against current earnings.

Economic Resources—The basic components of an economy, namely capital, labor, and land.

Edge Act—Federal Reserve Act amendment of 1919 that enables the Board of Governors of the Federal Reserve System to charter corporations that perform foreign banking functions.

Edge Act Corporation—A U.S. bank subsidiary that finances international trade. Also called *Edge Bank*.

Edge Bank—*See* Edge Act Corporation.

Effective—An offering is said to be effective once the SEC has passed on the issue.

Effective Date—Date a registered offering may be made, usually 20 days after the registration statement is filed with the SEC.

Effective Duration—An empirical measure of the sensitivity of a bond's price to changes in yield, computed by reference to recent market price movements relative to a benchmark security (e.g., a Treasury security). Effective duration is modified duration adjusted for the features of a specific security, such as embedded call options, put options, and sinking funds. The effective duration of a noncallable Treasury security is equivalent to its modified duration; these two measures of price sensitivity will diverge for callable and/or non-Treasury securities. *See* Modified Duration.

Effective Interest—Indicates that the interest due for a period equals the outstanding principal at the beginning of the period multiplied by the periodic interest rate. Effective interest is paid in arrears. Corporations, according to generally accepted accounting principles, must account for interest payments on debt using the effective interest method (where the periodic interest rate is the coupon rate). Also called *Actuarial Interest as Scheduled*.

Effective Margin—*See* Effective Spread.

Effective Rate—*See* Yield to Maturity.

Effective Sale—The price of a round lot that determines the price of the next odd lot.

Effective Spread—The spread to or margin over an index of a floating rate security, taking into consideration market price, payment basis, payment and reset frequency, and payment delay. Also called *Effective Margin*.

Effective Yield—The annualized rate of return realized by an investor who buys a security and subsequently sells it. It reflects coupon, interest on interest, principal payments, and capital gains or losses.

Efficient—Describes a market in which information is immediately available to all investors. Prices in an efficient market therefore reflect all available information.

Efficient Frontier—The collection of all efficient portfolios in a given market meeting given criteria. Each portfolio on the efficient frontier has a different degree of risk.

Efficient Portfolio—A portfolio with no unnecessary risk, or one with the highest expected return of all portfolios with the same total risk.

Either-Or Order—*See* Alternative Order.

Either-Way—Pertaining to a market in which a trader will buy or sell.

Elastic Demand—Economic condition in which a small increase/decrease in prices will cause a large decrease/increase in demand. Price elasticity is measured as the percentage change in quantity bought divided by the percentage change in price.

Elasticity—A measure of sensitivity to change in price of a product demanded or supplied.

Elastic Supply—Economic condition in which a small increase/decrease in prices will cause a large increase/decrease in supply. Supply elasticity is measured as the percentage change in quantity supplied divided by the percentage change in price.

Elbow—A peak in the yield curve.

Elect—A transaction that activates a stop order is said to elect the stop. Also called Trigger.

Eleemosynary—A charitable institution, which is required under the tax law to distribute 5.5% of its earnings each year. This is usually paid out of its interest earnings; if 5.5% is not available it must use funds from its principal.

Eleven Bond Index—Average yield of eleven out of the twenty bonds that make up the Twenty Bond Index. The eleven bonds are general obligation municipal bonds with a maturity of 20 years.

Eligible—1) Acceptable as collateral by the Fed at the discount window. 2) An investment that a FSLIC-backed Savings and Loan is authorized to purchase. 3) A security that may be used to meet margin requirements. 4) Registered securities as defined by Regulation T. *See* Regulation T. 5) Temporary investments of funds in a CMO collection account until the next bond payment date, including Guaranteed Investment Contracts, demand or time deposits, certificates of deposit, bankers' acceptances, repurchase agreements. *See* Collection Account.

Embedded Option Value—The difference in the yield to maturity of a callable or putable bond and the underlying bullet bond (positive for callable bonds, negative for putable bonds). *See* Underlying Bullet.

Eminent Domain—A government's power to condemn or take property. *See* Sovereign Risk.

Emolument—Compensation for work, such as wages, salary, and benefits.

Empirical Duration—The measured sensitivity of price to changes in yield. *See* Effective Duration and Modified Duration.

Employees Retirement Income Security Act (ERISA)—A law enacted in 1974 covering private pension plans, setting standards for fiduciary conduct and making fiduciaries personally liable for breaches of responsibility.

Encumbered—Property that has a lien or claim against it.

Endogenous Theory of Business Cycles—Economic theory that the causes of economic fluctuations are internal to the economy. Also called *Internal Theory of Business Cycles*. *See* Exogenous Theory of Business Cycles.

End Yield—The yield at which a security is liquidated prior to maturity.

Engel's Laws—Economic laws of Ernst Engel, Director of the Bureau of Statistics in Prussia, who stated in 1857 that, other things being equal: 1) family income is inversely related to percentage of income spent on food; 2) the percentage of income spent on clothing is constant; 3) the percentage of income spent on housing is constant; and 4) family income is directly related to the percentage of income spent on leisure, education, and luxury items.

English Auction—A competitive auction in which bidders buy securities at their bid price if they bid above the stop out price; if they bid below, they receive any unsold securities. *See* Stop Out Price.

Entry Age Normal—The most common funding method for U.S. pension funds, in which a level contribution is made each year that, with reinvestment income, is sufficient to accrue to the required benefit upon retirement. It is thus a more conservative method than the unit credit method, in which contributions increase over time.

Envelope System—*See* Stock Clearing Corporation.

Equal and Ratable Security Clause—*See* Pari Passu Clause.

Equalizing Sale—Short sale.

Equilibrium—Balance between the conflicting forces of supply and demand.

Equipment Trust Certificate—Form of borrowing secured by property, generally issued by railroads, to pay for new equipment. Title to the equipment is held in trust until the notes are paid off. It is usually secured by a first claim on the equipment.

Equity—1) *See* Common Stock. 2) The difference between the current value of a home and the mortgage balance. Equity increases when the mortgage balance declines, if the current value of the house increases, or if home improvements are made. 3) *See* Residual.

Equity Commitment Note—A form of mandatory convertible debt used as medium-term bridge financing for bank holding companies. The proceeds are counted as primary capital, the interest is tax deductible, and there is no initial dilution of earnings per share. Noteholders are paid in cash at maturity, from funds raised at intervals over the life of the note from stock issuance. Equity commitment notes are therefore not convertible per se but are considered convertible debt from a regulatory standpoint.

Equity Contract Note—A form of mandatory convertible debt used as medium-term bridge financing for bank holding companies. The proceeds are counted as primary capital, the interest is tax deductible, and there is no initial dilution of earnings per share. Noteholders are paid in cash or equities at maturity.

Equity Financing—Raising funds through stock issuance.

Equity-Linked Security—Any security whose value is dependent upon the price of one or more associated common stocks. Equity-linked securities include warrants, convertible bonds, convertible preferred stocks, and options.

Equity REIT—Real Estate Investment Trust that invests in real estate. *See* Mortgage REIT.

Equivalent Bond Yield (EBY)—A measurement of the rate of return on a security sold on a discount basis that assumes actual days to maturity and a 365-day year. *See* Interest Yield Equivalent.

Equivalent Contracts—The number of futures that has the same interest rate risk as a given position.

Equivalent Taxable Yield (ETY)—What the taxable yield on a corporate bond trading at par would have to be to equal the non-taxable yield on a municipal bond, calculated as non-taxable yield divided by (1-tax bracket). Also called *Taxable Equivalent Yield*.

Erroneous Report Rule—New York Stock Exchange rule that holds clients to the terms of a trade even if those terms have been reported erroneously.

Escheat—Reversion of property to the state in the absence of legal heirs.

Escrow—Money, securities, or other property held by a third party until the conditions of a contract are met.

Escrow Receipt—Bank receipt showing ownership of a security held by an option writer.

Escrowed to Maturity (ETM)—U.S. government securities held in escrow to provide debt service until maturity on the bonds issued in an advance refunding are said to be escrowed to maturity. *See* Advance Refunding.

Eurobond—A bond issued in a European country denominated in a currency other than that of the country of issuance.

Euro Certificate of Deposit—A certificate of deposit issued by a U.S. bank branch or foreign bank located outside the United States. Almost all Euro CDs are issued in London.

Euroclear—A book entry clearing facility for most Eurocurrency and foreign securities. Euroclear, which is owned by a large number of banks worldwide, mainly of North American and European origin, is located in Brussels and managed by Morgan Guaranty Trust. Euroclear is one of two clearing systems for the Eurobond market, the other being CEDEL.

Eurocommercial Paper—A generic term applied to Euronotes issued on a non-underwritten basis.

Eurocurrency—A pool of currency held in a European country, where that country is not the country of origin. Created when a banking office in one country accepts a deposit (or other evidence of debt) denominated in the currency of another. When the deposit is denominated in U.S. dollars, it is a Eurodollar deposit. In addition to bank deposits, Eurocurrency instruments may take the form of bankers' acceptances, letters of credit, certificates of deposit, and loans of various maturities. Hence the terms Eurodollar CD, Eurodollar bond, etc.

Eurodollar Bond—European or U.S. corporate bond issued in Europe, which pays interest and principal in U.S. dollars.

Eurodollar CD—*See* Eurocurrency.

Euro Equity Placement—*See* International Equity Placement.

Euro Floater—*See* Floating Rate Note.

Euro Issue—Term referring to any public offering or private placement of Eurosecurities. Such issues are typically placed with investors in more than one country by an international syndicate.

Euromarket—A general term for the international capital markets that encompasses, among others, the market for Eurobonds, Euro FRNs, Euro CDs/FRCDs, Euro interbank deposits, Euro foreign exchange and Euro syndicated credits. All transactions in the Euromarket are denominated in Eurocurrencies.

Euronote—A fully negotiable bearer promissory note. It is usually issued at a discount, and maturities are typically one, three, or six months.

Euronote Facility—A facility that allows a borrower to issue short-term discount notes via a variety of note distribution mechanisms, under the umbrella of a medium-term commitment from a group of banks that commit to purchase notes at a predetermined rate or maximum margin, usually expressed in relation to LIBOR, if they cannot be placed with investors at or under that margin. Also called *Revolving Underwriting Facility*.

European Currency Unit (ECU)—A basket of fixed amounts of European Economic Community currencies. The ECU is used to denominate debts and claims, and to facilitate settlement between EEC central banks.

European Depository Receipt (EDR)—A depository receipt issued and traded in Europe. *See* American Depository Receipt.

European Federation of Financial Analyst Societies (EFFAS)—The overall body for the various domestic European investment analyst societies. Holds a major conference biannually and has several standing commissions in order to regularize, optimize, and coordinate investment analysts.

European Monetary System (EMS)—A group of European countries (Belgium, Luxembourg, Denmark, Germany, France, Italy, Ireland, and the Netherlands) that agreed in March 1979 to keep their respective currencies within certain defined upper and lower limits in relation to each other. When one of these currencies is devalued, a realignment within the EMS takes place, and all the currency values are adjusted accordingly.

European Option—An option exercisable only on its maturity date.

European Unit of Account (EUA)—A composite currency unit, the value of which is expressed in terms of the ECU, at present the common denominator for the expression of central rates of the currencies of the countries participating in the exchange rate mechanism of the European Monetary System. *See* European Monetary System.

Eurosecurity—Any security issued in the Euromarket (e.g., Euroyen, Euro DM, Eurosterling).

Even Keel—Refers to stable monetary policy.

Even Par Swap—The sale of one block of bonds and the simultaneous purchase of the same principal amount of another block of bonds.

Event of Default—A default upon the occurrence of which an investor (or his trustee) is entitled to call in the outstanding amount of the related issue for immediate redemption. A borrower's failure to comply with any of a set of conditions specified in the terms of any of its issues of securities is called an event of default. Default includes non-payment and non-compliance with a covenant, such as a negative pledge, a cross-default, insolvency, and liquidation. *See* Liquidation Value and Grace Period.

Event Risk—Risk to bondholders that corporate activity such as mergers, acquisitions, takeovers, and restructurings will affect the quality of that corporation's securities.

Ex—Without. *See* Cum.

Exact Interest—Simple interest based an a 365-day year. *See* Ordinary Interest.

Ex-All—Sale of a security without any of the rights associated with it, such as dividends and warrants.

Ex Ante—Forward looking, or predicted, variables. *See* Ex Post.

Excess—The amount by which a margin account exceeds the margin requirement.

Excess Cash Flow—*See* Residual.

Excess Flow—Payments received from underlying mortgage collateral greater than the amount necessary to distribute to investors in a mortgage-related security.

Excess Loan Value—Describes a mortgage-backed security that is over-collateralized. In this situation, the value of the cash flow generated by the assets is greater than the value of the outstanding liability or what is required to service the obligation.

Excess Reserves—A bank's reserve balances at the Fed in excess of required amounts.

Excess Return—*See* Risk Premium.

Excess Servicing—Fees paid to a servicer in excess of the amount required to compensate for the servicing of a mortgage.

Exchange—1) A self-regulatory body where securities, futures and options, and commodities are traded. Exchanges regulate order execution, market making, trade reporting, trade clearing, and market surveillance. Stock exchanges are regulated by the Securities and Exchange Commission. The two major stock exchanges are the New York Stock Exchange (NYSE) and the American Stock Exchange (AMEX or ASE). The seven regional stock exchanges are Boston, Cincinnati, Intermountain (Salt Lake City), Midwest (Chicago), Pacific (Los Angeles and San Francisco), Philadelphia, and Spokane. Commodity exchanges are regulated by the Commodity Futures Trading Commission. The major futures exchange is the Chicago Board of Trade (CBT). There are twelve other commodity exchanges. Exchanges on which options are traded are regulated by the SEC. The major options exchange is the Chicago Board of Options Exchange (CBOE). 2) The money or currency of a country.

Exchangeable—Refers to convertible bonds or warrants that can be converted to common stock or another issue of the same issuer.

Exchange for Physicals—A futures transaction that takes place outside the trading pit in which two hedgers exchange futures and cash positions. Also called *Ex-Pit* and *Against Actuals*.

Exchange Distribution—*See* Cross.

Exchange Rate—The relative value of one currency in terms of another.

Exchange-Traded Option—An option for which the exercise price and expiration date are fixed by the exchange; only the premium is negotiated. In an over-the-counter option, the writer has a contract directly with the buyer. A broker negotiates the exercise price, the expiration date, and the premium. Also, OTC options are written for 35, 65, and 95 days, 6 or 9 months, or one year, while exchange-traded options are written for 3 months.

Ex-Coupon—*See* Ex-Dividend.

Ex-Date—*See* Ex-Dividend Date.

Ex-Dividend—Without dividend, because the owner bought the stock after the ex-dividend date.

Ex-Dividend Date—The first date an investor can sell a stock previously purchased, for regular way settlement, and still be entitled to the dividend payment for the preceding period. Conversely, the day prior to the ex-dividend date is the last day a buyer can purchase a preferred stock for regular settlement and still be entitled to the dividend payment for the current period. Also called *Ex-Date*.

Execute—Trade.

Exempt Securities—Instruments exempt from registration requirements of the Securities Act of 1933 and the margin requirements of the Securities & Exchange Act of 1934. Exempt securities include debt of the U.S. Treasury, U.S. Government agencies and municipalities, private placements, commercial paper, Title XI, equipment trust certificates, and new issues of $1.5 million or less.

Exercise—To use an option. When a call option is exercised the holder buys securities from the option writer. When a put option is exercised the holder sells securities to the option writer.

Exercise Content—The market content of any equity warrant adjusted for the exercise premium. *See* Market Content and Exercise Premium.

Exercise Limit—The maximum number of option contracts of a class of options that can be exercised during five business days.

Exercise Notice—Notice given by a broker to the Options Clearing Corporation (OCC) that a client wants to exercise an option. The OCC notifies the option writer.

Exercise Premium—The premium (expressed as a percentage) over current market price at which an equity warrant gives the holder the right to buy the underlying shares. *See* Exercise Content and Market Content.

Exercise Price—The price at which an option may be exercised for the underlying security. Also called *Strike Price*.

Exercise Rate of Return—The rate of return an investor would realize if an option's underlying security were called away at expiration.

Exhaust Price—Liquidation price of a security in a margin account, when margin requirements cannot be met.

Exhibit A—*See* Indenture Supplement.

Eximbank—Export-Import Bank.

Existing Holder—Owner of securities. With respect to STAR preferred stock, a person who has signed a purchaser's letter and is listed as the beneficial owner of shares of STAR preferred in the records of the trust company.

Exit Bond—Bond a bank buys from a debtor nation that absolves it from further contributions to that nation.

Exit Value—Current selling price.

Ex-Legal—A municipal security that does not have a legal opinion printed on the bond certificate.

Exogenous Theory of Business Cycles—Economic theory that economic fluctuations are caused by factors outside the economy. Also called *External Theory of Business Cycles. See* Endogenous Theory of Business Cycles.

Exotica—Any rarely traded, illiquid paper.

Expansion—Increase in the money supply and/or in production.

Expansive—Tending to heat up the economy. *See* Restrictive.

Expectations Hypothesis—Theory to explain the term structure of interest rates, in which the yield curve is determined by what investors expect. Assumptions about the yield curve are threefold: long-term rates are higher than short-term rates; short-term rates are more volatile than long-term rates; and all rates move pari passu.

Expected Maturity—The date on which the final principal payment of a variable maturity security (e.g., mortgage-related securities, callable bonds) is anticipated.

Expected Return—*See* Mean Return.

Expendable Goods—Goods that are consumed during use, as opposed to capital goods.

Expense—In accounting, to record an outlay of funds against revenue in the period in which the outlay occurs.

Experience—In the pass-through market, refers to a rate of prepayments, usually measured in terms of some norm. For example, "200% FHA experience" means prepayments occur at twice the rate predicted by the FHA model. *See* Interim Experience and Cumulative Experience.

Expiration Cycle—Successive expiration dates on futures and options contracts. There are three expiration cycles: January, April, July, October (JAJO); February, May, August, November (FMAN); and March, June, September, December (MJSD).

Expiry—Expiration.

Expiration Date—The date on which an option can no longer be exercised.

Ex-Pit—*See* Exchange for Physicals.

Export-Import Bank—An independent bank established by Congress in 1934 to encourage U.S. trade. The Export-Import Bank borrows from the Treasury to finance exports and imports, to give credit to foreign borrowers, and to provide insurance and guarantees.

Ex Post—Backward looking, or historical, variables. *See* Ex Ante.

Exposure—Risk.

Ex Redemption—Bonds traded between the drawing date and the redemption date, which will not be redeemed on the next drawing date. *See* Drawing.

Extel Card—In the case of an issue of securities being listed on the London Stock Exchange, two cards are prepared for The Extel Statistical Services Limited (a U.K. company) in compliance with the requirements of the Council of the Stock Exchange. One card gives information about the issue. In the case of a borrower whose securities and/or common stock are not already listed on The Stock Exchange, the second card gives information on the borrower and the borrower's guarantor, if any. For prime quality, frequent borrowers, whose issues and/or common stock are listed on the London Stock Exchange, Extel cards are sometimes used as substitutes for a prospectus, especially if time is of the essence in the transaction.

Extendable—Refers to ARM programs in which borrowers are allowed to extend the maturity of their loans instead of increasing the amount of the monthly payment when interest rates rise.

Extendable Maturity—Refers to a security whose maturity an investor has an option, exercisable on a specified date or dates, to extend to a date specified in the terms of the security, normally after a new coupon has been set. *See* Retractable.

Extendable Mortgage—A mortgage whose term may be extended under certain circumstances. For example, certain adjustable rate mortgages allow the borrower to extend the term of the loan when interest rates rise, in order to keep monthly payments constant.

Extension Risk—The risk that an investment's principal will be returned later than projected.

Extension Protected Floating Rate CMO Bond (E Bond)—A floating rate tranche of a CMO that is structured to moderate the extension of average life in a rising interest rate environment. In the event that rates rise and prepayments slow, failing to meet a specified minimum rate, residual cash flows are used to retire or sink the bonds. Unlike Planned Amortization Class bonds, E bonds do not have a specific sinking fund schedule.

Extension Swap—A swap that lengthens maturity.

External Debt—1) Debt issued by one economic entity to another. Issuing and redeeming external debt changes the aggregate wealth of each economic entity. Corporate debt is external debt, because the cash flows involved change the aggregate wealth of both the corporation and the bondholders (even if the bondholder is also a stockholder of the same corporation). Federal debt is considered internal debt, because the cash flows involved do not change the aggregate wealth of the nation. *See* Internal Debt. 2) Government securities owned by foreign investors.

External Option Overwriting—Using an options management firm to write options on another portfolio.

External Rate of Return—The yield of a security when the reinvestment rate is specified rather than assumed. *See* Internal Rate of Return.

External Theory of Business Cycles—*See* Exogenous Theory of Business Cycles.

Extra Dividend—Dividend paid in excess of a regular dividend. Typically made after an unusually profitable year.

Extra-Market Risk—Risk associated with specific groups of securities. *See* Specific Risk and Unsystematic Risk.

Extraordinary Dividend—A dividend payment that exceeds five percent of the taxpayer's basis (or, electively, the fair market value) in the stock.

Extraordinary Item—A nonrecurring or unusual material accounting item.

Extrinsic Value—The value of an option (or warrant) over and above its intrinsic value. The price of an out-of-the money option (or warrant) is entirely extrinsic value. Also called *Time Value*.

Ex-Warrants—A term for senior securities, originally issued with warrants, from which the warrants have been detached. These issues trade at a price reflecting investment merit that is independent of the warrant price.

F

Face Amount Certificate Company—A type of investment company that issues debt, the face amount of which will be paid on a fixed date more than 24 months after issuance.

Face Value—The principal amount the bondholder receives upon maturity. Alternatively, the amount which, when multiplied by the percentage coupon rate, gives the amount of interest payable to the bondholder. Also called *Par Value* and *Principal Value*.

Facilitation Order—Order for a broker/dealer's proprietary account.

Facility—A formal arrangement between an issuer of short-term securities (Euronotes or CDs) and a group of underwriting banks that commit to purchase such securities (at an agreed rate) throughout the life of a Euronote facility.

Factor—*See* Pool Factor.

Factoring—Buying notes at a discount from the holder. When the holder sells one note, it is called Discounting a Note.

Factor Slippage—When a hedge ratio for financial futures is distorted because of a change in the cheapest to deliver instrument. This causes the futures market to track another instrument with a different delivery factor. Not applicable to cash-settled contracts.

Faded—Describes a market with weakening prices.

Fail—A failure to receive or to deliver the proper amount of cash or securities in the proper form by the settlement date. Trades that do not clear on settlement date are said to fail.

Fair Market Value—Price on which a buyer and seller can agree; the current market value.

Fair Rate of Return—Profit level for utilities set by state and/or federal regulators.

Fallen Angel—Corporation whose debt ratings have significantly declined.

Family—Group of mutual funds with the same management company.

Fannie Mae—*See* Federal National Mortgage Association.

Farmer Mac—*See* Federal Agricultural Mortgage Corporation.

Farmers Home Administration (FmHA)—Agency of the Department of Agriculture that extends loans in rural areas for farms, homes, and community facilities. The FmHA finances its programs through the Federal Financing Bank. The sale of certificates of beneficial ownership (CBOs) to the public was discontinued in March 1975.

Farther In—An options expiration month closer to the present than another specified expiration month.

Farther Out—An options expiration month beyond another specified expiration month.

Fast—During an active trading session of a futures exchange, the tape may not be able to report every trade. When trades do not appear on the tape, "fast" will appear. Brokers cannot be held liable (e.g., for missing a stop order) when fast has appeared on the tape.

Fast Market—A market in which a large volume of futures or options are traded quickly.

Fast-Pay—A pass-through security that has prepaid faster than average pass-through securities of the same collateral and coupon. This prepayment experience does not necessarily indicate future prepayment patterns.

Father and Sons—An issue (father) with additional tranches (sons) issued.

Favorable Variance—When revenues are greater than expected, or when costs are less than expected.

FBC Yield—For floating rate notes, the internal rate of return (IRR) of an assumed future cash flow stream. IRR will be affected by current market price, the current coupon, and the timing and size of the assumed future coupon payments. The FBC yield is always stated in terms of corporate bond equivalent (CBE) yield.

Feasibility Study—Study done to determine the feasibility of a project associated with a new municipal revenue issue. *See* Engineering Report.

Feather Bond—Slang for a safe investment, that is, one with which an investor can sleep soundly.

Fed—Federal Reserve Board of the Federal Reserve Banking System.

Fed Action Time—Interval during which the Federal Reserve conducts open market operations (such as system repo and customer repo), traditionally between 11:20 a.m. and noon.

Federal Agricultural Mortgage Corporation (Farmer Mac)—U.S. federal agency that securitizes and guarantees farm mortgage loans.

Federal Deposit Insurance Corporation (FDIC)—Established in 1933 as a permanent instrumentality of the federal government, the Federal Deposit Insurance Corporation insures deposits that are in national banks, Federal Reserve member state banks, and non-member state banks that apply for Federal Deposit Insurance. FDIC is managed by a 3-member board of directors (two are appointed by the president for 6-year terms) and the Comptroller of the Currency. The FDIC currently insures up to $100,000 per deposit.

Federal Farm Credit Bank—*See* Federal Farm Credit System.

Federal Farm Credit System—Network of 12 Farm Credit districts, each of which has a Federal Land Bank, a Federal Intermediate Credit Bank, and a Bank for Cooperatives, all of which are consolidated under the Federal Farm Credit Bank. The system was created by the Farm Credit Act of 1971, and issues short-term discount notes and Federal Farm Credit System Consolidated Systemwide Bonds, the latter being sold on a monthly basis with maturities of six and nine months. The Federal Land Banks extend loans to farmers, who must buy stock equal to at least 5 percent of the loan in any local land bank association, which in turn buys an equal amount of stock in a Federal Land Bank. When the loan is repaid the stock is retired. The Federal Intermediate Credit Banks extend loans to institutions that extend loans to farmers, such as commercial banks and credit corporations.

Federal Financing Bank (FFB)—Government bank that consolidates financing costs of federal agencies whose debt is backed by the full faith and credit of the U.S. government.

Federal Funds—Non-interest deposit balances at the Federal Reserve, most of which represent legal reserves. Transactions that involve the sale of immediately available funds for one business day are federal funds transactions.

Federal Funds Rate—The interest rate charged to banks needing overnight loans to meet reserve requirements by banks with excess reserves at a Federal Reserve district bank. The rate is set daily by the market to be consistent with the desired rate of increases in reserves. It is monitored by the Fed in the process of regulating the growth of bank reserves and the money supply. As such, it is closely watched by market participants.

Federal Home Loan Bank Board (FHLBB)—*See* Federal Home Loan Banks.

Federal Home Loan Banks (FHLB)—Comprised of 12 District Banks throughout the country, the FHLB operate as a credit reserve system for the thrift industry, enhancing and stabilizing the flow of mortgage credit to the public. The banks are wholly owned by their member institutions, but are supervised by the Federal Home Loan Bank Board, an independent federal agency. The Bank Board issues all federal charters for savings and loan associations and mutual savings banks.

Federal Home Loan Bank System—*See* Federal Home Loan Banks.

Federal Home Loan Mortgage Corporation (FHLMC)—A corporate instrumentality of the United States, created by an act of Congress on July 24, 1970 in order to increase the availability of mortgage credit for the financing of housing. FHLMC raises funds by issuing securities backed by pools of conventional mortgages, either Participation Certificates (PCs), Guaranteed Mortgage Certificates (GMCs), or Collateralized Mortgage Obligations (CMOs). Also called *Freddie Mac.*

Federal Housing Administration (FHA)—Established on June 27, 1934, under the National Housing Act to encourage improvement in housing standards and conditions, to provide a system of mutual mortgage insurance, to provide aid to builders and buyers of homes and to mortgage-lending institutions, and for other purposes. The FHA is authorized to insure mortgage loans made for a variety of purposes, mostly related to residential housing.

Federal Intermediate Credit Bank—*See* Federal Farm Credit System.

Federal Land Bank—*See* Federal Farm Credit System.

Federal National Mortgage Association (FNMA)—A government-sponsored corporation owned entirely by private stockholders established in 1938 to provide additional liquidity to the mortgage market. In 1968, the original FNMA was broken into two corporations: the privately owned FNMA and the government owned GNMA. FNMA is subject to regulation by the Secretary of Housing and Urban Development. It purchases and sells residential mortgages insured by FHA or guaranteed by VA, as well as conventional home mortgages. Purchases of mortgages are financed by the sale of corporate obligations to private investors. Also called *Fannie Mae.*

Federal Reserve Act—Congressional Act of 1913 that created the Federal Reserve System, largely in reaction to the Panic of 1907.

Federal Reserve Bank—*See* Federal Reserve System.

Federal Reserve Board—*See* Board of Governors of the Federal Reserve System.

Federal Reserve Float—*See* Float.

Federal Reserve Open Market Committee (FOMC)—The Federal Reserve Board's arm for establishing and executing monetary policy. This committee is composed of the seven Governors of the Federal Reserve Board, the President of the Federal Reserve Bank of New York, and four of the presidents of regional Federal Reserve Banks. It normally meets on the third Tuesday of each month to issue guidelines to its trading desk at the Federal Reserve Bank of New York. A summary report of each meeting is released the Friday after the subsequent meeting.

Federal Reserve Open Market Operations—All of the Federal Reserve's activities in the marketplace. When the Fed is a buyer of securities, the quantity of bank reserves is increased. When the Fed sells securities, banks lose reserves. The purpose of most open market operations is merely to offset changes in the quantity of bank reserves arising from other factors, most notably changes in the Treasury's balance at the Federal Reserve.

Federal Reserve System—Established in 1913, it is the central banking system of the U.S. There are 12 regional Federal Reserve Banks but virtually all the policy-making powers are lodged in the Board of Governors of the Federal Reserve System in Washington. This has seven members appointed by the President of the U.S. for 14-year terms. The President chooses one of these to be Chairman for a 4-year term. All depository institutions must hold reserves at the Fed or in vault cash.

Federal Savings and Loan Insurance Corporation (FSLIC)—Institution that insures deposits at savings and loans, much as the Federal Deposit Insurance Corporation insures deposits at commercial banks.

Fed Wire—Computer system linking member banks, used to make payment of federal funds and deliveries of and payments for Treasury and agency securities. *See* Bank Wire.

FHA Experience—A statistical study done annually by the Actuarial Division of the Department of Housing and Urban Development describing the probability of an FHA-insured mortgage prepaying or defaulting in a given year of its life. The data, which date back to 1957, are updated annually and are compiled for each state as well as for the nation as a whole.

FHLMC—*See* Federal Home Loan Mortgage Corporation.

Fiat Paper—Paper money that cannot be redeemed in precious metal. Also called *Greenback* and *Soft Money*.

Fictitious Credit—Credit with a broker that a client may not withdraw. *See* Free Credit Balance.

Fictitious Order—Trade order given with the intention not of executing a trade but of creating the illusion of market activity.

Fidelity Bond—Insurance coverage that the SEC requires brokerage firms to have against losses due to loss of securities and employee fraud. Also called *Blanket Bond*.

Fiduciary—An individual or trust institution given the duty of acting for the benefit of another.

Fiduciary Money—*See* Credit Money.

Fifty-Five Percent Test—At least fifty-five percent of the principal amount of the mortgage certificates pledged to secure CMO bonds must consist of whole pools to avoid being considered an investment company and subject to regulation under the Investment Company Act of 1940, unless a 6(c) exemption has been obtained. Also called *Whole Pool Test.*

Fighter (FYTR)—Five-year Treasury note futures contract.

Figuring the Tail—Determining the effective yield of a future security.

Fill or Kill (FOK)—An order to be executed immediately or canceled.

Final Maturity—*See* Maturity.

Final Prospectus—*See* Prospectus.

Finance—1) The study of investment management. 2) To raise funds by issuing securities.

Finance Charge—Money needed to buy something on credit, including interest payments and service charges.

Finance Vehicle—An offshore subsidiary incorporated by the parent company for the purpose of issuing debt securities and lending the proceeds to the parent company or another subsidiary. The parent company generally guarantees the finance vehicle's issues.

Financial Accounting—Historical reporting of a corporation's assets, liabilities, equities, revenues, and expenses. *See* Managerial Accounting.

Financial Accounting Standards Board (FASB)—Board established in 1973 to establish and interpret generally accepted accounting principles.

Financial and Operations Principal (FINOP)—Supervisor in charge of compliance of recordkeeping, financial reporting, customer protection, and net capital requirements at a securities firm.

Financial Assistance Corporation (FAC)—U.S. federal agency that raises funds to recapitalize Farm Credit System banks.

Financial Distress—The possibility, however remote, that an entity may not be able to meet its liabilities.

Financial Futures—Futures contracts whose underlying securities are financial instruments. As such, they are sensitive to movements in interest rates. Also called *Interest Rate Futures.*

Financial Guaranty Insurance Company (FGIC)—A wholly owned subsidiary of FGIC Corporation that insures municipal debt.

Financial Leverage—Financing with debt and preferred stock to increase return on equity. Also called *Trading on the Equity.*

Financial Statement—Any record of a corporation's financial status, including the balance sheet and income statement.

Financial Year—British term for fiscal year.

Financing Cash Position—A dealer or trader's short-term borrowing to support inventory.

Financing Corporation (FICO)—Chartered by the Federal Home Loan Bank Board, FICO was authorized by the Competitive Equality Banking Act of 1987 to issue up to $10.8 billion in obligations and recapitalize the FSLIC by purchasing non-redeemable FSLIC capital certificates and redeemable capital stock.

Firm—Refers to an order to buy or sell a security that can be executed without confirmation for a stated period of time.

Firm Commitment—When an underwriter buys the issued securities. *See* Best Effort.

Firm Prices—Prices guaranteed by traders for a stated period of time.

First Call Date—The earliest date specified in the prospectus supplement on which optional redemptions may take place. When no date is specified, it is often the date on which a given condition is met, such as when a certain percentage of original principal amount remains.

First-In First-Out (FIFO)—An inventory valuation method that assumes that the oldest inventory (first in) is the first to be sold (first out). *See* Last-In First-Out.

First Mortgage Bond—A debt instrument secured by a first mortgage deed of trust containing a pledge of real property. More simply, a bond secured by property of the issuer.

First Notice Day—The first day during which the intention to deliver on a futures contract may be made known to the exchange. The first notice day is two business days before the first day in the delivery month.

Fiscal Agent—A bank appointed by a borrower as its agent for a new issue of securities when no trustee has been appointed. Its functions include those of a principal paying agent and a number of the clerical functions, but none of the fiduciary responsibilities, of a trustee.

Fiscal Policy—Federal government policies affecting government spending, taxation, and deficits (or surpluses) viewed from a macroeconomic standpoint.

Fiscal Year—Any consecutive twelve months chosen for an accounting period.

Fitch Investors Service, Inc.—Rating agency, based in New York and Denver, which assigns ratings to corporate and municipal debt, commercial paper, preferred stock, and other obligations.

Five Hundred Dollar Rule—Provision in Regulation T exempting a margin account from mandatory liquidation when the deficiency is $500 or less. *See* Regulation T.

Five Percent Policy—The NASD guide in establishing mark-ups and commissions. Dealer mark-ups and commissions should not normally exceed 5 percent of the price of the security.

Fix—To set the present or future price of a commodity.

Fixed Annuity—An annuity in which the insurance company makes fixed payments to the annuitant for the life of the contract, usually until the death of the annuitant.

Fixed Assets—Corporate assets used in business operations and not intended for sale such as buildings, machinery, office equipment, and furniture.

Fixed Benefits Plan—*See* Defined Contribution Benefit Plan.

Fixed Charge Coverage—Ability to pay fixed charges, which include actual interest incurred in each year on funded and unfunded debt, annual apportionment of debt discount or premium, and preferred dividends. Fixed charges are calculated as the sum of net income (adjusted for non-recurring gains or losses) plus total income taxes plus interest expense divided by interest expense. Also called *Times Fixed Charges*.

Fixed Charges—Actual interest incurred in each year on funded and unfunded debt and annual apportionment of debt.

Fixed Charges Earned Coverage Ratio—Income before interest and income tax expenses divided by interest expense.

Fixed Dates—In the Euromarket, the standard period for which Euros are traded (one month out to one year) are referred to as the fixed dates.

Fixed Deliverable Option—An option for which the deliverable security is known prior to the time the option is exercised. *See* Variable Deliverable Option.

Fixed-Dollar Security—A non-negotiable security that can be redeemed at a specified fixed price (e.g., bank deposits and government savings bonds).

Fixed Income—1) Constant income such as that from fixed rate bonds, annuities, and preferred stock. 2) Colloquially, refers to all sectors of the capital markets other than equity, equity-related, and option/warrant markets.

Fixed Liability—Long-term liability.

Fixed Price—Price at which syndicate members agree to sell an issue.

Fixed Rate Interest—Interest on a security that is calculated as a constant specified percentage of the principal amount and paid at the end of specified interest periods, usually annually or semiannually, until maturity.

Fixed Rate Loan—A loan for which the interest rate is fixed for life.

Fixed Trust—Unit investment trust that has a fixed portfolio. *See* Participating Trust and Unit Investment Trust.

Fixing—The determination and setting of the interest rate on a floating rate security or loan, usually two business days prior to the beginning of each interest period. *See* Agent Bank and Tender Panel Agent.

Flash GNP—An estimate for GNP made with only partial data for the quarter.

Flat—1) Excluding any accrued interest (so that only the dollar price is figured in the settling contract). Preferred stock, income bonds, and bonds in default are quoted and sold flat. Price without accrued interest is also called Clean Price. 2) Describes transactions executed for no profit. 3) A yield curve with an insignificant difference between short- and long-term yields.

Flat Market—*See* Sideways Market.

Flat Yield—*See* Current Yield.

Flat Yield Curve—*See* Yield Curve.

Flexible Loan Insurance Program Mortgage (FLIP)—A mortgage similar to a GPM from the borrower's point of view, but in which a portion of the down payment is used to create a pledged savings account that is used to subsidize the mortgage payment. The lender receives level payments comprised of loan payments plus savings account withdrawals.

Flexible Repurchase Agreement (Flex Repo)—A term repurchase agreement that provides for principal drawdowns prior to its maturity. This type of agreement is often used in structured municipal financings in which there is cash flow uncertainty.

Flight to Quality—Shifting capital to safe investments during financial crises.

Flip—To sell securities shortly after purchase for a trading profit.

Flip-Flop Security—Security in which the holder has the option to convert back and forth between the original issue and one of a shorter maturity, usually for a specified cost.

Flipper—An investor who frequently attempts to sell securities (typically new issue) for a profit shortly after purchasing them.

Float—1) Credits on the Fed's books to bank accounts during the process of check clearing without corresponding debits to other banks' accounts. Also called *Federal Reserve Float*. 2) Time between the deposit of a check and when the check clears. 3) The number of outstanding shares of a corporation. 4) The portion of an issue expected to trade actively in the secondary market. 5) Colloquially, to issue a security. Also called *Place and Distribute*.

Floatation—The amount of bonds outstanding in an issue.

Floater—Floating rate security.

Floating Debt—Municipal debt that will mature within 5 years. Also called *Bonded Debt*.

Floating Eurodollar Repackaged Assets of the Republic of Italy (FERARI)—Synthetic Eurodollar securities created by repackaging domestic Republic of Italy ECU bonds.

Floating-Floating—A version of the interest rate swap, in which each party pays a floating interest rate based on different indices (e.g., LIBOR vs. Treasury bill).

Floating Rate Certificate of Deposit (FRCD)—A bank liability on which the coupon rate changes periodically in accordance with a specified formula.

Floating Rate CMO—Collateralized mortgage obligation with one or more tranches that pay a floating rate of interest.

Floating Rate Interest—Interest on an issue of securities that is not fixed for the life of the issue, but which is periodically determined by an agent bank according to a formula specified in the terms of the issue. The rate is usually set at a margin or spread in relation to a specified money market rate.

Floating Rate Note (FRN)—Interest-bearing debt security, issued both in the U.S. and in the Euromarket, on which the interest rate is indexed to a short-term instrument, generally three- or six-month LIBOR or Treasury bills.

Floating Rate REMIC—Real Estate Mortgage Investment Conduit that pays a floating rate of interest.

Floating Supply—The amount of securities available for immediate purchase.

Floor—1) The trading floor of the central marketplace where a security or a commodity is traded, such as the Bond Room of the New York Stock Exchange. 2) An option contract in which the option buyer receives payments from the writer to the extent that an agreed upon index is lower than a specified rate (the "floor rate").

Floor Broker—A member of the New York Stock Exchange who executes orders received from member firms or for his own account on the floor of the Exchange.

Flowback—The sale of shares, originally placed with foreign investors, back into the domestic market.

Flower Bond—U.S. Treasury bond that can be applied to the payment of federal estate taxes at par when included in the estate of a deceased person.

Flow of Funds—A system of accounting that traces savings through various sectors of the economy.

Flow of Funds Accounts—A quarterly set of statistics compiled by the Federal Reserve estimating the sources and uses of funds for the major economic sectors and classes of financial institutions. They also show changes in holdings of various types of loans and securities.

Flow-Through Accounting—Method of accounting that shows all credits (or losses) from potential acquisitions or other extraordinary items in the income statement of the year in which the events occur.

Fluctuation—Change in yield or price.

FNMA—*See* Federal National Mortgage Association.

FNMA Major—FNMA security composed of loans from multiple lenders.

Forced Conversion—When an issuer calls a convertible security that is selling above its call price. The investor must take a loss by accepting the call price, convert to common shares, or sell the convertible.

Foreclosure—An authorized procedure taken by a mortgagee or lender, under the terms of a mortgage or deed of trust, for the purpose of having the value of the property applied to the payment of a defaulted debt.

Foreclosure Property—Property acquired due to default on a qualified mortgage. In relation to a REMIC structure foreclosure properties are permitted investments for a maximum of one year following foreclosure.

Foreign Bond—A security issued by a borrower in a domestic capital market other than its own and denominated in the currency of that market (e.g., Yankee bonds and Samurai bonds).

Foreign Currency Bond—An issue in which the coupon payments are made in a currency different from the currency of denomination, at the spot exchange rate.

Foreign Currency Options Principal (FCOP)—Supervisor of registered representatives involved in foreign currency options account activities.

Foreign Exchange Market—The market in which various currencies are traded.

Foreign Interest Payment Securities (FIPS)—Securities that are offered, paid for, and redeemed in one currency, with interest payments made in another currency at a specified fixed exchange rate. *See* Dual Currency Bond.

Foreign Sales Corporation (FSC)—Tax-saving vehicle created by the 1984 tax act as the successor to the domestic international sales corporation (DISC), allowing an exemption from federal income tax of 15 percent of export profits.

Foreign Targeted Note—Treasury notes available specifically to foreign investors, some of which are in bearer form with annual coupons.

Foreign Withholding Tax—A provision of the U.S. tax code that requires a 30 percent withholding tax on income other than compensation for services that is paid to a non-resident alien or foreign corporation. "Portfolio investment interest" received by non-resident aliens from obligations issued after July 18, 1984 is not subject to the tax. Foreign holders of regular interests in REMICs are also not subject to withholding. Foreign holders of residual interests in REMICs may be subject to withholding.

Forex-Linked Bond—An issue whose redemption proceeds are linked to the maturity spot exchange rate of another currency against the currency of denomination. *See* Heaven and Hell.

Form—The type of certificate(s) available for a bond issue. Possible forms are bearer, registered, or both bearer and registered.

Form 3—Form filed with the SEC by holders of 10 percent or more of the stock of a corporation, and by directors and officers of corporations. Information on Form 3 includes the number of shares owned as well as warrants, convertible bonds, rights, and options to buy stock.

Form 4—Form filed with the SEC by holders of 10 percent or more of the stock of a corporation, and by directors and officers of corporations, to reflect changes in stock ownership.

Form 8K—Form filed with the SEC to report any material change in a corporation's financial situation.

Form 10K—Annual financial report filed with the SEC by corporations with at least five hundred shareholders and assets of at least $1 million.

Form 10Q—Quarterly financial report filed with the SEC.

Form S-1—Used for registration under the Securities Act of 1933 for an initial public offering. Forms S-2 and S-3 are for use by larger and more seasoned issuers.

Formula Investing—Investment strategies based on preestablished rules, such as dollar cost averaging (periodic investment of equal amounts) and constant dollar (maintaining a fixed balance between debt and equity in a portfolio). Formula plans are based on price changes or periodic investments without regard to price.

Forward—A contract between a buyer and seller of a security or commodity for future settlement. A forward contract differs from a futures contract in that it can be for any amount of the security or commodity, it is non-transferable, and it is negotiated between buyer and seller.

Forward Exchange Contract—Agreement to exchange different currencies at the forward rate on a specified date.

Forward Fed Funds—Fed funds traded for future delivery—a cash forward transaction rather than a futures contract.

Forward Forward Contract—A currency deposit for future delivery.

Forward Interest Rate—The interest rate for a contract at a future (forward) time.

Forward Market—A market in which commodities, securities, or currencies are traded at a fixed price for delivery on a future date.

Forward Points—Basis point spread between a spot price and a forward price adjusted for interest rate differentials between countries.

Forward Pricing—SEC requirement that incoming buy and sell orders in a mutual fund be priced based on the next net asset valuation of fund shares.

Forward Rate—Rate for currency transactions (e.g., dollars necessary for a delivery of yen in one year).

For Your Information (FYI)—Indicates that a quote is given for valuation purposes, rather than for trading purposes.

Fourth Market—Over-the-counter transactions in listed or unlisted securities directly between institutional investors.

Four Tigers—Slang for the newly industrializing Asian economies of Korea, Hong Kong, Singapore, and Taiwan.

Fractional—1) Part of one share of common stock. 2) Currency unit less than the basic denomination, such as nickels, dimes, and quarters.

Fractional Note—Currency note with a denomination of less than one dollar.

Fractional Reserve System—A reserve system similar to that of the United States in which reserves required by the Federal Reserve are only a fraction of deposits, allowing deposits to expand by several times the amount of any change in the quantity of reserves.

Frankfurt Interbank Offered Rate (FIBOR)—The rate at which prime banks offer to make Eurocurrency deposits for a given maturity with other banks in Frankfurt.

Freddie Mac—*See* Federal Home Loan Mortgage Corporation.

Free and Open Market—Unregulated market in which prices are determined by supply and demand. *See* Controlled Market.

Free Box—Vault storing customer-owned securities.

Free Cash Flow—Cash flow from operations minus dividends minus capital expenditures.

Free Credit Balance—Credit with a broker that a client may withdraw. *See* Fictitious Credit.

Free Crowd—*See* Active Bond Crowd.

Free Delivery—Payment for securities which is not contingent upon the simultaneous delivery of the securities. *See* Delivery Versus Payment.

Freed Up—*See* Free to Trade.

Free On Board (FOB)—Indicates the location for which the price of a futures commodities contract includes delivery.

Free Payment—*See* Free Delivery.

Free Reserves—Excess reserves minus member bank borrowings at the Fed.

Freeriding—1) When a syndicate member withholds part of an offering to resell it at a profit. Freeriding is a violation of NASD Rules of Fair Practice. 2)When an investor trades without depositing a margin. *See* Regulation T.

Free to Trade—When members of a syndicate are no longer bound to sell a security at the agreed upon price. Also called *Freed Up.*

Friction—Costs associated with interest income, including trading costs, taxes, selling costs, information costs, and management costs.

Frictional Unemployment—Unemployment that is considered short term because the individuals included in this statistic are changing jobs. *See* Structural Unemployment.

Front Contract—*See* Nearby.

Front-Ending—When a broker-dealer agrees to buy part of an order to trade the rest.

Front End—1) Refers to payment at the beginning of a period (back end refers to payment at the end of a period). 2) Refers to the short maturity section of the yield curve.

Front End Load—A contractual purchase plan in which a mutual fund investor agrees that much of the first year's contributions will pay for total sales charges.

Front Month—Futures contract due to expire on the next expiration date.

Front Running—Trading with advance knowledge that an analyst will make a trade recommendation; it is a form of insider trading.

Frozen—Refers to an asset rendered illiquid by a legal restriction.

Frozen Account—An account in which the full purchase price of the transaction must be deposited in advance.

Full—*See* Handle.

Full Coupon Bond—Bond with a coupon at the market rate (therefore selling at or near par). *See* Current Coupon.

Full Disclosure—Principle that all material information be made available to potential investors in securities.

Full Employment—The maximum amount of individuals employed in a stable economy, taking into consideration factors such as seasonal demand for labor, population shifts, job changes, and technological changes.

Full Faith and Credit—Phrase used to describe the credit quality of government and municipal securities that are backed by the issuer's reputation and taxing power.

Full Price—*See* Dirty Price.

Fully Diluted—Refers to an earnings per share calculation that takes into consideration the possible exercise of all securities convertible into common stock, such as convertible bonds, preferred stock, warrants, and stock options. *See* Earnings per Share.

Fully Distributed—Describes a public offering that has been entirely sold to customers, as opposed to sold to dealers or not completely sold.

Fully Invested—Refers to a portfolio that has no assets in the form of cash or cash equivalents.

Fully Modified Pass-Through—*See* Modified and Pass-Through.

Fully Registered—Refers to a security whose principal and interest payments have been registered.

Fund—1) A large portfolio managed for a group of investors. 2) An asset set aside for a future purpose.

Fundamental Accounting Equation—*See* Basic Accounting Equation.

Fundamental Analysis—Market analysis based on quantitative financial information, such as a company's balance sheet and income statements, qualitative information, such as a company's management and goodwill, and/or supply and demand factors, such as raw materials, tax incentives, consumer trends, and money supply. *See* Classical Security Analysis and Technical Analysis.

Funded—Refers to an obligation such as a pension plan that has assets set aside to meet the obligation when due.

Funded Debt—Bonds and notes with at least five years to maturity.

Funded Interest—*See* Capitalized Interest.

Funded Ratio—Ratio of assets to liabilities.

Funding Agreement—A loan agreement collateralized by mortgage certificates or mortgage loans used to supply collateral for conduit CMOs.

Funds Flow—*See* Statement of Changes in Financial Position.

Funds from Operations—*See* Cash Flow from Operations.

Fungible—Interchangeable (e.g., delivery of one Treasury bill contract instead of another, one gallon of crude oil instead of another, etc.).

Fungible Securities—Commingled, identical securities in a bookkeeping system in which no specific securities are assigned by serial number to any one holder's account.

Funnel Sinking Fund—*See* Sinking Fund.

Future—A contract to buy or sell a specific amount of securities or commodities for a specific price or yield on a specified future date.

Futures Commission Merchant (FCM)—A broker who solicits or accepts buy or sell orders for futures contracts, and accepts payment to cover these orders.

Futures Contract—An exchange-traded contract, generally calling for delivery of a specified amount of a particular grade of commodity or financial instrument at a fixed date in the future.

Futures Delivery—The process of meeting an obligation to deliver or receive securities or commodities on a date and in a location as specified by terms of the contract. Not applicable to cash settled contracts.

Futures Market—A market in which contracts for future delivery of commodities or securities are traded.

Future Value (FV)—Value of present dollars at a future time, given as $P(1 + R)T$, where P = dollar amount, R = rate/compounding periods per year, T = number of compounding periods.

G

Gamma—Rate of change of an option's delta with respect to the price of the underlying security. *See* Delta.

Gap—1) A mismatch between the assets and liabilities of a balance sheet, usually defined as the difference between the dollar amount of assets maturing in a given time frame and liabilities coming due in the same time frame. When individual gaps are totaled across maturity categories, the result is known as "cumulative gap." 2) When the price movement of a security during one trading session does not overlap that of the next trading session.

Gap Analysis—An approach to asset/liability management for thrifts and other financial institutions. The traditional type of gap analysis involves comparing, on a periodic basis, the principal amount of maturing assets and maturing liabilities and implementing interest rate management strategies using swaps, futures, options, cash securities, and customized interest rate guarantees. More sophisticated forms of gap analysis involve computing the cash flow and duration of assets and liabilities under a variety of interest rate scenarios.

Gather in the Stops—To manipulate security prices to a level at which stop orders are known to exist, thus turning stop orders to market orders and encouraging further market movement.

Gearing—British term for financial leverage.

Geisha Bond—*See* Shogun Bond.

General Account—Margin account in which brokerage firms give credit to clients. General accounts are subject to Regulation T. *See* Regulation T.

General Fund—The main operating fund of a governmental entity.

General Mortgage Bond—A bond secured by a mortgage on the issuer's property that may be subordinate to one or more other mortgages.

General Obligation Bond (GO)—A federally tax-exempt bond backed by the "full faith, credit and taxing power" of the issuing municipality. *See* Limited Tax Bond and Unlimited Bond.

Gensaki—A Yen repo.

Geometric Return—Annualized compounded value of successive returns.

Gilt—A security denominated in Sterling backed by the full faith and credit of the United Kingdom and issued by the U.K. government.

Gilt Edged—Bonds with the highest credit rating (Aaa/AAA).

Gingy—Slang for a futures transaction unprofitable to the broker.

Ginnie Mae—*See* Government National Mortgage Association.

Give-Up—1) Yield give-up results from the sale of bonds at one yield and the purchase of an equivalent amount of bonds at a lower yield. 2) Name give-up involves NYSE bond trades only, whereby a broker notifies the seller of the buyer's identity upon execution so that delivery can be effected via the Stock Clearing Corporation.

Glass-Steagall Act—Congressional Act of 1933 forbidding commercial banks to own, underwrite, or deal in corporate stocks and bonds. Also called *Banking Act.*

Global Bond—A temporary certificate representing a whole issue, created to control the primary market distribution of an issue of securities in compliance with selling restrictions in certain jurisdictions when definitive bond certificates are not immediately available. *See* Lock-up Period.

GNMA—*See* Government National Mortgage Association.

GNMA Standby—GNMA put option.

GNMA I—A security issued by GNMA that is backed by a pool of FHA or VA mortgages, under the original GNMA guidelines.

GNMA II—A security issued by GNMA that is backed by a pool of FHA or VA mortgages. GNMA II securities differ from GNMA I securities by the use of a central paying agent and the availability of larger, geographically dispersed multiple issuer pools. The GNMA II program began in July 1983.

Gnome—1) A mortgage security issued by FHLMC with a 15-year maturity. 2) Bankers in Zurich, Switzerland, who engaged in foreign exchange speculation during the Sterling crisis of 1964.

GNP Deflator—A measure of inflation of current prices relative to those of a base year, currently 1972. The Department of Commerce calculates the GNP Deflator by estimating the value of all goods included in the GNP for the current year, dividing it by the value of those goods at prices during the base year, and multiplying that ratio by 100. *See* Gross National Product, Real GNP, and Money GNP.

Go-Around—When the Fed solicits competitive bids or offers from primary dealers in order to buy securities, sell securities, do repos, or do reverse repos.

Go-Go Fund—Investment company that is highly speculative.

Going Ahead—Violation of NASD rules of fair practice, whereby a broker trades for his own account before trading for a customer's account.

Going Away—Bonds purchased by dealers for immediate resale rather than for inventory are said to be going away.

Going Concern Assumption—*See* Continuity of Operations.

Going Public—Issuing shares to the general public.

Gold Clause—A common clause in prospectuses for bonds issued before 1933, promising payment in gold dollars of the same weight and fineness as those existing at the time of issuance. Such a promise has not been legal since 1933.

Golden Parachute—Financial benefits that corporate executives vote for themselves in the event of a hostile takeover.

Gold Standard—Fixing the price of domestic currencies in terms of gold. Countries under the gold standard pledge to buy and sell gold at the set price.

Good Delivery—A delivery with everything in order: certificates must be properly endorsed; any necessary legal papers must be attached; and the certificates must be in units of the proper denomination.

Good Due on Sale—Having a legally enforceable due on sale clause.

Good Execution—*See* Execute.

Good Faith Deposit—A cash deposit required on a competitive bid. Deposits usually range from one to five percent of the value of an issue, and are due at the time of the bid.

Good Money—Federal funds and cash; funds that are immediately available for payment.

Good Standing—Refers to preferred stock that is not in arrears as to dividends (if cumulative) or on which full dividends have been paid in each of the last three years (if non-cumulative), for which sinking fund payments are on a current basis.

Good-this-Month—Market order that expires at the end of the month.

Good-this-Week—Market order that expires at the end of the week.

Good 'Til Cancelled (GTC)—An open order to buy or sell securities that remains in effect until the order is executed or cancelled.

Good Trader—A Treasury bond or note issue that can easily be traded in large volumes.

Good Value—*See* Immediately Available Funds.

Go-Shugi—Japanese slang for large trades.

Governing Law—The jurisdiction to which the terms and conditions of a new deal are subject.

Governmental Accounting Standards Board (GASB)—Board that sets standards for municipal accounting.

Government Bond Basis—Refers to the method used to calculate accrued interest on U.S. government securities. The rate of interest is multiplied by the actual number of days elapsed and divided by the actual number of days in the year. Yields can be converted to a money market basis by multiplying by 360/365.

Government Broker—An agent of the Bank of England who acts in the gilt-edged market by issuing bonds and carrying out market transactions on behalf of the U.K. government and its departments. A government broker controls the new issue queue. *See* Tap.

Government Finance Officers Association (GFOA)—Board of state and local finance officials that oversees standards of municipal fiscal and debt operations. Formerly called Municipal Finance Officers Association.

Government in the Sunshine Law—*See* Sunshine Law.

Government National Mortgage Association (GNMA)—A wholly-owned U.S. Government corporation within the Department of Housing and Urban Development, established in 1968 as a spinoff from the Federal National Mortgage Association (FNMA). GNMA took over the assets and liabilities and operation of the Special Assistance Functions and the Management and Liquidating Functions of FNMA. GNMA can raise funds by issuing securities backed by pools of mortgages (*see* Pass-Through). Primary functions of GNMA are the purchase and sale of certain FHA and VA mortgages pursuant to various programs to support the housing market, and the guaranteeing of mortgage-backed securities issued against pools of FHA and VA mortgages.

Governments—U.S. Treasury securities.

Government Trust Certificate (GTC)—Certificates collateralized by U.S. government securities and guaranteed foreign military loans.

Govies—Slang for U.S. Treasury securities.

Grace Period—Period between a primary offering and the first sinking fund operation.

Grade—Refers to quality, as in high grade or contract grade.

Graduated Coupon—Coupons that regularly increase by a fixed amount or percentage for a specified period of time.

Graduated Payment Adjustable Rate Mortgage (GPARM)—Combines the features of graduated payment mortgages with those of adjustable rate mortgages.

Graduated Payment Mortgage (GPM)—A mortgage that calls for monthly payments that rise by a fixed percentage each year for a specified period of time. Early payments are insufficient to cover interest on the outstanding loan balance, resulting in negative amortization.

Graduated Payment Mortgage Reserve Fund—Fund established to cover interest accruing on graduated payment mortgages during their negative amortization period.

Graduated Tax—*See* Progressive Tax.

Granny—U.K. government savings bond that may be purchased only by retirees or recipients of governmental income.

Grant Anticipation Note (GAN)—Notes issued with the expectation of being repaid by federal grant money.

Grantor Trust—A special purpose vehicle set up to issue asset-backed or mortgage-backed securities, typically pass-through certificates. A legal entity, essentially ignored for tax purposes, that allows investors to hold interests in the trust and be taxed as if they owned their share of the trust assets directly. A Trust Agreement or Pooling and Servicing Agreement allows for the formation of a grantor trust by providing a contract between a depositor and a trustee. *See* Special Purpose Vehicle.

Grantor Underwritten Note (GUN)—An FRN facility, akin to a Euronote facility, whereby a group of banks, the "grantors," commit to purchase notes that investors put to them at fixed rates. These notes are then put up for auction.

Graveyard Market—Bear market in which holders of securities have incurred large paper losses and do not want to get out, and potential investors do not want to enter.

Gray Market—Market in which traders import foreign merchandise that bears a trademark of the importing country. Also called *Parallel Importation*.

Greater Fool Theory—Theory that an investor will always be able to sell a security at a profit to an even more gullible investor.

Greenback—*See* Fiat Paper.

Greenmail—Tendering a block of stock to the issuing corporation at a premium, with the implicit threat that a raider will buy the stock if the corporation does not.

Green Shoe—A provision in the underwriting agreement that allows the underwriter to purchase an additional amount (up to 15%) of the securities from the company on the same terms as the original offering. It provides the underwriter with a cushion against any short position incurred by the syndicate.

Gresham's Law—Sixteenth-century English economist's law that bad money drives out good (i.e., that if a country has two coins of equal face value but unequal intrinsic value, the one with higher intrinsic value will be hoarded or melted).

Grey Market—In the Eurobond market, the period of time during which an issue is traded from the date of its launch until allotment, i.e., during the primary market syndication on an "if, as, and when issued" basis. *See* When Issued.

Gross Coupon—The interest rate on the underlying collateral of a mortgage-related security. *See* Net Coupon.

Gross Debt—The amount of a debtor's total obligations.

Gross Domestic Product (GDP)—The total value of a nation's output produced within the country's borders. Like the Gross National Product, which is calculated as the Gross Domestic Product plus net income from abroad, it can be calculated either at current market prices or adjusted for inflation. When adjusted for inflation, it is said to be "at constant prices" or "real."

Gross Margin—Spread in basis points that is added to the index rate to compute the accrual rate and payment rate of an adjustable rate mortgage.

Gross National Product (GNP)—The total dollar value of final goods and services produced by the economy. When the proper accounting adjustments are made, this is equivalent to 1) total income and taxes in the economy, 2) total final sales plus the change in inventory stock, or 3) the total value of each industry's output. Real GNP is the figure derived by deflating each component of GNP for the increase in prices since an arbitrary base period (currently 1972) and adding the results. The relationship between this total and the actual dollar GNP yields the GNP price deflator that is commonly cited as a measure of general price change. *See* Money GNP and GNP Deflator.

Gross Redemption Yield—The redemption yield before tax.

Gross Revenue Pledge—*See* Pledged Revenues.

Gross Spread—1) The sum of management fees, underwriting fees, and the selling concession. 2) *See* Bid-Asked Spread.

Gross-Up—1) To increase a long position. 2) In Eurobond issues, additional payments made by a borrower to compensate for withholding tax or similar levies that reduce total return. 3) To calculate the yield before tax that equates to the yield after tax.

Group Net Order—An order to a municipal underwriting syndicate to allocate an issue at the public offering price without deducting the concession or takedown.

Growing Equity Mortgage (GEM)—A fixed rate, non-level payment mortgage in which monthly payments are increased each year. Unlike graduated payment mortgages, in which negative amortization occurs, early payments in GEMs are sufficient to cover interest on the outstanding loan balance.

Growth Fund—Mutual fund that invests in securities with a large potential for capital appreciation as opposed to large dividend or interest payments.

Growth Recession—*See* Recession.

Growth Stock—Stock of a company that has exhibited a fast growth in earnings and is expected to continue to do so.

Guarantee—A statutory or contractual obligation by a parent company or another entity (e.g., sovereign) to make interest, principal, or premium payments on a bond if the issuer defaults on such payments.

Guaranteed—Under the Uniform Securities Act, a guaranteed security is one whose payment of dividends or interest and principal is backed by an entity other than the issuer.

Guaranteed Bond—*See* Assumed Bond.

Guaranteed Coupon—In the GNMA forward market, a trade in which the seller guarantees the buyer delivery of a specific coupon GNMA at the agreed price, thereby avoiding the yield maintenance and par cap procedures associated with delivery of different coupons.

Guaranteed Investment Contract (GIC)—A contract with an insurance company that guarantees a rate of return.

Guaranteed Mortgage Certificate (GMC)—A bond issued by FHLMC backed by a pool of conventional mortgages. GMCs differ from pass-throughs in three ways: 1) FHLMC guarantees that some minimum principal amount will be paid each year; 2) GMCs pay interest semiannually and principal annually; and 3) investors have the option to put their remaining principal balance to FHLMC at par some time prior to maturity. FHLMC has not issued GMCs since 1979.

Guaranteed Sinking Fund—A sinking fund provision for a mandatory minimum schedule of bond retirements, regardless of prepayment rates on the underlying collateral in the case of CMOs. Usually the operation of a guaranteed sinking fund is based on a cumulative as opposed to a periodic basis. An agency (e.g., FHLMC) or a third party repurchase agreement backs the guarantee.

Guarantor—A party who by contract assumes liability for a debt in the event of a default.

Guarantor Program—Security issued under the auspices of FHLMC by mortgage lenders rather than FHLMC itself. *See* Swap PC.

Guerilla Group—Municipal syndicate.

Gun Jumping—1) Trading on inside information. 2) Soliciting orders for a security before SEC registration.

Gun-to-the-Head Tender—Tender offer whose terms are attractive compared to a threatened alternative, such as a call at a lower price.

H

Haircut—1) The lender in a repo transaction typically pays less than market value for the securities used as collateral, which are later repurchased by the borrower at market value. This margin is called a haircut. 2) The percentage of an asset's value that cannot be used to meet a collateral requirement.

Half-Life—The amount of time that must elapse until half the principal amount of a block of bonds has been retired (via a sinking fund or other process).

Half-PAC—*See* Targeted Amortization Class.

Half-Stock—Shares of common or preferred stock with a par value of $50 rather than $100.

Hammering—Intense selling, or selling short.

Handle—That part of a quote understood by all traders, usually the integer portion of a price quote. If a security is trading at 60-10 the bid may be 60-09 and the offer 60-11. The handle is 60. A trader would quote that market to another by saying he was at 9-11 (referring to 32nds). Also called *Big Figure.*

Hands-Off Economics—*See* Laissez-Faire.

Hang Seng Index—Index of 33 stocks on the Hong Kong Stock Exchange.

Hard Currency—*See* Hard Money.

Hard Dollars—Cash payment received for a service, such as research. *See* Soft Dollars.

Hard Money—1) Paper money that is backed by precious metal. 2) Coins or gold. 3) Currency in which there is international confidence. Loans taken out in hard money are typically repaid in hard money. Also called *Hard Currency.*

Harmless Income Warrant—A harmless warrant that pays its holder interest as long as it remains unexercised.

Harmless Warrant—A warrant attached to a bond that may be called during the period when the warrant may be exercised.

Head and Shoulders—A technical chart pattern consisting of a peak between two lower peaks. A head and shoulders pattern signals falling prices to a technical analyst. Conversely, a reverse head and shoulders pattern, consisting of a trough between two lesser troughs, signals rising prices. *See* Technical Analysis.

Heaven and Hell—A bond whose redemption proceeds are linked to the maturity spot exchange rate of another currency against the currency of denomination. The redemption proceeds may take any value between 5 percent and 200 percent of the face value.

Heavy—Refers to a market with selling pressure, and therefore falling prices.

Hedge—1) The technique of making offsetting commitments to minimize the impact of adverse movements in the price of a commodity or security. 2) A fixed commitment in a futures market that serves as a temporary substitute for an intended purchase or sale of a financial instrument for delivery and payment at a later date. 3) Any action taken to reduce risk in a portfolio.

Hedge Clause—A disclaimer that disavows legal claim of and responsibility for the accuracy of information obtained from outside sources.

Hedged Growth—*See* Risk-Controlled Arbitrage.

Hedged Tender—Selling short a percentage of securities being tendered, to protect against the possibility that all the securities tendered will not be accepted and that the price will consequently fall.

Hedge Fund—1) A mutual fund that uses hedging techniques. 2) An unregulated private investment partnership that is free to operate on either side of the market.

Hedge Period—The time interval between the transaction that creates an open position and the offsetting futures transaction.

Hedge Ratio—1) The number of futures or options contracts that are bought or sold in order to hedge the position in the underlying security. 2) The ratio of the price sensitivity of an option to that of the underlying security. *See* Delta.

Hell or High Water Obligation—Provision requiring a utility to make lease payments even if the plant does not operate.

Hemline Theory—Theory that securities prices move with women's hemlines.

Highballing—*See* Overtrading.

High Flyer—A highly volatile, highly speculative security.

High-Grade Bond—Bond rated double-A or above by Moody's or Standard & Poor's.

High-Low Floater—Hybrid capped floating rate security offering yields higher than other comparable credit quality floating rate securities as compensation for the short put option (cap) embedded in them.

High Powered Money—Refers to financial institutions' reserve balances on the books of the Fed, since each dollar of reserves supports several dollars of deposits. The total quantity of high powered money can be precisely controlled by the Federal Reserve. *See* Fractional Reserve System and Reserve Assets.

Highs—Security prices that have reached record levels for the current year.

High Yield Bond—All non-convertible debt securities rated Ba1/BB+ and below. The most common instruments issued and traded in the high yield market are straight subordinated debt and debt with an equity add-on or equity kicker of warrants and/or common stock. These instruments allow companies to raise capital without the highly restrictive covenants normally found when borrowing from banks. Also called *Junk Bond.*

Historical Cost—*See* Original Cost.

Historical Range—The range of prices within which a security has traded.

Historical Yield—The yield provided by a mutual fund, calculated as the dividend divided by the average monthly offering price.

Hit—To accept a bid.

Hoeckman—A jobber on the Amsterdam exchange.

Holder of Record—Owner of securities as recorded on the issuer's and/or paying agent's entry system.

Holding—Entering the market with enough buy orders to stabilize the price of the security. Holding is illegal according to the SEC, except in the case of new issue stabilization that is cleared with the SEC. *See* Stabilization and Pegging.

Holding Company—A parent company that has no business of its own. *See* Parent.

Holding Period—The time during which an asset is held by an investor; the interim between the purchase of a security and its sale.

Holding Period Return—An investor's gain (or loss) from interest and capital appreciation. Also called *Total Return.*

Holding the Market—*See* Holding.

Home Industry—*See* Cottage Industry.

Home Run—A large return received over a short period of time.

Honest-to-God (HTG) Yield—A term coined by First Boston for the yield computed on a mortgage-related security based on an actual or an assumed prepayment rate on the underlying mortgages. HTG is a monthly yield. It is typically semiannualized into HTG CBE yield for comparison with corporate bonds. Also called *Cash Flow Yield*.

Hook Order—*See* Cap Order.

Horizon Analysis—Total return analysis within a specified time period, taking into account nominal market conditions and departures from them. *See* Nominal Market Conditions.

Horizon Premium—*See* Liquidity Premium.

Horizontal Price Movement—Changes in price within a narrow range over an extended period of time.

Horizontal Spread—For a given option, a purchase or sale of the option is made for one expiration date at one strike price, while an offsetting purchase or sale is made at the same strike price but for a longer expiration date. Also called *Calendar Spread* and *Time Spread*. *See* Trading Against the Box.

Horizontal Yield Curve—*See* Yield Curve.

Horizon Volatility—A measure of price volatility within a specified time period.

Host Bond—A security issued with warrants.

Hot Issue—A security expected to trade at a premium after issuance.

House—1) An investment bank. 2) The London Stock Exchange.

House Call—Maintenance margin call, which is due on demand.

Household—An economic unit consisting of one or more individuals who act as a single unit in terms of consumption.

Household Industry—*See* Cottage Industry.

House Rules—An investment firm's internal policies, which may be more stringent than outside regulations.

Housing Starts—Number of residential buildings on which construction has begun, not including dormitories, mobile homes, hotels and motels, and housing units in nonresidential buildings. Housing starts is one of the twelve leading indicators. *See* Leading Indicator.

Human Capital—Spending for services that improve the labor force, such as education.

Human Resources—Labor and entrepreneurial resources.

Humped Yield Curve—*See* Yield Curve.

Hung Deal—A new issue of which a large portion remains unsold and in the hands of the underwriters.

Hung Up—Paper capital loss.

Hurdle Rate—Required rate of return in a discounted cash flow analysis.

Hybrid—A security with the characteristics of two different types of securities.

Hyperinflation—An extremely high rate of inflation, leading to economic collapse.

Hypothecation—The process of lending a customer money and using the customer's securities as collateral. The loans are typically used to purchase additional securities, cover shorts, or meet margin calls. *See* Rehypothecation.

I

Idiosyncratic Return—The part of an asset's return attributable to a particular company rather than to the market. Also called *Unsystematic Return.*

Illiquid—Refers to a security that does not have an active secondary market, and therefore cannot be easily traded or converted into cash.

Immediately Available Funds—Funds with immediate good value, such as federal funds and cash. *See* Same-Day Funds, Good Value, and Clearing House Funds.

Immediate or Cancel—Buy or sell limit order with the stipulation that if the order is filled only in part the rest is to be cancelled.

Immobilization—Elimination of movement of certificates through a book entry system.

Immunization—An asset management strategy in which a portfolio manager matches the duration of a bond portfolio with a specified investment horizon. This strategy is intended to lock in a return equal to the initial yield of the assets under the assumption of simple parallel shifts of a flat yield curve. Also called *Duration Matching.*

Impairment of Capital—Reduction of a corporation's value to a level below the legal value that must be maintained.

Imperfect Hedge—Unequal price changes on the two sides of a hedged position during a hedge period.

Implicit Interest—Unpaid interest.

Implied Dividend Rate—The dividend rate for Adjustable Rate Preferred (ARP) Stock that results from the same index rate, usually the current reference rate, being applied to all future dividend calculations. *See* Reference Rate.

Implied Forward Rate—The return over a future holding period implicit in the current cash market yield curve. For example, the implied forward rate one year from now is the rate that would make an invest-

135

or indifferent between owning a two-year security now and a one-year security now and investing the proceeds in a one-year security one year from now.

Implied Repo Rate—The rate of return earned by purchasing a security and delivering it into a futures contract.

Implied Volatility—The value of an option is a function of five variables: the price of the underlying security, time to expiration, the strike price, the short-term interest rate, and volatility. Volatility can be calculated if the other four variables as well as the market price of the option are known. If volatility is calculated in this way, it is called implied volatility. *See* Volatility.

Implied Yield—A forecasted yield derived from present yields and based on the theory that the yield curve on one day provides an unbiased estimation of itself in the future. *See* Term Structure Hypothesis.

Imprest—Petty cash.

In and Out—Buying and selling a security within a short period.

In-and-Out Trader—Day trader; a trader who keeps no overnight positions.

Incestuous Trading—Two corporations each buying and selling the other's securities.

Incidence—The ultimate burden of a tax.

Income—Revenues minus expenses for a period. Also called *Net Income, Earnings,* and *Profits.*

Income Bond—A bond that is guaranteed as to principal but for which interest payments are a contingent obligation. Failure to pay interest does not constitute default. Income bonds trade flat. *Also called* Adjustment Bond.

Income Fund—A mutual fund investing in income-producing securities rather than growth securities, with a large potential for capital appreciation.

Income Portfolio—A portfolio constructed to provide higher than average income.

Incomes Policy—Any governmental policy to directly influence or regulate prices, wages, profits, or dividends. Methods range from gentle moral suasion to rigid price and wage freezes.

Income Statement—A financial accounting statement that provides revenues, expenses, gains, and losses for a specified period, ending with net income.

Income Stock—Stock that pays high dividends.

Income Velocity of Circulation—*See* Velocity.

Income Warrant—A warrant that, while outstanding, pays a modest interest coupon on the warrant issue price. This current income tends to discourage early exercise and can be viewed as compensating investors if exercise privileges are limited.

Income Yield—*See* Current Yield.

In Competition—A situation in which two or more dealers compete for the purchase, sale, or swap of bonds for an account, with implicit agreement that the execution will be awarded to the dealer who provides the best price.

Incremental Capital-Output Ratio—*See* Capital-Output Ratio.

Indemnify—To guarantee against physical loss.

Indenture—For debt securities, the contract that specifies all legal obligations of the issuer with respect to the securities and any qualifications or restrictions that may exist. Also called *Deed of Trust.*

Indenture Supplement—A supplement to the indenture that authorizes a particular series of bonds. A CMO indenture supplement includes a listing of the underlying collateral (Schedule A or Exhibit A). Also called *Series Supplement.*

Independent—A standard usually imposed on accountants by a CMO indenture requiring that they be free from any obligation to or interest in the issuer, its management, or its owners.

Independent Broker—*See* Two-Dollar Broker.

Index—1) A market level off of which floating rate coupons are set, including federal funds, Treasury bills, cost of funds, LIBOR, commercial paper, Constant Maturity Treasury, and prime rate. 2) *See* Market Index.

Index Arbitrage—*See* Program Trading.

Index Duration—For adjustable rate mortgages, a measure of the sensitivity of price to a change in the index.

Indexed Bond—A bond in which the payment of interest is changed in line with an index, which is not itself an interest rate (e.g., the price of gold or the Retail Price Index).

Indexed Repo—A term repo in which the interest rate is reset periodically, generally as a function of federal funds, LIBOR, or Treasury bills.

Indexed Sinking Fund Debenture (ISFD)—Security whose sinking fund redemptions vary with changes in interest rates.

Index Fund—A portfolio structured so that its return will be close to that on a market index (e.g., Standard & Poor's 500 Stock Index).

Index Futures—A contract to buy or sell units of a specific index (e.g., the Corporate Bond Index) at a predetermined price on a specified future date (the delivery date).

Index-Linked Bond—*See* Index Bond.

Index Option—Option based on an underlying stock index rather than an individual security.

Indication of Interest—*See* Circle.

Indicated Market—Quotes that are subject, not firm.

Indicator—Any number or statistic giving information about the state of the economy. The U.S. government publishes an index of "leading economic indicators," including the unemployment rate, automobile sales, retail sales, housing starts, durable goods orders, personal income, and the money supply.

Indorsed Bond—*See* Assumed Bond.

Industrial Bond—Debt issued by a corporation.

Industrial Development Bond—*See* Industrial Revenue Bond.

Industrial Development Bond Insurance (IDBI)—Insurance for the financing of industrial and commercial development projects.

Industrial Revenue Bond—A bond issued by a municipality or development corporation to finance an industrial plant to be leased to a corporation. Also called *Industrial Development Bond. See* Conduit Financing.

Industrial Sector—*See* Business Sector.

Inefficient—A market in which asset prices do not reflect all available information.

Inelasticity—Market situation in which changes in price do not affect supply.

Inert—Refers to buy-and-hold investors.

Infinite Elasticity—*See* Perfect Elasticity.

Inflation—Increasing wages and prices and decreasing purchasing power. *See* Deflation.

Inflationary Gap—The difference between actual aggregate demand and the level of aggregate demand during a hypothetical period of full employment and price stability. *See* Recessionary Gap.

Information Date—The date on which the delivering party (the put buyer or the call writer) must tell what is being delivered on the settlement date. The information date is 48 hours prior to the settlement date, which is the third Wednesday of the delivery month.

Information Trading—The attempt to make a profit in the market by using information not yet discounted. *See* Discounted Information, Inefficient, and Liquidity Trading.

In Hand—*See* Firm.

Initial Margin—The amount of margin required in order to establish a position in a futures contract. *See* Margin. Also called *Performance Bond.*

Initial Public Offering (IPO)—The first offering to the general public of any class of a corporation's common equity securities.

Initial Rate—Interest rate that applies to an adjustable rate mortgage loan from origination to the first adjustment date.

Input-Output System—Economic analysis that analyzes what each industry buys and sells from every other industry. The idea for this kind of analysis comes from Francois Quesnay, the physician to Louis XV, whose *Tableau Economique* showed the trade among farmers, landlords, and merchants. In 1973, Wassily Leontif won the Nobel Prize in Economics for a similar kind of interindustry analysis.

Inside Information—Information that is not yet publicly available, and has therefore not yet affected market prices. It is illegal to trade on inside information.

Inside Market—The market defined by the highest actual bid and the lowest actual offering. An inside market may be tighter than a particular trader's market.

Insider—As defined by the Securities Exchange Act of 1934, an insider is a director, officer, or owner of 10% or more of the equity (stock or convertible securities) of a corporation. Anyone who becomes an insider must report this fact to the SEC within ten days. Insiders may neither sell the stock short nor sell the stock short against the box. If an insider sells the stock at a profit before holding it for at least six months, the corporation may sue for recovery of the profit. Also called *Affiliated Person* and *Control Person.*

Insider—*See* Affiliate.

Insolvent—Unable to pay debts.

Installment—Partial payment of debt.

Institutional Delivery (ID)—*See* National Institutional Delivery System.

Institutional Investor—An organization such as a pension fund, investment company, university, insurance company, or bank with a large amount of invested funds.

Institutional Pot—The percentage (usually 20%) of a new issue offering that is set aside by syndicate managers for large institutional orders. *See* Pot.

Instrument—A generic term for securities, encompassing a range of financial debt from negotiable deposits to bonds. Typically refers to short-term maturities, such as money market instruments.

Insured Bond—Municipal bond whose principal and interest payments are guaranteed by an insurance company.

In Syndicate—Refers to a new issue that is still subject to the price and trading restrictions as set forth in the agreement among underwriters. *See* Agreement Among Underwriters.

Intangible Asset—A nonphysical asset, such as goodwill, patents, and trademarks.

Interbank Rate—The rate at which banks bid for and offer deposits to each other, such as LIBID, LIMEAN, LIBOR, FIBOR, FIBID, FIMEAN, NIBOR, and SIBOR.

Intercommodity Spread—Purchase and sale of different commodities on either the same or different exchanges.

Intercorporate Debt—Debt of one corporation to either a corporation it controls or a corporation controlling it.

Inter-Dealer Broker—An intermediary between the primary or main dealers. Inter-dealer brokers allow dealers to perform anonymous transactions.

Interdelivery Spread—*See* Intermarket Spread.

Interest—An amount of money charged to a borrower by a lender for the use of money.

Interest Assumption—The actuarial expected rate of return on a pension plan's assets.

Interest Bond—Bond whose proceeds pay the interest on previously issued debt.

Interest Coverage—A measure of a borrower's ability to make interest payments out of its earnings or cash flow, calculated as net income before interest and taxes divided by interest charges. *See* Price-Earnings Ratio.

Interest Coverage—The ratio of pre-tax, pre-interest income to interest expense.

Interested—Refers to a shareholder who owns at least 10 percent of a corporation's outstanding capital stock.

Interest Equalization Tax (IET)—A special tax that was once imposed by the U.S. government on interest and other income from certain foreign securities in order to discourage the offering of such securities in the United States.

Interest Factor—One plus the interest rate.

Interest Only (IO)—Stripped mortgage-backed security in which the investor receives all of the interest and none of the principal of the underlying security.

Interest Only Period—Refers to a commercial loan in which there is a period when no principal is paid on the outstanding balance.

Interest Rate—The amount of money paid for borrowing money, expressed in terms of an annual percentage rate upon the principal amount. *See* Nominal Interest Rate and Real Interest Rate.

Interest Rate Cap—The maximum interest rate on a floating rate security.

Interest Rate Cycle—Periodic fluctuations of general interest rates resulting from macroeconomic factors.

Interest Rate Differential—The difference in the rate of interest offered for investments of identical maturities denominated in different currencies.

Interest Rate Exposure—Risk due to potential movement of interest rates.

Interest Rate Futures—Futures contracts for securities that have prices driven by interest rates.

Interest Rate Option—*See* Option.

Interest Rate Risk—*See* Basis Risk.

Interest Rate Shock—The psychological effect of paying a floating rate loan payment that is significantly higher than the previous payment.

Interest Rate Swap—An agreement between two parties to exchange payments that are based on specified interest rates and a notional amount. There is no transfer of principal. Swaps are simply cash flow exchanges and therefore can be applied to either assets or liabilities. Swaps allow parties to change their interest rate exposure from a floating to a fixed rate or vice versa, thereby allowing them either to access the fixed or floating capital markets indirectly or to manage their asset/liability structure.

Interest Yield—*See* Current Yield.

Interest Yield Equivalent (IYE)—A measurement of the rate of return on a security sold on a discount basis that assumes actual days to maturity and a 360-day year. *See* Equivalent Bond Yield.

Interim Experience—The rate of prepayments made between two specific points in time after a pass-through security has been issued (e.g., the experience for the latest three months).

Interim Financing—A short-term loan used before the closing of a long-term loan. Also called *Bridge Financing*.

Interim Statement—Accounting record for periods less than the annual period.

Intermarket Spread—Purchase and sale of the same security or commodity on different exchanges.

Intermarket Spread Swap—Swap done in anticipation of a change in the price or yield spread between two issues from two different sectors of the market.

Intermarket Trading—Purchase and sale of the same security or commodity on different exchanges. *See* Intramarket Trading.

Intermarket Trading System (ITS)—Six stock exchanges (New York, American, Boston, Midwest, Pacific, and Philadelphia) tied into an electronic communications network.

Intermediate—A bond with a maturity of intermediate length. Depending on the particular market, the range for this length may vary. In the corporate bond market, an intermediate has a maturity of one to twelve years.

Intermediate Bond—Bond with a maturity of between 2 and 10 years.

Intermediate-Term CD—Certificate of deposit with a maturity of one to five years. Also called *Term CD*.

Intermediation—Use of a broker or manager to invest funds.

Internal Debt—Debt for which the debtor and creditor belong to the same economic unit, so that cash flows do not change aggregate wealth. Federal debt is considered internal debt, because the cash flows do not change the aggregate wealth of the nation. *See* External Debt.

Internal Rate of Return (IRR)—The discount rate at which the sum of the discounted cash flows of a bond equals the price of the bond. In other words, the rate at which inflows and outflows for a given bond or portfolio, when discounted, exactly offset (i.e., net present value = 0). So called because the reinvestment rate is internal to the calculation. *See* External Rate of Return and Yield to Maturity.

Internal Theory of Business Cycles—*See* Endogenous Theory of Business Cycles.

International Bank for Reconstruction and Development (IBRD)—*See* Development Bank.

International Commodities Clearing House (ICCH)—An independent central guarantee organization used by the U.K.'s six largest clearing banks, acting as clearing agency for contracts on LIFFE.

International Equity Placement—A simultaneous placement of equity in two or more markets other than the issuer's domestic market. Also known as *Euro Equity Placement.*

International Monetary Fund (IMF)—System of international monetary reserves, established in 1944, to which over one hundred nations belong. The IMF acts as an international central bank by holding currency reserves and making loans to national central banks in order to facilitate trade and currency exchanges. *See* Special Drawing Rights.

International Primary Markets Association (IPMA)—An organization founded by Euromarket participants to provide a forum for discussion of standards and primary market practices.

International Securities Regulatory Organization (ISRO)—The regulatory organization set up for the monitoring and supervision of the international equities markets in London, created as a result of the U.K. Financial Services Act of 1986.

Interpositioning—When a broker uses a second broker, causing the client to pay for two transactions.

In the Black—Operating at a profit.

In the Box—When a dealer has a wire receipt for delivered securities. This phrase was used literally when Treasuries were physical securities stored in a rack.

In the Money (ITM)—An option that can be exercised profitably. A call option is in the money if its strike price is less than the value of the underlying security. A put option is in the money if the strike price is greater than the value of the underlying security. *See* Strike Price, Call, Put, At the Money, and Out of the Money.

In the Red—Operating at a loss.

In the Tank—Refers to a security whose price is rapidly declining.

Intramarket Trading—Purchase and sale of the same security or commodity on the same exchange, to take advantage of price movements. *See* Intermarket Trading.

Intra-State Offering—A securities issue that is restricted to investors residing in one state. Exempt from the filing provisions of the 1933 Securities Act.

Intrinsic Value—The amount by which a put or call option is in the money; out-of-the-money options have no intrinsic value. *See* Theoretical Value.

Inventory Turnover—*See* Turnover.

Inventory Valuation Adjustment (IVA)—A statistical estimate of what part of the national increase in the book value of inventories results from replacing identical items at higher or lower cost. The IVA is subtracted from the book value increase to obtain the inventory change component of the GNP.

Inverse Floater—*See* Reverse Floater.

Inverted—Refers to a descending yield curve, or one in which shorter maturities have higher yields than longer maturities. Also called *Negative Yield Curve. See* Yield Curve.

Inverted Market—Market in which prices for advanced months of futures contracts progressively decline. Also called *Discount Market. See* Backwardation.

Invested Capital—A corporation's outstanding securities (stocks and bonds) plus retained profits.

Invested Sinking Fund—Sinking fund for a term bond in which Treasuries are invested so that the term bond will be fully secured before maturity.

Investment—The use of money in the expectation of future returns in the form of income or capital gain.

Investment Act of 1940—Legislation passed by Congress to ensure that those investing in investment companies are fully informed and fairly treated. It requires that all publicly held investment companies register with the SEC.

Investment Banker—An individual or firm acting as the middleman between issuers of new securities and investors.

Investment Company—An institution that invests and trades in securities, including face amount certificate companies, unit investment trust companies, and management companies.

Investment Grade—Bonds rated in the top four rating categories (AAA, AA, A, BBB) are commonly known as investment grade securities and are considered eligible for bank investment under commercial bank regulations issued by the Comptroller of the Currency.

Investment Letter—The letter required in a private placement that declares the intent of the investor to hold the purchased securities as an investment rather than for resale.

Investment Letter Stock—An affiliated person's securities received through a merger or stock option plan.

Investment Portfolio—A portfolio in which the principal of the securities is considered relatively safe.

Invisible Trade Balance—Balance of trade in services plus net receipts of interest, profits, and dividends from abroad. *See* Trade Balance.

Invitation Telex—A telex to prospective syndicate members from the lead manager describing a primary market issue and its expected terms and inviting them to participate in the underwriting and/or distribution of the issue.

Invoice Amount—The settlement price of a futures contract for a specific month multiplied by the factor for the cash security being delivered (or divided by the factor in the case of GNMAs), plus any accrued interest as of the delivery date.

Invoice Price—The market price plus accrued interest for transactions in cash securities.

Involuntary Underwriter—Anyone who buys unregistered securities, offering them to the public without a registration statement. Also called a *Statutory Underwriter*.

Irish Dividend—Reverse split. Also called *Scottish Dividend* and *Polish Dividend*.

Iron Law of Wages—Economist David Ricardo's view that workers should receive only survival wages. Any excess would be wasted or lead to overpopulation.

Issue—1) Outstanding stock or bonds of a corporation. 2) The selling of new securities by a corporation, through an underwriter or by private placement.

Issue Bid—A bid to purchase securities at the initial offering price.

Issue Date—The date of an issue of securities from which interest accrues. The issue date is often incorrectly used as the date on which allotments are made for new issues of Eurosecurities. In fact, the issue date is frequently the same as the payment or closing date. Dated date is most often used in reference to Certificates of Deposit. *See* Closing Date, Launch Date, and Announcement Date.

Issue Price—The percentage of principal value at which the price of a new issue of securities is fixed.

Issuer—That corporation or government unit that borrows money through the sale of securities.

Issuing and Paying Agency—An agent for ensuring timely payment for and delivery of a security at the issue date. *See* Paying Agent.

Itaku Gensaki—A gensaki between two clients of a securities house, with the house acting as intermediary. *See* Gensaki.

J

James Bond—U.S. Treasury bond maturing in 2007.

January Barometer—Hypothesis that the market's movement in January will predict its direction for the remainder of the year.

January Effect—The typical rise in price of securities of small companies in the first few days of January. This is in effect a price rebound that occurs after tax-related selling at the end of the year.

Jawboning—The use of public pronouncements and persuasion to affect public policy.

J-Curve—An economic theory stating that a policy designed to have one effect will initially have the opposite effect. For example, currency may be devalued to increase exports. Before exports increase, however, the import bill may increase (because foreign goods are more expensive) and export earnings may fall (because export prices are lower in foreign currency terms). Therefore, the trade balance should initially become worse—the downward slope of the J—before it improves.

Jelly Roll Spread—A put and a call time spread. *See* Time Spread.

Jobber—A British term for a dealer who acts as a principal (i.e., acts for his own account).

Joint Account—An agreement by two or more firms to share in the purchase, sale, or ownership of securities with equal or proportionate risk and financial participation.

Joint and Several—In the context of a guarantee for which there is more than one guarantor, this term refers to each guarantor's liability to cover his own failure and the failure of any other guarantors to fulfill their obligation. Underwriters of a new Eurobond or FRN issue also have joint and several obligations to subscribe and pay for securities issued. *See* Several.

Joint Bonds—Bonds issued by two companies having a joint interest in a property.

Joint-Stock Company—Corporation.

Joint Tenants (JT)—An account held by two or more owners. May be With Rights of Survivorship (WROS), in which case one owner has total ownership in the case of the other's death; or as Tenants In Common (TIC), in which case one owner receives half the account in the case of the other's death with the remainder going to the estate of the deceased.

Juglar Cycle—Business cycle of 7 or 8 years, based on patterns of capital investment.

Jumbo—Mortgage loans that have principal balances greater than the amount eligible for purchase by FNMA or FHLMC. The Congressional limit is currently $153,100.

Junior Refunding—Refinancing government debt that matures in one to five years by issuing securities that mature in five or more years.

Junior Security—A security with a claim on a corporation's assets and income that is subordinate to that of a senior security. For example, common stock is junior to preferred stock, which is junior to a debenture, which is junior to secured debt.

Junk Bond—*See* High Yield Bond.

K

Kaffirs—A British term referring to shares in South African gold mines, which trade over the counter in the U.S. in the form of American Depositary Receipts. Kaffirs, under South African law, must pay out the vast majority of earnings as dividends.

Kangaroo Bond—An Australian dollar-denominated bond issued in the United States.

Kansas City Board of Trade (KCBT)—A futures exchange on which wheat contracts and Value Line Stock Index contracts are traded.

Kappa—The change in the price of an option with a one percent change in the volatility of the underlying security.

Kassenobligation(en)—A German financial instrument traded in the Euromarkets. It is normally issued in bearer form with a maximum maturity of four years by government agencies or Giro banks in Germany and is quoted on the domestic stock exchanges. Swiss Kassenobligationen are also traded.

Kassenvereine—Depository banks that form the German clearing system. *See* Clearing System, CEDEL, and Euroclear.

Keep Well Agreement—An agreement in which a parent company promises a third party that its subsidiary will maintain specified financial ratios.

Keynesian Economics—Economic theory based on the writings of John Maynard Keynes (1883-1946), primarily *The General Theory of Employment, Interest and Money* (1935). Keynes attacked the widely held Say's Law (1803), which states that supply creates its own demand and that unemployment is therefore theoretically impossible. Keynes argued that demand does not move in lock step with supply, and that imbalances in demand result in macroeconomic problems: insufficient demand results in unemployment, and excessive demand results in inflation. Aggregate demand, according to Keynes, should be manipulated by fiscal policy to ensure employment and economic growth. *See* Aggregate Demand, Laissez-Faire, and Monetarism.

149

Keynes' Law—Economic law that demand determines its own supply, as opposed to Say's Law, which states that supply determines its own demand.

Kicker—An inducement to buy a security, such as a warrant. Also called *Sweetener*.

Killer Bee—An entity, such as a law firm or bank, that helps a takeover target defend itself against a corporate raider.

Kind Arbitrage—Simultaneous purchase and sale of almost identical securities in the same market.

Kitchin Cycle—Business cycle of 39 months, based on fluctuations in business inventories.

Kiting—1) Manipulating security prices by creating artificial trading activity. 2)Writing checks against an account with insufficient funds, in an attempt to take advantage of the time it takes for the bank to clear checks. *See* Float. 3) Altering the amount written on a check.

Kiwi Bond—A New Zealand dollar-denominated Eurobond.

Know Your Customer—An ethical standard of conduct for registered representatives, defined in Article 3 of the NASD Rules of Fair Practice: "In recommending to a customer the purchase, sale or exchange of any security, a member shall have reasonable grounds for believing that the recommendation is suitable for such customer as to his other security holdings and as to his financial situation and needs." Also called *Rule 405*.

Kommunalobligation(en)—Bond issued by German banks to finance public sector loans. Kommunalobligationen are collateralized by a pool of public sector loans.

Kondratieff Cycle—*See* Kondratieff Wave.

Kondratieff Wave—Economic theory named after the Soviet economist who claimed that capitalist countries are prone to large swings in the economy called "supercycles," which last 50 to 60 years. Also called Kondratieff Cycle. *See* Kuznets Waves.

Kuznets Waves—Economic cycles, lasting approximately twenty years, generated by immigration patterns. Immigration leads to higher capacity utilization, which leads to rising real interest rates and expansionary monetary and fiscal policies. Kuznets waves are also based on generational population changes and consequent patterns of housing construction. *See* Kondratieff Wave.

L

Labor Force—Number of people who either have jobs or who are looking for work. The figures are obtained through monthly inquiry from a rotating sample of households.

Labor Force Participation Rate—The labor force as a percentage of the total population.

Labor Intensive—Pertaining to industries in which labor costs are high relative to capital costs.

Laddering—A fixed income portfolio strategy in which assets are distributed evenly over a range of maturities.

Lagging Indicators—*See* Leading Indicator.

Laissez-Faire—French for "allow to do," this doctrine states that government should not interfere in the economy. Laissez-faire is a cornerstone of classical economics. Adam Smith, for example, in *The Wealth of Nations* (1776), claims that an invisible hand in a laissez-faire economy will provide for the maximum good of all. *See* Keynesian Economics.

Lambda—The elasticity of the option price with respect to the price of the underlying security, calculated as the percentage change in the option's price divided by the percentage change in the price of the underlying security.

Lapping—*See* Ponzi.

Lapsed—Describes an option that has expired.

Last-In First-Out (LIFO)—An inventory valuation method that assumes that the newest inventory (last in) is the first to be sold (first out). *See* First-In First-Out.

Last Sale—The previous transaction in a security.

Last Trading Day—The day after which a futures contract cannot be offset and delivery must be arranged.

Latent Demand—*See* Potential Demand.

151

Launch—To issue a security.

Launch Date—The date on which a new issue's invitation telex is officially sent out to the syndicate.

Launder—To conceal the source of money through transfers.

Law of Comparative Advantage—David Ricardo's economic principle that the producer (individual, corporation, or nation) with the lowest opportunity cost will have the greatest profit, and that trading partners will both benefit if they exchange goods that they can produce at a low opportunity cost for goods they could produce only at a high opportunity cost.

Law of Demand—Economic principle that price and demand are inversely related.

Law of Diminishing Marginal Utility—*See* Utility.

Law of Supply—Economic principle that price and supply are directly related.

Lay Up—Easy execution of a trade order.

Leading Indicator—Economic statistic that in the past has moved up or down in advance of the general business situation. The Leading Indicator Index is a composite of several such statistics. There are also Coincidental Indicators (that move with the economic situation) and Lagging Indicators (that move after the economic situation). The twelve leading indicators are: average workweek of production workers; average weekly initial claims for state unemployment insurance; new orders for consumer goods and materials in 1972 dollars; vendor performance and the percentage of companies receiving slower deliveries; net business formation; contracts for plant and equipment in 1972 dollars; new building permits and private housing units; changes in inventories (on hand and on order) in 1972 dollars; change in prices of sensitive materials; change in business and consumer borrowing; prices of 500 common stocks; and money supply (M2) in 1972 dollars.

Lead Manager—The leading syndicate member of a new primary issue, responsible for its coordination, distribution, and documentation. The lead-manager runs the books and is primarily responsible for: 1) selecting the co-managers in consultation with the borrower; 2) determining the initial and final terms of the issue in consultation with the borrower and co-managers; 3) selecting the underwriters, generally in consultation with the borrower and co-managers; and 4) selecting the selling group. *See* Syndicate.

Leakage—An unforeseen side effect that causes an economic model to make slightly inaccurate predictions.

Left-Hand Financing—Borrowing that has as collateral assets listed on the left side of the balance sheet.

Leg—1) A position that hedges another. 2) One side of a spread transaction. *See* Spread and Lifting a Leg. 3) A sustained price trend.

Legal Defeasance—*See* Defeasance.

Legality—The legal status of a bond, generally used to indicate whether it is a legal investment for savings banks in Connecticut, Massachusetts, New Hampshire, New Jersey, and/or New York. Also called *Legal Status.*

Legal List—A state-approved list of securities in which fiduciary institutions such as savings banks, pension funds, and insurance companies may invest. Some states do not have a legal list but use the prudent man rule. *See* Prudent Man Rule.

Legal Opinion—A municipal bond counsel's written statement that an issue complies with all relevant laws. Legal opinion also specifies the tax-exempt status of the issue.

Legal Status—*See* Legality.

Legal Tender—Coin or currency accepted in the settlement of private and public debt.

Leg-In—To execute the first side of a spread trade. This presumes that each side is done separately to establish the spread. *See* Lifting a Leg.

Lender of Last Resort—The Federal Reserve Bank, whose role it is to support banks that face large withdrawals. Member banks may borrow from the Fed's discount window to maintain reserve requirements or cover large withdrawals.

Lender's Option—Borrower's Option (LOBO)—A municipal U.K. security for which a holder may choose a new coupon rate at any time. The borrower may then choose whether to pay the new rate or redeem the bonds.

Less the Re—*See* Less the Reallowance.

Less the Reallowance—Refers to a trade between two NASD member dealers of an item subject to syndicate restrictions at the maximum permissible discount. Often abbreviated as "less the re."

Letter Bond—*See* Letter Security.

Letter of Confirmation—*See* Due Bill.

Letter of Credit (LOC)—A commercial bank's guarantee to pay principal and interest on bonds, municipal notes, or commercial paper in the event the issuer cannot do so. A letter of credit gives the security it backs the creditworthiness of the bank that issues the letter.

Letter of Credit (LOC) Backed—Refers to U.S. commercial paper issued with a bank letter of credit agreement whereby the holder of the paper will be paid at maturity either directly ("direct pay" LOC) or, in the event of a default by the issuer, by the LOC bank.

Letter of Credit (LOC) Paper—*See* Documented Discount Note.

Letter of Intent (LOI)—1) Letter notifying another of the writer's intention to take a particular action, subject to the occurrence of a particular event or some other action. 2) Letter written by an investor in a mutual fund expressing the intention to buy enough shares to qualify for the minimum sales charge. *See* Breakpoint. 3) Agreement between two merging companies.

Letter of Notification—Issuers using Regulation A must file a letter of notification with their regional SEC office. *See* Regulation A.

Letter Security—A security that is not registered with the SEC and therefore cannot be publicly sold. Investors can buy such securities directly from issuers if they sign an investment letter that states that the securities are being bought for investment rather than for trading purposes.

Level—Prices or yields given by traders for analytical or indicative purposes only. Levels, or indications, are always prefaced by "bid side" or "offered side" to indicate whether the firm is buying or selling the security.

Level I, II, and III—*See* National Association of Securities Dealers Automated Quotations (NASDAQ).

Level Debt Service—A series of equal (or level) cash payments designed to exactly retire a debt. Most fixed rate mortgages are based on level debt service. Also, many municipalities prefer to pay off debt in equal installments, thereby creating a consistent and predictable tax burden.

Level Payment Mortgage—Amortization schedule in which payments are kept constant for the life of the loan. Also called *Level Debt Service.*

Leverage—1) The ratio of senior capital (bonds and preferred stocks) to junior capital (common stock), called the debt-to-equity ratio. Also called Financial Leverage and Trading on the Equity. 2) Ability to buy securities with borrowed money (e.g., buying on margin). 3) Prospect of a high return with little or no investment (e.g., buying futures or options). 4) *See* Gearing.

Leveraged Buyout (LBO)—Obtaining control of a company through financing. The financing is often done with high yield bonds; the debt is often paid by selling parts of the acquired company.

Leveraged Corporation—1) Corporation with large fixed charges (debt). 2) Corporation with high debt to equity ratio.

Leveraged Floater—A Floating rate security whose interest rate varies by a multiple of a specified index. There are two types of leveraged floaters: the super floater and the reverse floater. *See* Super Floater and Reverse Floater.

Leverage Ratio—A measure of the extent to which assets have been provided by common shareholders, calculated as average assets divided by average shareholders' equity.

Liability—Financial obligation.

Liability Management—*See* Asset/Liability Management.

Liability Partitioning—The practice of segregating different types of pension liabilities into different streams depending on the ability to predict future obligations.

Liability Swap—Type of swap that focuses on the liability side of a balance sheet. The liability swap allows an issuer to transform the cost of its liabilities from fixed to floating or vice-versa. The swap does not alter the principal amount of the liabilities on the balance sheet, because it is simply a cash flow exchange.

Liar—Bernard Baruch's term for anyone claiming to buy at the bottom and sell at the top.

Liberal School—*See* Classical School.

Lien—A claim against property.

Life-of-Loan Cap—Maximum interest rate for the life of an adjustable rate mortgage loan.

Life Spread—In preferred stock analysis, the basis adjustment available or required from the current reference rate to ensure that a quarterly dividend reset will not be constrained by the issue's collar rates. *See* Reference Rate and Collar.

Life-to-Call—The period remaining until the first call date.

Life-to-Put—The period remaining before an investor's first option to put a security. *See* Life-to-Call.

Lift—To take an offer at a given price.

Lifting a Leg—Closing out one side of a spread trade. *See* Leg-In.

Light Bid/Offer—Low bid/high offer.

Limit—The maximum daily price change of a futures contract above or below the previous day's settlement price allowed by the exchange.

Limitation on Liens—Indenture provision restricting a company's ability to pledge assets to secure borrowings.

Limited Liability—Refers to shareholders, who are not personally liable for corporate debts.

Limited Risk—Describes an options contract, in which the risk is limited to the premium.

Limited Tax Bond—General obligation bond secured by a specific tax that cannot exceed a specified rate or amount.

Limit Order——An order to buy or sell a security at a specified price or better. A buy limit order can be executed at or below a specified price; a sell limit order can be executed at or above a specified price. Also called *Resting Order.*

Line of Credit—A credit arrangement whereby a bank agrees to lend up to a certain limit (line) of money within a specified period. Also called Committed Facility. A demand line of credit enables a customer to borrow on a daily basis.

Liquid—Easily convertible into cash. Describes a security that can easily be bought or sold at the best available price. *See* Marketable.

Liquidating Market—*See* Open Interest.

Liquidation—1) Selling assets of a corporation to pay its debts. 2) Selling a client's securities to meet a margin call. *See* Sell Out. 3) Selling as opposed to exercising an option.

Liquidation Value—The amount a bondholder may receive in case of liquidation. It is the same as par value and face value.

Liquidity—The measurement of the ease with which an item can be sold at the highest available price.

Liquidity Diversification—Portfolio management strategy of investing in a variety of maturities to reduce market risk.

Liquidity Market—A technical condition of the futures market, in which open interest is decreasing and prices are declining. Open interest decreases when long and short contracts are closed out, or liquidated. If longs are more aggressive than shorts in liquidating their positions, then prices will decline.

Liquidity Preference—The desire of investors to hold issues that, other things being equal, are more liquid than others.

Liquidity Premium—The extent to which yields are lower on more liquid securities. Also called *Horizon Premium* and *Maturity Premium.*

Liquidity Ratio—*See* Cash Ratio.

Liquidity Risk—*See* Risk.

Liquidity Theory—Hicks' theory to explain the term structure of interest rates, in which investors expect a premium for longer debt to offset market risk.

Liquidity Trading—Trading based not on information but on changes in an investor's wealth or tolerance for risk. *See* Information Trading.

Liquidity Trap—Economic condition defined by Keynes in which monetary policy cannot stimulate aggregate demand. Keynes argued that when interest rates are relatively low, as they were during the Great Depression, investors will hold cash rather than invest in bonds. Expansionary monetary policy would cause interest rates to fall, and would therefore be unable to stimulate investment.

Listed Security—A security traded on a major stock or futures exchange.

Listing—The acceptance of an issue for trading on a stock exchange.

Load—A one-time sales fee charged by a mutual fund.

Load Factor—With respect to the electric utility industry, the ratio of the average load in kilowatts supplied during a designated period to the peak or maximum load in kilowatts occurring in that period.

Loaned Up—Condition of a bank that has no excess reserves. Also called *Fully Invested*.

Loan-to-Value (LTV)—The ratio of the outstanding amount of a mortgage loan to the appraised value of the property, expressed as a percentage.

Loan Consent—Margin clients authorizing their broker/dealer to lend their securities to a third party must sign a loan consent agreement.

Loan Value—The amount in a margin account that the broker can loan to the customer. It equals the complement of the Federal Reserve Board margin requirement times the market value of the securities in the account.

Lobster Trap—Takeover defense strategy prohibiting any holder or potential holder of 10% of a corporation's common stock from converting convertible securities into common stock.

Local—A person who trades for his or her own account on the floor of a futures exchange.

Local Authority Bond—A bond issued weekly by U.K. municipalities, not guaranteed by the government. Maturities are one to five years, typically one year.

Locked Market—When the bid equals the offer (i.e., when no one is willing to pay a commission).

Lock Limit—1) A situation in the futures market in which prices have moved up or down to the daily trading limit and there are still unfilled orders. *See* Trading Limit. 2) When the demand to buy or sell is so great that no one is willing to take the opposite position.

Lock Out—Period in which prepayments on a mortgage may not be made.

Lock-Up CD—A CD that the buyer will not trade.

Lock-Up Period—In the case of some issues, the period between an issue's closing date and the issuance of definitive certificates, during which a global bond usually represents the issuance of definitive certificates. *See* Seasoned.

Lombard Rate—The German Central Bank's rate of interest charged for a secured loan, usually about 1/2 percent above its discount rate.

London Interbank Bid Rate (LIBID)—The rate at which prime banks bid to take Eurocurrency deposits from other prime banks for a given maturity, which can range from overnight to five years.

London Interbank Mean Rate (LIMEAN)—The mean of LIBOR and LIBID. *See* Middle Price.

London Interbank Offered Rate (LIBOR)—The posted rate at which prime banks offer to make Eurodollar deposits available to other prime banks for a given maturity, which can range from overnight to five years.

London International Financial Futures Exchange (LIFFE)—The exchange in London for various futures and option contracts in currencies and bonds.

Long—Refers to the market position of an investor who has bought securities.

Long Bond—The most liquid (and usually the most recently issued) 30-year Treasury bond, which is used as the benchmark off of which other long maturity bonds are priced.

Long Coupon—A bond that has one coupon period, usually the first, longer than the others.

Long Hedge—Strategy to protect against rising prices, such as buying call options, selling put options, or buying futures. Also called *Buying Hedge*. *See* Short Hedge.

Long Leg—The long position in a hedge.

Long Straddle—Straddle in which an investor, anticipating increasing market volatility, buys both put and call options.

Long-Term—1) In the Eurobond market, refers to initial maturities longer than seven years. 2) Under standard accounting practice, often refers to debt with a remaining maturity of greater than one year. 3) A period of holding securities or realizing an investment strategy of at least six months.

Long-Term Debt Ratio—A measure of long-term liquidity risk indicating the proportion of long-term capital provided by creditors, calculated as long-term debt divided by long-term debt plus shareholders' equity.

Long-Term Debt to Long-Term Capital—Commonly used financial ratio, calculated as the name implies. It is the same as total debt to capital, excluding short-term debt from both the numerator and denominator.

Long the Basis—Buying a commodity or security and selling futures.

Look-Back Option—Option enabling the holder to buy or sell a commodity at the best price available during the life of the option.

Loose Credit—*See* Easy.

Lot Size—*See* Round Lot and Odd Lot.

Lower Floater—*See* Variable Rate Demand Note.

Low-Start Mortgage—*See* Graduated Payment Mortgage.

M

Macaulay Duration—*See* Duration.

Macroeconomics—Analysis of national or global economic conditions, such as income, employment, trade, prices, and money supply. *See* Microeconomics.

Macro-Hedge—Hedge designed to reduce the risk of an entire portfolio.

Mae West Spread—Short straddle and long strangle. *See* Straddle and Strangle.

Maintenance and Replacement (M&R) Fund—A fund provided in most electric utility mortgage bond indentures requiring minimal annual property additions based on a percentage of revenues and/or assets to maintain or replace depreciable property. Deficiencies must usually be made up by deposits of cash, bonds, or additional unfunded property. Deposited cash can often be used to redeem bonds at the special (lower) call price.

Maintenance Call—*See* Maintenance Margin.

Maintenance Margin—The margin level, usually lower than the original margin level, that the investor must maintain while a position is outstanding. When an investor's equity falls below the requirements set by the National Association of Securities Dealers, the exchanges, or the brokerage firm, the investor will receive a variation margin call. *See* Variation Margin.

Make a Market—To give a firm bid and asked price for a security.

Maker—Person who signs a check or note. Also called *Drawer*.

Maloney Act of 1938—An amendment to the Securities Exchange Act of 1934 giving the over-the-counter market the right to regulate itself. It was designed to protect the public from unfair practices and ensure continued public confidence in the securities industry. It is now section 15A of the Securities Exchange Act of 1934. The National Association of Securities Dealers and the Municipal Securities Rulemaking

161

Board are the only self-regulatory agencies for the over-the-counter market.

Management Company—A company that invests pools of investors' money in securities. Also called *Investment Company.*

Management Fee—1) A fixed percentage (usually 20 percent) of the gross underwriting spread that accrues to the managers of a syndicate. 2) An annual charge by a mutual fund for portfolio management and administration.

Management Group—The primary underwriters of a new issue.

Manager—A firm that deals with the issuer of securities on behalf of the underwriting group. There may be a number of co-managers, but only the one that runs the books is directly responsible for the distribution of securities throughout a syndicate. *See* Run the Books and Syndicate.

Manager's Fee—The fee paid to the lead manager of a syndicate out of the underwriting spread.

Managerial Accounting—Reporting of financial information designed to help management make strategic planning decisions. *See* Financial Accounting.

Mandatory Convertible Bond—A primary capital issue for a U.S. bank in which the borrower sells shares on maturity to provide cash for the redemption payments on the bonds. If it is not possible to sell shares, the holder will receive shares instead of cash.

Mandatory Redemption—A feature of an issue of securities that requires the borrower to retire a portion of an issue prior to its maturity, either by open market purchases at any price or by drawings by lot for payment at par through the operation of a sinking fund. *See* Purchase Fund and Sinking Fund.

Mandatory Security Valuation Reserve (MSVR)—A reserve, established by the National Association of Insurance Commissioners (NAIC), to absorb some of the principal loss of insurance companies' investments. The NAIC determines annual contributions to the reserve according to the quality of the assets in each insurance company's portfolio. All realized capital losses, as well as unrealized capital losses on common stock, are charged to the reserve. Realized capital gains are credited to the reserve if it falls below the required level.

Manipulation—To fraudulently influence market values. For example, a manipulator might trade a security to give it the appearance of greater liquidity, or sell it short to force the price down. *See* Wash Sale.

Margin—1) The spread between the coupon and index of a floating rate security. Also called *Coupon Spread.* 2) The percentage of market value required from an investor to finance securities, with the balance being loaned by a broker. The amount of margin on stocks and convertible bonds is controlled by the Federal Reserve Board under Regulation T and Regulation U. 3) Cash or securities deposits required for each futures contract to serve as a good faith deposit guaranteeing that both parties to the agreement will perform the transaction.

Margin Account—A brokerage account in which an investor may buy securities with money borrowed from the broker. *See* Cash Account, Regulation T, Hypothecation, Rehypothecation, and Maintenance Margin.

Margin Agreement—Rules governing a margin account, which cover hypothecation, equity requirements, and interest on loans. *See* Hypothecation, Maintenance Margin, and Regulation T.

Marginal—Refers to an economic decision that involves the effects of a change from a given condition.

Marginal Tax Rate—The tax rate paid on additional taxable income, calculated as the change in tax liability divided by change in income.

Marginal Utility—*See* Utility.

Margin Call—A call for cash in a margined position. *See* Maintenance Margin.

Margin Equity—The customer's ownership interest in a margin account—the total market value if there is no debit balance. In a long account, equity equals market value minus the debit balance. In a short account, equity equals the proceeds from the short sale plus the deposited margin minus the market value.

Margin of Profit—Operating income divided by net sales.

Margin of Profit Ratio—One hundred percent minus the operating ratio. *See* Operating Ratio.

Margin Security—A security that may be traded in a margin account. *See* Regulation T.

Markdown—1) Dealer's spread. 2) Drop in a dealer's quote.

Market—1) The prices at which a security can be bought and/or sold. 2) A locale where a security is traded.

Marketable—Describes securities that can easily be bought or sold (not necessarily at the best price). *See* Liquid.

Marketable Debt—Securities sold in the open market.

Market Analysis—*See* Technical Analysis.

Market Content—The value of the shares that are added to a host bond to make up the unit of an equity warrant issue. *See* Exercise Content.

Market If Touched (MIT)—An order to buy or sell a security or commodity at a specified price. When the market reaches that price, the order becomes a market order. Also called *Stop Order* and *Board Order*.

Market Impact Cost—A measure of the quality of execution, it is the difference between the realized market price on a trade and the subsequent price behavior of the traded security.

Market Index—A level derived from the weighted average of the values of the components that make up the index, used to measure market movement. Market indices include the Corporate Bond Index, Standard and Poor's 500 Stock Index, and Value Line.

Market Maker—A dealer who consistently gives both bid and offer prices for a security. *See* Make a Market.

Market Multiple—*See* Price-Earnings Ratio.

Market Order—An order to buy or sell a security at the best immediately obtainable price.

Market Out Clause—Underwriting agreement that the underwriter may terminate its firm commitment if certain events change the investment quality of the offered securities.

Market Price—The price that can be obtained by selling a security in the market.

Market Price Adjustment Ratio—For price adjusted rate preferred stock, it is par value divided by the average market price.

Market Raid—*See* Dawn Raid.

Market Rate—The current rate of interest that an entity must pay to issue debt.

Market Risk—*See* Systematic Risk.

Market Segmentation Hypothesis—Theory to explain the term structure of interest rates, in which investors have a preferred habitat, or preference for the maturity of their investments, and will change only for a yield premium.

Market Value—The current or prevailing price of a security or commodity.

Marking—Executing an option contract at the close, thereby obtaining a price better than the fair value of the contract.

Mark to Market—The revaluing of a security, commodity, or futures contract to reflect the most current market value.

Markup—To increase the price of a security.

Married Put—A put option bought on same day as the security. The put is labeled "hedged position" by the dealer, allowing the holding period to begin. Buying a security and then buying a put terminates the holding period.

Master Note (MN)—A floating rate unsecured promissory note that is privately placed by a borrower with an institutional investor. The transaction is documented by a Master Note Purchase Agreement signed by both parties. This agreement defines the formula by which the note is priced, the principal amount, the range within which the principal amount can fluctuate (if applicable), the liquidity provisions, and maturity.

Master Servicer—An entity that administers and supervises servicers (mortgage lenders). Master servicers collect monthly mortgage payments on the collateral of a structured financing from several servicers.

Matched Book—1) The collection of repurchase and reverse repurchase agreements done by a dealer with customers. Securities acquired through reverse repurchase agreements are "matched," or paired off, against a repo on the same security for the same period of time. The investment banker running the matched book acts as principal in all transactions and incurs any liabilities. Repos done to finance dealer positions are not considered part of the matched book. Also called *Repurchase Book*. 2) Any collection of agreements or contracts with customers (e.g., interest rate swaps or OTC options) in which purchases and sales can be paired off. 3) When the maturities of a bank's assets equal that of its liabilities. The opposite is called an Unmatched Book, an Open Book, or a Short Book.

Matched Funding Program (MFP)—A fixed rate/flexible drawdown demand note. The note is fully secured as to principal and interest by a matching note issued by a corporation enjoying a rating equivalent to that of the bond issuer. The corporate obligation is held by an escrow agent, thus creating a perfected security interest in the underlying note.

Matched Growth—Adding assets and liabilities with the same or similar maturities or durations to the balance sheet.

Matched Orders—1) Similar to a wash sale, except that two investors act in concert to manipulate the price of a security. *See* Wash Sale. 2) A specialist's attempt to create an opening price similar to the previous closing price.

Matched Sales—1) Reverse repurchase agreements. 2) In reference to Federal Reserve actions, a means of temporarily absorbing reserves by selling securities under an agreement to subsequently repurchase them. This subtracts cash from the financial system and pushes rates upwards.

Match Fund—Matching a loan (asset) with a deposit (liability) of the same maturity.

Matching—Convention in accrual accounting in which asset expirations (expenses) are recognized in the period in which the associated revenues are recognized.

Material—Significant information that must be disclosed in standard formats, such as accounting statements and prospectuses. Information is considered material if "the judgment of a reasonable person relying on the information would have been changed or influenced by the omission or misstatement."

Matrix Price—Price derived from a formula, given other variables such as sector, maturity, rating, and coupon.

Matrix Trading—Trading that takes advantage of changes in yield spreads.

Mature Economy—1) Pertaining to a population that has stabilized or is declining. 2) Pertaining to an economy that is no longer strong or expanding.

Maturity—The date on which the principal or stated value of a debt security becomes due and payable in full to the holder.

Maturity Premium—Premium investors demand for assuming the interest rate risk of long-term bonds. Also called *Horizon Premium* and *Liquidity Premium*.

Maturity Value—Principal, or principal plus interest, to be paid to a bondholder at maturity. *See* Face Value.

Maximum Margin—1) The margin, usually expressed in relation to LIBOR, at or under which tender panel bids must be made. 2) The margin at which facility underwriters commit to purchase notes in the event of insufficient tender panel bids.

May Day—May 1, 1975, when fixed brokerage commissions ended in the United States.

Mean Return—The average of all possible returns of an investment. Also called *Expected Return*.

Measure of Economic Welfare (MEW)—A measure of national economic performance that differs from GNP in three ways: the cost of bad economic side effects, such as pollution, are subtracted from GNP; the cost of "regrettable necessities," such as local and national defense, are excluded from GNP; and the value of non-market goods, such as leisure, are added to GNP.

Medium Bond—*See* Intermediate Bond.

Medium Term—1) A bond with a maturity of two to ten years. 2) In the Eurobond market, refers to maturities of two to seven years. 3) In the Euro money markets, refers to maturities in excess of one year.

Medium-Term Note (MTN)—Debt instrument with a maturity ranging from one to fifteen years, offered under a program agreement through one or more dealers. MTNs have fixed coupons and maturities that can be targeted to meet investor requirements. They are issued in the capital markets either publicly under an SEC Rule 415 shelf registration or privately without such a registration. Euro MTNs have shorter maturities of one to five years.

Member Bank—A bank that is a member of the Federal Reserve System. A member bank must buy stock in its district's Federal Reserve Bank equal to 6% of its paid-in capital and paid-in surplus, and must maintain a percentage of its deposits as reserves. Reserves consist of currency in bank vaults and deposits at the Fed district banks.

Member Firm—A securities firm having one or more partners or officers who are members of a major stock exchange.

Member Order—A sale order credited to a single member of a municipal bond syndicate.

Mercantilism—Economic system that replaced feudalism in Europe, based on national accumulation of wealth (bullion). Colonies were founded and navies built for this purpose. Adam Smith revolutionized political economics by claiming that the wealth of nations was based not on bullion but on capitalist production.

Merchant Bank—1) A U.S. bank that accepts merchants' deposits. 2) A European bank that performs investment banking services.

Merger—A combination of companies in which only one retains its legal identity. *See* Consolidation.

Mezzanine—The second largest bracket in an underwriting syndicate.

Mickey Mouse—Walt Disney Corporation securities.

Microeconomics—Analysis of units within an economy, such as individuals, products, and corporations. *See* Macroeconomics.

Micro-Hedge—Hedge designed to reduce the risk of a security.

Middle Price—The arithmetic mean of a bid and an offered price. *See* London Interbank Mean Rate.

Midget—A mortgage pass-through security issued by GNMA with a 15-year maturity.

Mill—One 1,000th of one dollar.

Mini-Max Bond—A collared floating rate security in which the maximum and minimum coupon rates are very close, so that the bond resembles a fixed rate issue.

Minimum Rate—In the context of floating rate notes, that interest rate below which the coupon may not be fixed.

Mini-Refunding—Treasury auction of four-year and seven-year notes, held in the second half of the last month of each quarter.

Mini Tap—*See* Taplet.

Minority Interest—The proportionate interest of a minority stockholder in a majority-owned subsidiary that is consolidated.

Mintage—*See* Brassage.

Minus Tick—A downward price movement of a security. Investors cannot sell short on a minus tick. Also called *Downtick*.

Mirror Warrant—Warrant on a callable bond enabling the holder, once the bond is called, to call the bond back from the issuer.

Misappropriation—Illegal use of insider information.

Mismatch—*See* Gap.

Miss the Market—To fail to execute a transaction.

Mixed Account—A brokerage account with both long and short positions.

Mixed Bag—Repurchase agreement in which collateral is not specified during the trading day but is allocated by computer after the close of business. The collateral is then held in safekeeping by the seller.

MJSD—March, June, September, December—an options expiration cycle.

Mobile Home—Mobile home mortgage pass-through security, usually issued by GNMA.

Modern Portfolio Theory (MPT)—The theoretical framework for designing investment portfolios based upon the risk and reward characteristics of the entire portfolio, which is held not to be equivalent to the cumulative risk of the individual securities of the portfolio. The major tenet of the theory holds that reward is directly related to risk, which can be divided into two basic parts: 1) Systematic risk (market risk), and 2) Unsystematic risk (risk of individual securities). Because unsystematic risk can be largely eliminated through diversification, the portfolio will be subject principally to systematic risk. *See* Capital Asset Pricing Model and Classical Security Analysis.

Modified—In reference to a pass-through security, modified means that interest payments will be made to the security holder whether or not they were actually collected from the mortgagors. The cash flow is "modified" by the issuer to include interest payments that may be absent. If principal payments are also made whether or not they are collected, the security is said to be fully modified. FHLMC PC securities are modified. GNMAs are fully modified. *See* Pass-Through.

Modified Cash Basis—An accounting method that is the same as the cash basis method except that capital assets are treated as assets rather than as expenses when purchased; a portion of the cost is then depreciated as an expense. *See* Cash Basis.

Modified Duration—A measure of the sensitivity of a bond's price to changes in yield. For example, if a bond has a modified duration of 4 years, for every 100 basis point change in yield in one direction the price will change 4 percent in the other direction. Modified duration is computed by dividing a bond's unmodified duration by one plus the bond's periodic yield. A bond's periodic yield is its yield to maturity divided by the discounting frequency per year. Also called *Adjusted Duration. See* Option-Adjusted Duration.

Mom and Pop—U.S. slang for individual investors. European slang is Belgian Dentist.

Monetarism—Economic policy based on the assumption that macro-economic factors such as business cycles and employment are a function of money supply rather than fiscal policy.

Monetary Aggregate—Any one of a number of statistics generally used to describe the nation's money supply. *See* Money Supply.

Monetary Base—Reserve balances held at the Federal Reserve Banks plus balances held for services plus currency in circulation (i.e., currency outside the Fed and the Treasury).

Monetary Items—In accounting, amounts fixed in terms of dollars, such as cash accounts receivables, accounts payable, and debt.

Monetary Policy—Central bank policies affecting the growth of monetary and credit aggregates.

Monetize—To make liquid.

Monetized Gold—The total of gold certificates issued by the Treasury to Federal Reserve Banks.

Monetizing the Debt—An open market operation in which the Federal Reserve Board buys U.S. government securities from member banks, thereby increasing the money supply. The phrase is usually used by critics of easy or accommodative monetary policy.

Money—Currency and demand deposits.

Money Back Warrant—A warrant that the holder may exercise or exchange with the issuer for cash.

Money Bonds—Bonds with an S&P rating of AAA or AA.

Money Center Bank—A bank with most of its assets from the capital markets and relatively few from depositors. *See* Regional Bank.

Money Crunch—*See* Credit Crunch.

Money GNP—GNP valued at current prices. *See* Real GNP and GNP Deflator.

Money Market—The market for assets maturing in less than one year, such as federal funds, Treasury bills, bankers' acceptances, commercial paper, certificates of deposit, federal agency discount paper, and repurchase agreements.

Money Market Basis—Refers to the method used to calculate accrued interest on CDs, FRCDs, and FRNs. The rate of interest is multiplied by the actual number of days elapsed and divided by the number of days in the accounting year (365 in the U.S. and U.K., 360 in many European markets). *See* Bond Basis.

Money Market Certificate (MMC)—A six-month CD with a minimum deposit of $10,000. The maximum interest is tied to the rate of the most recent six-month Treasury bill.

Money Market Fund—Mutual fund that invests exclusively in money market instruments.

Money Spread—*See* Vertical Spread.

Money Supply—The amount of privately-owned money balances. Holdings of the federal government and banks are excluded. The money supply is divided into the following components:

M_1A: Currency +
Demand deposits
M_1B: M_1A +
Other checkable deposits
M_2: M_1B +
Overnight RPs issued by commercial banks +
Overnight Eurodollar deposits held by U.S. nonbank residents at Caribbean branches of U.S. banks +
Money market mutual fund depositary institutions +
Savings deposits at all depositary institutions +
M_2 consolidation components
M_3: M_2 +
Large time deposits at all depositary institutions +
Term RPs issued by commercial banks +
Term RPs issued by savings and loan associations
L: M_3 +
Other Eurodollars of U.S. residents other than banks +
Bankers' acceptances +
Commercial paper +
Savings bonds +
Liquid Treasury obligations

Money Yield—Nominal yield, derived by calculating all future income payments and redemption proceeds using an assumed rate of inflation. *See* Real Rate of Return.

Monopoly—The control of a market by one seller; the absence of competition. *See* Monopsony, Oligopoly, Oligopsony, and Cartel.

Monopsony—Situation in which one buyer controls prices. *See* Monopoly, Oligopoly, and Oligopsony.

Moody's—A U.S. credit rating agency. Moody's defines its rating categories as follows, allowing for gradations within categories:

> **Aaa**—Bonds that are judged to be of the best quality. They carry the smallest degree of investment risk and are generally referred to as gilt-edged. Interest payments are protected by a large or exceptionally stable margin and principal is secure. While the various protective elements are likely to change, such changes are unlikely to impair the fundamentally strong position of such issues.

> **Aa**—Bonds that are judged to be of high quality by all standards. Together with the Aaa group, they comprise what are generally known as high grade bonds. They are rated lower than Aaa bonds because protection may not be as great, fluctuation of protective elements may be of greater amplitude, or there may be other elements that make the long-term risks appear somewhat larger.

> **A**—Bonds that possess many favorable investment attributes, considered upper medium grade obligations. Factors giving security to principal and interest are considered adequate but elements may be present that suggest a susceptibility to impairment.

> **Baa**—Bonds that are considered medium grade obligations, that is, they are neither highly protected nor poorly secured. Interest payments and principal security appear adequate for the present but certain protective elements may be lacking or may be characteristically unreliable over any great length of time. Such bonds lack outstanding investment characteristics and have speculative characteristics. Bonds rated below Baa are not considered investment grade.

> **Ba**—Bonds that are judged to have speculative elements; their future cannot be considered well assured. Often the protection of interest and principal payments may be very moderate, and therefore not well safeguarded.

> **B**—Bonds that generally lack the characteristics of a desirable investment. Assurance of interest and principal payments or maintenance of other terms of the contract over any long period of time may be small.

Caa—Bonds of poor standing. Such issues may be in default or there may be elements of danger with respect to principal or interest.

Ca—Bonds that are highly speculative. Such issues are often in default.

C—The lowest rated class of bonds. Issues so rated can be regarded as having extremely poor prospects of ever attaining any real investment standing.

Moody's Investment Grade (MIG)—Rating system for municipal debt, in which each issue is rated MIG1 (the highest rating) to MIG4.

Moral Obligation Bond—A tax-exempt security backed by a pledge of a state or local government that is not legally binding.

Moral Suasion—One of the Fed's tools to control the money supply whereby it tries to persuade member banks to comply with its policy voluntarily.

Mortality Table—Actuarial table of life expectancies for age groups of either sex.

Mortgage—A conveyance of an interest in real property given as security for the payment of a debt.

Mortgage-Backed Security (MBS)—An ordinary bond backed by an undivided interest in a pool of mortgages or trust deeds. Income from the underlying mortgages is used to pay off the securities.

Mortgage Banker—A firm that supplies its own funds for mortgage loans that are later sold to investors. Usually they continue to service the loans for a specified fee.

Mortgage Banking—The origination, servicing, and securitization of mortgages.

Mortgage Bond—A bond backed by a lien against real property.

Mortgage Cash Flow Obligation (MCF)—A multi-class, mortgage-backed corporate bond with a sequential payment structure similar to that of a CMO. Payments of principal and interest, however, are not secured by a lien on the underlying collateral, as is the case with a CMO. Holders of MCFs rely on the issuer's contractual obligation to apply the cash flow from the underlying collateral and reinvestment income thereon to the payment of principal and interest.

Mortgage Certificate—A GNMA, FNMA, FHLMC, or private pass-through certificate, representing interests in pools of underlying mortgage loans.

Mortgagee—A person or firm to whom the title to property is conveyed as security for a loan.

Mortgage Insurance—A type of term life insurance often bought by mortgagors. The amount of coverage decreases as the mortgage balance declines. In the event that the borrower dies while the policy is in force, the debt is automatically repaid by insurance proceeds. *See* Private Mortgage Insurance.

Mortgage Pool—Group of mortgages, usually on the same type of property with the same or similar interest rate and maturity.

Mortgage REIT—Real Estate Investment Trust that lends stockholder capital to builders and buyers of real estate. *See* Real Estate Investment Trust and Equity REIT.

Mortgage Servicing—Administration of a mortgage loan, involving such duties as notification and collection of payments from mortgagors and sending payments to investors.

Mortgage Swap—An interest rate swap with fixed rate cash flows that match the flows on a pass-through security and floating rate cash flows that approximate the variable cost of financing that security.

Mortgage Yield—*See* Prepaid Life.

Mortgagor—One who borrows money, giving as security a mortgage or deed of trust on real property.

Most Active List—Securities that have the largest trading volume in a particular period.

Motorcycles—Guaranteed Mortgage Certificates issued by FHLMC.

Moving Average—A series of average prices of a security over a specified interval.

Multicurrency Clause—A clause on a Euro loan permitting the borrower to switch currencies on a rollover date.

Multifamily—Residential property with five or more dwelling units.

Multi-Option Financing Facility (MOFF)—A facility that allows for the issuance of Euronotes and short-term bank advances by competitive bidding against a variety of funding bases in permissible currencies. If the notes or advances cannot be issued at an acceptable rate the issuer typically draws on a revolving credit facility.

Multiple Pool—Security issued under the GNMA II program in which multiple issuers contribute to a mortgage security.

Multiple Servicing—More than one servicer for a mortgage-backed security pool.

Multiplier—The factor by which a deposit in a bank is multiplied as it expands into loans throughout the banking system. The theoretical value of the multiplier is the reciprocal of the Fed's reserve requirement.

Multiplier Bond—A municipal zero coupon bond whose maturity value is a multiple of $100.

Multiply-Traded Options—Identical options simultaneously trading in more than one options market.

Muni—Municipal security.

Municipal Bond—Long-term debt issued by state and local governments and their agencies.

Municipal Bond Insurance—A private guarantee protecting against a municipal bond default.

Municipal Bond Insurance Association (MBIA)—Association of five insurance companies that guarantees principal and interest payments on municipal debt.

Municipal Finance Officers Association (MFOA)—*See* Government Finance Officers Association.

Municipal Investment Trust (MIT)—A unit investment trust that invests in municipal securities. *See* Unit Investment Trust.

Municipal Note—Short-term municipal debt (6 to 12 months).

Municipal Over Bond (MOB) Spread—The price of municipal bond futures minus the price of Treasury bond futures.

Municipal Securities Rulemaking Board (MSRB)—A self-regulating organization established by the Securities Acts Amendments of 1975, which makes rules governing municipal brokers and dealers.

Munifacts—Municipal bond industry news service that reports both news and secondary market offerings.

Mutilated—Pertaining to a security certificate that has been damaged.

Mutual Fund—Investment vehicle in which many investors pool their money to act as a large single investor. Investment strategies vary among mutual funds. All mutual funds charge a management fee; some charge a one-time sales fee (load).

N

Naked—1) An unhedged position in the cash or futures market. 2) An uncovered option. 3) A warrant unaccompanied by either a host bond or other form of debt. *See* Cum Warrant.

Naked Warrant—A warrant without a host bond. *See* Cum Warrant.

Narrowing the Spread—Bidding higher or offering lower than the previous bid or offer. Also called *Closing a Market*.

Narrow Market—*See* Thin.

National Association of Bond Lawyers (NABL)—Association of bond counsel that settles legal problems related to municipal securities.

National Association of Securities Dealers Automated Quotations (NASDAQ)—NASD computerized quotation system. Provides quotations for securities traded over the counter and many NYSE-listed securities. Organized as a three-level system: level I shows highest bid and lowest offer; level II shows individual quotations; level III is used to enter quotes into the system.

National Association of Securities Dealers (NASD)—A self-regulating body of the securities industry designated to establish rules of fair practice for the protection of the investing public, formed in 1939 under the auspices of the Maloney Act.

National Bank—A nationally chartered commercial bank, which is required to be a member of the Federal Reserve System. *See* Member Bank.

National Board for Prices and Incomes—A British organization established by the National Plan to administer measures to fight inflation.

National Debt—Money owed by the federal government. In the U.S., national debt includes interest owed on Treasury securities.

National Income—A measure of the monetary value of the total flow of goods and services produced in an economy over a specified period of time. *See* Gross National Product.

175

National Income and Product Accounts—A description of the economy, detailing the value and cost of goods and services.

National Institutional Delivery System (NIDS)—Automated system for transmission of dealer confirmations and investor affirmations of trades.

National Market System (NMS)—National Association of Securities Dealers (NASD) system for trading over-the-counter stocks. National Market System stocks must meet certain size and profitability guidelines. Trading information for NMS stocks is displayed on the NASDAQ system.

Nationalization—Transfer of property or industries from private to public ownership.

National Quotation Bureau—A subsidiary of the Commerce Clearing House that provides daily quotes for over-the-counter securities. Quotes are printed on pink sheets for stocks and yellow sheets for corporate bonds.

Natural—*See* Clean.

Natural—1) Refers to the holder of a security who is willing to sell it. 2) Refers to a trade for which there is no inventory risk. Block trades in which there is no such risk are called Clean.

Natural Business Year—Any 12-month period used for accounting cycles. The end of the natural business year typically coincides with a winding down of activity and a decline in inventory.

Natural Hedge—A cash security for which a long position acts as a hedge for a long position in another cash security.

Natural Rate of Growth—Growth rate of the labor force, adjusted for changes in technology and productivity.

Natural Rate of Unemployment—*See* Normal Unemployment.

Natural Spread—A vertical call spread with one long call at one price and two short calls at a higher price.

Nearby—The futures or options contract month trading for the most immediate delivery. Also called *Front Contract*.

Near Money—1) A security that is close to its call date. 2) Demand deposits (i.e., money that is only one step away from being used).

Near the Money—Refers to an option whose strike price is close to the market price of the underlying security or commodity.

Negative—Bearish.

Negative Amortization—Refers to a loan whose principal balance grows over time. A Graduated Payment Mortgage (GPM) in its early years is a loan with negative amortization. Because initial payments in a GPM are not sufficient to cover interest charges, the shortfall accrues to the principal.

Negative Amortization Cap—Maximum limit on the increase in principal balance of an adjustable rate mortgage due to negative amortization.

Negative Carry—*See* Carry.

Negative Covenants—Restrictive covenants in a bond indenture. Such covenants prevent the corporation, in effect, from benefiting the shareholders at the expense of the bondholders.

Negative Convexity—*See* Convexity.

Negative Duration—A measure of a security's price sensitivity to changes in yield, in the atypical situation in which price and yield move up or down together. For example, if a bond has a duration of -4 years, for every 100 basis points change in yield the price will change by 4 percent in the same direction.

Negative Exports—Imports.

Negative Free Reserves—Net borrowed reserves.

Negative Gap—*See* Unmatched Book.

Negative Income Tax—Payments to individuals who earn below a specified level.

Negatively Sloped—Refers to a declining yield curve, or one on which shorter maturities have higher yields than longer maturities.

Negative Pledge Clause—A promise in an indenture that the corporation will not pledge any asset at the expense of bondholders. Also called *Covenant of Equal Coverage.*

Negative Yield—When an investment's return is less than the rate of inflation.

Negative Yield Curve—*See* Yield Curve.

Negotiable—Refers to a security that is transferable.

Negotiable CD—A large denomination CD that can be sold before maturity. A non-negotiable CD is comparable to a savings account.

Negotiable Order of Withdrawal—Interest-bearing checking account.

Negotiated Market—A market in which one buyer negotiates with one seller. The over-the-counter market is a negotiated market. *See* Over-the-Counter and Two-Sided Market.

Negotiated Offering—A method of syndication by which the terms of an offering are determined by negotiation between the issuer and the underwriter.

Net—Adjusted, usually by subtracting items from gross. In a fixed income context, net implies deduction of brokerage fee or tax from an investment's return. *See* Flat.

Net Assets—Owner's equity, defined in the basic accounting equation as total assets minus total liabilities.

Net Asset Value (NAV)—1) The bid price of mutual fund shares. 2) A corporation's total assets minus intangible assets minus liabilities and securities having prior claim, divided by the number of outstanding securities (bonds, preferred shares, or common shares).

Net Bank Position—Deposits in a bank minus loans payable to that bank.

Net Borrowed Reserves—*See* Borrowed Reserves.

Net Capital Formation—Expenditures on capital goods minus capital goods used up in the manufacturing process.

Net Capital Requirement—Ratio of a broker-dealer's indebtedness to liquid capital. The Security and Exchange Commission's net capital requirement is currently 15 to 1. *See* Rule 15c3-1.

Net Cash Flow—Cash flow from operations minus dividends.

Net Change—The difference between the closing price of a stock on one day and the closing price on the previous day. Reported in the financial section of the newspaper.

Net Coupon—The coupon rate on a mortgage-related security. Net coupon is equal to the gross coupon minus servicing fees. *See* Gross Coupon.

Net Current Assets—Current assets minus current liabilities. Also called *Working Capital*.

Net Current Asset Value—Working capital divided by the number of outstanding common shares.

Net Debt—Gross debt minus sinking fund accumulations and self-supporting debt.

Net Earnings—Income, before deducting interest on funded and unfunded debt, and after deducting operating and maintenance expenses, depreciation and depletion, and all taxes (including income taxes). Extraordinary, non-recurring items of income or expense are excluded.

Net Income—Revenues minus expenses for a defined period. Also called *Income, Earnings,* and *Profits*.

Net Interest Cost (NIC)—The weighted average coupon rate for a new municipal issue. Sometimes bids on a municipal issue are made by potential underwriters in the form of an NIC.

Net Interest Margin—Fundamental measure of a bank's earning power, calculated as fully taxable equivalent net interest income divided by average earning assets.

Net Margin—For securitized adjustable rate mortgages, net margin is gross margin less cost of mortgage insurance and other securitization expenses; for whole loan ARMs, it is gross margin less servicing fees.

Net Operating Loss (NOL)—A loss carried forward and amortized against income in future years, computed differently for book and tax purposes. Certain security transactions, most notably the issuance of preferred stock, may take advantage of net operating losses for tax purposes.

Net Order—*See* Basis Order.

Net Pension Liability—Pension benefit obligation less net assets available for benefits plus or minus the measurement valuation allowance.

Net Position—A trader's or a firm's position in a given issue, maturity, or other parameter (e.g., a trader can be $10 million long on Treasury bills). The net position is determined by subtracting the short position from the long position.

Net Present Value—Value of all cash flows of an investment discounted at a specified interest rate minus the initial investment. *See* Pledged Revenues.

Net Quick Assets—Cash, marketable securities, and accounts receivable minus current liabilities.

Net Revenue Pledge—*See* Pledged Revenues.

Net Tangible Assets to Long-Term Debt—Commonly used financial ratio, calculated as the sum of total assets minus intangible assets minus non-debt liabilities divided by long-term debt.

Net Tangible Assets to Total Debt—Commonly used financial ratio, calculated as the sum of total assets minus intangible assets minus all non-debt liabilities divided by total debt.

Net Worth—The sum of stock, capital surplus, and retained earnings. Also called *Owners' Equity*.

Net Writer—Market maker who has written or sold more options than he or she has purchased.

Net Yield—Yield or cost of capital taking into consideration such costs as commissions, markups, and tax.

Neutral—Refers to an opinion or position that is neither bearish or bullish. Neutral option strategies are generally designed to perform best if there is little or no change in the price of the underlying security.

Neutral Hedge—A hedge balanced to give the highest return when the price of the underlying asset remains unchanged. The upside and downside breakeven points are generally equidistant from the entry price.

Neutral Period—The period during which Eurodollars are sold if it does not start or end on a Friday or the day before a holiday.

Neutral Price—For a floating rate security, the price on the next coupon date that will produce a yield equal to the index rate (e.g., LIBOR) plus the discounted margin between now and the next coupon date.

Neutral Spread—*See* Ratio Bull Spread.

New Housing Authority Bonds—Bonds issued by local public housing authorities, backed by the U.S. government, to finance public housing.

New Issue—A security sold by a corporation for the first time. Distribution of a new issue is regulated by the Securities and Exchange Commission.

New Money—In a refunding, the amount by which the principal amount of securities offered exceeds the principal amount maturing.

New Money Preferred—A preferred stock of a public utility that was issued on or after October 1, 1942 that did not refund or replace any bond, debenture, or other preferred stock issued prior to October 1, 1942. In accordance with the laws regarding investment by one corporation in the stock of another corporation, corporations are entitled to an 80% tax exclusion on the dividends from new money preferred stocks.

New York Clearing House Funds—*See* Clearing House Funds and Same Day Funds.

New York Futures Exchange (NYFE)—A division of the New York Stock Exchange devoted to financial futures contracts trading.

New York Interbank Offered Rate (NIBOR)—NIBOR represents the same interbank market as LIBOR, but the rate is usually quoted at about 11:00 a.m. New York time and reflects the activities of a larger proportion of New York market makers.

New York Stock Exchange (NYSE)—Largest and oldest stock exchange in the United States by trading volume. Located in New York City at 11 Wall Street, it is also referred to as the Big Board or the Exchange. *See* Exchange.

New York Stock Exchange Composite Index—Composite index of all NYSE-listed common stock prices relative to their aggregate market value as of the market's close on December 31, 1965. Point changes from the index' base value of $50 are calculated each half hour and listed in dollars and cents.

Nickel—Five basis points.

Nikkei—An index of 225 Japanese stocks.

Nine Bond Rule—New York Stock Exchange rule that all orders for nine bonds ($9000 par amount) or less in listed issues must be sent to the floor for execution unless the customer directs the broker to go to the OTC market. Also called *Rule 396*.

Noah's Ark Portfolio—A portfolio with too much diversification (two of everything).

No Load—An open-ended investment company that does not have a commission (load) charge.

Nominal Amount—1) Par amount. 2) Face amount of currency, not adjusted for inflation. *See* Real Amount.

Nominal Interest Rate—The actual interest rate, not adjusted for inflation.

Nominal Market Conditions—Constant yield over time. *See* Horizon Analysis.

Nominal Owner—Owner in name only (e.g., a broker who has physical possession of a customer's securities). *See* Beneficial Owner.

Nominal Quotation—Trader's non-firm quote. Also called *Numbers Only*.

Nominal Rate—*See* Nominal Yield.

Nominal Value—The value stated on the face of a security. *See* Face Value.

Nominal Yield—Yield calculated as the annual payout divided by the par value. It is the rate listed on the face of a bond. Also called *Nominal Rate* and *Coupon Rate*. *See* Real Rate of Return.

Nominative Security—*See* Bearer Security.

Nominee—The registered name given by the Comptroller of the Currency into which a bank or a trust company registers the securities it holds as an investment agent for its trust department portfolios, thereby facilitating a good delivery to brokers at time of sale or exchange. *See* Street Name.

Non-Affiliated Persons—Non-insiders who own restricted investment letter stock. *See* Investment Letter Stock.

Non-Amortization Period—Period during the life of a credit card asset backed security during which principal received from payments on credit card receivables is reinvested in additional receivables. Investors receive only interest during this period. Also called *Revolving Period.*

Non-Bank Bank—A limited service financial intermediary—one that either takes demand deposits or gives commercial loans, but not both. A commercial or industrial company can not own a bank, but can own a non-bank bank. For example, Sears Roebuck owns Greenwood Trust (a non-bank bank), which it uses as the vehicle to fund its Discover Card loan portfolio.

Noncallable—Exempt from any kind of redemption for a stated time period.

Non-Competitive Auction—Treasury auction at which all bidders receive securities at the average price. *See* Competitive Auction.

Non-Competitive Bid—*See* Competitive Bid.

Non-Conforming Loan—A mortgage loan that does not conform to FNMA or FHLMC standards. The most common non-conforming features include principal balance, documentation, and underwriting standards.

Noncontributory—Refers to a pension plan into which only the employer contributes.

Non Cumulative—Refers to preferred stock on which unpaid dividends do not accrue.

Non-Cumulative Sinking Fund—A sinking fund in which any unapplied monies for the sinking fund may not be used in the following year.

Noncurrent Assets—Corporate assets not expected to be converted into cash. Noncurrent assets include fixed assets, intangible assets, notes receivable after one year, and certain investments.

Non-Exempt Security—Security subject to the Securities Act of 1933.

Non-Gnome—A 15-year swap security issued by mortgage lenders through FHLMC, as opposed to gnomes, which are issued directly by FHLMC.

Nonhuman Resources—Non-labor inputs needed to produce goods, including capital (e.g., machines and buildings), raw materials, and land. Also called *Physical Capital.*

Non-Issuer Transaction—*See* Secondary Transaction.

Non-Litigation Certificate—Certificate stating that no pending or foreseeable litigation would affect the security of an issue of municipal bonds.

Non-Marketable Debt—Debt that cannot be transferred or used as collateral (e.g., U.S. Savings Bonds).

Non-Participating Preferred Stock—Preferred stock with no voting rights.

Non-Recourse—Refers to a loan with no insurance or guarantee.

Non-Recourse Commodity Loan—U.S. government loan to farmers using stored crops valued at government supported levels as collateral. Farmers can repay the loan with the crop if the crop's market value falls below the supported level.

Non-Recurring—A one-time corporate gain or loss appearing in the financial statement.

Non-Refundable—Debt that cannot be retired by funds from another borrowing. Bonds with refunding protection are still subject both to regular redemption through sinking funds and to being called for cash.

Non-Underwritten Euronote—Issue of Euronotes without the support of a group of banks who commit to purchase the notes if they cannot be placed at a certain margin, usually expressed over LIBOR. *See* Eurocommercial Paper or Note Issuance Facility.

No Par—Refers to stock without a par value.

Normal Cost—Expenses for a pension plan during an accounting period.

Normalized Accounting—Method of accounting that amortizes extraordinary gains (such as acquired investment tax credits through a merger) over the expected life of an asset or liability. Normalized accounting recognizes a deferred tax liability when straight line depreciation is used for reporting purposes and accelerated depreciation is used for tax purposes; flow-through accounting does not recognize this liability. Normalized accounting also recognizes and matches expenses and revenues through time rather than at the exact time the cash movement occurs. For example, bond interest is accrued on a corporation's books each month, even though it is paid semiannually. Also called *Accrual Accounting.*

Normal Market—Market in which prices for advanced months of futures contracts progressively increase. Also called *Carrying Charge Market* and *Premium Market. See* Discount Market.

Normal Trading Unit—*See* Round Lot.

Normal Unemployment—The unemployment rate due to inefficiencies in the job market, such as lack of mobility, limitations to union membership, and time necessary for job search. Also called *Natural Rate of Unemployment.*

Normal Yield Curve—*See* Yield Curve.

North—Slang for an increase in a variable, such as risk, yield, or income.

Note—A promise to pay as distinguished from an order to pay. A written promise by the maker to pay a certain sum of money to the person named as payee, on demand or at a fixed or determinable future date. In the government securities market, a note is a coupon issue with a maturity of one to ten years. In contrast to Treasury bonds, coupon rates on Treasury notes are not restricted by law.

Note Issuance Facility (NIF)—A medium-term arrangement enabling borrowers to issue short-term paper, typically of three or six month maturity, in their own names. Usually a group of underwriting banks guarantees the availability of funds to the borrower by purchasing any unsold notes at each roll-over date, or by providing a standby credit. Facilities produced by competing banks are called revolving underwriting facilities, note purchase facilities, and Euronote facilities.

Not Held (NH)—An order giving the broker full discretion (the broker is not held responsible).

Notice of Sale—Notice used when an issuer will accept competitive bids for municipal bond underwriting, printed in the Daily Bond Buyer.

Notional Amount—The agreed upon principal amount on which interest rate payments are based in an interest rate swap.

Not Rated (NR)—Pertaining to a corporation or a security that a rating agency has not rated.

Novation—1) Replacing an obligation with newer debt. 2) Transferring the rights and duties stated in a contract from one party to another.

Nuisance Call—Indenture provision allowing the issuer to call bonds when only a small percentage (e.g., 10%) of original principal is outstanding. Also called *Cleanup Call*.

Nuisance Lawsuit—Libel suit against an investor (typically a short seller) whose rumors lower a security's market value.

Nuisance Tax—Tax whose revenues are needed to administer the tax.

Numbers Only—*See* Nominal Quotation.

Numeraire—1) A unit of value that is not legal tender, but which is composed of other units which themselves are legal tender. 2) A standard unit of measurement.

NV SUB—A company established in the Netherland Antilles as a wholly-owned subsidiary of an overseas parent company that is used to raise funds either through loan syndication on the Eurodollar market, Eurobond issues, or direct bank loans. Establishment of this type of financing intermediary enables a corporation to take advantage of tax treaties (or the lack of treaties) between the Netherland Antilles and other countries and reduces the tax liability associated with international operations.

O

Odd Coupon—A coupon for a period other than six months, typically the first or last coupon.

Odd Lot—1) Less than a round lot; technically, an amount of bonds of less than $100,000 par amount. 2) Colloquially, a block of bonds too small for a large institutional investor. For obscure securities, an odd lot is less than 100 bonds; for active issues, it is less than $1 million par amount.

Odd Lot Theory—Garfield Drew's theory, often invalidated, that the market trend will oppose that of odd-lot transactions. *See* Contrarian.

Off-Balance Sheet Financing—Corporate assets and liabilities not on the balance sheet. Off-balance sheet liabilities include lease obligations, interest rate swaps, project finance, and take-or-pay contracts.

Off Board—An over-the-counter transaction.

Offer—1) The price at which someone will sell a security. 2) Under the Uniform Securities Act, an attempt to dispose of a security for value, or a solicitation to buy or sell a security. *See* Sale. 3) The practice of issuing a security by public subscription. *See* Placement and Oversubscribed.

Offer for Sale—1) Issuing a security by public subscription. *See* Placement. 2) The legally required public advertisement that must be printed within a specified time period prior to the sale of a new security.

Offering Circular—*See* Prospectus.

Offering Date—Date on which a new security is available to the public.

Offering Memorandum—*See* Prospectus.

Offering Scale—Initial prices of the different maturities of a serial bond issue. *See* Serial Security.

Offer Wanted (OW)—Signifies that the security referred to is desired by a buyer, and prospective sellers are requested to submit offers for it. The inference is that the security will be bought for the lowest price offered.

Off-Floor—Customer trade orders, as opposed to orders from members trading for their own accounts (on-floor orders).

Official Discount Rate—*See* Discount Rate.

Official Notice of Sale—A municipality's request for competitive bids for a bond issue, printed in the *Daily Bond Buyer*.

Official Reserve Account—Part of the balance of payments, defined as reserves held with the International Monetary Fund. Reserves consist of foreign currencies, gold, and special drawing rights. *See* Balance of Payments and Special Drawing Rights.

Official Statement—A prospectus of a municipal offering.

Offset—1) To transfer the obligation to make or take delivery of a commodity or security by selling or buying futures contracts. 2) To terminate an option position. An opening sale transaction is offset by a closing purchase. An opening purchase is offset by a closing sale. 3) To hedge.

Offshore—1) In respect of taxation, any location where levels of taxation or regulations governing operations are sufficiently favorable to attract borrowers and lenders of funds from major financial centers. 2) Pertaining to any location foreign to an investor or borrower's country of residence and/or nationality.

Off-the-Run—Refers to a Treasury or agency security that is not the most recently issued of its maturity.

Off to Off—Refers to a trade made from one retail account to another (off-the-street to off-the-street).

Oil Depletion Allowance—The percentage of income an investor in an oil and gas limited partnership is allowed to receive tax free from the sale of oil and gas produced.

Oil Indexed Notes—Securities issued with or without coupons that, upon maturity, pay principal plus an amount determined by the difference between an oil index and a specified strike price.

Okun's Law—Economic law that at full employment levels, for each one percent change in the unemployment rate the nation's total output will change by three percent.

Old Lady of Threadneedle Street—Bank of England.

Old Money Preferred—A preferred stock of a public utility that was issued prior to October 1, 1942, or that refunded or replaced a bond, debenture, or other preferred stock issued prior to October 1, 1942.

Oligopoly—A small number of corporations that controls a market. *See* Monopoly, Monopsony, and Oligopsony.

Oligopsony—A small number of buyers that controls prices. *See* Monopoly, Monopsony, and Oligopoly.

Omnibus Account—A single account of two or more investors.

Omnibus Account on an Undisclosed Basis—*See* Conduit-Type.

One Cancels Other (OCO)—*See* Alternative Order.

One-Decision Issue—A security thought to have such potential for price appreciation that it is bought and held.

One-Man Picture—When both the bid and asked prices come from the same source.

One-Sided Market—A market in which only the bid or the offer price is firm. Also called a *One-Way Market*. *See* Two-Sided Market.

One-Way Market—*See* One-Sided Market.

On-Floor—*See* Off-Floor.

On the Hook Order—*See* Cap Order.

On-the-Run—Refers to current Treasuries. Of regularly auctioned Treasury issues, the most recently issued.

Open—1) Willing to accept bids or offers. 2) Willing to accept indications of interest. 3) Unfilled orders.

Open Book—*See* Unmatched Book.

Open Contract—*See* Open Interest.

Open-End—1) Mortgage bonds with an indenture that allows corporations to issue additional bonds on the same property. 2) To liquidate all or part of a portfolio and to hold cash or cash equivalents.

Open-Ended—An investment company that continually issues shares. An open-ended company that hires a management company is called a mutual fund. *See* Closed-End.

Opening—1) Beginning of a trading session. 2) Price of a security at the beginning of a trading session. 3) An opportune time to invest in or issue securities.

Opening Purchase—A transaction in which the buyer creates or adds to a long position in an option.

Opening Range—Range of prices at which orders may be filled at the opening of the market.

Opening Rotation—The order in which the markets for different contracts are opened each day on the options exchange.

Opening Sale—A transaction in which the seller creates or increases a short position in an option.

Open Interest—Number of futures contracts not yet offset by opposite transactions or fulfilled by delivery. In a technically strong market, open interest either increases as prices increase or decreases as prices decrease. The market in the latter case is called a liquidating market. In a technically weak market, open interest either increases as prices decrease or decreases as prices increase. Also called *Open Contract* and *Open Position. See* Volume.

Open Market Committee—*See* Federal Reserve Open Market Committee.

Open Market Operations—Monetary tool whereby the Federal Reserve trades Treasury securities in the secondary market to affect the money supply and interest rates. *See* Coupon Pass, Customer Repo, Matched Sales, and System Repo.

Open Mortgage—A mortgage that can be prepaid without penalty.

Open on the Print—A block trade that appears on the consolidated tape and that leaves the block trader with some risk. A block trader who sells a position short to complete a transaction is open on the print.

Open Order—An order to buy or sell entered at a certain price and designated good until cancelled. An unexecuted trade. Also called *Good 'Til Cancelled.*

Open Outcry—Trading done through vocal bids and offers or hand signals in the pit.

Open Position—*See* Open Interest.

Open Repo—A repurchase agreement with no specified term.

Open Up—To widen the bid-asked spread. *See* Narrowing the Spread.

Operating Cash Flow to Current Liabilities—Ratio useful in predicting bankruptcies, calculated as cash provided by operations divided by average current liabilities.

Operating Income—Net sales minus total expenses.

Operating Profit Margin—A company's operating income divided by its net sales.

Operating Ratio—Operating income divided by cost of goods sold. *See* Margin of Profit Ratio.

Operative Date—Date that is appropriate for redemption, based on calculations of the yield-to-operative date. *See* Yield to Operative Date.

Operative Yield—*See* Yield to Operative Date.

Opinion—Auditor's report.

Opportunity Cost—The cost of a project or investment in terms of the loss of the return on the best investment alternative. Also called *Alternative Cost.*

Optimization—The process of selecting securities in a portfolio in order to maximize or minimize a criterion specified by the investor (e.g., yield, coupon, duration, convexity, cost of the portfolio), subject to constraints (e.g., credit, diversification, maturity, duration).

Option—A contract that gives the holder the right to buy from or sell to the writer a specified amount of securities at a specified price, good for a specified period of time. An American option may be exercised at any time prior to its expiration; a European option is exercisable only on its expiration date.

Option-Adjusted Convexity—Convexity calculated by using an option-based model rather than cash flows, to take into consideration embedded options.

Option-Adjusted Duration—Modified duration calculated by using an option-based model rather than cash flows to take into consideration embedded options.

Option-Adjusted Spread—Yield spread over the Treasury yield curve adjusted for the value of the option embedded in the security.

Option-Adjusted Yield—Yield adjusted for the value of the option embedded in the security.

Optional Dividend—A dividend that the investor may receive as cash or additional stock.

Optional Payment Bond—Bond whose principal and/or interest the investor may receive in any specified currency.

Optional Redemption—A borrower's option to retire or call the whole or part of an issue of its securities prior to its maturity at prices at or above par.

Option Holder—The buyer (owner) of an option. The holder pays a premium to the option writer.

Option Mutual Fund—A mutual fund that trades options.

Option Overwriting—*See* Overwriting.

Option Premium—The price of an option. The option buyer pays the premium to the option seller.

Option Program—Any option strategy used systematically.

Options Clearing Corporation (OCC)—Corporation that issues and guarantees option contracts on the New York Stock Exchange, the

American Stock Exchange, the Pacific Stock Exchange, the Philadelphia Stock Exchange, and the Chicago Board of Options Exchange.

Option Series—Options of the same type (put or call), underlying security, exercise price, and expiration month.

Option Spread—A simultaneous long and short option position.

Option Swap—1) The right to enter into a swap agreement on or before a specified date. 2) *See* Contingent Swap.

Option to Double—A feature of an indenture that allows a sinking fund to purchase twice the normal principal amount of bonds for the sinking fund, at the sinking fund call price. Such additional purchases are not considered buying ahead. *See* Buying Ahead.

Option Warrant—A warrant that may be exercised for either equity or debt securities.

Option Writer—The seller of an option, who receives the option premium from the option holder.

Or Better (OB)—*See* At or Better.

Order—Instructions to trade a security. *See* Market Order, Limit Order, and Stop Order.

Order Book Official (OBO)—The individual who maintains a book of public orders for future execution on the Chicago Board of Options Exchange.

Order Room—A brokerage firm department that receives buy and sell orders for securities.

Order Support System (OSS)—Automated system for executing orders used on the Chicage Board of Options Exchange. *See* Automated Order Entry System.

Ordinary Annuity—An annuity in arrears.

Ordinary Income—Compensation, including wages and fees, taxed according to the individual's tax bracket.

Ordinary Interest—Simple interest based on a 360-day year. *See* Exact Interest.

Ordinary Shares—British for common stock.

Original Cost—Acquisition cost. Also called *Historical Cost.*

Original Face—*See* Original Principal.

Original Issue Discount (OID)—A bond issued at a discount from par. The discount must be greater than 1/4 point per year of maturity. The IRS treats the accretion of this discount over the life of the security as current income.

Original Issue Premium (OIP)—A bond issued at a premium to par. The premium must be greater than 1/4 point per year of maturity.

Original Maturity—Interval between issuance date and maturity date. Also called *Original Term*. *See* Current Maturity.

Original Principal—The principal amount of a pass-through pool at issuance. Also called *Original Face*.

Original Term—*See* Original Maturity.

Originator—1) A person who solicits builders, brokers, and others to obtain applications for mortgage loans. Origination is the process by which the mortgage banker brings into being a mortgage secured by real property. 2) Manager of a syndicate.

Orthodox School—*See* Classical School.

Other Income—Section of an income statement that includes income not generated from the main course of business, such as interest and sale of assets.

Out Firm—Signifies that a trader has already given someone else an option to buy or sell the security at a given price, for a specified period of time.

Outlier—1) A term used in statistics to refer to an observed element or data point that falls outside the usual range of such elements. 2) A person or thing that is classified or situated away from the main group of such people or things.

Out of the Money—An option that has no intrinsic value. A call option is out of the money when the underlying security is worth less than the exercise price; a put option is out of the money when the underlying security is worth more than the exercise price. *See* In the Money.

Outside Broker—Broker who is not a member of an exchange.

Outstanding—1) Uncollected debt. 2) A corporation's stock held by investors.

Outstanding Contract—An option contract that has not been closed out by a closing purchase or sale, has not been exercised, and has not expired.

Out the Window—Pertaining to a rapidly sold new issue. Also called *Blowout*.

Out-Trade—A futures trade by a floor trader that the clearing house cannot match with the other party to the trade, as recorded at the time of the trade.

Overallotment—Selling more securities in the primary market than are issued. Overallotment is, in effect, selling a new issue short.

Overbanked—Situation in a syndicate in which more securities are allotted to syndicate members than are to be issued.

Overbooked—Situation in a syndicate in which client demand exceeds available registered securities. *See* Oversubscribed and Syndicate.

Overbought—Market or security whose price rise is unsupported by fundamental factors. The market is overbought when long interest increases rapidly and short interest decreases sharply. An overbought market or security is susceptible to a downward price correction. *See* Oversold.

Overcollateralization—Providing more collateral than is needed to support the principal amount of bonds.

Overhang—Unsold securities remaining in dealers' inventories.

Overheating—Pertaining to an economy with a growing money supply and rising inflation.

Overlapping Debt—That part of the debt of one municipality for which the residents of another are responsible.

Overlying—Subordinated.

Overnight—Refers to a repurchase agreement with a maturity of the next business day.

Overnight Delivery Risk—When settlement centers are in different time zones, payment or delivery on one side of a transaction may be insufficient when received the next day in an account on the other side.

Overnight Position—Trader's or dealer's position at the end of a trading session.

Oversold—A market or security that is susceptible to an upward correction in price levels. Implies that prices have fallen more than fundamentals would dictate. *See* Overbought.

Oversubscribed—In response to an offer for sale, the total amount subscribed for exceeds the total amount offered. Under these circumstances, applicants will receive only an allotment or proportion of the amount applied for. *See* Overbooked and Allotment.

Over the Counter (OTC)—A market in which buyers and sellers seek each other out and negotiate terms. Over the counter securities include: U.S. government, state, and municipal securities; most industrial, rail, and utility securities; most bank and insurance company securities; mutual funds; American Depositary Receipts; and securities of corporations that can not or will not meet the requirements of an exchange. Also called *Negotiated Market,* as opposed to the Auction Market of the listed securities exchanges.

Over-the-Counter (OTC) Deliveries—Securities that are delivered by messenger to members and agents against payment. Delivery hours are between 9:00 a.m. and 11:30 a.m.

Over-the-Counter (OTC) Option—An option for which the writer has a contract directly with the buyer. A broker negotiates the exercise price, the expiration date, and the premium. In an exchange-traded option, the exercise price and expiration date are fixed by the exchange; only the premium is negotiated.

Over the Bridge—The delivery against payment statement of a trade between a Euroclear and a CEDEL participant by a book-entry transfer.

Overtrading—1) The practice of allowing illegal concessions by paying substantially more than the market value for one security in order to affect the sale of another. Also called *Highballing. See* Papilsky. 2) As defined by Adam Smith, buying assets at inflated prices during the euphoria of a speculative boom, overestimating profits, or buying on margin.

Overvalued—A security whose market price is higher than what a fundamental analyst judges to be its true value.

Overwriting—Selling more options than one owns.

Owners' Equity—Paid-in capital plus retained earnings of a corporation. In terms of the basic accounting equation, owners' equity equals assets minus liabilities. Also called *Residual Interest,* because shareholders have a claim on the assets of the firm after the creditors' claims are met.

Owner Trust—An entity established to issue CMOs. Ownership of the entity may be sold in the form of shares of beneficial interest.

P

Package Trading—Weekly or monthly trades to rebalance index funds so they will match the percentages of a market index.

Pac-Man—Defensive strategy whereby a takeover target threatens to acquire the raiding corporation.

Paid in Arrears—Refers to a loan whose payments are made at the end of each accrual period. *See* Effective Interest.

Paid-In Capital—Capital a corporation raises by selling stock.

Paid-In Surplus—The difference between the capital raised by selling stock and the stock's stated, or par, value (if the stock is sold in a primary offering for greater than face value). Also called *Additional Paid-In Capital* and *Capital Surplus*.

Painting the Tape—A form of manipulation whereby a number of investors trade a security among themselves to give the appearance of an active market.

Pair Off—1) To offset a position in the GNMA forward market by buying an issue previously sold or selling an issue previously bought. Both buy and sell sides must be in the same delivery month, and both must be for the same guaranteed coupon. 2) To offset a trade in the match book, that is, to do a repurchase agreement on securities acquired through a reverse repurchase agreement or vice-versa. *See* Matched Book.

Paper—1) Securities of a particular industry or sector. 2) Commercial paper.

Paper Barrel—Oil futures.

Paper Dealer—Commercial paper securities dealer.

Paper Gain—*See* Paper Profit.

Paper Gold—*See* Special Drawing Rights.

Paper Loss—Unrealized capital loss.

195

Paper Profit—Unrealized capital gain. Also called *Paper Gain*.

Papilsky—Plaintiff whose name is associated with certain underwriting practices. Paulette Papilsky, who owned 40 shares (about $300) of Affiliated, a mutual fund, filed suit in 1971 against Lord, Abbett & Co., who managed the fund. She sued the investment firm for violating its fiduciary responsibility to the fund by not trying, in a securities offering, to have itself designated as a member of the selling group and thereby receive a discount on the selling concession. The 1976 verdict was in favor of Papilsky. The NASD responded by ending all discounts off the fixed price of a new offering, including soft dollar payments for research and the already illegal but common practice of overtrading, or swapping new securities for less expensive issues. *See* Overtrading.

Par—1) A price of 100 (percent of face value). 2) The face value assigned by a corporation to common or preferred stock. 3) The principal amount or denomination at which the obligor (issuing corporation) contracts to redeem the bond at maturity. The par value amount is stated on the face of the bond.

Paradox of Thrift—Economic situation in which an increase in personal savings leads to a decrease in economic activity, causing actual total savings to decrease.

Parallel Importation—*See* Gray Market.

Parallel Pay—*See* Concurrent Pay.

Parallel Shift—A movement in a yield curve such that the shape (slope) of the curve remains unchanged.

Par Bond—A bond selling at par.

Par Bond Yield Curve—*See* Par Yield Curve.

Par Cap—1) In a GNMA certificate delivery contract, a stipulation that no cash securities priced above par can be delivered against a short position. 2) A restriction that prohibits the delivery of an issue in the GNMA forward market to satisfy a yield maintenance contract if the equivalent price of the security delivered is over par. The only exception is when the issue bought for yield maintenance was at a price over par. In this case, the issue delivered may be at the contracted price or lower.

Par Compression—The pressure on the price of a mortgage-related security, once it has risen above par, to fall back to par, due to the effect of prepayments in a falling interest rate environment. The phenomenon of prices falling, or not increasing to the extent predicted by modified duration, is called negative convexity.

Parent—A corporation that owns or controls another. *See* Holding Company.

Pareto's Law—Theory named after the economist who claimed that income tends to be distributed the same way, regardless of social, political, or fiscal policy. Also called the law of the trivial many and the critical few, or the 80-20 law (80% of a nation's income tends to be distributed to 20% of the population).

Pari Passu—Latin for with equal step. In the context of unsecured debt, it means equal in right of payment to other debt.

Pari Passu Clause—Clause in an indenture stating that if a prior lien is placed on corporate assets that have been designated as collateral, the bonds issued will be provided an equal and pro rata share in the prior lien. Also called *Equal* and *Ratable Security Clause*.

Parity—1) In a convertible bond, parity refers to the comparison of market price of the underlying stock to the theoretical value of the convertible bond. Parity is the price at which the convertible bond would have to sell in order to be equal in value to the underlying stock. For example, if a stock were selling at $50 and the conversion ratio were 15, parity for the bond would be $750. *See* Conversion Ratio. 2) An option is said to be trading at parity with the underlying security if its price is equal to its intrinsic value.

Parity Price—The price at which yield equals the coupon rate for bonds with payment delays, such as pass-throughs.

Parking—1) Temporarily placing assets in a safe investment. 2) Illegally hiding assets.

PAR Preferred—Price Adjusted Rate Preferred Stock. The dividend rate on PAR preferred is reset periodically based on a short-term index such as the bond yield equivalent of the three-month or six-month Treasury bill. The rate is then further adjusted if the recent trading range of the security has, on average, deviated from its par value. These adjustments, based on both rate and price, should ensure that the security trades at or near par.

Partial—Partial delivery, that is, when a broker delivers fewer securities than agreed upon.

Partial Dedication—Construction of a dedicated bond portfolio to fund only a portion of a liability stream.

Partially Funded—Refers to a pension plan in which earned benefits have not all been funded.

Partially Paid—Refers to U.S. dollar-denominated bonds sold to foreign investors who put up less than the Federal Reserve Board's margin requirement.

Participant—A firm that uses a registered clearing agency to confirm, clear, and settle securities transactions.

Participating Preferred—A preferred stock entitled to a specific dividend before dividends are paid to common stockholders and participates with the common stock in additional corporate earnings distributed as dividends. The form of participation differs among issues, though the most common form permits the preferred stockholder to share in future dividend distributions with common stockholders. Usually a participating preferred stock is entitled to some stated maximum percentage over the common stock dividend, but not less than its own fixed rate.

Participating Trust—An investment company that issues shares reflecting an interest in another investment company.

Participation—A purchase of a beneficial interest in mortgage loans. Although the purchaser does not actually purchase the notes themselves and the seller remains the mortgagee of record, the purchaser has the right to the cash flows and is deemed to be the owner from a financial perspective. This ownership interest is evidenced by a participation certificate.

Participation Certificate (PC)—1) A security issued by FHLMC representing an undivided interest in a pool of conventional mortgages. Principal and interest payments on the mortgages are passed through to the certificate holders each month. Participation certificates qualify as "loans secured by an interest in real property" and as "qualifying real property loans" with respect to certain thrift institutions' investment restrictions. 2) Stock that has no voting rights.

Partly Paid Bond—Bond on which a partial payment is due at the closing of syndication, with the balance payable in one or two installments on predetermined dates. Also called *Deferred Purchase Note*.

Par Value—1) The principal amount the bondholder receives upon maturity. Also called *Face Value*. 2) The amount due the preferred shareholder in the event of a liquidation. Unlike common stock, preferred stock usually does have a par value, which is specified in the issuer's corporate charter. The usual preferred stock par value is $100, $50, or $25 per share. If a preferred stock has a par value, the dividend rate on the security will be stated as a percentage of the par value (e.g., Pacific Gas and Electric, 8.00% preferred, $25 par). If the preferred stock does not have a par value, the dividend rate will be stated in dollars. 3) Ratio of one currency unit to another.

Par Yield Curve—A yield curve drawn by estimating the coupon rates for bonds of different maturities that would be priced at par. Also called *Par Bond Yield Curve. See* Spot Rate Curve.

Passed Dividend—An omitted dividend on common stock or cumulative preferred stock. In the case of the latter, the passed dividend is in arrears.

Passive—Not owning a large enough percentage of a corporation's stock to exert influence on that corporation. According to generally accepted accounting principles, investment in less than 20 percent of a corporation's stock is considered a passive investment. *See* Active.

Passive Bond—Bond that pays no interest.

Passive Management—1) Investment strategy designed to earn market returns. Passive management tries to maximize the expected return-to-risk ratio and to avoid diversifiable risk. Index funds are examples of passive management. *See* Diversifiable Risk. 2) Buy and hold strategy.

Passive Portfolio—A portfolio whose objective is to minimize transaction costs and taxes rather than to beat the market. A passive portfolio avoids risk through diversification.

Pass-Through—A mortgage-backed security for which the payments on the underlying mortgages are passed from the mortgage holder through the servicing agent (who usually keeps a portion as a fee) to the security holder. There are three types of pass-through securities: 1) Straight Pass-Through. The security holder receives principal and interest actually collected by the servicing agent. 2) Modified Pass-Through. The security holder receives interest due, whether or not it has been collected, and principal as collected. 3) Fully Modified Pass-Through. The security holder receives principal and interest due, whether or not they have been collected.

Pass-Through Rate—The coupon rate of a pass-through security.

Pass-Through Yield—The conventional yield of a pass-through security, which is computed based on cash flow that assumes no principal prepayments occur for a specified number of years (12 for a 30-year security) followed by the total prepayment of all outstanding principal. Cash flow yield, or Honest-to-God (HTG) Yield, on the other hand, assumes prepayments occur every month according to a prepayment model.

Payable—A debt that is unpaid but not necessarily due.

Payback Period—Interval needed to recover an investment.

Pay Date—Date on which quarterly dividend payments are made.

Paydown—1) Payment of principal on a loan. 2) In a Treasury refunding, the amount by which the principal amount of securities maturing exceeds the principal amount offered.

Paying Agent—A trustee, typically a commercial bank, responsible for the mechanical task of disbursing payments of principal and interest to a holder of a security when the security or its coupons are presented.

Pay-in-Kind (PIK)—Stock that pays dividends in the form of additional shares for a specified period of time, typically three to six years.

Pay-in-Kind stock may be either publicly underwritten or offered as cram down paper. *See* Cram Down Paper.

Payment Cap—Maximum amount by which an adjustable rate mortgage borrower's monthly principal and interest payment can increase. A payment cap, if invoked, can cause negative amortization. *See* Negative Amortization.

Payment Date—1) The date in a primary issue on which syndicate members pay the lead manager for their allotment of securities. 2) Date on which a dividend or interest payment is made. 3) A settlement date in respect to secondary market transactions.

Payment Delay—1) When the coupon payment is made after the coupon period ends, thereby reducing yield. 2) The time lag between the date a pass-through issuer receives payments of principal and interest from the mortgagors and the date the security holder receives them. "Stated delay" refers to the interval from the time interest begins to accrue until the payment is made to investors. Since interest is calculated monthly, the interest-free delay periods ("actual delay") are one month less than the stated delays, resulting in actual delays of 14, 19, 24, and 44 days for GNMA I, GNMA II, FNMA, and FHLMC pass-through securities, respectively.

Payment Frequency—The number of times per year that interest payments are made on a floating rate security or a mortgage security.

Payment in Advance—Mortgage obligation in which the first payment is due at the time of origination. This payment schedule results in lower payments in the future.

Payment in Arrears—When interest is due at the end of the payment period.

Payment Shock—Psychological reaction that could result if interest rates were to rise sharply, causing adjustable rate mortgage borrowers to face large monthly payment increases.

Payout Event—An event that allows the issuer of an asset-backed security to end the non-amortization period. Payout events include a decline in yield and a change in prepayment patterns. *See* Non-Amortization Period.

Payout Ratio—1) The percentage of an underwriting fee that is paid by the lead manager to the managers and sub-underwriters of a new issue after adjustment for profits or losses, if any, on the stabilization of the issue in the primary market and deduction of any costs incurred by the lead manager in preparation of the issue insofar as such costs are not reimbursed by the borrower. 2) Annual common stock dividends divided by net income to common stock for the same period.

Pay-Through Bond—A general obligation bond secured by mortgage collateral. Also called *Cash Flow Bond*.

Pay-Up—The difference in price when a block of securities is purchased at a higher price than another block of securities sold. The buyer pays up the difference.

Pegging—An investment bank's attempt to stabilize the price of a new issue by buying it at or above the offering price. Pegging is allowed by the SEC up to ten days after the offering date.

Pennsylvania Bond—Slang for a bond likely to default.

Penny Stock—Stock that is issued at less than one dollar per share.

Pension Assets—The current value of net assets set aside to pay pension benefits.

Pension Benefit Guaranty Corporation (PBGC)—Self-financing government corporation that was established by ERISA to provide pension plan termination insurance. Plan sponsors make annual contributions to PBGC to establish a reserve fund. If a plan is terminated and there are insufficient assets, the PBGC becomes the trustee for the plan to ensure that participants receive their guaranteed payments.

Pension Fund—A tax-exempt fund established by any entity with employees to ensure payment of pension benefits.

Pension Reform Act—*See* Employees Retirement Income Security Act.

Per Capita Debt—Total bonded debt, typically of a municipality, divided by the population.

Percentage Order—A market or limit order to trade a specified number of securities after another specified number of the same security has been traded.

Perfect Elasticity—Market situation in which price does not change with quantity supplied or demanded. Also called *Infinite Elasticity*.

Perfect Hedge—Equal price changes on both sides of a hedged position during a hedge period.

Perfect Inelasticity—Market situation in which quantity does not change as price changes. Also called *Complete Inelasticity*.

Performance—The total return of a portfolio.

Performance Bond—1) An initial margin deposit. 2) A surety bond, given by one party to a contract to protect the other against loss or violation of the contract.

Performance Fee—Compensation to investment advisors based on returns.

Performance Fund—A mutual fund that invests in securities that offer growth rather than income.

Peril Point—Tariff level at which any reduction, according to protectionists, would hurt domestic industry.

Periodic Payment—1) Consecutive equal sinking fund payments. 2) Regular investments in a mutual fund.

Periodic Purchase Deferred Contract—An annuity contract with regular fixed payments, or premiums, that begins to pay out at a specified date.

Periodic Rate Caps—Maximum amount by which an adjustable rate mortgage loan rate may change per reset interval.

Permanent Income—Expected average lifetime income.

Permitted Investments—Cash flow investments, qualified reserve funds, and foreclosed property that can comprise up to five percent of a REMIC's assets. *See* Real Estate Mortgage Investment Conduit.

Perpendicular Spread—*See* Vertical Spread.

Perpetual—A fixed income security with no maturity date (e.g., British consul or a preferred stock with no sinking fund).

Perpetuity—An annuity whose payments never stop.

Person—Under the Uniform Securities Act, "a corporation, a partnership, an association, a joint stock company, a trust where the interests of the beneficiaries are evidenced by a security, an unincorporated organization, a government, or a political subdivision of a government."

Personal Income—Total individual income from all sources, minus total personal payments to social security.

Personal Property—Personal assets other than real estate.

Personality Bond—Security whose performance depends in part on the market's perception of corporate officials.

Peruvian Bond—Slang for a worthless security, so called because National City Bank president Charles E. Mitchell endorsed two ill-fated Peruvian bond issues in 1928 and 1929.

Petrocurrency—*See* Petrodollars.

Petrodollars—U.S. dollars received for oil and deposited in Western banks. Also called *Petrocurrency*.

Pfandbrief(e)—A bond issued by German banks to finance mortgages. Pfandbriefe are collateralized by a pool of mortgages.

Phantom Income—Taxable, non-cash income, such as the interest accreted on a zero coupon bond.

Phantom Shelf—*See* Convenience Shelf.

Philadelphia Automated Communication and Execution (PACE)— Automated system for executing orders used on the Philadelphia Stock Exchange. *See* Automated Order Entry System.

Philadelphia Plan—A means of financing equipment purchases used by American railroads whereby a trustee, acting for the benefit of trust certificate owners, holds title to the equipment involved and leases it to the railroad at a fixed rental that is sufficient to cover principal and interest payments. *See* Equipment Trust Certificate.

Phillips Curve—Curve that shows that unemployment and inflation are inversely related (at least in the short term). *See* Accelerationist Theory.

Physical Capital—*See* Nonhuman Resources.

Physicals—*See* Actuals.

Physical Strip—The bearer bond or note of a U.S. Treasury zero coupon bond or note. In 1982 a law mandated that all future U.S. Treasury bonds and notes be in registered book entry form, thereby eliminating future bearer issue securities. Physical strips therefore refer to pre-summer of 1982 issues. New stripped zeros are in registered form.

Physiocrat—Economist who believes that all wealth originates in agriculture.

Pick-Up—The gain in yield resulting from the sale of one block of bonds and the purchase of another block with a greater yield.

Pick-up Payment—*See* Balloon Payment.

Picture—A broker's bid and asked prices for a security. A picture is an indication of market levels, and is therefore subject to confirmation. *See* Quotation and Subject.

Piece—A trading unit.

Pip—One 1/100th of one percent of principal value, or 10 cents per thousand dollars face amount. It is a measure of price differential (a basis point is a measure of yield differential).

Pipeline—1)Underwriting procedures taken before the public offering. The pipeline for municipal securities is called the Thirty Day Visible Supply. 2) Potential mortgage loans on which applications have been made but not closed. Loans in the process of being approved and entering the mortgage-related securities market are said to be "in the pipeline."

Pit—A trading area on the floor of an exchange where only one kind of security is traded. In the futures market, it is a trading area on the floor of an exchange where one or more types of futures contracts may be traded.

Pit Broker—A person who executes the trading orders of other parties on the trading floor of a futures exchange.

Place—To sell securities during an issue's primary market distribution. Also called *Distribute* and *Float.*

Placee—1) An investor who purchases a new issue. 2) A broker-dealer who purchases a bought deal. *See* Bought Deal.

Placement—One bank depositing or selling Eurodollars to another.

Placement Ratio—Percentage of municipal issues sold by issuers selling at least $1 million par value of securities, published weekly in *The Bond Buyer.* Also called *Acceptance Ratio.*

Placing Memorandum—*See* Private Placement Memorandum.

Placing Power—A bank's or a broker's ability to sell (place) securities.

Plain Vanilla—An issue with no additional features such as calls, puts, and warrants. *See* Bells and Whistles.

Plain Vanilla Swap—A U.S. dollar interest rate swap in which one party makes floating rate payments based on three- or six-month LIBOR and receives fixed rate funds expressed as a spread over the rate on U.S. Treasury securities. The maturity is usually one to ten years. Deal size is typically $10-$15 million, although it ranges from $5-$150 million.

Plan III GPM—A graduated payment mortgage whose payments increase by 7.5% for each of the first five years of the mortgage. Over 80% of FHA/VA GPMs are issued as plan III. Because the early payments are usually not sufficient to pay the interest due on the outstanding balance, negative amortization occurs in early years (the interest shortfall being added to the outstanding principal balance). After the fifth year, the payment is constant and sufficient to fully amortize the mortgage to maturity.

Planned Amortization Class (PAC)—A type of Controlled Amortization Bond, or CMO tranche that has a planned amortization schedule. Principal payments are made on a priority basis to the PAC bonds before being made to the other tranches. The payment schedule causes the weighted average life of the PAC bond to remain relatively constant over a wide range of prepayment experience. Also called *Controlled Amortization Bond (CAB)*, *Planned Redemption Obligation (PRO) Class*, and *Scheduled Redemption Obligation (SRO) Class.*

Planned Redemption Obligation (PRO)—*See* Planned Amortization Class.

Plan Termination—A company may terminate an entire employee benefit plan, or it may institute a split plan whereby the active portion is fully funded and the residual assets enter the retired portion, which is then terminated.

Pledge—*See* Hypothecate.

Pledged Revenues—Pledge that either all revenues (Gross Revenue Pledge) or all revenues after specified expenses (Net Revenue Pledge) will be used to service municipal debt.

Plow Back—To reinvest earnings in the business.

Plus—One sixty-fourth. To quote a bid or offer a dealer will omit the handle, quoting only the number of 32nds and, when necessary, a plus sign to indicate 1/64. For example, a quote of 2+ means the handle plus 2/32 plus 1/64.

Plus Tick—*See* Uptick.

Point—One percent of the face amount of a bond; $10 for each $1000 face amount. Bond prices are quoted in points and fractions of points. (For stocks, one point is one dollar.)

Points—Loan fee (one point equals one percent of the loan), paid in advance by the borrower to the lender.

Poison Pill—The right given to shareholders to buy discounted shares in the event of a hostile takeover attempt.

Poison Put—A bondholder's option to sell bonds back to the issuer at par in the event of a hostile takeover.

Polish Dividend—*See* Irish Dividend.

Ponzi—Fraudulent scheme that uses funds from new investors to pay earlier investors. Also called *Lapping*.

Pool—An aggregation of investment instruments into a single security. Most commonly used in reference to mortgages.

Pooled Financings—Financing that allows a group of unaffiliated borrowers to accept funds from a central bond issuing authority, thereby reducing their borrowing costs. Also called *Bond Pool*.

Pool Factor—The ratio of the outstanding principal amount of a pass-through pool to its original principal amount. *See* Z Factor.

Pooling of Interest Method—Combining the balance sheets of two corporations involved in a merger. *See* Purchase Acquisition Method.

Pool Insurance—Insurance carried to guarantee the payments of principal and interest on the mortgages comprising a mortgage pool. Pool insurance covers a specified percentage of credit losses (typically 5% to 15%); it does not cover special hazards, such as earthquakes, and bankruptcy.

Pork Bellies in Pinstripe—Slang for financial futures.

Portfolio—The securities owned by an investor.

Portfolio Insurance—Technique of dynamically allocating funds between a risky and a riskless portfolio. When the risky portfolio is performing well, funds are shifted to it, and vice versa. The effect is to synthetically replicate a put option on the portfolio.

Portfolio Optimization—The process of selecting securities in a portfolio in order to maximize or minimize a criterion specified by the investor (e.g., yield, coupon, duration, convexity, cost of the portfolio), subject to constraints (e.g., credit, diversification, maturity, duration).

Position—1) Used as a noun, a position is the amount an investor is long or short in a security. 2) Used as a verb, to position oneself is to go long or short a security.

Position Limit—The maximum number of futures contracts that may be held by speculators overnight. *See* Reporting Level and Trading Limit.

Position Trader—A speculator who buys or sells securities because of anticipated market moves, and holds positions at least overnight. *See* Scalper.

Positive Carry—*See* Carry.

Pot—The portion of an offering not retained for distribution by members of the syndicate account but set aside for discretionary distribution by the manager running the books—either to institutions (institutional pot) or to dealers (dealer pot).

Potential Demand—An unsatisfied need that is expected to be satisfied when some condition is met. Also called *Latent Demand.*

Potential Holder—Any person, including any existing holder, who has executed a purchaser's letter and who may be interested in buying shares of STAR preferred stock. *See* Existing Holder and Purchaser's Letter.

Pot Protection—Obtaining commitments to buy a specified amount of a new issue of stocks or bonds.

Power of Attorney—Document signed by account owners authorizing a third party to transact business within the account on behalf of the owners. Also called *Trading Authorization.*

Praecipuum—A portion of the management fee calculated on the full principal amount of an issue taken by the lead manager(s) as compensation for assuming responsibility for the coordination and distribution of a primary market issue.

Preemptive Right—The right a corporation gives to holders of its securities to purchase new shares or bonds before the general public can participate.

Preference Stock—Preferred stock that has all the priveleges of other preferred issues of the same issuer but is junior in right of payment.

Preferred Habitat—*See* Market Segmentation Hypothesis.

Preferred Stock—A corporate equity security that, while junior to all debt instruments, is senior to common stock in the payment of dividends and the liquidation of assets. The dividend can be fixed or floating rate, and is usually stated in dollar terms or as a percentage of the preferred's issue price. Preferred stock has no maturity, and usually has no voting rights.

Preferred Stock Ratio—Ratio of preferred stock to total long-term capitalization.

Preliminary Official Statement (POS)—*See* Red Herring.

Preliminary Prospectus—A prospectus prepared by the lead manager of an issue in conjunction with the borrower and distributed on the launch date. It contains most relevant details about the securities and the borrower but excludes certain final terms. It is subject to revision. *See* Prospectus. Also called *Preliminary Official Statement* and *Red Herring*.

Premium—1) The difference between the price of an issue and par, for issues selling above par. 2) An amount that must be paid above par in order to call or refund an issue (e.g., call premium, refunding premium). 3) The price of an option. 4) A premium bond.

Premium Bond—A bond selling above par. The excess over par is called the premium.

Premium Cash—1) For securities selling above par, the difference between the price of the security and par. 2) An amount that must sometimes be paid above par in order to call an issue. 3) Margin or spread in the sense of a percentage above a given amount or rate. *See* Conversion Premium.

Premium Convertible—A convertible bond whose market price is greater than its conversion value expressed as a percentage over current equity price.

Premium Debt Repurchase—Significant retirement of premium debt prior to expiration of call protection.

Premium Market—*See* Normal Market.

Premium Raid—*See* Dawn Raid.

Prepaid Life—A method of analyzing mortgage cash flows that assumes no principal prepayments occur for a specified number of years (12 for a 30-year security) followed by the total prepayment of all outstanding principal. The yield to prepaid life also assumes that the security is new, even if it has been outstanding for years.

Prepaid Syndicate Expense (PPSE)—Expenses   incurred   by   the managers in preparing an offering for market.

Prepayment—Any payment made before its originally scheduled payment date. In particular, the full or partial repayment of a mortgage loan before such payment is due.

Prepayment Experience—Historical rate of mortgage prepayment.

Prepayment Model—Predictive model of prepayment rates. Models include Twelve-Year Life or Prepaid Life, FHA Experience (of various vintages, including Old, New, and New New), Single Monthly Mortality (SMM), Conditional Prepayment Rate (CPR), Constant Percent Prepayment (CPP), the PSA (Public Securities Association) Standard Prepayment Model, and the Absolute Prepayment Model (ABS) for asset-backed securities. *See* entries for each model.

Prepayment Reserve Fund—Fund established to protect CMO investors in the event a large percentage of principal is prepaid early in a bond period. *See* Calamity Call.

Prepayment Risk—*See* Risk.

Prepayment Table—*See* Decrement Table.

Prerefunding—Issuing securities to refund an outstanding security that is not yet callable. *See* Arbitrage Bond.

Presale Order—A buy order for a portion of a municipal offering before the details are known. Such orders are legal for municipal securities, which are not registered with the SEC.

Prescribed Period—The period of time determined by the relevant governing law that must elapse before the amounts due under a contract become no longer payable. Also called *Prescription Period.*

Prescription Period—*See* Prescribed Period.

Present Value—The current worth of a cash flow. Future value is converted to present value through the process of discounting.

Presidential Effect—Stock market lore that prices rise in an election year and fall the year after, that prices are better in the second two years of an administration than in the first two years, and that the market does better in a Republican administration than in a Democratic one.

Presold—An issue that is sold out before it is announced.

Price—1) Used as a noun, the value of anything offered for sale expressed in monetary terms. Prices of bonds are expressed as percentages of par or face value. 2) Used as a verb, to determine the value of a new issue.

Price-Earnings Ratio—Market price of a share of stock divided by annual earnings per share.

Price Effect—The effect that a trade has on the price of a security.

Price Elasticity—A measure of how much a unit change in price will cause a change in quantity supplied or demanded.

Price Limit—Price fluctuation allowed on a futures contract in one trading day.

Price-Sales Ratio (PSR)—A company's stock price divided by its sales revenue per share.

Price Spread—*See* Vertical Spread.

Price Talk—Talk among underwriters about the price range of a negotiated issue.

Pricey—Expensive, usually referring to an underpriced bid or an overpriced offer.

Price-Yield Curve—Curve that plots price as a function of yield.

Pricing Date—The date on which the structure and price of a CMO is determined.

Pricing Speed—The prepayment assumption used to project the cash flows on the underlying collateral of a mortgage-related security when initially priced and offered to investors. These cash flows in turn determine the expected maturities and average lives of the securities.

Primary Capital—Stockholders' equity, loan loss reserves, and qualifying subordinated debt. Primary capital must be 5.5% of bank assets.

Primary Dealer—A dealer that makes a market in government securities. The Fed conducts open market operations only through primary dealers.

Primary Distribution—Sale of new securities. Also called *Primary Offering*.

Primary Earnings Per Share—Net income to common shareholders plus after-tax interest or dividends on common stock equivalents divided by the number of common shares outstanding plus potential increase in common shares should all dilutive instruments be exercised.

Primary Market—The market in which new issues are initially distributed.

Primary Offering—*See* Primary Distribution.

Primary Underwriter—The manager of an issue who agrees to underwrite a new issue of securities in its entirety before the issue is officially launched and before the sub-underwriters participate. To the extent that such underwriters participate, the manager's "primary underwriting commitment" is reduced pro rata. After such a pro rata reduction, each manager's remaining underwriting commitment is referred to as its "secondary underwriting commitment."

Primary Underwriting Commitment—*See* Primary Underwriter.

Prime Bank—A bank of the highest standing.

Prime Commercial Paper—Commercial paper with a Moody's rating of P (P-1, P-2, or P-3).

Prime Rate—The rate of interest at which a commercial bank offers to lend money to its most creditworthy customers.

Prime Underwriting Facility (PUF)—Rare facility in which the Euronote facility concept is adapted to pricing on a U.S. prime rate basis.

Principal—1) The face amount or par value of a security; the amount exclusive of interest or premium due the holder at maturity. It is the sum used to compute interest. Also called *Face* or *Nominal Amount.* 2) A legal term used to designate one who employs another person to act as an agent. 3) According to the NASD, a person actively engaged in the management of a firm's business. 4) One who acts as a dealer in a transaction for his or her own account at net prices.

Principal Balance—The outstanding balance of a mortgage, sinking fund bond, or other debt, exclusive of interest and any other charges. *See* Original Principal.

Principal Only (PO)—Stripped mortgage-backed security in which the investor receives all of the principal and none of the interest on the underlying security. *See* Interest Only.

Principal TR—*See* Corpus TR.

Principal Value—*See* Face Value.

Principle Paying Agent—The bank responsible for coordinating the operations of an issue's paying agents. Such an agent is usually appointed only when there is a trustee to the issue of securities. *See* Fiscal Agent.

Priority—A system of filling market orders in which the first bid or offer is executed first, and in which off-floor orders have priority over on-floor orders.

Prior Lien—Bonds issued with a lien that has priority over a first mortgage bond (issued only with permission of the first mortgage bondholders).

Prior Preferred—A preferred stock issue that is senior to another preferred issue of the same company.

Private Activity Bond—A taxable municipal bond.

Private Mortgage Insurance (PMI)—Insurance written by a private company protecting a mortgage lender against loss due to a mortgage default. The insurance is typically written on mortgage loans having an initial loan-to-value ratio greater than 80 percent.

Private Pass-Through—A pass-through not issued by a government agency and therefore not containing a government or agency guarantee. Private pass-throughs are also referred to as AA pass-throughs, reflecting the credit rating of issuers such as Citicorp and Bank of America.

Private Placement—An issue that is sold to one or a few investors as opposed to being publicly offered and sold. Private placements avoid many of the delays, legal complications, and costs of public issues, and are not subject to the registration provisions of section 4-2 of the Securities Act of 1933. Private placements must meet the following conditions: 1) The issuer has reason to believe that each buyer is experienced enough to evaluate the risks involved. 2) Each buyer has access to the same financial data that would normally appear in a prospectus. 3) The issuer does not sell securities to more than 35 persons in any consecutive 12-month period. 4) The issuer is assured that the buyer does not intend to make a subsequent sale for quick trading profit; this is usually accomplished by having each buyer sign an investment letter.

Private Placement Memorandum (PPM)—A confidential document that is provided for a private placement syndicate and for its clients. It is prepared by the lead-manager and contains all the relevant information about the borrower and the placement. Also called *Direct Placement Memorandum* and *Placing Memorandum. See* Prospectus.

Proceeds—Money received from the sale of a security or from the issuance of securities.

Proceeds Sales—*See* Swap.

Pro-Cyclical—An economic force that tends to reinforce fluctuations in the business cycle, turning slowdowns into recessions and expansions into booms. Also called *Cyclically Perverse. See* Counter-Cyclical.

Producer Goods—Capital goods used to produce consumer goods.

Producer Price Index (PPI)—A measure of wholesale prices, broken down by commodity, industry sector, and stage of production, and published by the Bureau of Labor Statistics. *See* Consumer Price Index.

Professional—A counterparty in a security transaction who is not a retail investor.

Profitability Ratio—A measure of a corporation's profitability, such as return on capital.

Profit and Loss Statement—Income Statement.

Profit Margin Ratio—A measure of a corporation's ability to control costs relative to revenues, calculated as the percentage of net income plus interest net of taxes to sales.

Profits—*See* Net Income.

Profit Taking—When traders or investors sell for profit after a rise in the market, pushing prices down.

Pro Forma Statement—A hypothetical accounting statement.

Programme—A formal arrangement generally between a single dealer or a group of banks and an issuer for the sale of the issuer's short-term Euronotes or CDs on a best efforts basis. A programme is not underwritten. *See* Facility.

Program Trading—The simultaneous purchase or sale of large amounts of securities that make up a basket or index when a specified market level is reached, often while taking offsetting positions in stock index futures or index options, in which case it is called Index Arbitrage. *See* Block Trade.

Progressive Tax—A method of taxation in which tax rates increase with income. Also called *Graduated Tax*. *See* Regressive Tax.

Prohibited Transaction—In relation to a REMIC, prohibited transactions include receiving fees for services, liquidating assets improperly, and earning income on assets other than qualified mortgages and permitted investments. A 100% tax rate applies to income earned from prohibited transactions. *See* Real Estate Mortgage Investment Conduit and Permitted Investments.

Project Loan—A mortgage on commercial property or a multi-family dwelling, with a maturity of up to forty years. Also refers to pass-through pools containing project loans.

Project Note (PN)—A short-term, federally tax-exempt note backed by the U.S. government, issued by local authorities to finance low-cost housing.

Promissory Note—An unconditional promise in writing, signed by the debtor, undertaking to pay a specific sum on demand or at a fixed or determinable future time.

Promissory Notes Rate—One of four Dutch central bank rates, used as a reference level to set the rates at which commercial banks lend to their clients.

Property Additions Sinking Fund—A sinking fund that gives the borrower the option of satisfying the sinking fund requirements by crediting some percentage of net property additions rather than delivering cash or bonds to the trustee.

Property Dividend—A dividend in kind.

Proportional Representation—*See* Cumulative Voting.

Pro Rata—In proportion; a method of proportional allocation.

Pro Rata Sinking Fund—A sinking fund in which each investor loses an equal percentage of holdings to the issuer when the issue is called for sinking fund retirements.

Prospectus—A statement filed with the SEC containing all of the pertinent information about a security being offered and about the issuer of the securities. A preliminary prospectus (Red Herring) is filed prior to the final prospectus, which is not filed until the final pricing.

Prospectus Supplement—A document, sometimes improperly referred to simply as the prospectus, that contains specific financial information about bonds being issued, including stated maturities, repayment periods under different scenarios, financial assumptions, price, composition of the underlying collateral for mortgage-related securities, and the capitalization of the issuer. A prospectus supplement is used for shelf registrations, when a corporation issues securities that have been previously authorized by the SEC.

Protect—To guarantee a customer an execution at a certain price (the "protect price"). The customer has the option of accepting the execution or refusing it.

Protection—During an issue's distribution in the primary market, the guarantee on an "if, as and when issued" basis to sell another party a specified amount of securities. It is normally given by a lead-manager to the syndicate members. They in turn may offer protection to their clients. After protection has been granted, the sale is considered to have been executed subject to the issue being completed on the closing date. Protection may be the pricing indemnity amount in whole or in part.

Protectionism—Government policy to limit imports in order to strengthen domestic industry. Protectionist legislation includes the Dingley Act, in effect from 1897 to 1909, and the Smoot-Hawley Tariff, in effect during the early 1930s. Pejoratively called Beggar-Thy-Neighbor. *See* Peril Point.

Protective Covenant—1) A municipality's promise to protect investors in its securities. The covenant may, for example, promise that the financed project be insured and maintained, that there be adequate accounting, that its rents, fees, tolls, etc. be adequate for debt coverage. 2) *See* Covenant.

Protective Put—A position consisting of a put and the underlying security.

Proxy—1) Written authorization given by a corporate shareholder giving someone else the right to vote on his or her behalf at a shareholder meeting. 2) Person authorized to vote on behalf of a corporation shareholder at a shareholders' meeting.

Proxy Statement—Information provided to shareholders about a company and its board of directors before they vote by proxy. Required by the SEC.

Prudent Man Rule—A standard of conduct that requires fiduciaries to discharge their duties with care, skill, prudence, and diligence. The Prudent Man Rule was defined by the Supreme Court of Massachusetts in 1830 in the case of Harvard College versus Amory: "All that can be required of a trustee to invest is that he shall conduct himself faithfully and exercise a sound discretion. He is to observe how men of prudence, discretion and intelligence manage their own affairs, not in regard to speculation, but in regard to the permanent disposition of their funds, considering the probable income, as well as the probable safety of the capital invested."

PSA Standard Prepayment Model—FHA experience specifies standard prepayment percentages for each year of a mortgage's life. PSA, on the other hand, specifies a standard percentage for each month, and annualizes that percentage. 100% PSA calls for prepayment rates of .2% CPR in the first month, .4% CPR in the second month, .6% CPR in the third month, and so on until, in months 30 and beyond, the mortgage (or mortgage pool) will prepay at an annual rate of 6% CPR. Also called *Standard Prepayment Assumption.*

Public Choice—Theory that self-interest determines fiscal policy. Elected officials, according to the theory, are likely to pursue popular, expansionary fiscal policy.

Public Debt—Government debt.

Public Goods—Goods that are consumed jointly, such as national defense, highways, and the legal system.

Public Housing Authority (PHA) Bonds—Federal tax-exempt bonds that are issued by local housing authorities to finance public housing and are backed by the U.S. government.

Publicly Held—Refers to a corporation that sells shares to the public.

Public Offering—A new listed issue of securities offered to the public. *See* Private Placement.

Public Utility Holding Company Act—Act passed by Congress in 1935 requiring registration with the SEC for all publicly owned holding companies engaged in the electric utility business or in the retail distribution of natural gas.

Purchase Acquisition Method—Accounting method in which an acquiring corporation treats the acquired corporation as an investment, adding the latter's assets to its own at fair market value, and treating any premium paid over fair market value as good will. *See* Pooling of Interest Method.

Purchase Agent—A bank designated by a borrower to use its best efforts to purchase bonds on the borrower's behalf to satisfy the borrower's purchase fund obligation.

Purchase Fund—A provision of certain issues of preferred stock. A purchase fund is similar to a sinking fund, though redemptions of the preferred shares are not mandatory, are non-cumulative, and are generally executed through a tender offer. Under this provision, a company is periodically obligated to attempt to purchase a specified number of securities from investors at or below par value or stated value. No obligation is made to call securities for retirement if they cannot be purchased at scheduled prices.

Purchaser Representative—As defined in Regulation D of the Securities Act of 1933, anyone who represents a potential non-accredited investor who has been solicited to purchase securities pursuant to Regulation D. Purchaser representatives may not own 10 percent or more of the stock of the issuer and may not be an affiliate, director, officer, or employee of the issuer unless they are related by blood to the offeree. *See* Regulation D.

Purchaser's Letter—Letter addressed to the trustee and broker-dealers acting as underwriters, in which a person agrees, among other things, to offer to purchase and/or sell shares of STAR preferred stock.

Purchasing Power Parity (PPP)—The exchange rate at which a dollar will buy the same quantity of goods and services in the U.S. as it will in other countries. The economic theory of PPP states that in the absence of unexpected policy changes or other unanticipated events, exchange rates will tend gradually to move towards the PPP level.

Purchasing Power Risk—The inflation-related risk that a dollar returned on an investment today will not be worth as much as a dollar used to purchase the investment in the past.

Pure Play—Investing in a corporation that specializes in one type of product or service.

Purgatory and Hell—An issue whose redemption proceeds are linked to the maturity spot exchange rate of another currency against the currency of denomination. The redemption proceeds are constrained to lie between 0 and 100 percent. *See* Heaven and Hell.

Purpose Loan—Loan used to trade or carry securities subject to the Fed's credit regulations.

Purpose Statement—Form filed with the lender when a loan is collateralized by margin securities.

Put—An option that gives the holder the right to sell a certain amount of securities to the option writer at a specified price for a specified period of time.

Putable—A security whose indenture contains a provision for investor redemption prior to maturity.

Put-Call Parity—Relationship between put and call prices in which the call price is equal to the security price plus the put price minus the present value of the exercise price.

Put Date—The date on which an investor may exercise the right to put a security.

Put Harmless Warrant—A harmless warrant that the investor may put back to the issuer at a pre-designated price at the end of the fifth year. Subsequent investor puts may also be permitted.

Put Price—1) The price at which a put option may be executed. 2) The price, usually par, at which an investor may ask an issuer to purchase a putable bond on the put date.

Put Warrant—A warrant that gives the right to the holder to redeem the underlying security at a specified price and at a specified time.

Pyramiding—Using profits from a position as margin for adding to that position.

Q

Qualified Bid—A bid subject to conditions (e.g., delivery date).

Qualified Legal Opinion—Legal opinion concerning a pending municipal bond issue that expresses reservations about the advisability of the issue, such as when there is a lawsuit in effect that may affect the issue.

Qualified Mortgage—Real estate interest that is eligible as a REMIC asset, including single-family, second mortgages, and multifamily and commercial real estate mortgages. Non-mortgage assets are not eligible. *See* REMIC.

Qualified Opinion—An auditor's qualification to a financial statement or an audit. When there are no qualifications, the opinion is called a clean opinion.

Qualified Replacement Mortgage—Any real estate interest that meets the qualified mortgage definition, and is substituted for a qualified mortgage within three months of REMIC election or for a defective mortgage within two years of REMIC election.

Qualified Reserve Fund—In relation to a REMIC, a fund that is designed to provide credit enhancement for qualifying mortgages, and is reduced when credit claims are paid and as principal pays down. *See* Real Estate Mortgage Investment Conduit.

Qualified Terminable Interest Property (Q-TIP) Trust—Trust in which the surviving spouse receives the decedent's assets, which, upon the death of that spouse, pass on to whomever the original decedent chose.

Qualifying Real Estate Investment—ERISA regulation specifying mortgage asset investments in which a pension fund can invest.

Qualitative Analysis—Security valuation based on non-financial information, such as management expertise, goodwill, and labor relations.

Qualitative Controls—*See* Selective Controls.

Quality—The degree of creditworthiness of a security or issuer, commonly denoted by the rating(s) given to a security. *See* Moody's and Standard & Poor's.

Quantitative Analysis—Security valuation based on financial information.

Quantitative Controls—Monetary policy tools that affect the commercial banking system, including the reserve requirement, discount rate, and open market operations.

Quantity Theory of Money—Monetarist theory that prices are a function of the money supply.

Questioned Trade (QT)—*See* Don't Know.

Quick Asset Ratio—*See* Acid Test Ratio.

Quick Assets—Current assets minus inventory.

Quick Ratio—*See* Acid Test Ratio.

Quid Pro Quo—One thing (of value) for another.

Quiet Period—Ninety-day period, required by the SEC, between an initial public offering and when the underwriters may distribute research about the issuer.

Quotation—A price (bid and/or offer) in a subject market. A quotation is not necessarily the price at which a security can be bought or sold; it is an indication of market levels.

Quoted Margin—The margin over the index rate at which the coupon of a floating rate security is fixed.

Quoted Price—The price of the previous trade in a security.

R

Raider—An investor who attempts to buy a controlling interest in a corporation's stock. *See* Williams Act.

Rally—A rise in prices following a flat or declining trend.

Ramping—Increasing, especially with respect to coupon rate. The coupon on a zero-fixed coupon security, for example, is said to be ramping up. *See* Zero-Fixed Coupon.

Random Walk—A behavior pattern, normally associated with prices or yields, in which the value at one point in time is equal to the previous value plus a number chosen at random. Colloquially, refers to any trading pattern that is inherently unpredictable.

Range—High and low prices of a security over a specified time interval.

Rate Base—For monopolies, a pool of assets upon which rate charges to the public are based. Such assets may consist of capital equipment, property, and capitalized construction costs.

Rate Base/Phase In—Accounting system devised to ease utility rate increases arising from additions to, or capital improvements of, the rate base. When new assets are placed into the pools, the costs are amortized to protect consumers from extraordinarily high rate hikes. Also called *Rate Moderation Plan*.

Rate Cap—1) Maximum rate of interest for a period or lifetime of a loan. 2) A series of put options on a floating interest rate (such as LIBOR, commercial paper, or Treasury bills). A cap agreement specifies the floating rate to be used (e.g., 3-month LIBOR), the length of time of the agreement (maturity), and a predetermined strike level or rate. If rates go above this strike level, the seller of the cap must pay the buyer the difference between the actual rate and the strike rate.

Rate Change—Refers to a change in the mortgage rate offered on FHA-insured and VA-guaranteed loans. Since these loans are packaged into GNMA securities, the rate change affects the current coupon on GNMAs, or the nominal rate at which GNMAs are issued.

Rate Covenant—An agreement in a municipal revenue bond indenture stating that the rate charged by the facility being financed will be sufficient to pay interest and principal on the bond.

Rate Moderation Plan—*See* Rate Base/Phase In.

Rate of Return—Coupon rate divided by the purchase price.

Rating—Any evaluation of a security's investment quality and creditworthiness. The best-known credit rating agencies are Moody's and Standard and Poor's.

Ratio Analysis—The study of a corporation's or government's financial situation by using financial statement ratios and comparing them to those of previous periods or to other corporations. *See* Acid Test Ratio, Capitalization Ratio, Common Stock Ratio, Current Ratio, Preferred Stock Ratio, Price-Earnings Ratio, Quick Ratio, and Return on Equity.

Ratio Bull Spread—Option spread consisting of one long call at one exercise price and two short calls at a higher exercise price. Also called *Neutral Spread.*

Ratio Calendar Spread—An options strategy in which an investor sells an amount of near-term options and buys a different amount of longer-term options with the same strike price.

Rational Expectations—The assumption that investment decisions are made taking all relevant, available information into account.

Ratio Spread—An options strategy in which an investor buys an amount of options and sells a different amount of out-of-the-money options.

Ratio Strategy—An options strategy in which an investor has an unequal number of long and short positions, typically more short options than long options or securities.

Ratio Writing—Writing call options for more securities than one owns. Also called *Variable Ratio Writing.*

Reaction—A fall in the price of a security after a sustained price increase. Also called *Correction.*

Reaganomics—Supply side economic policy introduced by President Reagan in 1981 to spur economic growth and reduce inflation by reducing taxes, government expense, business regulations, and the growth of the money supply.

Real—Refers to property. *See* Tangible.

Real Amount—Face amount of currency, adjusted for inflation. *See* Nominal Amount.

Real Capital—*See* Capital.

Real Economic Growth Rate—*See* Economic Growth Rate.

Real Estate Investment Trust (REIT)—A public corporation that manages real estate assets. *See* Equity REIT and Mortgage REIT.

Real Estate Mortgage Investment Conduit (REMIC)—A mortgage securities vehicle, authorized by the Tax Reform Act of 1986, that holds commercial or residential mortgages and issues securities representing interests in those mortgages. A REMIC can be formed as a corporation, partnership, or segregated pool of assets. The REMIC itself is generally exempt from federal income tax, but the income from the mortgages is reported by investors. For investment purposes, REMIC securities are nearly indistinguishable from CMOs.

Real GNP—Gross national product adjusted for inflation, calculated as money GNP multiplied by the GNP deflator for a base year (currently 1972), divided by the GNP deflator for the current year. *See* Money GNP and the GNP Deflator.

Real Income—Income adjusted for inflation.

Real Interest Rate—The nominal rate of interest minus the inflation rate.

Real Money—Gold held as reserves in bank vaults.

Real Property—Real estate, including land and buildings.

Realizable Tail—The yield at which a synthetic forward money market instrument is purchased. It is created by buying an existing instrument and financing the initial portion of its life with a term repurchase agreement.

Realizable Value—Market value.

Realize—To convert into money. *See* Recognize.

Realized Compound Yield—*See* Realized Return.

Realized Return—The return a bond earns over a stated period of time, based on the purchase price and a reinvestment rate assumption. Also called *Realized Compound Yield.*

Reallowance—The maximum portion of the selling concession that an underwriter may give up, or reallow, to another NASD member, who need not be a syndicate member. The reallowance is specified at the time of pricing. Analogous to concession in the municipal bond market. *See* Concession.

Real Rate of Return—Nominal rate of return minus the inflation rate. Also called *Real Yield. See* Nominal Yield.

Real Yield—*See* Real Rate of Return.

Rebalancing—The periodic re-optimization of a dedicated, immunized, or other structured portfolio, in which the assets and liabilities are realigned by shifting funds to bonds with the most desirable durations and yields.

Recapitalization—1) Issuing new securities in exchange for old ones. 2) Exchange of one type of security for another (e.g., convertible bonds for common stock).

Recast—To recompute the adjustable rate mortgage principal and interest schedule in order to fully amortize the unpaid principal balance over the life of the loan. ARM loans must be recast whenever their interest rate changes.

Receipt Versus Payment (RVP)—Payment for securities when they are received and accepted. *See* Delivery Versus Payment.

Receivable—*See* Account Receivable.

Receive Balance Order (RBO)—*See* Balance Order.

Receivership—Corporate situation in times of financial difficulty, in which the court appoints directors to replace those elected by the stockholders.

Recession—A decline in total physical output that lasts at least six consecutive months. A growth recession is marked by a slowdown rather than a decline in the growth rate.

Recessionary Gap—The difference between aggregate actual demand and the level of aggregate demand necessary to expand output to the level that supports full employment. *See* Inflationary Gap.

Reciprocal Immunity—Supreme Court ruling that the federal government cannot tax interest on state or municipal securities, and state governments cannot tax interest on federal securities.

Recision—To cancel a contract.

Reclamation—A claim for the right to return, or a demand for the return of, securities previously delivered and accepted.

Recognize—To record a gain or loss without necessarily realizing it.

Reconstitution—Reassembling stripped coupon and principal only securities into full coupon securities.

Record Date—The date used by the issuer to record those holders who are entitled to the coupon or dividend payment for a particular period. Also called *Date of Record*.

Recovery—1) A price advance following a decline. 2) An expansion in the business cycle.

Red—Refers to a futures contract month more than 12 months away (e.g., the red June is the June after the next one). So called because the quote listed at the Chicago Board of Trade is surrounded by a red box.

The green June refers to the contract that expires the following year, because its quote is surrounded by a green box.

Redemption—The cancellation of an outstanding debt through a cash payment. Called bonds that are not surrendered cease to earn interest. Also called *Cash Call.*

Redemption Fee—*See* Back-End Load.

Redemption Price—The price at which a bond may be redeemed (at the option of the company) prior to its maturity date. Redemption prices are determined when the bond is issued and are usually based on the original coupon and offering price.

Red Herring—A preliminary prospectus giving the advance details of an expected offering of corporate securities, subject to amendment, with the sale contingent upon clearance by the SEC. So-called because it contains a disclaimer printed in red. Also called *Preliminary Prospectus* and *Preliminary Official Statement.*

Rediscount Rate—*See* Discount Rate.

Reduction Option Loan—Conventional 30-year, fixed rate mortgage with an option to reduce the rate once between the thirteenth and the fifty-ninth monthly payments. The initial rate is slightly above market rates, but the refinancing cost is substantially below typical fees. The refinancing option can be exercised only if interest rates have fallen a specified amount from time of origination.

Reference Bank—A prime bank whose quotations for deposits in money market accounts are used by an agent bank in determining the interest rate on a floating rate instrument.

Reference Rate—A market-determined interest rate benchmark to which the dividend rate of adjustable rate preferred stock is indexed. *See* Implied Dividend Rate.

Refinancing—1) The retirement of existing securities and issuing of new securities to save interest costs, consolidate debt, lengthen maturity, or otherwise alter the capitalization of a company. 2) The prepayment of a mortgage with funds borrowed at a lower interest rate.

Reflation—Restoring deflated prices to higher levels.

Refunding—A redemption with funds raised through the sale of a new issue.

Refunding Protection—A period from issuance during which bonds can not be called with proceeds from lower cost debt. The bonds can be called, however, with cash proceeds from an equity issuance. This refunding protection is typically five years for utility debt and ten years for industrial debt.

Regional Bank—A bank that primarily accepts deposits and makes loans to customers in its geographic region, rather than rely on the national or international money markets as its primary funding source. *See* Money Center Bank.

Regional Holding Company—One of the seven regional telephone companies formed after the breakup of AT&T.

Registered Bond—*See* Registered Security.

Registered in Legal Form—Registered in a name that is not a good street name. When securities are registered in the name of a corporation, they must be accompanied by a corporate resolution to effect a good transfer.

Registered Options Principal (ROP)—Supervisor of registered representatives involved in options account activities.

Registered Representative (RR)—A full-time employee of a New York Stock Exchange member organization who has met the requirements of the exchange. Also called *Account Executive, Customer's Broker,* and *Customer Man.*

Registered Security—A bond registered on the issuing company's books in the name of the owner. Although interest can be collected upon presentation of the coupon, the principal can be transferred only with the endorsement of the registered owner. A fully registered bond pays interest to the owner by check from the issuer's agent. Also called *Nominative Security. See* Bearer Bond.

Registrar—An agent of the borrower who records the ownership of registered securities. *See* Registered Security.

Registration Statement—A document including a prospectus with exhibits prepared primarily by the issuing company, its counsel, and independent accountants, with the help of the managing underwriter and its counsel. The registration statement is filed with the SEC. The registration statement contains information about the securities being registered, the business of the issuer, and the latest financial results of the issuer. *See* Prospectus.

Regressive Tax—A method of taxation in which tax rates decrease with income, or one in which the poor pay a larger percentage of taxable income than the rich. *See* Progressive Tax.

Regular Interest—A class of securities that has fixed terms with regard to interest rate and principal amount. The interest rate cannot be significantly above market rates (e.g., super-premium mortgage strips are not considered regular interests).

Regular Settlement—The customary process by which purchases and sales of securities are determined and the balance paid. Regular settlement of a corporate security is on the fifth full business day after the transaction date; on a government security, it is the first full business day after the trade date. Cash delivery is same day settlement.

Regulated Futures Contract (RFC)—Futures contracts traded on or subject to the rules of an exchange. Regulated futures contracts are marked to market to determine margin account equity.

Regulation A—Securities Act of 1933 regulation exempting new issues of $1.5 million or less from SEC registration. *See* Letter of Notification.

Regulation D—Securities Act of 1933 regulation exempting private placements from SEC registration and defining insiders and purchaser representatives.

Regulation G—Federal Reserve Board regulation limiting the amount of credit extended to a customer for the purpose of purchasing securities by a lender other than a broker, bank, or dealer.

Regulation M—Federal Reserve Board regulation requiring member banks to hold reserves against net borrowings from their foreign branches over a 28-day averaging period.

Regulation Q—Federal Reserve Board regulation limiting the rates banks may pay on savings and time deposits. Time deposits over $100,000 are exempt.

Regulation T—Federal Reserve Board regulation that sets initial margin requirements and defines registered, unregistered, and exempt securities. Initial margin is currently 50 percent for listed securities and 100 percent for unlisted securities. Registered securities are listed on a national exchange, and may be bought or sold short in a margin account. Unregistered securities are not listed, and cannot be traded in a margin account. Exempt securities may be traded in margin accounts; they include U.S. government securities, municipal securities, and World Bank securities.

Regulation U—Federal Reserve Board limit on credit for buying securities on margin.

Regulation Z—Federal Reserve Board truth in lending disclosure requirements.

Rehypothecation—The practice of using a customer's securities as collateral for a bank loan. *See* Hypothecation.

Reintermediation—Transfer of money from debt securities to the banking system.

Reinvestment Rate—The rate at which an investor assumes that cash payments can be reinvested over the life of an issue.

Reinvestment Risk—*See* Risk.

Rejection—Refusal to accept securities delivered to fulfill a contract usually because the securities do not meet the standards of good delivery. *See* Good Delivery.

Relationship Trading—*See* Basis Trading.

Relative Value—The attractiveness of one instrument relative to another measured in terms of risk, liquidity, and return.

Remaining Term—*See* Current Maturity.

Remargining—Meeting a margin requirement.

Remarketed Preferred—Preferred stock whose dividend periods and rates are set through a remarketing process. Available terms are seven-day and 49-day dividend periods with optional and special terms available at the option of the issuer.

REMIC—*See* Real Estate Mortgage Investment Conduit.

Renegotiated Rate Mortgage (RRM)—*See* Rollover Mortgage.

Rentes—French perpetuity bonds, representing the national debt of France.

Reoffer—The syndicate that buys the bonds offered by an issuer is said to reoffer them to the public.

Reopening—The offering by the issuer of an additional amount of an outstanding security.

Repo—*See* Repurchase Agreement.

Repo Rate—*See* Repurchase Rate.

Reporting Level—The point at which a futures speculator is required to file notice with the CFTC for every subsequent trade. *See* Position Limit and Trading Limit.

Repurchase Agreement (RP)—1) A method of borrowing using a security as collateral for a loan. The interest rate and term of the loan are agreed upon in advance, and upon repayment of the loan the same security is returned to the owner. The borrower retains possession of the security and continues to receive any interest payments during the term of the agreement. Also called *Repo* and *Buy Back*. 2) In reference to Federal Reserve actions, a means of temporarily adding to reserves. When the Fed is said to be doing RP, it is lending money (i.e., increasing bank reserves by buying Treasuries from the banks). The Fed buys securities under a contract to sell them back at an agreed price and date. General repurchase agreements mature within one to seven days, the maximum term being 15 days. *See* Dollar Repo and Matched Sales.

Repurchase Book—*See* Matched Book.

Repurchase Rate—The rate at which a holder of securities sells them to an investor with an agreement to repurchase them at a fixed price on a fixed date. The security "buyer" in effect lends the "seller" money for the period of the agreement. Also called *Repo Rate.*

Required Net Yield (RNY)—The amount of interest a servicer sends to FHLMC for each mortgage purchased, which equals the PC coupon plus the management and guarantee fee. RNY is expressed as an annualized percentage of the unpaid principal balance.

Required Rate of Return—The minimum rate of return needed for an investment to break even, or to avoid losing value due to systematic risk.

Reserve—An accounting term meaning any provision for future payments. For example, a corporation can establish a reserve for future tax liabilities, depreciation, pensions, or claims in litigation. Reserves are often confused with funds. *See* Fund.

Reserve Assets—Assets that can be used to satisfy the Fed's reserve requirements. The Federal Reserve Act of 1913 allows for only two kinds of assets: vault cash, which is the currency and coin held by depository institutions, and reserve balances held at Federal Reserve Banks. Also called *High Powered Money.*

Reserve Bank of Australia—Central bank of Australia, which controls and regulates domestic money and bond markets.

Reserve for Depreciation—*See* Accumulated Depreciation.

Reserve Fund—A fund established by a bond issuer that may be used by the trustee to make principal and interest payments or to pay administrative expenses when funds are not otherwise available. Also called *Debt Service Fund.*

Reserve Margin—For electric utilities, the difference between the maximum output of a generating unit and the system load requirement (peak load). Also called *Capability Margin.*

Reserve Requirements—The percentage of deposits that member banks must hold on deposit (at no interest) at the Fed. The requirement is set by the Fed, within limits legislated by Congress. Generally, reserve requirements are higher on demand deposits than on savings deposits. Reserve requirements are changed infrequently.

Reset Frequency—Time between coupon adjustments in floating rate debt.

Reset Margin—The spread by which an investor's net coupon will exceed the index rate at each reset date.

Residual—Cash flows resulting from the difference between the cash inflow generated by a pool of mortgage collateral and the cash outflow necessary to fund bonds that are entirely supported by that collateral. Also called *Excess Cash Flow* and *CMO Equity.*

Residual Interest—*See* Owners' Equity.

Resolution—*See* Indenture.

Resistance Level—The level above which prices tend not to rise.

Resting Order—*See* Limit Order.

Restricted—1) Refers to a margin account in which the equity falls below the Federal Reserve Board initial margin requirement. A restricted account has no loan value, and no money or securities may be withdrawn. *See* Undermargined. 2) Refers to retained earnings not legally available for dividends. 3) Refers to an unregistered security. *See* Letter Security.

Restrictive—Tending to slow down the economy. *See* Expansive.

Restrictive Covenant—*See* Covenant.

Retail—1) Individual investors. 2) An account that does relatively little trading.

Retail Price Index (RPI)—In the United Kingdom, a measure of price changes at the retail level. *See* Consumer Price Index.

Retail Repo—Repurchase agreement between a bank and a depositor.

Retained Earnings—Corporate profits after dividends are paid, which are put back into the business. Also called *Undistributed Profits* and *Earned Surplus*. *See* Shareholders' Equity.

Retention—A syndicate member's underwriting participation that is retained for retail sales, the balance of the underwriting commitment being set aside for the pot.

Retention Requirement—Fed requirement that 50 percent of the proceeds of a sale in a restricted margin account remain in the account.

Retire—To eliminate a debt obligation. A corporation may retire bonds through refunding, a sinking fund, open market purchase, exercising a call, or conversion (exchanging debt for equity).

Retractable—Refers to a bond whose maturity may be shortened, typically with a put option.

Return—1) Capital appreciation plus interest payments, usually expressed as a percentage of initial price. 2) The rate that equates the present value of future cash flows to the purchase price.

Return on Assets (ROA)—A measure of a corporation's performance in using assets to generate earnings, independent of the financing of the assets, calculated as net income plus interest net of taxes divided by average assets. ROA is equal to the profit margin ratio multiplied by the asset turnover ratio. *See* Asset Turnover Ratio.

Return on Equity (ROE)—A measure of a corporation's performance in generating earnings based on shareholders' equity, calculated as net income minus preferred dividends divided by average shareholders' equity. ROE is equal to the profit margin ratio (net of interest and preferred dividends) multiplied by the asset turnover ratio multiplied by the leverage ratio. *See* Leverage Ratio.

Return on Permanent Capital—Earnings before interest and taxes divided by the average of the current and the prior year's short-term debt (including the current portion of long-term debt) plus long-term debt (including capitalized lease obligations) plus deferred taxes plus stockholders' equity (including preferred stock).

Revaluation—Increasing the value of one currency in relation to others.

Revenue—Actual or expected cash inflows from ongoing enterprises or operations.

Revenue Anticipation Note (RAN)—State and municipal notes used to finance current expenditures in anticipation of non-tax revenues.

Revenue Bond—A bond that is funded by revenues from the project being financed (e.g., toll bridges).

Revenue Bond Index—Average yield of 25 particular revenue bonds, each with a maturity of 30 years. Computed and published weekly in the Bond Buyer.

Reversal—1) Arbitrage strategy of buying a call and selling a put with the same expiration and strike price, and selling short the underlying security. 2) A bond swap that is the "reverse" of a prior bond swap. If the initial bond swap consisted of selling bond A and buying bond B, the reversal is the sale of B and the purchase of A.

Reverse Annuity Mortgage (RAM)—A means of receiving fixed annuity payments for some fixed period of time using the equity value of the property as collateral.

Reverse Conversion—A market position of being short the underlying security and buying a call and selling a put on the same security, with both options having the same strike price and expiration date.

Reverse Crush Spread—The sale of futures of a primary commodity (e.g., soybeans) and purchase of futures of products derived from the primary commodity (e.g., soybean oil and meal). *See* Crush Spread.

Reverse Floater—A type of leveraged floater in which the coupon moves inversely with a specified index. The coupon rate is quoted as a relationship between a constant and the index (e.g., 14% - LIBOR). When the coupon resets at a negative multiple of a specified index (e.g., 20% - 2 × LIBOR), the security is called a Reverse Super Floater. Also called *Yield Curve Note* and *Bull Floating Rate Note*.

Reverse Hedge—1) Long a call and short the underlying security. 2) Long a common stock and short a security that can be converted into that common stock. Also called *Chinese Arbitrage*.

Reverse Repurchase Agreement (Reverse RP)—*See* Matched Sale.

Reverse Stock Split—A stock split that decreases outstanding shares.

Reverse Straddle—*See* Short Straddle.

Reverse Super Floater—*See* Reverse Floater.

Reverse Swap—A swap that offsets the interest rate or currency exposure on an existing swap.

Reverse to Maturity—A repurchase agreement in which the term is the same as the maturity of the collateral. The customer has in effect sold the collateral, although it remains on the books.

Reversion—Taking surplus money out of a corporate pension plan to finance other corporate projects.

Revolver—1) *See* Revolving Line of Credit. 2) Credit card holder who pays less than the entire account balance, thereby incurring a finance charge.

Revolving Line of Credit—A line of credit for which the borrower pays a commitment fee and can take down and repay funds on his own schedule. Also called a *Revolver*.

Revolving Period—*See* Non-Amortization Period.

Revolving Underwriting Facility (RUF)—Most commonly used generic acronym to describe a Euronote facility.

Revulsion—Stage of a speculative cycle in which investors seek to sell assets that were the cause of the boom. The sell-off can turn into a panic, during which there may not be enough money for everyone to sell. "Revulsion" against these assets has historically led banks to stop issuing loans that use these assets as collateral, further decreasing liquidity.

Reward—The financial benefit from holding a security. Reward is usually expressed in terms of an expected rate of return.

Rho—The dollar change in the option price with a one percent change in the interest rate.

Rich—Expensive; having a price perceived to be overvalued. Also called *Dear*. *See* Cheap.

Riding the Curve—As a security ages, the investor who owns it is said to ride down the (positively sloped) yield curve.

Right—An option to subscribe to new shares issued by a corporation. Rights enable a stockholder to maintain a proportionate ownership in the corporation.

Right of Payment—Refers to a security's priority in terms of receiving interest payments or dividends and its claims in case of liquidation. Right of payment is ranked as follows: senior debt, senior subordinated debt, subordinated debt, preferred stock, preference stock, common stock.

Rights of Accumulation—The right that related mutual fund investors have to combine their purchases in order to qualify for the minimum sales charge. *See* Breakpoint.

Rising Star—An entity whose debt ratings have significantly improved. *See* Fallen Angel.

Risk—A measure of the probability and/or severity of financial loss. In the fixed income markets there are several types of risk:

Credit Risk: The risk that an issuer will default on its bonds.

Currency Risk: The risk associated with exchange rate fluctuations in the value of a security.

Market Risk: The risk that current interest rates may change and thus adversely affect current market prices of a security.

Liquidity Risk: The risk that an issue will be thinly traded and consequently trade at a wide bid-asked spread.

Prepayment Risk: The risk that a pass-through mortgage security will have an adverse pattern of prepayments (e.g., low prepayments for discount issues, high prepayments for premium issues).

Reinvestment Risk: The risk that an investor will be forced to reinvest cash flow from an issue at substantially lower rates than expected.

Risk can be either systematic or unsystematic. *See* Modern Portfolio Theory, Systematic Risk, and Unsystematic Risk.

Risk-Adjusted—Modified to account for risk. For example, if a yield were lowered to account for the probability of default, it would be a "credit risk-adjusted rate of return."

Risk Arbitrage—Buying shares of a takeover candidate and selling shares of the acquiring corporation.

Risk Aversion—The tendency of investors to avoid risk, or to want to be compensated for taking risks.

Risk-Controlled Arbitrage—A strategy for thrifts that involves buying mortgage-related securities funded by short-term borrowings, typically reverse repurchase agreements. The purchase is then hedged, typically with interest rate swaps, caps and collars, futures, and options, in order to protect against interest rate risk. Also called *Hedged Growth* and *Controlled-Growth Arbitrage.*

Risk Disclosure Statement—A statement required by CFTC Rule 1.55 to be signed by customers of futures brokerage firms prior to commencement of futures trading, indicating that they are aware of the risks inherent in the futures markets.

Risk Free Return—The theoretical return earned on a riskless investment.

Riskless—1) Without credit risk. Treasury issues and government-guaranteed issues are regarded as the only riskless securities. 2) With respect to bond trading, simultaneous buying and selling so as to eliminate market risk.

Risk Premium—The difference between the yield or expected return of a security and the riskless rate. Also called *Excess Return.*

Rocket Bond—A non-PAC tranche of a CMO that consists of several PAC tranches, so that the yield volatility is concentrated in the non-PAC tranche. *See* Planned Amortization Class.

Roll—Selling the previous on-the-run Treasury issue and buying the corresponding new issue during its "when issued" period. The transaction often involves a small yield give-up. *See* On-the-Run and Liquidity.

Roll Down—Closing a futures or options position and opening another with a lower exercise price.

Roll Forward—Closing a near futures or options position and opening a deferred futures or options position.

Rolling Call—A call feature that an issuer can use at any time after a specified date. *See* Stepped Call.

Rolling Down the Curve—As a security ages, it is said to roll down the (positively sloped Treasury) yield curve as it is priced off of progressively shorter Treasury issues.

Rolling Forward the Hedge—When a hedger liquidates a futures position in one delivery month and buys a similar position in a later delivery month. Also called *Switch.*

Rolling Yield—The return from a bond purchased at one yield and sold at a different yield after it has rolled down the yield curve.

Rollover—Taking principal from matured securities and reinvesting it in the same instrument.

Rollover Mortgage (ROM)—A method of financing property with consecutive short-term loans. Each loan is generally three to five years in term. At maturity, the loan is renegotiated (rolled over) at a new rate for the next period. Principal is amortized over the entire period of all loans, which is generally thirty years. Also called a *Renegotiated Rate Mortgage (RRM)*. When there are no restrictions upon the lender as to the rates that may be renegotiated, the ROM is referred to as a Canadian Rollover.

Rollover Price—For a floating rate security, the price at the next coupon date (ex accrued interest).

Rollover Yield—*See* Breakeven Yield.

Roll Up—Closing a futures or options position and opening another with a higher exercise price.

Round Lot—1) An amount of bonds of $100,000 par amount. For trades involving par amounts greater than $100,000, a good delivery requires that the bonds delivered be in units that are multiples of $100,000 or units that can be grouped into blocks of $100,000. 2) Colloquially, the smallest amount of bonds acceptable for dealing, ranging from $100,000 to $5 million, depending on the liquidity of the issue and the size of the institution involved. 3) The smallest amount of bonds traded in a tight market without a price differential or adjustment.

Round Trip—The completed transaction cycle of both buying and selling a security.

Round Turn—Commission for both purchase and sale of a futures contract.

Rule 3b-3—SEC definition of a short sale as the sale of a borrowed security.

Rule 10a-1—SEC short sale rule, stating that a short sale must be made on an uptick.

Rule 10b-2—SEC rule prohibiting the solicitation of orders for a primary or secondary distribution without a prospectus or an offering circular.

Rule 10b-4—SEC rule prohibiting a short tender, or selling short to a person making a tender offer.

Rule 10b-5—SEC rule against securities fraud, including untrue statements and omission of material fact.

Rule 10b-6—SEC rule prohibiting distributors of a security from buying the security or rights to it during the distribution process.

Rule 10b-7—SEC rule limiting the use of an underwriter's stabilizing bid.

Rule 10b-10—SEC rule setting disclosure requirements for trade confirmations.

Rule 10b-13—SEC rule prohibiting a person making a cash tender offer from taking a position in the security being tendered until the offer expires.

Rule 10b-16—SEC rule concerning margin loan disclosure requirements.

Rule 12b-1—SEC rule allowing a mutual fund to deduct an annual amount from its assets to pay for marketing and distribution costs. The charge is called the "12b-1 fee."

Rule 13D—SEC rule requiring disclosure of beneficial interest, or of acquisition of 5 percent or more of any class of registered stock.

Rule 13E—SEC rule prohibiting an issuer from purchasing its own shares during a tender offer. *See* Tender Offer.

Rule 15c2-1—SEC rule concerning margin accounts. *See* Commingling and Hypothecation.

Rule 15c3-1—SEC rule concerning capital requirements for broker-dealers.

Rule 15c3-2—SEC rule concerning credit balances for broker-dealers.

Rule 15c3-3—SEC rule requiring that fully paid securities be segregated and that money on deposit be placed in a special account that can be used by all customers of the broker-dealer.

Rule 16b—*See* Short Swing Rule.

Rule 19b-3—SEC rule prohibiting fixed brokerage commissions.

Rule 144—SEC rule permitting the sale of restricted investment letter stock by affiliated persons in small amounts without first registering the stock with the SEC. The rule is designed to prohibit the creation of public markets in securities of issuers for which adequate current information is not available to the public. It permits the public sale in ordinary trading transactions of limited amounts of securities owned by persons controlling, controlled by, or under common control with the issuer and by persons who have acquired restricted securities of the issuer. For listed stocks, the maximum amount that may be sold is the greater of one percent of the total shares outstanding or the average weekly volume of the past four weeks. For over-the-counter stocks, the maximum is one percent of the total shares outstanding. The limitation on sales applies for 90-day periods.

Rule 237—SEC rule permitting the sale of non-registered, restricted investment letter stock by non-affiliated persons.

Rule 254—SEC rule allowing the sale of securities worth $1.5 million or less without registration.

Rule 396—*See* Nine Bond Rule.

Rule 405—*See* Know Your Customer.

Rule 415—SEC rule permitting shelf registration.

Rule 425—SEC rule requiring that the following statement be on the front cover of every prospectus in capital letters: "These securities have not been approved or disapproved by the Securities and Exchange Commission nor has the Commission passed upon the accuracy or adequacy of this prospectus. Any representation to the contrary is a criminal offense."

Rule 425A—SEC rule requiring that the following statement be on the front or back page of every prospectus: "Until [date] all dealers effecting transactions in the registered securities, whether or not participating in this distribution, may be required to deliver a prospectus. This is in addition to the obligation of dealers to deliver a prospectus when acting as underwriters and with respect to their unsold allotments or subscriptions."

Rule 433—SEC rule allowing a preliminary prospectus, or red herring, to be used before the effective registration date if it contains the same information required in the final prospectus except the offering price and certain other items.

Rule of 69—Formula stating that money invested at r percent per period will double in approximately 69/r + .35 periods.

Rule of 72—Formula stating that money will double in a certain number of years if the rate multiplied by the number of years equals 72 (e.g., money invested at 9 percent will double in 8 years).

Rule of 78—Method used to calculate interest on an installment loan for each month of a year. Assuming equal principal payments, the interest for the first month is 12/78ths of the annual interest, 11/78ths for the second month, 10/78ths for the third month, and so on.

Rules of Fair Practice—NASD rules governing conduct of member institutions, specifically in their transactions with the public.

Run—1) A series of bid and asked quotes. 2) A rapid increase in a security's price. 3) Massive withdrawals of a bank's deposits.

Run Bonds Through the Pot—Should the institutional or dealer pot be clean (sold out), the manager running the books may take unsold securities back from an account and place them into the pot for additional pot distribution.

Running Ahead—When a registered representative improperly trades for his or her own account before filling customer orders.

Run the Books—To administer the marketing, allocation, and payment and delivery of a syndicate offering. Only one manager can run the books.

S

Safe Custody—*See* Custodian.

Safe Harbor—1) Financial action that avoids legal or tax consequences. 2) Shifting investments to a less volatile area of the market. *See* Flight to Quality.

Safekeeping—Segregating or otherwise protecting a customer's fully paid securities. *See* Commingling.

Salary—Annual compensation, not based on hourly rates. *See* Wage.

Sale—Under the Uniform Securities Act, every contract of sale, contract to sell, or disposition of a security or interest in a security for value. *See* Offer.

Sale Date—The date a security is offered in the primary market. *See* Award.

Sales Load—*See* Load.

Sallie Mae (SLMA)—*See* Student Loan Marketing Association.

Same Day Funds—Funds with good value (available for withdrawal) at the end of the business day on which the order to transfer the funds is made. *See* Immediately Available Funds and Clearing House Funds.

Same Day Settlement—Cash settlement.

Samurai Bond—A yen-denominated bond issued in Japan by a foreign issuer.

Sandwich Bond—A tranche of a CMO situated between shorter and longer maturity tranches. The shorter maturity tranche has a targeted minimum sinking fund. The sandwich bond has a targeted maximum sinking fund, with principal payments allocated to both tranches simultaneously. The sandwich bond ensures against maturity extension of the first tranche and offers call protection to later tranches.

Saturday Night Special—A surprise takeover attempt.

Savings and Loan (S&L)—In the United States, an association whose primary business is to take local deposits and to lend those funds for residential mortgages. *See* Thrift.

Savings Bond—Non-transferable U.S. government bond purchased at a fifty percent discount, which has a face value from $50 to $10,000. Income tax on the interest may be paid as it accrues or at redemption. Also called *Series EE. See* Series HH.

Savings Certificate—A deposit of a fixed maturity and amount, usually earning a higher rate of interest than a savings deposit.

Say's Law—Economic law named after Jean Baptiste Say, the French interpreter of Adam Smith, positing that production always provides the income to buy whatever is produced (i.e., supply creates its own demand). Although Malthus took exception to Say's Law, it became economic dogma until Keynes and the Depression. *See* Keynes' Law.

Scale—1) Interest rates of an issuer's serial debt securities. 2) Designation of the number of bonds, maturity date, coupon, and offering price of one issue of a serial bond. 3) Designation of all the bonds, maturities, coupons, and offering prices of a serial debt issue.

Scale Order—An order consisting of several limit orders with different prices. For example, "SELL 100 XYZ 96, and 100 each half point up. Total: 500" means sell 100 XYZ securities at a price of 96, 100 at 96 1/2, and so on until 500 securities are sold.

Scalper—A speculator who trades for his or her own account. A scalper will usually open and close a position during the same trading session. *See* Position Trader.

Scalping—Trading for small gains, usually with day trading rather than position trading. Scalping often has the connotation of unethically recommending a security for trade in order to profit on the consequent price movement. *See* Position Trading.

Scenario Analysis—1) An evaluation method that provides holding period expected returns for a security under various projected interest rate environments. The calculation of expected returns considers the receipt of principal and interest, reinvestment income on interim cash flows, and price appreciation or depreciation of the remaining principal balance over the holding period. 2) More generically, any evaluation method that separately considers the impact of more than one future outcome with respect to some economic event.

Schedule A—*See* Indenture Supplement.

Schedule 13D—Form filed with the SEC by purchasers of at least five percent of an equity security.

Scheduled Redemption Obligation (SRO) Class—*See* Planned Amortization Class.

Schuldscheindarlehen—Loans in the German domestic market that are evidenced by a promissory letter.

Scorched Earth—Any defensive strategy of a takeover target to make itself look unattractive, such as selling assets or restructuring debt. *See* Poison Pill.

Scottish Dividend—*See* Irish Dividend.

Scrip—Certificate representing a fractional share of a corporation.

Scripophily—Collecting old security certificates.

Seasonal—Describes a company whose sales and operations vary regularly due to changes in the climate, vacations, or holidays.

Seasonally Adjusted Statistics—Economic data adjusted for expected seasonal fluctuations. For example, data that take into account that mortgage prepayments typically decrease from January to February or that retail sales typically rise sharply between November and December are seasonally adjusted.

Seasoned—1) A non-exempt security that has been outstanding in the secondary market for over 90 days. 2) A mortgage on which payments have been made for a relatively long period, typically 2-3 years. *See* Vintage.

Seasoned Private—Shares of private preferred stock for which the intent of original investment resale limitations have been met and from which restricted legends have been removed.

Seat—Membership on an exchange.

Secondary Distribution—An offering of existing securities held by the issuing corporation itself or by bondholders.

Secondary Market—Trading in securities after their primary distribution. Also called *After Market.*

Secondary Private Placement—A private placement is an original issue security sold in accord with Regulation D of the Securities Act of 1933; as such it is not required to be registered under the Act. An issue is private in the sense that it can be offered not to the general investing public but only to sophisticated investors (usually insurance companies, banks, and pension funds) who can analyze the security and the issuer. The offerings are made on a private basis. A secondary private placement is an issue that trades from one sophisticated investor to another after it has become seasoned, that is, after the original purchaser has owned it for a period of one to three years. *See* Regulation D.

Secondary Transaction—Sale of a security from one party to another, neither of which is the issuer.

Secondary Underwriting Commitment—*See* Primary Underwriter.

Second Generation Duration—A measure of duration that discounts cash flows at the yields of zero coupon bonds that mature with each cash flow, rather than at the yield to maturity of the security.

Second Liberty Bond Act—Congressional Act of 1917 that prohibited the issuance of U.S. Treasury bonds with a coupon greater than 4 1/4%. The Act also limited the outstanding total face value of obligations issued under authority of the Act or guaranteed as to principal and interest by the U.S. government to an amount set by Congress. Obligations issued on a discount basis and subject to redemption prior to maturity at the option of the owner are included in the statutory debt limit at current redemption values.

Second Market—Over-the-counter transactions in unlisted securities by registered broker-dealers. *See* Primary Market.

Sector—1) A group of securities with similarities (e.g., industry type, coupon rate, maturity date and/or rating). 2) Group of the population exhibiting similar economic behavior.

Sectoral Inflation—*See* Bottleneck Inflation.

Sector Rotation—Timing the holding of securities to the parts of the business cycle during which they have historically performed well.

Secular—In the context of the bond market, secular is used literally to mean once in a generation. A secular change in interest rates would be large and unusual.

Secular Trend—A long-term movement in the price of a security or of interest rates, which is not related to seasonal or technical factors. *See* Cyclical Trend.

Secured Debt—Debt backed by specified assets or revenues of the borrower. If there is an event of default, the lenders can force the sale of such assets to meet their claims. *See* Debenture.

Secured Lease Obligation Bond (SLOB)—A bond that is secured by a lien on, and security interest in, a utility, which is payable from rentals and leases.

Securities Act of 1933—A law designed to ensure that new securities offered to the public are clearly and completely described in the registration statement and prospectus. The SEC does not guarantee that the statements are accurate, but attempts to make certain that all relevant information is fully disclosed.

Securities and Exchange Commission (SEC)—An agency created by Congress to provide laws for the protection of investors in security transactions. The SEC administers the Securities Act of 1933, the Securities Exchange Act of 1934, the Trust Indenture Act, the Investment Company Act, the Investment Advisers Act, and the Public Utility Holding Company Act. Members of the SEC are appointed for a five-year term by the President with the advice and consent of the Senate. They must engage in the full-time business of the Commission.

Securities Exchange Act of 1934—A law that extended the disclosure principle to trading in existing securities. It also regulates broker-dealers, exchanges, and corporate insiders. This act established the Securities and Exchange Commission. *See* Williams Act.

Securities Industry Automation Corporation (SIAC)—Jointly owned subsidiary of the New York Stock Exchange and the American Stock Exchange that provides communication services and computer systems for the two organizations.

Securities Investor Protection Act (SIPA)—Congressional Act of 1970 that created the Securities Investor Protection Corporation (SIPC). SIPC provides protection to customers of investment firms (maximum $500,000 per customer, $100,000 for cash claims).

Securitization—The process that structures non-tradable financial transactions such as bank loans into tradable securities. *See* Asset Backed Security and Collateralized Mortgage Obligation.

Section 8 Program—Government program that subsidizes rent payments made by low-income individuals under Section 8 of the U.S. Housing Code.

Security—Any document that can be traded for value. A security is an instrument of ownership or debt, such as stocks and bonds, used to finance government and corporate entities. Fixed annuities, life insurance or endowment policies, IRA and Keogh plans, commodity futures contracts, and shares issued by non-profit organizations are not securities.

Seek a Market—Look for a trade.

Segregation—Keeping customer accounts separate. *See* Commingling, Hypothecation, and Rule 15c3-3.

Selective Controls—Monetary policy tools used to control particular sectors of the economy. The only selective control currently in use is the margin requirement. Also called *Qualitative Controls*. *See* Quantitative Controls.

Self Regulatory Organization (SRO)—An association or organization such as the National Association of Securities Dealers that sets standards for and regulates the activities of the securities and commodities industries. The national securities and commodoties exchanges are also considered SROs. *See* Exchange and National Association of Securities Dealers (NASD).

Self-Supporting—Refers to a bond used to finance a project that needs no tax support other than a specific tax for that project.

Sellers' Inflation—*See* Cost-Push Inflation.

Seller's Market—Market in which demand far exceeds supply.

Seller's Option—An option allowing delivery to be made at the office of the purchaser on or after the sixth full business day following the trade, but prior to or on the expiration date of the option. Seller's options are not used with Treasury securities.

Selling Agreement—An agreement between the borrower and each member of the selling group specifying the selling restrictions imposed upon the initial distribution of the securities.

Selling Climax—A downward price trend that shows a sudden increase in volume and consequently a relatively large decrease in price.

Selling Concession—The portion of the gross spread paid to an underwriter for each bond or share of stock it retains for distribution. Analogous to the "takedown" in the municipal bond market.

Selling Group—The group of securities dealers that receives securities less the selling concession from the managing underwriter for distribution at the public offering price.

Selling Hedge—*See* Short Hedge.

Selling Off—Selling securities to avoid losses due to further price declines.

Selling Period—The period of time, stipulated by the book running manager, in which new issue orders are taken from both syndicate and non-syndicate members. *See* Subscription.

Selling Restriction—Any limitation imposed upon the managers and selling group of a new issue.

Selling Short Against the Box—Selling short a security an investor owns, but delivering a borrowed security. This may be done to postpone the realization of capital gains, or when the long and short positions are in different accounts.

Selling the Basis—Selling a cash bond and buying an appropriate number of futures contracts (as determined by the delivery factor).

Selling the Spread—*See* Bear Spread.

Selling the Yield Curve—A duration-weighted spread trade consisting of buying a short maturity and selling a long maturity security to take advantage of an anticipated steepening of the yield curve. *See* Buying the Yield Curve.

Sell-Out—1) When a new issue is fully distributed. 2) The sale of a security to complete delivery of a failed transaction. If the original buyer refuses to accept a good delivery, the seller can, on notification to the buyer and after a period of time, effect a sell-out through a third party. *See* Buy-In. 3) Liquidation of a margin account, when an investor fails to meet a margin call.

Sell Stop—*See* Stop Order.

Sell the Book—Investor's order to a broker to sell as much of a security as possible at current prices.

Sell the Fact—*See* Buy Bullish News.

Semiannual Yield—*See* Yield.

Semi-PAC—*See* Targeted Amortization Class.

Senior Security—The class of securities that occupies the highest priority claim for principal and interest or dividend payments.

Senior/Subordinated Pass-Through—A pass-through security in which claim to the collateral pool is divided into two classes. The senior, or A, class has priority over the subordinated, or B, class. In the event that the collateral loans default, losses are absorbed first by the B piece, thus providing credit protection to the A piece. Also called *A/B Structure.*

Senior/Subordinated Security—A security whose priority in terms of right of payment is between that of a senior issue and a subordinated issue of the same issuer.

Sensitivity—A measurement of how much one variable changes in relation to another. For example, price sensitivity refers to how much a security changes in price for a given change in market yield.

Sentiment Indicator—Any measure of the mood (bullish or bearish) of the market. *See* Contrarian.

Separate Account—The account used with a variable annuity in which investors' payments are invested in securities. The securities that comprise a separate account are kept separate from the insurer's investments.

Separately Traded Registered Interest and Principal Security (STRIPS)—Treasury zero coupon security. The cash flows are based on the principal or interest payments of Treasury bonds. Coupon STRIPS are available in physical or certificate form.

Serial Note (SN)—GNMA pass-through security program in which pools of single family mortgages are used to collateralize 100 to 200 consecutively numbered notes. As principal is retired on the underlying mortgages, the notes are retired sequentially.

Serial Security—An issue of securities consisting of a series of blocks of securities maturing sequentially, or serially. Each block may have a different coupon and issue price, but the entire issue is covered by the same prospectus and documentation.

Serial Sinking Fund—*See* Pro Rata Sinking Fund.

Series—1) A class of options with the same expiration date and exercise price. 2) A set of bonds issued at different times (as opposed to bonds, whose issues mature periodically). 3) The designation that distinguishes one CMO and its tranches from another CMO of the same issuer. A CMO series is typically noted by a letter (e.g., CMSC Series A) or a number (e.g., ASW Series 1). Each series of a CMO issuer is unique, having different collateral and various coupons and maturities as set forth in its prospectus supplement.

Series E—Government savings bonds issued from World War II to December 31, 1979.

Series EE—*See* Savings Bonds.

Series HH—Government savings bonds that pay interest semiannually, acquired only in exchange for Series EE bonds (prior to 1982, Series HH bonds could be purchased directly). Also called *Current Income Bonds. See* Series EE.

Series Supplement—*See* Indenture Supplement.

Servicing—1) The administrative and record-keeping functions performed by mortgage lenders. The servicer receives a fee for sending payment notices, keeping track of the principal balance, ensuring that property taxes and mortgage insurance are paid, and remitting payments to mortgage investors. 2) The equivalent functions for loans other than mortgages, such as automobile loans and credit card receivables.

Servicing Fee—The fee paid to the servicer of a mortgage or other loan. It is usually a fixed percentage of the outstanding principal balance of the loan, and is taken from the interest portion of the payment.

Settle—*See* Clear.

Settlement—An arrangement between brokerage houses for payment or receipt of cash or securities. Settlement may be handled through a clearing corporation.

Settlement Date—The date a transaction is completed; the customer is debited or credited normally five business days after the trade date for corporates, the next day for governments.

Settlement Price—The price received for a security or commodity delivered in satisfaction of a futures contract. The settlement price is determined each trading day as the general price level at which the contract was trading at the close of trading (although it is not necessarily the price of the last trade).

Several—In the context of a guarantee, for which there is more than one guarantor, it is the limitation of each guarantor's liability to only that portion of the debt it has guaranteed. *See* Joint and Several.

Severally and Jointly—*See* Eastern Account.

Severally but not Jointly—Refers to a syndicate in which underwriters are responsible only for their own portion of unsold securities. Also called *Western Account.*

Shadow Calendar—Issues registered with the SEC but with no effective date. *See* Effective Date.

Shadow Market—Trading in derivative securities, such as futures and options.

Shakeout—1) When speculators are forced to sell at a loss. 2) When several competing corporations go out of business, leaving fewer, more efficient competitors.

Share—Unit of common stock or equity.

Share Adjusted Broker Remarketed Equity Shares (SABRES)—Preferred stock whose dividend periods and rates are set through a remarketing process. Dividend periods may range from one day to infinity.

Shared Appreciation Mortgage (SAM)—A mortgage in which the lender receives some percentage of any appreciation in the value of the property, upon sale or maturity of the loan, in return for offering the borrower a below market interest rate.

Shareholders' Equity—Total assets minus total liabilities of a corporation. Shareholders' equity consists of contributed capital and retained earnings. Also called *Net Worth. See* Retained Earnings.

Shark Repellant—A change in a corporation's charter designed to make the corporation less attractive to a raider.

Shelf Registration—The sale of securities on a continuous basis with various maturities and interest rates, allowed by SEC Rule 415. When an issuer expects to enter the market several times during the year, an official statement is developed that contains information not expected to change over the course of that year. When the issuer does come to market, it supplements the Master Official Statement with information specific to the issue. This process bypasses the original filing step and allows the issue to be brought to market faster.

Shibosai Bond—A foreign bond placed privately in Japan. *See* Samurai Bond.

Shipping Certificate—Delivery paper for plywood in its futures contract.

Shogun Bond—U.S. dollar bond issued in Japan.

Shop—1) Money market or bond dealer. 2) To look for a better bid or offer after having received a firm bid or offer from a dealer.

Short—To become an ower; to have sold without ownership in anticipation of subsequently purchasing at a lower price.

Short Against the Box—A perfect hedge, with offsetting long and short positions in the same security, sometimes used to delay the tax consequences of the long position.

Short Bond—Bond with a short current maturity.

Short Book—*See* Unmatched Book.

Short Coupon—1) Security whose first coupon period is less than six months. 2) Bond with a relatively short remaining maturity.

Short Covering—The action taken by a trader or investor in buying securities previously sold short and thereby closing out a short position.

Short Exempt—A short sale that need not be made on a plus tick, because it is part of an arbitrage transaction.

Shortfall—The amount by which a scheduled payment is less than the amount anticipated.

Short Hedge—Strategy to protect against falling prices, such as selling call options, buying put options, or selling futures. Also called *Selling Hedge*. *See* Long Hedge.

Short Interest—Total short positions in listed securities (i.e., both regular shorts and shorts against the box).

Short Interest Ratio—The average number of days of trading, at a security's average volume, needed to equal a security's short position.

Short Interest Theory—Theory that when the short interest exceeds 1 1/2 to 2 times the security's average daily volume, the price of that security will rise.

Short Leg—A short position that is part of a hedge.

Short Position—A position established by selling borrowed securities.

Short Sale—The sale of a borrowed security with the expectation of its repurchase at a lower price.

Short Squeeze—1) Being unable to cover a short position. 2) Rising prices resulting from short covering rather than fundamental demand. Also called *Bear Squeeze*.

Short Straddle—Straddle in which the investor sells put and call options. Also called *Reverse Straddle*.

Short Swing Rule—Rule 16b of the 1934 Securities and Exchange Act that prohibits insiders and owners of 10% or more of a corporation's stock from buying low and selling high (or vice versa) within six months. *See* Insider.

Short Tender—Illegal practice of using borrowed securities to accept a tender offer. *See* Rule 10b-4.

Short Term—Refers to obligations with a maturity of less than one year.

Short-Term Auction Rate (STAR) Preferred Stock—Preferred stock whose dividend rate is adjusted every seven weeks through a Dutch auction. With yields adjusted this frequently, STARPs trade at or near par, providing a current market return.

Short-Term Note Issuance Facility (SNIF)—Generic term for Euronote facility. Also called *Revolving Underwriting Facility*.

Short the Basis—Strategy of buying a futures contract and selling the underlying commodity or security.

Short the Board—Sell futures listed on the Chicago Board of Trade.

Side by Side—Trading a security and an option on that security on the same exchange.

Side of the Market—Long or short.

Sideways Market—A market characterized by narrow price movements. Also called *Flat Market.*

Sight Draft—Draft payable upon presentation.

Simple Interest—Interest calculated only on the original principal amount. Compound interest is calculated on the original principal amount as well as on accrued interest.

Simple Margin (SM)—A refinement to Spread for Life (SFL) to calculate yield spreads on floating rate securities. Like SFL, SM has been replaced by YTM Spread. *See* YTM Spread.

Simple Option—An option contract for which the exercise price and the amount of underlying securities are fixed. *See* Complex Option.

Simple Yield to Maturity—A measure of a bond's yield commonly used in the Japanese domestic market. It assumes that any capital gain or loss occurs uniformly over the life of the bond.

Simultaneous Transaction—*See* Riskless.

Sin Bonds—Alcohol and tobacco company debt.

Singapore Interbank Offered Rate (SIBOR)—The posted rate at which prime banks offer to make Asian dollar deposits available to other prime banks.

Single Family (SF)—Refers to mortgages on one- to four-family dwellings.

Single Issuer Pool—*See* Custom Pool.

Single Monthly Mortality (SMM)—A prepayment model originally developed as an alternative to FHA experience. The SMM rate of a mortgage pool is the percentage of outstanding mortgages assumed to terminate each month. Unlike the FHA model, the SMM model assumes that a pool of mortgages will prepay at a fixed percentage rate, regardless of the age of the mortgages. SMM is more accurate for high coupon pass-throughs, which are influenced more by interest rate levels than by the age of the underlying mortgages. Other advantages of SMM are that it is mathematically simple and does not need to be updated annually. Other prepayment models, such as CPR and CPP, are similar to SMM, but express prepayments on an annual basis. CPR and CPP differ from each other in the way they annualize the SMM figures.

Single Point Adjustable Rate Preferred—Preferred stock whose dividend is reset relative to a single reference rate. These issues usually reset quarterly, although some reset more frequently. Single point reference rates include three-month Treasury bill, 60-day AA commercial paper composite, and three-month LIBOR.

Sinker—Bond with a sinking fund.

Sinking Fund—Money, either cash or an acceptable substitute, regularly set aside by a company out of its earnings at stated intervals to redeem all or part of its long-term debt as specified in the indenture. The creation of a sinking fund provides for an orderly amortization of debt over the life of an issue. A cash sinking fund can be satisfied by cash or bonds purchased in the open market or called at the sinking fund call price. A property additions sinking fund is generally satisfied by pledging a stated portion of the value of unmortgaged property. Most indentures restrict the issuer to calling a pro rata amount of each series eligible for the sinking fund. A funnel sinking fund allows the issuer to satisfy the entire sinking fund requirement with any series. *See* Canadian Sinking Fund.

Size—1) The number of securities available. "In size" means the number is large. 2) To determine the amount of securities available for trading.

Skip-Day Settlement—Settlement of a trade one business day after the normal settlement date.

SLD Last Sale—Sold Last Sale. Signifies that a security has been sold for a price significantly higher than that of the previous transaction.

Sleeper—An overlooked investment opportunity. Also called *Sleeping Beauty*.

Sleeping Beauty—A potential takeover target.

Slippage—Side effect of monetary policy that prevents it from achieving its desired effect. *See* Leakage.

Slow Asset—Asset that cannot be liquidated without a loss. *See* Under Water.

Slow Pay—A pass-through security that has prepaid more slowly than average pass-through securities with similar collateral and coupon. This prepayment experience does not necessarily indicate future prepayment patterns.

Small Business Administration (SBA)—Government agency that provides loans to small businesses, whose debt is backed by the full faith and credit of the U.S. government.

Small Investor—Investor who typically trades in odd lots.

Small Order Execution System (SOES)—Automated system for executing orders used in the over-the-counter market. *See* Automated Order Entry System.

Snake—Superseded by the European Monetary System, a colloquial term for an agreement among certain members of the European Economic Community to link their currencies to each other and thus permit them to trade only within a relatively narrow range of exchange rates.

Snowball—When a price trend is intensified by trading pressure.

Snugging—Refers to Federal Reserve operations that tighten the money supply.

Social Goods—Goods and services that benefit society as a whole, such as the armed services and interstate highways.

Soft—1) Describes profits that are declining, or at least not increasing. 2) Describes a market with more supply than demand, wide bid-offer spreads, inactive trading, and declining prices. Also called *Buyer's Market*.

Soft Currency—*See* Hard Currency.

Soft Dollars—*See* Hard Dollars.

Soft Money—*See* Fiat Paper.

Solvency—Ability to meet financial obligations.

South—Slang for a decrease in a variable, such as risk, yield, or income.

Sovereign—A security issued by a foreign government outside of its capital market.

Sovereign Immunity—An historical doctrine of law in operation in certain jurisdictions under which sovereign governments may not be sued or their assets seized. In certain instances, a sovereign government may waive its immunity, or its immunity with respect to commercial activities may be limited by local law.

Sovereign Risk—Any risk associated with the government of the country in which there is an investment. Also called *Country Risk*.

Special Advances Rate—One of three discount rates at which Dutch commercial banks can borrow from the Dutch central bank. The other two rates are the Discount Rate and the Secured Loans Rate. The Special Advances Rate is available only to banks holding Treasury securities and State loans as collateral.

Special Arbitrage Account—Margin account for hedging activity, which typically has lower margin requirements than regular margin accounts.

Special Assessment Bond—Bond payable from tax assessments against those who will benefit from the project being financed.

Special Bracket—The group of underwriters that appears between the manager(s) and the major bracket and whose members underwrite the largest amount of securities after the manager(s).

Special Depository—Bank in which the Treasury deposits proceeds from the sale of federal securities.

Special Drawing Rights (SDR)—A composite currency unit designed by the International Monetary Fund (IMF) and based upon a standard basket valuation system. Special drawing rights are reserves held in the form of accounting entries in the IMF. As such, they can be used, like foreign currencies and gold, to make international payments. Also called *Paper Gold*.

Specialist—Member of an exchange whose function is to maintain an orderly market. Specialists are obliged to act as both agent and principal. As agent, a specialist receives orders from broker-dealers, enters them in a book, and executes them if and when the market reaches appropriate levels. As principal, a specialist trades for his or her own account, making bids and offers when there are none in the market.

Specialist's Quote—*See* Bid-Asked Spread.

Specialist's Sale—The sale of a large block of stock by private placement that occurs off the floor.

Special Miscellaneous Account (SMA)—A margin sub-account of funds in excess of the margin requirement that may have resulted from an increase in market value, dividends, or sale of securities. A customer is not free to withdraw funds from a special miscellaneous account without the broker's permission.

Special Offer—A sale of a large block of stock in the secondary market announced on the consolidated tape, in which the sale's price is fixed by the selling member, and buyers are limited to New York Stock Exchange members.

Special Order Routing and Execution System (SOREX)—Automated system for executing orders used on the Pacific Coast Stock Exchange. *See* Automated Order Entry System.

Special Purpose Vehicle—An entity that buys assets from an originator and insures debt securities collateralized by the assets. Special purpose vehicles used for credit securitization are typically corporations, trusts, partnerships, or REMICs. *See* Grantor Trust.

Special Redemption—A call feature allowing for the retirement of principal earlier than scheduled. A special redemption in corporate securities typically occurs when interest rates have declined, allowing the issuer to retire relatively high coupon bonds by issuing new bonds with a lower coupon. A special redemption in mortgage-related securities occurs when the cash flow generated from the underlying collateral is insufficient to support scheduled principal and interest payments; the amount of principal redeemed is limited to the amount that would have been retired at the next scheduled payment date. In the latter case, it is also called Calamity Call.

Specials—Securities that are in great demand.

Special Tax Bond—A bond secured by a special tax, typically on luxury items.

Specie—Coined money.

Specific Issues Market—The market in which dealers do reverse repos in securities they expect to short.

Specific Option—An option for which only one specific security is deliverable when the option is exercised.

Specific Risk—Risk associated with individual securities, as opposed to the market. *See* Unsystematic Risk and Extra-Market Risk.

Speculator—High risk investor.

Spike—Burst in prepayment activity, usually not sustainable and often occurring after a decline in interest rates.

Spillover—An indirect benefit.

Spiv—A speculator with very short-term investment horizons.

Split Offering—An issue with different kinds of bonds (e.g., serial and term bonds, or primary and secondary distribution in the same offering).

Split Rating—Different credit ratings given to the same security by different rating agencies.

Sponsor—1) Underwriter of a mutual fund. 2) A host entity whose duty is to manage the investment of pension funds in a responsible manner.

Spot—*See* Actuals.

Spot Delivery—Delivery at the time the contract is made.

Spot Market—Market in which trades have immediate delivery. Also called Cash Market.

Spot Month—*See* Cash Market.

Spot Price—1) The price of a security or commodity in the cash market, especially for securities or commodities that underlie various futures contracts. 2) The price of the spot month on a futures contract.

Spot Rate—1) Any prevailing money market yield. 2) Any prevailing currency exchange rate. 3) Theoretical Treasury STRIPS yield at which neither a profit nor a loss is generated by stripping on-the-run Treasury issues.

Spot Rate Curve—Yield curve in which every point represents the yield to maturity of a zero coupon bond.

Spread—1) The yield or price differential between two different securities. 2) Underwriting spread; the difference between the price to the public and the issuer. 3) The difference between the bid and the asked price or yield in the quotation of a security. 4) Simultaneous purchase and sale of different but related futures contracts. 5) The difference in premium between the purchase and sale of two option contracts. 6) The margin over an index of a floating rate security.

Spread Banking—Commercial bank strategy of matching assets and liabilities and profiting from the spread between the interest rate at which it lends and borrows money.

Spread Duration—A measure of the sensitivity of price to a change in the spread or effective margin above the index of a floating rate security.

Spread for Life (SFL)—A calculation of the spread over the index rate each year from the settlement date until the maturity date of a floating rate security. SFL requires no forecasting of interest rates. Call dates are substituted for floaters trading at a premium, and put dates are used for those at a discount. SFL has been replaced by YTM. *See* Yield to Maturity for Floating Rate Securities.

Spreading—The simultaneous purchase and sale of different futures contracts.

Spread Load Contractual Plan—A periodic investment program in which the load (sales charge) is equally distributed among monthly payments.

Spread Option—A long put and a long call with the same expiration and different exercise prices.

Spread Order—An order to buy and sell two related futures contracts. *See* Intermarket Spread and Intercommodity Spread.

Spread Position—The simultaneous purchase and sale of options on the same underlying security, differing only in maturity and/or strike price.

Spread Price—Price calculated on a security by adding a margin to the price of another security.

Spread-to-Maturity—A measure of return from a floating rate note relative to that of its index rate, calculated by discounting future cash flow on a bond basis. *See* Discount Margin and Simple Margin.

Squeeze—*See* Short Squeeze.

Stabilization—The process by which a lead manager supports the immediate secondary market performance of a new issue of securities. Stabilization can be accomplished as follows: 1) the lead manager may over-allot securities (i.e., go short), the shortfall being covered through secondary market purchases by the lead manager; and/or 2) the lead-manager may go long for the syndicate account, the long position being subsequently either distributed to the syndicate or sold in the secondary market for the account of the syndicate. Stabilization may be used only to prevent or retard a price decline. If an issuer intends to stabilize the price of a security during distribution, this fact must be disclosed on the inside front cover of the prospectus. The broker-dealer must notify the SEC when stabilization begins (within three days) and when it is terminated. *See* Rule 10b-7.

Stabilizing Bid—The bid that the manager running the books keeps posted on the specialist's book during syndication. The purpose of the bid is to prevent the price of the security from going below the issue price while the offering is still in syndicate. *See* Run the Books.

Stag—To buy and sell a security quickly, without paying the full price.

Stagflation—Economic condition characterized by slow growth, high unemployment, and inflation.

Staggering Maturities—Investing in securities with a wide range of maturities, to hedge market risk.

Stagging—Applying for a new U.K. issue that is expected to be over-subscribed on the expectation of selling at a profit on the first trading day.

Stagnation—Slow economic growth.

Stale Date—The current maturity of a swap when that maturity renders the swap illiquid (e.g., eight years and three months).

Standard & Poor's (S&P)—A U.S. credit rating agency. S&P's debt rating is a "current assessment of the creditworthiness of an obligor with respect to specific obligations where creditworthiness is the capacity to make timely payments of interest and principal." The ratings are attached to individual bonds. S&P defines its rating categories as follows, allowing for gradations within categories:

AAA—Debt rated 'AAA' has the highest rating assigned by S&P. Capacity to pay interest and repay principal is extremely strong.

AA—Debt rated 'AA' has a very strong capacity to pay interest and repay principal and differs from the highest rated issues only to a small degree.

A—Debt rated 'A' has a strong capacity to pay interest and repay principal although it is somewhat more susceptible to the adverse effects of changes in circumstances and economic conditions than debt in higher rated categories.

BBB—Debt rated 'BBB' is regarded as having adequate capacity to pay interest and repay principal. Whereas it normally exhibits adequate protection parameters, adverse economic conditions or changing circumstances are more likely to lead to a weakened capacity to pay interest and repay principal for debt in this category than in higher rated categories.

BB   Debt rated 'BB', 'B', 'CCC', or 'CC' is regarded, on balance,
B   as predominately speculative with respect to capacity to pay
CCC interest and repay principal in accordance with the terms of
CC   the obligation. 'BB' indicates the lowest degree of speculation and 'CC' the highest degree of speculation. While such debt is likely to have some quality and protective characteristics, these are outweighed by large uncertainties or major risk exposure to adverse conditions.

C—This rating is reserved for income bonds on which no interest is being paid.

D—Debt rated 'D' is in default, and payment of interest and/or principal is in arrears.

Standard & Poor's 500 Index—*See* Market Index.

Standard Basket—System of valuation of a composite currency whereby the value of one unit is deemed to be equal to the sum of the values of specific amounts of stated currencies. *See* European Currency Unit.

Standard Prepayment Assumption (SPA)—*See* PSA Standard Prepayment Model.

Standby Commitment—1) In mortgage sales, a loan purchase commitment by an investor for which the mortgage banker pays a non-refundable commitment fee and retains the right, but not the obligation, to deliver such mortgages. Also called *Standby Contract.* 2) An underwriter's promise to purchase unsold securities. Also called *Standby Underwriting Agreement.*

Standby Underwriting Agreement—*See* Standby Committment.

Standstill Return—Annualized return on a covered call position, assuming the price of the bond remains constant and the option expires at its intrinsic value. *See* Yield Standstill Return.

State and Local Government Series (SLGS)—Non-marketable U.S. government securities that the Treasury sells to municipal governments, typically deposited in an escrow account in order to refund bonds.

Stated Delay—*See* Payment Delay.

Stated Maturity—The date on which a security is originally scheduled to repay principal.

Stated Value—Value of a corporation's stock that is credited to the capital stock account.

Statement of Cash Flows—A financial statement that focuses not on net income and net worth but on available cash. The statement proceeds from beginning cash to ending cash.

Statement of Changes in Financial Position (SCFP)—A financial statement that focuses not on net income and net worth but on available cash. The statement lists the source of funds and the use of funds. Also called *Funds Flow*. This statement is being superceded by the Statement of Cash Flows.

Statutory Underwriter—*See* Involuntary Underwriter.

Statutory Voting—Corporate voting procedure in which shareholders cast one vote per share owned for or against board of director nominees. *See* Cumulative Voting.

Steenth—One-sixteenth of a point. Also called *Teenie.*

Step Down Floating Rate Note—A floating rate note whose margin over the index rate decreases over time.

Stepped Call—A call option that may be exercised only on coupon payment dates after the first call date. *See* Rolling Call.

Stepped Coupon—A type of deferred interest security whose coupon resets at specified intervals to specified interest rates. *See* Deferred Interest Security and Zero-Fixed Coupon.

Stepped Up Put Notes—Short-term (3-5 year) notes with a coupon lower than current levels. The investor has the option to extend the note at a higher coupon.

Step Up Floating Rate Note—A floating rate note whose margin over the index rate increases over time.

Sterilization—Domestic monetary policy intended to offset international policy. For example, after selling dollars and buying yen to bolster the yen against the dollar, Japan's central bank engaged in open market operations to put more yen in circulation.

Stickering—Supplementing an official statement, so called because the new information is printed on paper with an adhesive backing and stuck onto the official statement.

Sticky Deal—A difficult underwriting to market.

Stimulative—Tending to speed up the economy.

Stochastic Duration—Duration adjusted to reflect the yield volatility of a security. Stochastic duration compensates for the assumption of parallel yield curve changes.

Stock—1) Ownership of a corporation. A share of common stock is a claim on the earnings and assets of a corporation. Common stock confers voting rights. Preferred stock confers no voting rights but has a senior claim on earnings and assets. 2) In the U.K. domestic market, it refers to specific fixed income Treasury securities. 3) In the context of local authority stock, the term refers to securities with an initial maturity of more than five years. 4) Inventory.

Stock Ahead—When more than one order for stock at the same price arrives at an exchange simultaneously and one of the orders cannot be executed. In this case, New York Stock Exchange priority rules state that the larger order must be executed first. The broker of the smaller order receives notice that the trade was not completed because there was "stock ahead."

Stock Clearing Corporation (SCC)—A means of receiving and delivering physical securities through a central clearing corporation. This is commonly called the Envelope System. Securities are placed in envelopes and are deposited with the clearing house for distribution to members and non-members of the New York Stock Exchange between the hours of 9:00 a.m. and 11:30 a.m.

Stock Dividend—A dividend payment made in the form of additional shares, which results in a debit to retained earnings and a credit to capital stock accounts in the amount of the market value of the issued shares.

Stock Exchange—A physical location where trading in listed securities is carried out by professional members of the stock exchange. *See* Listing.

Stockholder of Record—Person shown on the issuing company's books as owning stock.

Stockholders' Equity—*See* Shareholders' Equity.

Stock Index Arbitrage—Simultaneous purchase of stock index futures and sale of underlying stocks in the index, or vice versa, to take advantage of temporary discrepancies in prices.

Stock Index Future—A futures contract, the value of which is based on general market performance or on a specific market index, such as the New York Stock Exchange Composite Index or Standard & Poor's 500 Index. Settlement of stock index futures is in cash.

Stock Jobbing—Eighteenth-century British term denoting every kind of activity in the market. The term soon acquired pejorative overtones of self-interest and corruption, as in Defoe's 1701 pamphlet *The Villainy of Stock-Jobbers.*

Stock Repurchase—Corporate strategy to buy back common shares, typically when the stock is undervalued or when the company wants to increase its control.

Stock Split—An increase in outstanding common shares resulting from the distribution of additional shares to shareholders at no cost. A stock split decreases the value per share.

Stock-Value Ratio—1) Total market value of a corporation's capital stock divided by the par value of its funded debt. 2) Total market value of a corporation's common stock divided by the total par value of all bonds plus preferred stock.

Stop—1) To agree to trade a specific block of securities at a certain price or better. 2) In a Treasury auction, the last competitive bid accepted (i.e., the bid with the highest yield or lowest price).

Stop Limit Order—An order to buy or sell at the limit price once the stop price is reached. *See* Stop Order.

Stop Loss—*See* Stop Order.

Stop Order—An order to buy or sell when a given price is reached or passed. A stop order to buy always specifies a price above the present market price. A stop order to sell always specifies a price below the present market price. When the stop price is reached or passed, the stop order becomes a market order. Also called *Stop Loss.*

Stop Out Price—The lowest price the Treasury accepts in an auction.

Stopped Call—A call feature that an issuer may use only on coupon dates. *See* Rolling Call.

Stopped Out—When a stop order is executed.

Story—The fundamentals used to sell a bond. *See* Fundamental Analysis.

Story Bond—*See* Color.

Straddle—1) An option position that is a combination of a put and a call on the same security at the same strike price for the same expiration date. *See* Volatility Spread. 2) A futures position that is a combination of long and short contracts of the same security for different delivery months, with a net position of zero.

Straight—Fixed rate security not convertible to another security.

Straight Debt Value—Market value of a convertible bond if the bond has no conversion right.

Straight Line—Method of depreciation in which equal portions of a qualifying asset's value (calculated as cost minus salvage value) are depreciated every year of its useful life.

Straight Pass-Through—*See* Pass-Through.

Strangle—Combination option strategy with strike of the put below the price of the underlying security and the strike of the call above the price of the underlying security. Investors who believe the market is overestimating volatility sell strangles, and vice versa.

Strap—An option position that is a combination of two calls and one put on the same security at different strike prices for the same expiration date.

Street—The New York Financial Community in the Wall Street area, or the broker/dealer community in general.

Street Name—Registration of securities in the name of a broker bank or other third party instead of the owner. Facilitates transfer of ownership records and the clearance and settlement of securities transactions. *See* Nominee.

Street Practice—Any procedure generally agreed upon and in use by the financial community, such as the conventions regarding calculations of yields or prices.

Street Sweeping—Slang for the takeover strategy of buying large blocks of a target corporation's stock.

Strike Price—The price at which an option may be exercised for the underlying security. Also called *Exercise Price*.

Strip—1) A mortgage-backed security created by altering the distribution of interest and principal on a pass-through from a pro rata to an unequal allocation. 2) An option position that is a combination of two puts and one call on the same security at different strike prices for the same expiration date. 3) A position consisting of a series of futures contracts for consecutive delivery months.

Strip Order—Order for successive maturities of a serial bond.

Stripped Bond—The principal portion of a coupon security, which is traded independently from its coupons. The holder of a stripped bond receives the face amount of the bond at maturity. The coupon payments are traded as separate instruments, either separately or together.

Stripped Price—Market price minus the theoretical accrued interest. Also called *Clean Price*.

Stripped Yield—Yield of a unit stripped of warrants.

STRIPS—*See* Separately Traded Registered Interest and Principal Security.

Strong—Describes a market with good demand and rising prices. *See* Firm, Soft, and Weak.

Structural Unemployment—Unemployment due to major, long-term changes in industry and labor. *See* Frictional Unemployment.

Stub Period—The period between now and the next floating rate reset date in a swap transaction.

Student Loan Marketing Association (SLMA)—Publicly traded corporation that guarantees student loans for sale in the secondary market. Federally chartered in 1972 to increase liquidity in the student loan market. Also known as Sallie Mae.

Sub—*See* Edge Act Corporation.

Subject—1) Short for subject to confirmation. Refers to a quote or indication of price that is not firm and cannot be relied upon as the basis for a transaction. 2) In new issue terminology, an indication to potential buyers that all securities have been circled and will be sold subject to availability.

Subordinated—Refers to a promise to pay or a security with a promise to pay that cannot legally be fulfilled until payments on certain other obligations have been made and any other conditions (defined in the indenture) have been met. These other obligations are said to be senior to the subordinated obligation. Subordinated securities rank behind other debt in right of payment in liquidation. *See* Senior Security and Junior Security.

Subordinated Variable Rate Notes—Floating rate debt that ranks junior to other debentures currently outstanding.

Sub Right—Right to change the collateral of a repo.

Subrogate—To transfer debt from one creditor (the subrogor) to another (the subrogee).

Subscription—An order to buy primary market securities, given by investors to syndicate members who relay these orders to the lead manager.

Subscription Agreement—An agreement (to which is appended the underwriting and selling group agreements) between the borrower and the managers, under the terms of which the managers agree to subscribe to and to procure subscribers for a primary market issue and the borrower agrees to issue such securities.

Subscription Period—The period during which syndicate members solicit subscriptions from investors for a primary market issue and indicate this demand to the lead manager. Also called *Selling Period*.

Subscription Warrant—*See* Warrant.

Subsequent Event—An event that occurs after an accounting statement period.

Substitution Swap—Swap done in order to improve upon one or more characteristics of the original bonds, such as yield pick up, quality improvements, or change in call protection.

Sub-Underwriter—A member of a syndicate who is invited by the lead manager to contract severally with the managers to sub-underwrite a specific portion of a new issue. Sub-underwriters receive both an underwriting fee or commission on the principal amount of the securities they sub-underwrite and a selling concession on the principal amount of the securities for which they may subscribe. Sub-underwriters fall into the following categories, in descending order of amount of securities underwritten: major, sub-major, and minor. All sub-underwriters are listed alphabetically on a tombstone. *See* Primary Underwriter and Special Bracket.

Sum-of-the-Years' Digits—Method of depreciation in which the amount to be depreciated is calculated as the asset's value (cost minus salvage value) multiplied by the number of the year of useful life, counting backward, divided by the sum of the years of useful life. For example, in the first year of an asset's useful life of four years, the amount to be depreciated would be equal to the asset's cost multiplied by four (the number of the year of useful life, counting backward) divided by ten $(1 + 2 + 3 + 4)$.

Sunshine Law—State or federal laws requiring regulatory bodies to hold meetings in public and to disclose records. The SEC and Commodities Futures Trading Commission are subject to sunshine laws. The Freedom of Information Act is the most prominent sunshine law. Also called *Government in the Sunshine Law*.

Sunshine Trading—Making no attempt to disguise one's market strategy.

Super Floater—A type of leveraged floater in which the coupon resets at a positive multiple of a specified index. The coupon rate is quoted as a multiple of the index and a constant (e.g., 2 × LIBOR - 7%). *See* Leveraged Floater.

Super Put—A put option that allows the investor to put back a corporate bond to the issuer at par in the event of a change in control, defined as the purchase of 20 percent or more of outstanding stock by a third party, whether that party is deemed friendly or hostile. *See* Poison Put and Change of Control Bond.

Super Sinker—Bond with long stated maturity but with short expected maturity. Super sinkers are typically mortgage-related instruments. For example, a single family housing revenue bond issue in which all mortgage prepayments are used to retire a specified percentage of the bonds is a super sinker. Prepayments make the average life shorter than the stated maturity.

Supplemental Agreement—*See* Transfer Authorization.

Supply Elasticity—A market environment in which a rise or decline in price causes a rise or decline in production. *See* Demand Elasticity.

Support Level—Price level below the market level at which price declines have historically tended to stop, used by technical analysts to predict market supply and demand patterns.

Supranational—An entity that does not belong to only one country (e.g., the European Economic Community).

Surety Bond—*See* Performance Bond.

Surplus—The amount by which revenues exceed expenditures.

Sushi Bond—Non-yen denominated debt issued outside of Japan by Japanese entities.

Suspended—Describes an interval during which trading is halted on an exchange. Exchanges have the right to suspend trading to give the market time to absorb information.

Swap—1) The sale of one security for the purchase of another. *See* Intermarket Spread Swap and Substitution Swap. 2) *See* Interest Rate Swap.

Swap PC—Participation certificate (PC) issued in conjunction with FHLMC. Swaps are formed when mortgage originators exchange a pool of loans with FHLMC for a certificate. Because swaps are formed by a single originator, they tend to be smaller, less diversified pools than regular FHLMC Participation Certificates.

Sweetener—*See* Kicker.

Swing Line—Demand line of credit. *See* Line of Credit.

Swissy—Slang for Swiss franc.

Switch—1) *See* Rolling Forward the Hedge. 2) British for swap.

Switching—*See* Churning.

Switch Order—Extending the delivery month of a futures contract by offsetting a position and buying another contract.

Syndicate—1) A limited partnership agreement among underwriters. 2) A group of investment bankers who underwrite and distribute a new issue of securities or a large block of an outstanding issue.

Syndicated Credit—*See* Syndicated Loan.

Syndicated Loan—A loan by more than one bank to one borrower, usually on a floating rate basis, at a specified margin over short-term interest rates. Also called *Syndicated Credit.*

Syndicate is Terminated—Phrase signifying that all underwriters have been freed from all price and trading restrictions imposed during syndication and that the security is trading or is expected to trade at or over its initial offering price. *See* Break.

Syndicate Letter—Letter that lays out the rules of a syndicate, inviting a broker-dealer to join the underwriting syndicate.

Syndicate Restrictions—The contractual obligations placed on the underwriting group relating to distribution, price limitations, and market transactions.

Synthetic—Any transaction that replicates the cash flows of a desired asset, liability, or risk management tool.

Synthetic Call—Buying a put and buying the underlying instrument.

Synthetic Long—Buying a call and selling a put.

Synthetic Position—An option or futures position that has the same risk/reward characteristics as another kind of position. For example, buying a call and selling a put with the same expiration and strike price is the equivalent of owning the underlying security and is therefore called a synthetic position that replicates the underlying security.

Synthetic Put—Buying a call and selling the underlying instrument.

Synthetic Short—Selling a call and buying a put.

Systematic Risk—Risk that includes uncertainty of prices and interest rate volatility. Beta is a measure of systematic risk. Systematic risk is that part of total risk that cannot be reduced by diversification. Also called *Market Risk. See* Diversifiable Risk, Unsystematic Risk, and Total Risk.

System Repo—Federal Reserve open market operation in which the Fed buys collateral for its own account, adding cash to the system. This will exert downward pressure on short-term rates.

T

T Account—*See* Double Entry.

Tag Ends—The amount of a security that remains unsold from an underwriting.

Tail—1) The difference between the average price and the stop price (the lowest bid price) in Treasury cash auctions. 2) An increment added to a bid or offer in competition to avoid ties. 3) The decimal places in a competitive underwriting bid amount. 4) For pass-through securities, the difference between the principal amount of securities actually delivered and the amount contracted for at the time of purchase.

Tailgate—To trade a security after another investor places an order in that security, hoping to profit in the price movement caused by the original trade.

Tainted—Refers to a position whose holding period has legally ended. For example, if an investor buys a put option on a security owned for less than one year, the position is tainted (i.e., the holding period of the security for IRS purposes starts again when the put is sold or expires).

Take—To accept an offering. *See* Hit and Lift.

Take a Bath—To incur large trading losses.

Take a Flier—To make a speculative investment.

Take a Position—To go long or short in a security.

Take Delivery—To accept the underlying security or commodity of a futures contract.

Take-Down—Discount allowed to a syndicate member on any bonds sold. *See* Selling Concession.

Take-or-Pay—Utilities contract stating that a purchaser of fuel or power agrees to pay a certain amount whether or not the fuel or power is purchased.

263

Take-Out—Cash retained as a result of the sale of one block of bonds and the purchase of another block at a lower price. *See* Pay-Up.

Takeover—1) To gain control of a corporation. 2) The act of gaining control, or the attempt to gain control, of a corporation.

Talon—The physical strip of paper on a bearer security that is exchanged for payment of interest.

Tandem Spread—Buying one security and shorting another.

Tangible—Refers to personal property as opposed to land. *See* Real.

Tanking—*See* In the Tank.

Tap—1) To approach a market for funding purposes. 2) To issue securities on an "as required" basis, often in irregular amounts. The term is used primarily to describe issues of U.K. gilt edged bonds, CDs and FRCDs.

Tape—Electronic display of trades, with each item consisting of the symbol, volume, price, and price change.

Tape Dancing—When a broker/dealer sells at an artificially high price on block trades in return for a larger commission. This bumps up the sale price reported on the tape, thereby creating upward momentum in the security.

Taplet—In the context of the gilt edged market, a small, additional issue of an existing bond. Also called *Mini Tap*.

Target—The object of a takeover attempt.

Targeted Amortization Class (TAC)—A CMO tranche that has a planned amortization schedule. Like PAC bonds, TAC bonds are structured to improve call protection during periods of accelerated prepayments. Unlike PAC bonds, TAC bonds are subject to extension of average life should collateral prepayments decline below the pricing speed. Also called *Semi-PAC* and *Half-PAC*. *See* Planned Amortization Class.

Tariff—Import or export tax.

Taxable Equivalent Yield—Yield on a taxable security that equates it to that of a non- taxable security, calculated as after-tax yield divided by [100% - tax bracket]. Also called *Equivalent Taxable Yield*.

Tax Anticipation Bill (TAB)—Treasury bills maturing on quarterly corporate income tax dates, used by corporations to pay taxes.

Tax Anticipation Note (TAN)—State or municipal notes issued in anticipation of tax revenue.

Tax Basis—Price at which a security was purchased, including any commission.

Tax Credit—A direct dollar-for-dollar reduction of taxes as opposed to a tax deduction, which reduces taxes on a percentage basis depending upon the taxpayer's tax bracket.

Tax Deferred—Describes an investment, such as an annuity or an IRA, whose accumulated earnings are delayed for a specified period of time and cannot be taxed until they are distributed to the investor.

Tax Equity and Fiscal Responsibility Act of 1982 (TEFRA)—An act of taxation legislation containing revisions to the Internal Revenue Code generally effective January 1, 1983. Major changes affect business taxpayers by curtailing certain tax benefits and capital formation incentives (including some enacted in 1981) and affect individual taxpayers by reducing medical and casualty deductions and strengthening "alternative minimum tax" provisions. In addition, the Act requires withholding on interest and dividends and provides for other measures designed to improve compliance with existing laws.

Tax-Exempt Bond—Municipal bond, the interest on which is exempt from federal income tax.

Tax Opinion—An opinion given by the issuer's tax counsel stating how an issue would be treated for federal income tax purposes.

Tax Selling—Selling securities at a loss to offset capital gains.

Tax Swap—Arranging taxable gains and losses for the most advantageous tax treatment.

T-Bill—Treasury bill.

T-Bond—Treasury bond.

T Call—Margin call. *See* Regulation T.

T-Note—Treasury note.

Teaser—Below market initial interest rate used on an adjustable rate mortgage to attract and/or qualify mortgage borrowers.

Technical Analysis—Market analysis based on market data and trends such as price, volume, and moving averages. *See* Fundamental Analysis.

Technical Condition—Supply and demand forces that have only short-term influence on the market.

Technical Correction—A price movement generated by internal market variables, such as the number of short positions, as opposed to one generated by fundamental economic or credit factors.

Technical Rally—A price rise created by technical factors in the context of a larger market decline.

Technical Reaction—A market tendency to retrace up to 50 percent of a major move in either direction.

Technicals—Market information such as prices, volume, and moving averages used to forecast security prices. *See* Fundamentals.

TED Spread—The spread between Treasury bills and Eurodollar CDs (LIBOR).

Teenie—One-sixteenth of a point. Also called a *Steenth*.

Tenant—Part owner of a security.

Tenants in Common (TIC)—*See* Joint Tenants.

Tender—1) To sell one's shares in a corporation in response to a tender offer. 2) A medium of exchange. Also called *Legal Tender*.

Tender Offer—A cash offer to the public, usually at a premium over current market price (or call price), for a specific aggregate amount of securities as an inducement to surrender the securities. A fee is generally paid to the dealer who solicits the tender and to the dealer manager.

Tender Panel—A group of financial institutions that bids among themselves by quoting yields at which they will purchase an issuer's securities.

Tengoku/Jigoku Bond—Japanese heaven and hell bond. *See* Heaven and Hell.

Tennessee Valley Authority (TVA)—Government agency whose debt is used to fund development around the Tennessee River.

Tenor—Maturity.

Ten Percent Rule—General guideline stating that a municipality's debt should not exceed 10 percent of its real estate value.

Term—1) Maturity. 2) Refers to a repurchase agreement with a maturity of at least two days, generally less than three months.

Term Bond—1) A long-term bond issue with one maturity date. *See* Serial Security. 2) A callable Treasury bond. 3) A municipal bond quoted and traded in price (or dollars) rather than yield. Also called *Dollar Bond*.

Term CD—*See* Intermediate-Term CD.

Term Cost Method—An actuarial cost method that values ancillary benefits (those payable on early retirement, death, disability, termination of service, etc.) using one-year costs. Valuation of death and disability benefits by the term cost method is analogous to insurance company practices that calculate, for each participant, the probability and value of a claim occurring in a year.

Term Fed Funds—Fed funds sold for a period longer than overnight.

Terminated—*See* Syndicate Is Terminated.

Term Loan—Loan extended for more than 90 days.

Term Repo—A repurchase agreement for longer than overnight.

Term Structure—The relationship between a security's interest rate and its term to maturity. The three hypotheses that explain term structure are the liquidity hypothesis, expectations hypothesis, and segmentation hypothesis. *See* Liquidity Preference, Expectations Hypothesis, and Market Segmentation Hypothesis.

Term Structure Curve—Yield Curve.

Term Structure Hypothesis—The theory that the market is priced in such a way that an investment in a riskless issue of any maturity is expected to produce roughly the same total return over any given holding period. The hypothesis enables investors to imply a market forecast for interest rates based on the shape (or term structure) of the existing yield curve. *See* Expectations Hypothesis, Liquidity Preference, and Market Segmentation Hypothesis.

Texas Hedge—Any strategy that increases risk.

Theoretical Time Value—Theoretical value of an option minus its intrinsic value.

Theoretical Value—The price of an option, calculated using a mathematical model. *See* Black-Scholes.

Theta—The change in the price of an option with a decrease of one day in time to expiration.

Thin—Pertaining to a market with low trading volume and poor liquidity.

Third Market—Over-the-counter transactions of listed securities by non-member broker-dealers of an exchange.

Thirty Day Visible Supply—*See* Visible Supply.

Three-Handed Deal—Municipal issue that combines serial maturities with two term maturities.

Thrift—A financial institution, the most common of which are savings and loans, savings banks, and credit unions, that accepts personal savings and then loans these funds in the residential mortgage market. Thrifts are legally barred from offering demand deposit accounts. *See* Federal Home Loan Banks and Savings and Loan.

Throughput and Deficiency Agreement—A form of indirect credit support used in connection with pipeline projects, whereby users undertake with the borrower to pass an amount of oil or gas through the pipeline system owned by the borrower at a price sufficient for the borrower to meet all its obligations. Any cash deficiencies arising from the operation of the pipeline have to be satisfied by the users who are required to pay, on demand, their pro rata share of the deficiency.

Through the Market—Having a yield that is below market levels. When a new bond offering has come to market and the yield to maturity is lower than that of comparable outstanding bonds, the new bond is said to be offered "through the market."

Through Treasuries—*See* Trading Through the Curve.

Throwaway—A nominal quote, that is, an estimate rather than a firm quote.

Tick—Minimum price movement on a security.

Ticker—Automated system that provides a report of stock exchange trading activity, including price and volume of securities traded. Also known as the tape. *See* Consolidated Tape.

Tiffany List—Issuers of the highest quality commercial paper.

Tight—1) A market with heavy trading volume and narrow spreads between bid and ask prices. 2) An economic condition of high interest rates and relatively little credit. The Fed can create this condition by decreasing the money supply. *See* Easy.

Till Money—Vault Cash.

Time Decay—The loss of an option's time value as its expiration date approaches.

Time Deposit—A deposit with a maturity fixed by law of at least 30 days. Savings accounts at commercial banks are also regarded as time deposits. *See* Demand Deposits.

Time Draft—*See* Draft.

Time Order—An order to be executed within a specified time period.

Times Fixed Charges—*See* Fixed Charge Coverage.

Times-Interest Earned—Pre-tax corporate income plus interest charges divided by interest charges.

Time Spread—An option position created by selling one call and buying another with a longer expiration date at the same strike price. Also called *Calendar Spread* and *Horizontal Spread*.

Time Value—The portion of the option premium that is not intrinsic value. It is the total option premium less the amount the option is in the money. Out-of-the-money options have premiums consisting entirely of time value.

Tip—*See* Inside Information.

Title XI—A bond backed by a ship mortgage and guaranteed by the U.S. government according to the Ship Financing Act of 1972, of which Title XI is a section.

Toehold—The accumulation of less than 5 percent of a corporation's stock.

Tokkin Fund—Japanese money market fund.

Tombstone—An advertisement that states the name and terms of a security, the underwriters, and where a prospectus can be obtained. It does not constitute an offer to buy or sell securities.

Tom Next—Tomorrow next (the next business day).

Tone—Refers to prices remaining firm (positive or good tone) or falling (negative or bad tone). Good tone characterizes a market in which there is active trading on narrow bid-asked spreads.

Top—To make a higher bid.

Top-Down Manager—Portfolio manager whose decisions are based on the economy rather than on fundamental analysis of individual corporations. *See* Bottom-Up Manager.

Total Debt to Capital—Commonly used financial ratio, calculated as total borrowings divided by total capital.

Total Financing-to-Value Ratio (TFTV)—The unpaid principal balance of the first mortgage plus the original amount of the second mortgage divided by the market value of the home.

Total Liabilities to Tangible Worth—Commonly used financial ratio, calculated as all liabilities divided by the sum of equity (common and preferred) minus intangible assets.

Total Loan-to-Value Ratio (TLTV)—The sum of all outstanding mortgage balances on a property divided by the market value of the property.

Total Output—*See* Aggregate Supply.

Total Reserves—Reserve balances held at the Federal Reserve Banks plus vault cash used to satisfy reserve requirements. Total reserves include both required and excess reserves.

Total Return—Coupon income, retired principal, reinvestment income, and change in the market value of a bond over a certain time period divided by the initial price, expressed as a percentage rate of return. *See* Effective Yield.

Total Return Buyer—Investor who trades to increase income and capital gains. *See* Yield Buyer and Cash Flow Buyer.

Total Return Optimization—The technique of constructing a bond portfolio to achieve maximum total return over a given investment horizon, across a set of interest rate scenarios and subject to constraints.

Total Risk—Systematic plus unsystematic risk.

Total Spending—*See* Aggregate Demand.

To the Buck—For U.S. government securities, the bid-offer spread if the bid is close to the offer and the offer is a round number. For example, if a quote is 98-29/32 bid, 99 offered, a trader might quote the spread as "29 to the buck."

Trade—A completed agreement to buy and sell securities. Also called *Deal* and *Transaction*.

Trade Balance—The difference in value between exports and imports. Usually refers to the balance of trade in merchandise only (i.e., it excludes services, interest payments, profits, and dividends, or the invisible balance).

Trade Date—The date on which a transaction is executed. Also called *Acquisition Date*. *See* Settlement Date.

Trade Deficit—The amount by which the value of imports exceeds that of exports, or the net outflow of money from a nation.

Trade on Top of—Trade with little or no spread to another instrument.

Trader—A person whose intention is to profit from buying and selling, rather than holding, of securities.

Trade Surplus—The amount by which the value of exports exceeds that of imports, or the net inflow of money to a nation.

Trade Weighting—Method of determining the amount of one security to swap for another. Investors who want to take advantage of a yield spread and not change their portfolio's exposure to interest rate risk (i.e., change the portfolio's duration) will swap blocks of bonds with equal dollar duration, not equal par amounts. *See* Duration-Weighted Trade.

Trading Against the Box—A strategy expression derived from the way options prices are reported in the newspaper: the strike prices are listed vertically along the left and the expiration dates are listed horizontally along the top, thus creating a "box." Buying and selling different options for a given underlying security is thus "trading against the box."

Trading Authorization—*See* Power of Attorney.

Trading Limit—The maximum price change allowed in one futures trading session. Once the trading limit has been reached trading may be done only at or within the limit level. *See* Lock Limit, Position Limit, and Reporting Level.

Trading Market—The secondary market for securities.

Trading on the Equity—*See* Financial Leverage.

Trading on the Wind—Making a profit on a series of transactions without investing any money.

Trading Over the Curve—Selling above the Treasury yield level.

Trading Post—Location on a stock exchange floor where specific securities are bought and sold. The New York Stock Exchange has 22 trading posts, with about 100 stocks traded at each post.

Trading Profits—Profits or losses from information trading. Interest payments and risk premiums are not part of trading profits.

Trading Range—High and low prices of a security over a specified time interval.

Trading Through the Curve—Selling below the Treasury yield level.

Trading Unit—*See* Round Lot.

Traditional Mortgage—A mortgage with a fixed interest rate and term to maturity, requiring level payments of principal and interest. *See* Alternative Mortgage Instrument.

Tranche—A part of a security, typically a CMO, that shares documentation with other parts but has different terms (e.g., in a $200 million issue, one tranche of $100 million may have a maturity of five years and the second tranche of $100 million may have a maturity of ten years). Also called *Class*.

Transaction—*See* Trade.

Transfer Agent—Institution, typically a commercial bank, that a corporation appoints to maintain security ownership records.

Transfer Authorization—Part of the customer agreement allowing the broker to transfer funds that relate to regulated commodities into another account without further customer consent. Also called *Supplemental Agreement*.

Transfer Payment—A government payment or other payment for which the recipient renders no current services. Social security, unemployment compensation, and welfare benefits are the largest types of transfer payments.

Translation Gain—Foreign exchange gain.

Trapper—Registered representative.

Treasury Bill—A non-interest-bearing obligation, fully guaranteed by the U.S. government, payable to the bearer. Bills are sold on a discount basis, in three-month, six-month, and one-year maturities, in book entry form only, and in denominations of $10,000, $15,000, $100,000, and $1 million. Interest is calculated on an actual/360 basis, and quoted in discount yield terms.

Treasury Bond—A U.S. Treasury coupon security that generally has a maturity of more than ten years. Interest is calculated on an actual/365 basis. Price is quoted as a percentage of par to the nearest 1/32. Bonds are sold in registered and book entry form in denominations of $1,000, $5,000, $10,000, $100,000, and $1 million.

Treasury Certificate—Short-term U.S. government debt, no longer issued publicly, that was occasionally issued to facilitate transfers from the Fed to banks. Also called *Certificate of Indebtedness.*

Treasury Note—A coupon security issued by the U.S. Treasury with a maturity of between one and ten years. Interest is calculated on an actual/365 basis. Price is quoted as a percentage of par to the nearest 1/32. Notes are sold in registered and book entry form in denominations of $1,000, $5,000, $10,000, $100,000, and $1 million.

Treasury Receipt (TR)—Custodial receipt evidencing ownership of future interest or principal payments on certain U.S. Treasury notes or bonds. Such interest and principal payments are direct obligations of the U.S. government. No payments are made on TRs prior to the point at which corresponding principal or interest payments on the underlying Treasury security are made. *See* Coupon TR and Corpus TR.

Treasury Refunding—A redemption of Treasury securities with funds raised through the sale of one or more new issues. Refundings are currently held quarterly, on the three consecutive business days at the beginning of the second month of each quarter, when the Treasury auctions 3-year notes, 10-year notes, and 30-year bonds.

Treasury Stock—Previously issued stock that a corporation reacquires through purchase or donation. Treasury stock is not considered outstanding stock for accounting purposes. It neither receives dividends nor has voting privileges. A corporation can repurchase its own stock to bolster its value, to use in exchange for the shares of another corporation with which it would like to merge, to put into pension or profit- sharing plans, or to resell (the capital gain is not taxable).

Treasury STRIPS—*See* Separately Traded Registered Interest and Principal Security.

Trend—A movement in the direction of prices, earnings, or another measurement over a period of time.

Trick—A transaction executed on a securities exchange.

Trigger Level—Level at which an investor is willing to trade a security.

Trigger Puller—An individual with direct responsibility for executing trades and for deciding with whom they will be executed.

Trigger Rate—Rate in a drop-lock issue at which a floating rate issue becomes a fixed rate bond.

Triple Exempt—Bonds exempt from federal, state, and local taxes (e.g., bonds issued by Puerto Rico and territories and possessions of the U.S.).

Triple Witching Hour—The four Fridays each year when stock, index, and futures options come due at 4 p.m.

True Interest Cost (TIC)—Semiannually compounded rate needed to discount interest and principal payments on a security to the purchase price.

Trust Deed—*See* Trust Indenture.

Trustee—An individual or institution that holds assets for the benefit of another.

Trust Indenture—A trust deed (English terminology) or indenture (U.S. terminology) is an agreement between a borrower and the security holders concerning the terms of the security, the powers of the trustee, and investor meetings.

Trust Indenture Act of 1939—Requires bonds to have an indenture filed with the SEC as part of the registration statement. Governments, municipals, and bonds of foreign governments are exempt.

TT&L Account—Treasury tax and loan account at a bank.

Turkey—A poorly performing investment.

Turn—Cost of financing a position from the end of one year into the beginning of the next year.

Turnaround—Refers to the ability to clear securities that are bought and sold for same-day settlement. Good turnaround is considered receiving and delivering the security within the established delivery period (between 9:00 a.m. and 11:30 a.m.).

Turnover—1) The dollar amount of trading done in a portfolio. 2) The volume of business done in a security or the entire market. 3) Ratio of annual sales to inventory. Also called *Inventory Turnover*. 4) Ratio of annual sales to a corporation's net worth. Also called *Capital Turnover*.

Turnover Tax—*See* Cascade Tax.

Twelve-Year Life—The traditional cash flow assumption used to compute 30-year mortgage yields. It derives from an accounting practice used by mortgage bankers in keeping their books. It assumes that there are no prepayments or defaults for the first 12 years. At the end of 12 years, the unamortized principal balance is assumed to be redeemed at par.

Twenty Bond Index—Average yield to maturity of twenty particular general obligation bonds, each having a twenty-year maturity. The index is calculated weekly and published in the Bond Buyer.

Twenty-Five Percent Rule—Guideline that a municipality's bonded debt should not exceed 25 percent of its annual budget.

Twisting—*See* Churning.

Two-Dollar Broker—A broker who executes transactions for other brokers. Also called *Broker's Broker* and *Independent Broker*.

Two-Fer—One long and two short calls, where the long call has the lowest exercise price and all have the same expiration date. *See* Ratio Writing.

Two-Handed—Refers to an underwriting syndicate with two co-managers.

Two-Sided Market—Synonymous with market, which consists of a bid and an asked price, both of which are firm and operable for the standard unit of trading. Also called *Two-Way Market. See* One-Sided Market.

Two-Way Market—*See* Two-Sided Market.

U

Ultra Vires—Refers to a corporation's actions that are unauthorized by its charter. *See* Charter.

Unamortized Bond Discount—The part of the original issue discount that has not yet been amortized or charged off against earnings.

Uncovered—Refers to the writer of a call option who does not own the underlying security. Also called *Naked*.

Undated—A security with no final maturity that may be converted into a dated security by the holder subject to some penalty (e.g., a lower margin in floating rate notes). *See* Perpetual.

Underbanked—A syndicate that needs other members to share the risk of underwriting.

Underbooked—An underwriting with insufficient public interest.

Undercut—To sell securities at below market levels.

Underlying Bullet—A callable or putable bond without the call or put features. *See* Embedded Option Value.

Underlying Debt—Debt of a municipality that is under the jurisdiction of another government entity. *See* Overlapping Debt.

Underlying Security—The security on which an option or futures contract is written.

Undermargined—Pertaining to an account that has fallen below maintenance margin. *See* Maintenance Margin, Restricted, and Variation Margin.

Undervalued—A security or currency whose market price is lower than the price an analyst judges to be its true value. *See* Fundamental Analysis.

Under Water—Refers to a security whose market value is less than its book or acquisition value. Also called *Below Water*. *See* Above Water.

Underwrite—To agree to buy an issue of securities on a given date at a specific price, or to agree to buy the unsubscribed securities of an issue, thus guaranteeing the issuer the full anticipated proceeds.

Underwriter—The firm that agrees to buy an issue of securities on a given date at a specific price, or agrees to buy the unsubscribed securities of an issue, thus guaranteeing the issuer the full anticipated proceeds.

Underwriter's Agreement—The agreement between the issuing corporation and the underwriters wherein the terms of the purchase of the securities are formally stated. This agreement is separate from the Agreement Among Underwriters.

Underwriting Fee—A percentage of the gross spread that accrues only to the members of the syndicate on a pro rata basis.

Undigested—Refers to new issue securities that have not been distributed. *See* Absorbed.

Undistributed Profits—Retained earnings.

Undivided Account—*See* Eastern Account.

Unearned Income—Income that results from fortuitous events rather than from sales.

Uneconomic Trade—A trade in which the investor cannot make a profit.

Unemployment Rate—The percentage obtained by dividing the number of persons looking for work by the total labor force.

Unencumbered—A fully owned asset that has no lien against it.

Unfunded—An obligation, typically of a pension fund, that has no assets set aside to meet it.

Uniform Gifts to Minors Act (UGMA)—Act governing the administration of assets held in the name of a minor adopted by most U.S. states. Sets up rules for custodianship of assets, transfer of assets when the minor reaches the age of majority, and taxation of assets held by a minor.

Uniform Practice Code—National Association of Securities Dealers rules governing standards and procedures of over-the-counter securities trading. Also provides for the settlement of disputes via Uniform Practice Committees.

Unifying Bond—*See* Consol.

Unissued—Stock authorized by a corporation's charter but not issued.

Unit—1) Minimum trading quantity. Common units are 25 for municipal bonds, 100 for government bonds, 250 for corporate bonds, and 100 shares of common stock for options. 2) Securities sold together. A bond and a warrant may constitute a unit, as may a share of common stock and a share of convertible preferred.

Unit Credit—*See* Entry Age Normal.

Unit Credit Method—With regard to pension plans, a method under which the benefits (projected or unprojected) of each individual included in an actuarial valuation are allocated by a consistent formula to valuation years.

United Account—*See* Eastern Account.

Unit Investment Trust (UIT)—A fixed portfolio of bonds, units of which are sold to investors.

Unit Investment Trust Company—An investment company organized under a trust indenture rather than a corporate charter.

Unlimited Tax Bond—General obligation bond secured by the unlimited taxing authority of the municipality.

Unlisted—Refers to a security that is not registered on an exchange.

Unmatched Book—Asset/liability maturity imbalance. Also called *Gap* and *Open Book*.

Unmodified Duration—*See* Duration.

Unpaid Dividend—A dividend that has been declared by a corporation but has not yet been paid.

Unrealized Gain/Loss—*See* Paper Gain/Loss.

Unrestricted—Pertaining to an account whose equity equals or exceeds the Federal Reserve's initial margin requirement.

Unsecured Bond—*See* Debenture.

Unsystematic Return—*See* Idiosyncratic Return.

Unsystematic Risk—Risk unique to particular assets, which can be reduced by diversification. *See* Systematic Risk and Total Risk.

Unwind—To gradually reduce a position in a security.

Upgrade—1) An improvement in credit rating. 2) The sale of one block of bonds and the purchase of another block with a higher rating.

Upside—The potential for price appreciation.

Upstairs Market—Market in which block trades are done away from the exchange floor.

Uptick—A term used to designate a transaction done at a price higher than the preceding transaction in the same security. Also called *Plus Tick*.

Usable—Pertains to bonds that can be tendered at par in payment of the exercise price of certain warrants.

Useful Life—Period during which an asset can be of service.

Usury—An excessively high rate of interest.

Utility—1) Corporation that provides a public service, such as electricity, gas, or communications. These corporations are subject to public regulation of earnings and rates and of the service provided in return for being granted a virtual monopoly in a region. 2) In economics, the benefit from using a consumer good. Marginal utility is the additional benefit received from using an additional unit of the consumer good within a unit of time.

Utility Theory of Value—Theory that for necessary items, such as air and water, availability rather than the fact that they are a necessity should determine the price.

V

Validation—1) Endorsement of a mutilated certificate or coupon by the issuer. 2) Determination of the legality of a municipal issue.

Value Date—Delivery date of funds traded in the Euromarket, usually two days after a trade.

Value of a Basis Point—*See* Value of an 01.

Value of an 01—The price change in a bond caused by a one basis point change in yield. Also called *Value of a Basis Point.*

Vanilla—*See* Plain Vanilla.

Variable Annuity—An annuity for which a life insurance company makes periodic, variable payments during the subscriber's lifetime.

Variable Deliverable Option—An option for which the maturity date of the most deliverable security is unknown or will depend on when the option is exercised. *See* Fixed Deliverable Option.

Variable Duration Note (VDN)—A coupon-bearing security that gives the investor the option, on each coupon payment date, to take the coupon in cash or to reinvest the coupon income in additional VDNs at par.

Variable Rate CD—Short-term CD with an interest rate that is reset at certain intervals.

Variable Rate Demand Note—A note carrying a floating interest rate, priced at par. The investor has the option to redeem the security at par at any time after giving the required notice. Also called *Lower Floater.*

Variable Rate Mortgage (VRM)—Predecessor to the adjustable rate mortgage, originated during the late 1970s in California. VRMs reset semiannually off the Semiannual Cost of Funds Index for California members of the FHLB of San Francisco. VRMs have a maximum final maturity of 40 years from origination. Periodic rate resets are limited to 25 basis points, and the lifetime cap is 250 basis points.

Variable Rate Note—*See* Floating Rate Note.

Variable Ratio Writing—*See* Ratio Writing.

Variable Term Preferred (VTP)—Preferred stock that has an initial fixed dividend rate and term, both of which are subject to redetermination on term anniversaries through Dutch auction or remarketing.

Variation Margin—Additional margin required from an investor when the equity in a margin account falls below the maintenance margin level. Variation margin brings the account back up to the initial margin level. *See* Maintenance Margin.

Vault Cash—Currency kept in a bank for use by depositors; vault cash is considered part of the bank's reserves.

Vega—A measure of the sensitivity of an option's price to a change in volatility.

Velocity—The number of times per year that each dollar in the money supply is spent on goods and services. Velocity is usually calculated as the ratio of nominal GNP to the money supply (M2). A decline in velocity means that people are saving rather than spending.

Vendee—Veteran Administration loans on properties on which the previous VA loan was foreclosed. GNMA securities backed by VA vendee loans carry the same guarantee of timely payment of principal and interest as any other GNMA security and are deliverable for generic GNMA trades.

Vertical Call Bear Spread—Buying a higher strike call and selling a lower strike call with the same expiration.

Vertical Call Bull Spread—Buying a lower strike call and selling a higher strike call with the same expiration.

Vertical Integration—Merger of businesses at different stages of the manufacturing and distribution cycle.

Vertical Put Bear Spread—Buying a lower strike put and selling a higher strike put with the same expiration.

Vertical Put Bull Spread—Buying a higher strike put and selling a lower strike put with the same expiration.

Vertical Spread—A position created by trading against the box. For a given option, a purchase or sale of the option is made for one expiration date at one strike price while an offsetting purchase or sale is made for the same expiration date but at a different strike price. Also called *Price Spread* and *Money Spread*. *See* Trading Against the Box.

Vested—Refers to a pension plan in which an employee has full benefits at retirement (or death) even if the employee is no longer employed by the employer.

Vested Benefits—The estimated current legal obligations of a pension plan (and therefore of the company itself), that eventually must be paid whether or not the employee leaves or the plan is terminated.

Vested Funding Position—The difference between pension assets and vested benefits. A positive number means that vested benefits are fully funded as of the plan valuation date; a negative number means that vested benefits are underfunded as of the plan valuation date.

Vesting—The right of an employee under a retirement plan to retain part or all of the annuities purchased by the employer's contributions on his or her behalf. In some plans, it is the right to receive a cash payment of equivalent value on termination of employment after certain qualifying conditions have been met. In essence, vesting means a non-forfeitable right to a retirement income.

Veteran's Administration (VA)—A United States government agency that executes all laws for the benefit of war veterans. Included in these benefits are loans, education, insurance, and medical care.

Vintage—Year of issuance, especially of a mortgage. The vintage of a mortgage, along with the interest rate pattern to which the mortgage has been exposed, in large part determines the likelihood of prepayment. *See* Seasoned.

Virgin Bond—*See* Back Bond.

Visible Supply—Municipals scheduled to be issued within thirty days.

Vneshtorgbank—The Soviet foreign bank.

Volatility—The susceptibility of a quantity or entity to change. For securities, volatility is typically stated as the standard deviation of possible ending prices (or yields, or returns) over a one-year period.

Volatility Spread—Options strategy of buying a put and call on the same security. If the market moves significantly in either direction, the profit on one leg will be greater than the loss on the other leg. If the market does not move, both options will expire at a loss. *See* Straddle.

Volume—Number of securities traded during a trading session.

Voluntary Underwriter—An investment banker who buys securities from a company or an insider, offering the securities to the public under an effective registration statement.

Vulture Fund—A real estate mutual fund that buys distressed properties and sells them at a profit.

W

Wage—Employee compensation based on time worked or products produced. *See* Salary.

Wage-Price Spiral—Inflation caused by wages and prices chasing each other.

Waiter—British for floor clerks on an exchange.

Waiting Period—Interval specified by the SEC, currently 20 days, between the filing of the registration of a securities offering and the offering itself. Also called *Cooling-Off Period*.

Wall Flower—A thinly traded security.

Wall Street—The street on which the New York Stock Exchange is located. Also refers to the entire financial community.

Wanted for Cash—Announcement on the ticker tape signifying that a bidder is willing to pay cash for a security for same day settlement.

War Babies—Securities of corporations that are defense contractors.

Warehouse Receipt—Delivery paper for grain in a futures contract.

Warehousing—The borrowing of funds by a mortgage banker on a short-term basis at a commercial bank using permanent mortgage loans as collateral. This form of interim financing is used until the mortgages are sold to an investor.

Warrant—A certificate giving the holder the right to purchase a security from the issuer at a stipulated price, either for a specified period of time or perpetually. Also called *Subscription Warrant*.

Washington Metropolitan Area Transit Authority—Government agency that finances and operates mass transit in Washington, D.C., whose debt is backed by the full faith and credit of the government.

Wash Sale—The purchase and sale of securities by an individual without any beneficial change of ownership for the purpose of raising or depressing the price of a security. Section 9 of the Securities Exchange Act of 1934 prohibits price manipulation, including wash sales.

The Wash Sale Rule prohibits the deduction of capital losses if an investor sells a security and repurchases it within 30 days.

Wasting—1) Pertaining to assets that have no value after expiration, such as option contracts. 2) Refers to tangible assets subject to depletion, such as oil, forests, and metals.

Watered Stock—Shares that represent assets worth less than par or stated value.

Weak—Describes a market in which there is selling pressure and falling prices.

Wealth Effect—Stimulation of the economy during a depression by consumer spending. The wealth effect is a counter-cyclical force that occurs when individuals with discretionary income and savings realize the relative increase in their wealth and begin to spend, which in turn stimulates the economy. *See* Counter Cyclical.

Wedding Warrant—A warrant issued with a callable host bond. The warrant may be exercised to give a bullet back bond with the same coupon and final maturity date as the host bond. The warrants expire on the maturity date of the bonds. From the issue date until the first call date of the host bond, the warrant may be exercised only by surrendering the host bond. After the call date, the warrant may be exercised with cash. *See* Harmless Warrant.

Weekend Effect—*See* Blue Monday.

Weighted Average Coupon (WAC)—WAC is calculated by multiplying the coupon of each mortgage in a given pool by its remaining balance, summing the products and dividing the result by the total remaining balance.

Weighted Average Maturity (WAM)—WAM is calculated by multiplying the maturity of each mortgage in a given pool by its remaining balance, summing the products, and dividing the result by the total remaining balance.

Weighted Average Remaining Maturity (WARM)—The weighted average remaining maturity of a mortgage-related security, recalculated each month.

Weighting the Trade—Buying and selling par amounts of two securities that will result in the same absolute value of price movement for each. That is, for a given interest rate movement, the price of a security will move a specified amount. Since this amount differs from security to security, buying and selling equal amounts of two different securities will usually result in unequal price movements if interest rates move.

Western Account—A corporate syndicate in which members are responsible only for the securities that they individually underwrite. Also called *Divided Account*. *See* Eastern Account.

When Issued (WI)—Securities traded between the announcement of the issue and the auction date. The entire phrase is "when, as, and if issued."

Whipsawed—Refers to rapid, volatile price movements, making trading difficult or impossible.

White Knight—A friendly acquirer of corporations, that is, a corporation or takeover specialist who is not hostile to the management of the takeover target.

Whole Loan—A mortgage that is not part of an agency pool whose terms may not conform to GNMA, FNMA, or FHLMC underwriting standards.

Whole Pool—Ownership of an entire pool of mortgage loans.

Whole Pool Test—*See* Fifty-Five Percent Test.

Wholesale Price Index (WPI)—A weighted average of prices that retailers pay manufacturers.

Wide Open—An underwriting that needs more syndicate members. *See* Underbanked.

Wide Opening—Large spread between bid and asked prices at the beginning of a trading session.

Widow and Orphan—A security that is considered safe, usually pertaining to blue chip stocks that pay high dividends.

Williams Act—Law requiring those making a tender offer to file a statement with the SEC and the target company specifying the terms of the offer, the source of funds to make the offer, and takeover plans if appropriate. The offering period must be at least 20 days, and the tendering shareholders must be given 15 days to make a final decision. Any person acquiring at least 5 percent of the shares of a corporation must file the same information with the SEC as one making a tender offer. The Williams Act is now Sections 13(d) and 14(d) of the Securities Exchange Act of 1934.

Windfall—A profit that results from an event not in an investor's or corporation's control.

Window—1) Interval during which there is a market opportunity. 2) Discount window at a Federal Reserve bank.

Window Dressing—Making a portfolio or a financial statement look good to investors.

Window Settlement—Method of clearing and settling securities in which securities are delivered and paid for at a dealer's cash window. *See* Continuous Settlement.

Window Warrant—Warrant exercisable with cash only at the end of a specified period, such as the end of the fifth year.

Wire House—A brokerage firm that can transmit financial information through a computer network among branch offices.

Withholding—1) Action by a dispersing agent whereby a portion of dividends and interest paid by a U.S. corporation to non-resident alien holders of its securities is withheld in payment of U.S. taxes. 2) Failure to make complete distribution of a hot issue. *See* Freeriding.

With or Without—Used on an odd-lot limit order to instruct the broker to do a trade based on the last effective sale or the quote for the security, whichever comes first.

Without—A bid or offer without the opposite position. A one-way market. The phrase "50 bid without" means there is a bid of 50 without any offers.

With Rights of Survivorship (WROS)—*See* Joint Tenants.

Wooden Ticket—A fraudulent confirmation.

Working Capital—Current assets minus current liabilities.

Working Control—Effective control of a corporation by a person or persons holding less than 51 percent of a company's voting stock. Usually occurs when ownership of shares of stock is widely dispersed.

Working Order—Large trade order to be executed slowly so as not to influence the market.

Work-Out—*See* Best Effort.

Workout Market—An indicated market given on an active security with the inference that, over time, either one or both sides could be made firm by the trader.

Workout Order—1) A firm order in response to a workout market. 2) A firm swap order, usually involving two rare issues or at a level away from the current market levels.

World Bank—*See* Development Bank.

Worth—*See* Net Worth.

Wrap-Around Mortgage—A junior lien that is written for the entire mortgage indebtedness of the borrower. The wrap-around lender assumes responsibility for the original lien, and the borrower thereby makes only one monthly payment to the wrap-around lender.

Writer—Seller of an option contract.

Y

Yankee Bond—A bond of a foreign issuer payable in U.S. dollars and registered with the SEC.

Yellow Sheet—Sheets listing the bid and ask prices for corporate bonds.

Yen Certificate of Deposit—Short-term, negotiable instrument issued in Japan by Japanese financial institutions and foreign banks with Japanese branches.

Yen Government Securities—Securities issued by the Japanese government, including: 1) Interest-bearing bonds with maturities of two, three, four, and ten years. 2) Discount bonds, usually with a maturity of five years. 3) Short-term securities of maturities of 60 days and over (usually 60-62 days). These discount bills are of three kinds: Treasury bills, Food bills, and foreign exchange fund bills.

Yield—The effective annual rate of return expressed as a percentage. For stocks, it is the dividend divided by the price.

Yield Basis—A method of expressing the value of a security. In a market made on a yield basis, the dealer states both a bid yield and an offered yield.

Yield Buyer—An investor who trades to increase yield. *See* Cash Flow Buyer.

Yield Curve—A graph showing the relationship between yield and maturity for a set of similar securities. Generally refers to the U.S. Treasury market if not otherwise specified. There are four basic yield curve shapes: 1) Ascending. Characterized by short-term rates that are lower than long-term rates. Indicates risk aversion to the increased price volatility and/or decreased liquidity of longer-term issues. Also called *Positive* and *Normal*. 2) Flat. Characterized by approximately constant yield levels for all maturities. Indicates that investors expect that interest rates in the future will be approximately the same as current levels. Also called *Horizontal*. 3) Descending. Characterized by short-term rates that are higher than long-term rates. Indicates that short rates are expected to fall relative to long rates in the immediate future. Also called *Negative* and *Inverted*. 4) Humped. Characterized by a bulge at some point of the yield curve with lower yields on either side. Indicates a positive long-term outlook for interest rates despite a high degree of short-term uncertainty; occurs in markets undergoing some type of major stress.

Yield Curve Arbitrage—1) Buying an off-the-run security if it is relatively cheap and selling a comparable on-the-run security, or vice versa. 2) Buying a short-term security if it is relatively cheap and selling a longer-term security on the same yield curve, or vice versa.

Yield Curve Note—*See* Reverse Floater.

Yield Curve Swap—*See* Constant Maturity Swap.

Yield Differential—*See* Spread.

Yield Maintenance—For a GNMA or other mortgage security bought under a futures contract or standby commitment, the adjustment of the price upon delivery necessary to provide the same yield to the buyer that was specified in the original agreement. Yield maintenance becomes necessary when the coupon on the GNMA that is delivered is different from the coupon that had been expected at the time the agreement was made. *See* Par Cap.

Yield Premium—Extra yield to compensate an investor for assuming risk.

Yield Spread—The difference between the yield of two securities.

Yield Standstill Return—Annualized return on a covered call position, assuming the yield of the bond remains constant and the option expires at its intrinsic value. *See* Standstill Return.

Yield-Tilted Index Fund—Fund that invests in a broadly diversified portfolio of high dividend-paying stocks.

Yield to Adjusted Minimum Maturity—A measure designed to give the yield to the shortest possible maturity of a bond. It is based on the assumption of maximum sinking fund operation and a call on the bond as early as possible. Also called *Yield to Crash*.

Yield to Average Life—1) The yield derived when the average life date (average maturity) is substituted for the maturity date of the issue. 2) *See* Prepaid Life.

Yield to Call—The yield computed assuming the cash flow is the coupon stream to the call date, at which time the issue is redeemed at its call price.

Yield to Crash—*See* Yield to Adjusted Minimum Maturity.

Yield to Maturity (YTM)—The discount rate at which the present value of future payments (coupon flow and repayment of principal) equals the price of the security. The calculation takes into consideration the number of times per year cash flows are paid to the investor. Semiannual yield, for example, assumes two payments per year, annual yield assumes one payment, and so on. Also called *Effective Rate* and *Internal Rate of Return*, because of the implicit assumption that coupon payments can be reinvested at the yield to maturity rate.

Yield to Maturity for Floating Rate Securities (YTM)—A yield to maturity calculation that accounts for all the variables of floating rate securities, including price, accounting method, index rate, margin, coupon refix frequency, payment delay, and refix spread formulas. YTM is a refinement of previous methods, and is the standard formula for U.S. floaters. *See* Discounted Margin.

Yield to Operative Date—Higher of the maximum yield to put or minimum yield to call or maturity. *See* Operative Date.

Yield to Put—The return a bond earns assuming that it is held until a certain date and then put (sold) to the issuing company at the put price.

Yield to Worst—The yield resulting from the most adverse set of circumstances from an investor's point of view; the lowest of all possible yields.

Yield Trading—*See* Basis Trading.

YTM Spread—The difference between the YTM of a floating rate security and that of an index rate. *See* Yield to Maturity for Floating Rate Securities.

Z

Z—Signifies that a number represents the total number of shares and not to multiply by one hundred.

Z Bond—*See* Accrual Bond.

Zerial—Serial zero coupon bond.

Zero Coupon Bond—Debt instrument that does not pay periodic interest. Rather, it is issued without a coupon at a deep discount and is redeemed at par when held to maturity. The difference between the original issue discount price and the par value represents an accretion of interest.

Zero-Fixed Coupon—A type of stepped coupon security whose coupon is initially set at zero and moves after specified intervals to other specified rates. *See* Stepped Coupon.

Zero-Minus Tick—Refers to a trade that is made at the same price as the previous trade in the same security but at a lower price than the last trade done at a different price. *See* Minus Tick.

Zero-Plus Tick—Refers to a trade that is made at the same price as the previous trade in the same security but at a higher price than the last trade done at a different price. *See* Plus Tick.

Z Factor—The ratio of the outstanding accreted principal amount of an accrual bond to its original principal amount. Also called *Accrual Factor*. *See* Accrual Bond and Pool Factor.

Appendix 1

A Guide to U.S. Taxable Fixed Income Securities

Public Debt of the United States

U.S. Treasury securities, backed by the full faith and credit of the federal government, are sold to finance discrepancies between the Treasury's income and outflow. Such deficits may be planned and foreseen or they may arise unexpectedly when receipts or expenditures deviate from the budgeted targets. Some shortfalls are seasonal in nature, reflecting differences in timing of expenses and receipts. In addition to financing budget deficits, Treasury securities are also issued to raise funds on behalf of "off-budget" federal programs with expenditures, revenues, and borrowings that are not included in the budget.

The Treasury has several types of marketable and nonmarketable securities outstanding. Marketable issues, consisting of bills, notes, and bonds, differ mainly in the length of time to maturity from issuance: Treasury bills are issued with an original maturity of one year or less; Treasury notes are issued with maturities ranging from two to ten years; and Treasury bonds are issued with original maturities greater than ten years and up to 30 years. In addition, bills are issued on a discount basis while the others carry interest coupons. Nonmarketable issues consist mainly of savings bonds and special issues to Treasury trust funds, foreign monetary authorities, and state and local governments.

Marketable Treasury securities may be exchanged at any Federal Reserve Bank or branch for an equal amount of any authorized denomination of the same issue. Bearer bonds are interchangeable with registered bonds. Treasury bills and a large portion of all other marketable securities are now in book-entry form, which means they exist as computer entries only. Obligations issued by the United States or any agency or instrumentality thereof after December 31, 1982 (September 3, 1982 in the case of certain long-term U.S. obligations) are required to be in registered form. The registration requirement does not apply to obligations not offered to the public, obligations with a maturity at issuance of not more than one year, and obligations designed to be sold to non-United States investors.

Treasury Auction Schedule

Because of the large amount of Treasury financing needed to fund the government deficit over the last few years, the Treasury has established a regular auction schedule to sell its securities to the public. This schedule calls for a particular auction day for each Treasury maturity. At the announcement of each auction—usually one week before the auction date—the Treasury reveals the amount of each maturity to be sold.

Treasury Bills

Three-month, six-month, and one-year bills are auctioned regularly by the Treasury. Cash management bills, however, are auctioned intermittently to carry the Treasury through periods during which it temporarily falls short of cash.

Three-month and six-month bills are normally auctioned on Mondays, with payment due the following Thursday—the day on which the issues that were sold three and six months earlier mature. The amounts to be auctioned, ordinarily announced late in the afternoon on the Tuesday preceding the auction, can be greater than, less than, or equal to the amounts maturing, depending on the Treasury's current and anticipated cash needs.

Year bills, or 52-week bills, are auctioned every fourth Thursday. Payment is due the following Thursday, when the issues sold 52 weeks earlier mature. Similar to bills with shorter maturities, the amounts of 52-week bills auctioned can exceed, fall below, or equal the amount maturing. The size of the offering is usually announced in the late afternoon of the Friday preceding the Thursday auction. Once every four weeks the payment dates for the 52-week, three-month and six-month bills coincide.

Cash management bills, which raise new cash, are issued at irregular intervals with maturities ranging from a few days to about six months. Typically, these bills are issued early in the month when government spending tends to be heaviest, and mature shortly after one of the major mid-month tax receipt dates (March, April, June, September, or December). The Treasury usually sets the maturities of cash management bills to coincide with those of bills already outstanding, so that once issued they will be interchangeable for trading purposes. Most often, cash management bills are announced only a few days before sale. On occasion, however, an issue may be announced and sold on the same day.

Treasury Coupon Securities

The schedule by which the Treasury auctions its seven coupon issues at various maturities is displayed in the chart below. Treasury notes have original maturities of up to ten years, and Treasury bonds have original maturities ranging from over ten years to 30 years. Currently, the Treasury issues only 30-year bonds. The Treasury eliminated the 20-year bond on April 30, 1986.

Exhibit I Treasury Auction Schedule

Month				Maturities			
	2[1]	3[2]	4[3]	5[4]	7[3]	10[2]	30[2]
January	■						
February	■	■		■		■	■
March	■		■		■		
April	■						
May	■	■		■		■	■
June	■		■		■		
July	■						
August	■	■		■		■	■
September	■		■		■		
October	■						
November	■	■		■		■	■
December	■		■		■		

Footnotes

[1] 2-year—Auctioned second half of every month, except in March, June, September, and December when the 2-year will be auctioned as part of the End of Quarter financing operation.

[2] 3-, 10-, 30-year—Auctioned first week of second month in calendar quarter.

[3] 4-, 7-year—Auctioned second half of last month in calendar quarter.

[4] 5-year—Auctioned late in second month of calendar quarter.

Two-year notes are auctioned during the second half of the month, usually on the second to the last Wednesday of the month. When the Treasury conducts its End of Quarter financing operation, however, the 2-year note is auctioned as part of the package, together with the 4-year and the 7-year notes. They are dated and mature as of the month's end. The size of the issue, typically announced a week before the auction, may be greater than, less than, or the same as the amount maturing, depending on the Treasury's cash position.

Five-year notes are auctioned on either the last Tuesday or Wednesday of the second month of each calendar quarter with payment in the beginning of the final month of the quarter. Five-year notes mature mid-month.

Treasury Quarterly Refunding

In three consecutive days at the beginning of the second month of each calendar quarter, the Treasury conducts its regular refunding operation and auctions three- and ten-year notes and 30-year bonds. The Treasury's announcement, usually on the last Wednesday of the preceding month, breaks down the proportion of the package that is refunding of maturing debt and the portion that represents new money for the Treasury. At the same announcement, the Treasury estimates its cash needs for the balance of the quarter and discloses the specific types of financing that it is considering.

As part of the quarterly refunding, the three-year and ten-year notes are dated on or near, and mature on, the 15th of the month.

The 30-year bond, the last auction of the package, is also dated and scheduled to mature on the 15th of the month. Prior to 1985, the Treasury auctioned the bond as a callable security, callable at par five years prior to maturity at the option of the Treasury. Beginning with the Treasury refunding operation in February 1985, however, all 30-year bonds have been auctioned as non-callable securities.

Treasury End of Quarter Financing

The Treasury's end of quarter financing, an operation similar to the quarterly Treasury Refunding, is conducted during the second half of the last month of each calendar quarter. The securities sold in this package are four- and seven-year notes. The Treasury announces the details of the financing package on the Tuesday preceding the auctions. The auctions are usually held during the last week of the quarter.

The four-year notes generally are dated and mature at month's end, while the seven-year notes generally are dated at the beginning of the month and mature mid-month.

Method of Sale. *Treasury Bills.* Treasury Bills are sold at a discount—that is, the dollar price charged to the investor is less than the redemption value at maturity. The difference, or the discount, constitutes the payment of interest to the investor. Prior to an offering of Treasury bills, the Treasury issues a notice that invites tenders under competitive and noncompetitive bidding. When tendered competitively, the price bid must be expressed on the basis of a par value of 100; noncompetitive bids without a stated price are accepted in full at the average price of the accepted competitive bids.

All bills are issued in book-entry form and pay face amount at maturity. The minimum order for regular three-month, six-month, and one-year bill auctions is $10,000; above the initial $10,000, orders must be in multiples of $5,000. For cash management bills, minimum orders range from $10 million for very short maturities to $1 million for longer maturities.

Coupon Offerings. While the auction procedures for Treasury notes and bonds are similar to those for bills, bidding is in terms of yield rather than price. On the day of a given auction, bids can be submitted to the Treasury until 1:00 p.m. New York time. Competitive bidders submit the yield and the amount of the new issue that they wish to buy at that yield to the Treasury. After the books are closed, the Treasury sets the coupon on the new issue based on the range of bids it received and on the amount of the security it wants to issue. The coupon is set to the nearest one-eighth of one percent, resulting in an average price equal to or less than 100. After the coupon is set, the price that each accepted bid represents is calculated. This price also equals the amount that must be paid to the Treasury. Noncompetitive bids are accepted at the average price of the accepted competitive bids.

In auctions of outstanding issues being reopened by the Treasury, the coupon and maturity date are already known; therefore, bids for the issue are made in terms of price. The average price can be above or below 100, depending on how the coupon compares with prevailing market rates. Those bidding on the issue submit the prices and the amount that they wish to buy to the Treasury. After all bids have been received, the Treasury determines the average price and the yield based on that price.

Treasury notes and bonds are available in registered, bearer, and book entry form. As of December 31, 1982 (September 3, 1982 in the case of certain long-term U.S. obligations), however, obligations issued by the United States or any of its agencies are required to be in registered form. Registered book entry obligations are transferable only pursuant to regulations prescribed by the Secretary of the Treasury. The minimum order for Treasury notes and Treasury bonds at auction time is $5,000 and $1,000, respectively. Both notes and bonds also are available in denominations of $10,000, $100,000, and $1,000,000.

Stripped Treasury Bonds

A Treasury bond or note represents a series of coupon payments and a principal payment at maturity. The process of "stripping" is the separation of unmatured coupons and corpus (principal payment). Thus, the component stripped securities are essentially zero-coupon bonds: investors pay specific sums of money in return for single payments of proceeds at a later date with no payments in the interim. In stripped securities, each coupon and principal payment is sold separately and subsequently traded separately. If the bond that has been stripped is of bearer form, then physical coupon and corpus strips are in bearer form and can be transferred. If the Treasury security stripped is in registered form, the strips created must be kept in registered form.

There is a large secondary market for Treasury strips. This market developed in July 1982 after the amendment of the Internal Revenue code, at the request of the Treasury, required that stripped coupons and corpus be treated in the same manner as corporate original issue discount securities for tax purposes.

Initially, physical strips represented the majority of strip securities. Thus, a bearer Treasury note or bond, backed by the full faith and credit of the United States, was stripped into its component pieces by physically separating the coupons and the corpus from each other and then selling the individual pieces as zero coupon Treasury strips to investors. Delivery of the individual coupon or corpus to the buyer completed the stripping process.

In addition to physical strips "growth receipts" or "certificates of accrual" have been issued by various securities dealers in the United States. These receipts represent direct ownership of an individual cash flow or a group of serially maturing cash flows: the receipt entitles the investor to receive the proceeds of an individual coupon, corpus, or callable corpus of a Treasury security held by a custodian for the receipt holders. One disadvantage of this form of stripping was that it was offered, and thus traded by, only one firm.

In 1982, the revised Internal Revenue code mandated that all future U.S. Treasury notes and bonds be issued in registered, book-entry form. This eliminated any future issuance of bearer physical securities—the raw material of the physical strip market—and reduced the availability of physical issues. As a result, certificate offerings using registered securities as the underlying collateral began to proliferate.

In response to the need for a generic strip product in registered receipt form, Treasury Receipts (TRs) were created. Treasury Receipts represent ownership of future interest and principal payments on certain U.S. Treasury notes or bonds held in custody by State Street Bank and Trust company on behalf of the holders of the related TRs. The interest and principal payments on the Treasury securities underlying the TRs are direct obligations of the United States. TRs of the semiannual interest payments due on the Treasury securities are offered as Coupon TRs, and those of the principal payments due on the Treasury securities are offered as Principal TRs. TRs that evidence ownership of both the principal payments due on redeemable Treasury securities and any interest payments due thereon (following the earliest redemption date) are offered as callable TRs.

Any depositor of Treasury securities who is acceptable to the custodian can offer the related TRs. When TRs initially were developed, it was intended—though not required—that all depositors would make markets in all TRs, irrespective of which depositor originally offered them. TRs are offered in registered form in denominations and at prices negotiated between the purchaser and the depositor at the time of sale. Delivery is made by the depositor in New York against payment by the purchaser.

The latest addition to the U.S. Treasury zero coupon market is Treasury STRIPS (Separately Traded Registered Interest and Principal Security). These securities, first made available by the Treasury at the end of January 1985, are wire transferable, $1,000 denominated interest and principal payments on U.S. Treasury securities. As is true of most other zero coupon instruments, they are traded in terms of yield to maturity and generally quoted on a 10 basis point spread between bid and offer. STRIPS are created by delivering bonds to the Federal Reserve with instructions to return the bonds with their component pieces separated and identified on the customer's account with a Federal member bank. They are available only in registered form.

U.S. Government Agencies and Sponsored Enterprises

In addition to U.S. Treasury securities, which are fully backed by the federal government, there are several government agencies and government-sponsored enterprises that also issue debt directly to the public. The capital raised from these issues supports a variety of public programs and activities in the United States. Some of these issues are backed by the full faith and credit of the United States and many are guaranteed by the Treasury or supported by the issuing agency's right to borrow from the Treasury. Others, however, lack any formal government backing.

Currently, there are five regular issuers of straight debt securities. In addition, there are securities currently outstanding by issuers that are no longer active in the public debt market. A brief description of each agency or enterprise and the types of securities that it issues follows.

Federal Farm Credit Banks

The Farm Credit System is a cooperatively owned nationwide system of banks and associations. The system provides mortgage loans and short- and intermediate-term credit to farmers, ranchers, rural homeowners, and agricultural and rural cooperatives. These credit services are provided through the Federal Land Banks, Federal Intermediate Credit Banks, and Banks for cooperatives in each of the 12 Federal Farm Districts in the United States.

The Farm Credit System relies solely on the money markets and the credit markets for funds. Prior to 1979, each of the bank groups issued securities on their own behalf. In January 1979, however, the banks established the Federal Farm Credit Bank Funding corporation in New York to issue all their public offerings of securities.

The Federal Farm Credit Bank currently issues two types of securities, consolidated systemwide discount notes and consolidated systemwide bonds.

The U.S. Treasury maintains revolving funds. These funds permit the Governor of the Farm Credit Administration to make temporary investments in the stock of the Federal Intermediate Credit Banks and the Banks for Cooperatives, amounting to $112 million and $149 million. The Secretary of the Treasury may deposit up to $6 million with the Federal Land Banks. On December 23, 1985, President Reagan signed legislation providing indirect federal support of the Farm Credit System. The law established the Federal Farm Credit Capital Corporation for the purpose of redistributing assets among the profitable and financially pressed System banks. Additionally, the Act permits the Secretary of the Treasury to infuse funds into the farm credit system in the event of credit difficulties.

The Governor of the Farm Credit Administration follows a policy of cooperative consultation with the U.S. Treasury when securities are issued. The Farm Credit Banks also have a close relationship with the Federal Reserve Banks. The Federal Reserve Banks maintain accounts and act as clearing agents for each of the 37 farm banks.

Although the government assumes no direct liability for these securities, they are the obligations of banks operating under federal charter. The securities sold to the public are secured by collateral consisting of notes or other obligations of the borrowers, obligations of the United States or any agency thereof, other readily marketable securities approved by the Farm Credit Administration, or cash, in an aggregate value equal to the bonds outstanding. Furthermore, the Farm Credit

Banks are authorized to issue notes and bonds up to an amount equal to 20 times the capital and surplus of the banks.

Consolidated systemwide discount notes are issued periodically—most often to provide temporary funding between the sale of bonds. These discount notes are issued with maturities ranging from five to 360 days in denominations of $50,000, $100,000, $500,000, $1,000,000, and $5,000,000 in definitive form. Six- and nine-month systemwide bonds are issued every month and longer-term bonds, maturing in as many as ten years, are issued approximately eight times a year. The bonds are issued in multiples of $1,000 for maturities over 13 months and $5,000 for shorter maturities. Bonds are issued in book-entry form only.

Federal Home Loan Banks

The Federal Home Loan Bank System (FHLB) is comprised of 12 District Banks located throughout the country. The FHLB operates as a credit reserve system for the thrift industry, enhancing and stabilizing the flow of mortgage credit to the public. The banks are wholly owned by their member institutions, but are supervised by the Federal Home Loan Bank Board, an independent federal agency. The Bank Board issues all federal charters for savings and loan associations and mutual savings banks.

Membership in the Federal Home Loan Bank System is mandatory for all federally chartered institutions. Other state chartered thrift institutions are eligible to become members provided they meet specific requirements. To join the system, a qualified institution must purchase capital stock in its regional District Bank in an amount equal to at least one percent of the aggregate of the unpaid principal of its mortgage loans.

The purchase of stock by member banks provides the equity base used to support the debt of the FHLB system. This debt is issued as consolidated discount notes and bonds. Although the debt of the FHLB is not guaranteed by the U.S. government, the Banks operate under federal charter and supervision. Furthermore, the Secretary of the Treasury is authorized to purchase up to $4 billion of these securities. Consolidated obligations of the System are limited to an amount of up to 12 times the total paid-in capital stock and legal reserves of all the Banks.

The District Banks must maintain secured advances, guaranteed mortgages, U.S. government securities, or cash in an amount at least equal to their obligations outstanding. The FHLB bonds are issued for long-term funding requirements with maturities of between one and ten years. Bonds are issued at least once a month, but the system may enter the market more often if additional funding is required. The bonds are issued only in book entry form for a minimum of $10,000 with multiples of $5,000 thereafter.

Discount notes are issued periodically to enhance the cash management of the FHLB system. Discount notes are issued with maturities of 30 to 360 days and are issued on a discount basis. The notes are issued in book entry form in denominations of $100,000, $150,000, and $1,000,000 through six dealers in the United States.

Federal Home Loan Mortgage Corporation

The Federal Home Loan Mortgage Corporation (FHLMC), a corporate instrumentality of the United States, was created by an Act of congress in 1970. Its purpose is to increase the availability of mortgage credit for the financing of housing, primarily by developing and maintaining an active nationwide secondary market in conventional residential mortgages.

The capital stock of the Corporation, $100 million of non-voting common, is owned entirely by the 12 Federal Home Loan Banks. FHLMC purchases residential mortgages and participations in mortgages from members of the Federal Home Loan Bank System and from other authorized financial institutions whose deposits or accounts are insured by agencies of the U.S. government. The system also purchases other mortgages approved by the Department of Housing and Urban Development. FHLMC packages these mortgages and sells them to the public as mortgage-related securities.

FHLMC sells two types of mortgage-related securities: Participation Certificates and Collateralized Mortgage Obligations. Periodically, FHLMC also issues straight long-term debt securities. Until 1979, Freddie Mac also sold Guaranteed Mortgage Certificates or GMCs. GMCs represent undivided interest in conventional residential mortgages, which pay principal annually in guaranteed minimum amounts and interest semiannually.

Participation Certificates. Participation Certificates (PCs) issued by FHLMC represent undivided interests in conventional or Federal Housing Administration/Veteran's Administration mortgages bought by FHLMC from eligible sellers. FHLMC guarantees the timely payment of interest to each certificate holder every month. Principal, both scheduled and unscheduled, is "passed through" as it is collected by FHLMC, and the payment of all collected principal is guaranteed to be paid no later than one year after it becomes payable. Although the final payment date is 30 years after issuance, prepayments and other factors have shortened the expected average lives of these securities.

FHLMC issues two different types of PCs: regular PCs and guarantor or "swap" PCs. In its regular PC program, FHLMC purchases mortgages from eligible sellers in weekly auctions. These mortgages may be held in the FHLMC portfolio or put into pools and sold directly as PCs in weekly auctions or through a dealer group. In the guarantor program, FHLMC exchanges or swaps a certificate for mortgages directly with the mortgage originator, who is then free to sell the PC. Guarantor program PCs are smaller than regular PCs and are usually concentrated with a single mortgage originator. Regular PCs consist of mortgages from FHLMC's entire national portfolio, and the pools are generally broad-based geographically and contain thousands of loans.

FHLMC PCs are sold in registered form only and FHLMC acts as the registrar and transfer agent. PCs are sold in original unpaid principal balances of $25,000, $100,000, $200,000, $500,000, $1,000,000, and $5,000,000.

Collateralized Mortgage Obligations. Collateralized Mortgage Obligations (CMOs), a recent innovation in mortgage securities, are designed to provide investors with a greater range of coupon, maturity, and expected average life alternatives. In a standard CMO offering, the issuer constructs a series of bonds that are fully collateralized by an underlying group of mortgages. Each CMO offering is broken out into several classes or tranches. The cash flows generated by the mortgages in the collateral pool are used first to pay interest on each tranche of bonds outstanding. Residual cash flows are then used to retire principal. Principal payments are made exclusively to the first tranche of bonds outstanding until they are all retired. Principal payments are then made to the holders of the second tranche. The sequential retirement process continues until all bonds are retired. In no case does any tranche receive principal before all previous tranches are fully retired.

The sequential approach to the retirement of tranches increases the predictability of cash flows on CMOs relative to pass-throughs. A pass-through holder receives principal and interest each month. The investor, however, risks early retirement of the security because of prepayments. In contrast, a CMO tranche enjoys call protection provided by prior tranches. Additionally, since all but the last tranche of bonds will be retired before the underlying mortgage collateral matures, most CMO tranches have guaranteed final maturities that are shorter than those available on pass-throughs.

CMOs have been popular among U.S. investors because they provide incremental yield over Treasuries over a broad array of maturities and average lives. Most CMOs have semiannual payments as opposed to the monthly payments typical of pass-throughs. CMOs often are structured more like Treasuries than are pass-throughs; some investors view this as an advantage.

Federal National Mortgage Association

The Federal National Mortgage Association (FNMA) is a federally chartered Association and privately owned corporation. FNMA was established in 1938 as a United States government agency to provide additional liquidity to the mortgage market. In 1968, the original FNMA was broken into two corporations——the privately owned FNMA and a government-owned corporation, the Government National Mortgage Association.

FNMA was originally authorized to deal only in the secondary market in federally guaranteed or insured mortgages. In 1970, however, FNMA was authorized to deal in conventional mortgages as well. FNMA supplies funds to the mortgage market by purchasing home mortgage loans from local lenders. The funds for these purchases are raised by the sale of short-term notes and debentures to the public.

FNMA's debentures and notes do not represent U.S. government obligations and are not federally guaranteed. The President of the United States, however, has the authority to appoint five of FNMA's fifteen directors. The Secretary of Housing and Urban Development, representing the Executive Branch, also has general regulatory authority, as well as specific regulatory and supervisory functions, which include reviewing dividend policies, examining financial reports, approving changes in the legal debt to capital ratio of FNMA, and approving issuance of stock. In addition, the Secretary of the Treasury exerts authority over FNMA by approving the issuance and terms of any debt securities, and by possessing the discretionary authority to purchase $2.25 billion of FNMA obligations.

Debentures and Notes. FNMA sells short-term discount notes to the public with maturities ranging from 30 to 360 days. Frequently, these maturities are negotiated between the investor and FNMA. The rates at which the notes are sold are established by FNMA. These rates are subject to change and are generally held in line with other prevailing short-term rates such as Treasury bills and commercial paper. The minimum denomination for FNMA discount notes is $50,000 with additional increments of $5,000, $10,000, $25,000, $100,000, $500,000, and $1,000,000. The notes are issued in bearer form only.

FNMA debentures, backed by the general credit of FNMA, are issued periodically with maturities ranging from three to 25 years and generally are not callable. The debentures are issued in book-entry or bearer form in denominations of $10,000, $25,000, $50,000, $100,000, and $500,000 with a minimum order of $10,000.

Guaranteed Mortgage Pass-Through Certificates. In 1981, FNMA began packaging pools of mortgages as pass-through securities called

FNMA Guaranteed Mortgage Pass-Through certificates. FNMA purchases mortgages from approved sellers and servicers, including state and federally chartered savings and loan associations, mutual savings banks, commercial banks, and similar institutions whose deposits or accounts are insured by the FDIC, FSLIC, or the National Credit Union Association.

FNMA can issue its pass-through certificates in several ways. When FNMA is the issuer of the security, sales may be direct from the originator of the pool to the investor. FNMA may also contribute loans from its own portfolio to a pool. When there is more than one originator contributing to a pool, the pool may be offered through a dealer group. FNMA guarantees the timely payment of principal and interest.

FNMA mortgage pass-through certificates are issued in registered form only in minimum denominations of $25,000 original principal amount. There are no restrictions as to increments above this minimum.

Government National Mortgage Association

The Government National Mortgage Association (GNMA) was created in 1968 as a government corporation within the U.S. Department of Housing and Urban Development (HUD) to administer mortgage support programs that could not be carried out in the private market.

Structured as a corporation, GNMA functions as part of HUD and is, by law, subject to the overall direction of the Secretary of HUD. The President of GNMA ranks as an Assistant Secretary and is nominated by the President of the United States and confirmed by the U.S. Senate. GNMA's budget is part of the budget of the U.S. government.

GNMA's most important ongoing activity is its Mortgage Backed Securities (MBS) program. In this program, GNMA guarantees privately issued securities backed by pools of federally insured or guaranteed mortgages on residential properties. The purpose of the MBS program is to increase the availability of mortgage credit by attracting new sources of funds for the mortgage market and by increasing liquidity in the secondary mortgage market.

Through the MBS program, GNMA guarantees privately issued securities backed by pools of mortgages. Security holders receive a pass-through of the principal and interest payments from the pool of mortgages, less amounts needed to cover servicing costs and certain GNMA fees. The GNMA guaranty assures the registered security holder of the timely payment of monthly principal and interest payments and early recovery of principal on the underlying mortgages. The investor receives these payments whether or not they are made by the homeowners.

GNMA neither loans the funds for the underlying mortgages nor issues the pass-through securities. GNMA's function is limited to acting as a guarantor of the performance of the security. The underlying mortgages are insured by other government agencies. The funds are ultimately raised by the sale of securities in the capital markets.

The MBS program is a means for channeling funds from the domestic and international securities markets into the American housing market. The U.S. government's backing of the securities makes them acceptable in those sectors of the capital markets that otherwise would not be likely to invest in the residential mortgage market. Statutory authority for the MBS program is provided in Section 306(g) of the National Housing Act. It authorizes GNMA to guarantee the timely payment of principal and interest on securities that are based on and backed by a trust or pool composed of mortgages that are insured by the Federal Housing Administration (FHA), or guaranteed by the Farmers Home Administration (FmHA) or the Veterans Administration (VA).

GNMA's guaranty of mortgage backed securities carries the full faith and credit of the United States. GNMA has the statutory right to borrow without limit from the U.S. Treasury if necessary to make payments to security holders.

The MBS program has helped finance over four million housing units. As of year-end 1985, over $267.4 billion in securities had been issued and more than $212.1 billion of the aggregate principal balances was still outstanding. There are approximately 110,000 GNMA mortgage pools in existence. More than one thousand firms are approved GNMA issuers with about 90 securities dealers authorized to market the securities. The majority of the issuers are mortgage bankers, though many savings and loan associations, commercial banks, and other financial institutions are active as issuers.

GNMA administers two mortgage-backed securities programs, each of which has several sub-programs. The GNMA I program was initiated in 1970. The GNMA II program, introduced in July 1983, takes advantage of many technological improvements that have emerged since the first GNMA I securities were introduced. The key features of the GNMA II program include the use of a central paying agent and the availability of larger and more geographically dispersed, multiple issuer pools. The central paying agent provides consolidated monthly payments (one check for all GNMA II holdings) to investors. GNMA II multiple issuer pools provide investors with improved prepayment consistency.

In order to become an approved issuer of GNMA securities, a firm must be in the business of originating or servicing mortgage loans. It must be an FHA approved mortgagee (lender) in good standing and have a net worth that assures GNMA of the firm's financial capacity to pay security holders when mortgagors (homeowners) fail to make their mortgage payments on time.

Each issuance, or mortgage pool, must total at least $1 million in principal amount. All the loans in a single pool will bear the same interest rate. Typically, the issuer also makes arrangements with a securities dealer to market the mortgage-backed securities when they become available.

Settlement Procedures

Treasury and Agency

The delivery and clearing process of U.S. Treasury and agency debt securities has been facilitated greatly by the change to book-entry form. This has enabled over 90% of government securities transactions to be cleared over the Federal Reserve Wire System.

All of the large New York banks now clear most of their transactions with each other and with the Federal Reserve through the use of computers and the book-entry custody system maintained by the Federal Reserve Bank of New York. Virtually all transfers for the account of the banks, as well as for the government securities dealers and their customers, are now processed solely by bookkeeping entries. Also, most corporations and non-bank financial institutions active in the securities markets maintain accounts at major New York banks through which they clear their securities transactions. This system reduces the costs and risks associated with physical handling and speeds the completion of transactions.

The normal settlement date for Treasury and agency securities is the next full business day after the trade is executed. Each major dealer retains a New York bank for clearing specific securities. Such clearing banks are responsible for the receipt of payment and delivery of securities if securities are sold by the dealer and the reverse if securities are bought by the dealer. For example, when First Boston sells Treasury bills to a customer, our clearance agent, Manufacturers Hanover, is responsible for receiving payment for the bills and delivering them to the customer. If the customer clears through Morgan Guaranty, then Manufacturers Hanover and Morgan Guaranty handle the clearing process. The customer must advise Morgan Guaranty of the trade and instruct it to pay for and take delivery of the bills from First Boston; if not, the trade will "fail." All of the money involved in the transaction is transferred over the Federal Wire System, as are the securities involved once payment is made.

GNMA Pass-Through Securities

The day that a GNMA pass-through trade is transacted, confirmation of the specific terms of the trade (including amount, coupon, price, and the date on which the trade will settle) is made over the telephone between the purchaser and the seller. On the day following the trade, formal written confirmation of the trade is sent to the purchaser specifying the details of the trade.

Coupons less than or equal to 10% settle on the Monday following the third Wednesday of the month. Coupons over 10% and all 15-year maturity GNMAs settle on the third Wednesday of the month. Trades can also be specified for other settlement (five business days later). Five business days prior to the standard settlement date, final closing figures that specify the pool number and the original face amount of the GNMA certificate and that month's pool factor are determined and relayed to the purchaser. Based on the original face amount and the current factor, the final proceeds of the trade are calculated by multiplying the current amortized amount of the certificate by the price paid for the pool plus accrued interest. Formal written confirmation with the final settlement figures is sent the following day. On the settlement date, the purchaser must have federal funds in the amount of the final proceeds at its New York correspondent bank. After payment is made, the GNMAs are received at the correspondent bank on behalf of the purchaser and the GNMAs become registered in the purchaser's name by Chemical Bank, the transfer agent for GNMA. On the 15th day of the following month, the investor receives the principal, interest, and prepayments collected from the pool the preceding month.

Due to the monthly payment of principal, interest, and prepayments, there are two key dates that determine who will receive a given month's payments from a GNMA pool. The cut-off date is the last day of the month during which a principal prepayment received by the issuer will be remitted to the security holder in the forthcoming payment. For GNMA securities, this date is the 25th day of the month. Any GNMA prepayments that are collected after the 25th day will be paid in the following month's payment. The 30th day of the month or the last business day of the month is the record date for the GNMA payment process. The registered holder of the GNMA on this day receives that month's payments of principal, interest, and prepayments.

U.S. Corporate Bond Market

Corporates are the second largest fixed income sector, exceeded in quantity only by Treasuries. Most corporate bonds outstanding are registered in the name of the owner for both principal and interest payments. Payments are sent directly to the registered owner of the securities, providing protection from loss or theft.

Most corporate bonds pay interest semiannually and generally come in denominations of $1,000 and above. The bonds usually are traded in round lots of $100,000 par amount; many firms are reluctant to trade odd lot (less than $100,000 par value) over-the-counter orders. Corporate bond delivery and payments normally are effected through clearing house funds, five business days after the transaction. Earlier payment, or payment in federal funds, must be arranged before the transaction takes place. Accrued interest from the last coupon payment date through the day prior to the delivery date must be paid by the purchaser of the bonds to the seller. Interest payments on corporate bonds are calculated based on 30-day months and 360-day years.

Most industrial and bank/finance bonds are unsecured debentures backed by the general credit of the issuing corporation. Subordinated debentures are issued infrequently by finance companies and rank behind bank debt and debentures but ahead of preferred and common stock.

Industrial issues usually carry refunding protection for ten years from the date of issuance and include sinking funds that begin approximately eleven years after the initial offering. These features are designed to retire a portion of the issue before its final maturity, effectively shortening the average life of the issue. Portions of an issue can be called away from the holder by lot to satisfy sinking fund requirements. This occurs most often when the issue is trading above its sinking fund price.

Public electric utility issues are generally backed by a first mortgage lien on a utility plant. The majority of utility indentures provide for earnings coverage of interest expenses before financing is permitted. Special redemption features are included in selected electric utility indentures, which should be accounted for prior to purchase. Typically, most utility issues have five-year refunding protection and no or minimal sinking fund provisions.

Telephone issues generally have been issued with long maturities, ranging from 30 to 40 years, and carry five years of call protection.

Rating Agency Definitions

The quality of corporate bonds is measured by three independent rating agencies: Standard & Poor's Corporation, Moody's Investors Service, Inc., and Duff & Phelps, Inc. The top four categories for each agency are considered investment-grade bonds. Moody's and S&P rating definitions for these categories indicate a low level of risk relative to payment of interest and repayment of principal on a timely basis. The investment grade ratings fall into the following categories:

Moody's	S&P	Duff & Phelps	FBC Ranking
Aaa	AAA	1	09.0-10.0
Aa1, Aa2, Aa3	AA+, AA, AA-	2, 3, 4	08.0-09.0
A1, A2, A3	A+, A, A-	5, 6, 7	07.0-08.0
Baa1, Baa2, Baa3	BBB+, BBB, BBB-	8, 9, 10	06.0-07.0

Moody's Investors Service, Inc. Bonds rated Aaa are judged to be of the best quality. They carry the smallest degree of investment risk and are generally referred to as "gilt edged." Interest payments are protected by a large or exceptionally stable margin and principal is secure. While the various protective elements are likely to change, such changes are unlikely to impair the fundamental strength of such issues.

Bonds that are rated Aa are judged to be of high quality by all standards. Together with the Aaa group they comprise what are generally known as high grade bonds. They are rated lower than the best bonds because margins of protection may not be as large or there may be other elements present that make the long-term risk appear somewhat higher than for Aaa securities.

Bonds rated A possess many favorable investment attributes and are to be considered upper medium grade obligations. Factors giving security to principal and interest are considered adequate, but elements may be present that suggest a susceptibility to impairment sometime in the future.

Bonds that are rated Baa are considered medium grade obligations, i.e., they are neither well protected nor poorly secured. Interest payments and principal security appear adequate for the present, but certain protective elements may be missing or characteristically unreliable over any extended period. Such bonds lack outstanding investment characteristics and in fact have speculative characteristics as well.

Standard & Poor's Corporation (S&P). Debt rated AAA has the highest rating assigned by Standard & Poor's. Capacity to pay interest and repay principal is extremely strong.

Debt rated AA has a very strong capacity to pay interest and repay principal and differs from the higher rated issues only in a small degree.

Debt rated A has a strong capacity to pay interest and repay principal although it is somewhat more susceptible to the adverse effects of changes in circumstances and economic conditions than debt in higher rated categories.

Debt rated BBB is regarded as having an adequate capacity to pay interest and repay principal. Whereas it normally exhibits adequate protection parameters, adverse economic conditions or changing circumstances are more likely to lead to a weakened capacity to pay interest and repay principal for debt in this category than in higher rated categories.

Both Moody's and S&P assign additional modifying ratings within each rating category from double A through triple B. S&P uses a plus (+) or minus (–) to show the relative standing within the rating category. Moody's assigns numerical modifiers (1, 2, and 3) to indicate the standing within each category. The modifier 1 indicates that the security ranks in the higher end of the category, modifier 2 indicates mid-range ranking, and the modifier 3 indicates that the issue ranks in the lower end of the rating category.

Duff and Phelps, Inc. (D&P). Debt rated 1 is the equivalent of triple A and is the highest credit quality. The risk factors are negligible, being only slightly more than those of risk-free U.S. Treasury debt.

Debt rated 2, 3, and 4 is the equivalent of high, medium, and low double A, respectively, and is considered to be of high credit quality. Protection factors are strong. Risk is modest but may vary slightly from time to time because of economic conditions.

Debt rated 5, 6, and 7 is the equivalent of high, medium, and low single A, respectively. Protection factors are average but adequate. Risk factors, however, are more variable and greater in periods of economic stress.

Debt rated 8, 9, and 10 is the equivalent of high, medium, and low triple B, respectively. Such debt offers below average protection, but is still considered sufficient for institutional investment. There is considerable variability in risk during economic cycles.

First Boston Ranking. First Boston has devised its own numerical ranking scale to help investors compare secondary issues in the corporate bond market and to compare corporate sectors. The scale also aids in the selection process when isolating groups of securities within a narrow credit quality range.

Corporate Bond Pricing

The pricing of a corporate bond takes into consideration the individual features of the security such as maturity, put and call provisions, credit quality, sinking fund features, size of the issue, and the technical aspects of the credit markets.

Industrial and finance company issues are typically handled by the negotiated offering method involving one or more investment banking firms. These firms, acting as manager on behalf of the underwriting syndicates, negotiate the terms of the offering. Competitive bidding is frequently used by utility companies and railroads offering equipment trust certificates.

Yield spreads and yield premiums to Treasuries are frequently used as guidelines in pricing new issues and assessing relative value in the secondary market. For lower grade sectors, absolute target yield levels may have a strong influence in attracting investor interest. Yield spreads for corporate bonds have generally widened as yield levels rise. A dramatic rally, however, may also cause a short-term widening of corporate spreads as investors seek the liquidity and call protection of the Treasury market. Greater variability in spread is generally found among lower grade securities due to the impact of interest rate levels on their debt quality. Relative spreads can vary widely over a period of years, and can materially influence the total return realized by investors.

Historically, high quality industrial credits have traded closest to Treasury levels due to their superior credit quality and stability. In recent years, however, leveraged buy-outs, corporate balance sheet restructuring, and heightened levels of merger and acquisition activity have led to a deterioration of credit perceptions of the industrial sector. Collectively known as "event risk," these phenomena have caused industrial spreads to widen, approaching or exceeding traditional credit spreads of other corporate sectors. Event risk affects not only the acquiror as it increases its leverage but also the target company if it tries to avert a takeover. The deterioration of credit perceptions is measured not only in absolute basis points but also on a percentage basis commonly referred to as yield premiums to Treasuries.

Technical factors operating in the market may also influence corporate bond pricing. Among these factors are volatility and supply of new issues. Volatility negatively affects variable cash flow instruments such as callable corporates as the issuer's call option increases in value to the detriment of the investor. Heavy new issue supply may also have an adverse impact on yield spreads.

The structure of corporate bonds may have a significant impact on return performance. In most instances, bonds are cash callable at some premium upon issuance but may carry refunding protection for a period of years. During this period, a bond issue may be called only through using internally generated cash. When refunding protection ends, debt issues may be retired by using proceeds from the issuance of lower coupon debt.

Cash call and refunding features may limit a bond's price appreciation in a market rally. As interest rate levels decline, bond prices may increase toward their call or refunding price. Bond prices may become "cushioned" due to the market's reluctance to bid on a bond that may be called at a predetermined price. Investors assessing yield spreads on corporates should evaluate both the call and credit components of the spread. Option valuation techniques may be used to quantify the basis point value of issuers' call options.

Over the near term as corporate debt is refunded, the market will most likely witness a change in the composition of issuers. Utilities formerly were among the largest class of issuers. They may actually become net generators of cash in the near future. As a result, their new issue volume may subside as will the percentage of utility issues within the corporate bond spectrum.

Appendix 2

Money Market Instruments

Bankers' Acceptances

A bankers' acceptance is a unique credit instrument used to finance both domestic and international self-liquidating transactions. By definition, it is ". . . a draft or bill of exchange, whether payable in the United States or abroad and whether payable in dollars or some other money, accepted by a bank or trust company, or a firm, company, or corporation engaged generally in the business of granting bankers' acceptance credits." [1]

Creation and Life of an Acceptance

Consider a coffee processor in the United States who wishes to finance the importation of Colombian coffee on an acceptance basis. The American importer, after negotiating with the exporter in Colombia, arranges for his American commercial bank to issue an irrevocable letter of credit in favor of the exporter. The letter of credit specifies the details of the shipment and states that the Colombian exporter may draw a time draft for a certain amount on the American bank. The Colombian exporter, in conformity with the terms of the letter of credit, draws a draft on the American bank and negotiates the draft with his local bank, receiving immediate payment. The Colombian bank then forwards the draft to the United States for presentation to the bank that issued the letter of credit. This bank stamps the draft "accepted" thus incurring an obligation to pay the draft at maturity. An acceptance has been created.

The new acceptance is typically discounted for the Colombian bank by the accepting bank and the proceeds credited to the account of the Colombian bank. The accepting bank in turn may either sell the

---

1   Advances and Discounts by Federal Reserve Banks, Regulation A. Board of Governors of the Federal Reserve System.

315

acceptance to a dealer or hold it in its own portfolio. Whatever the case, the shipping documents are released to the American importer against a trust receipt, thus allowing the importer to process and sell the coffee. The importer is obligated to deposit the proceeds of the coffee sales at the accepting bank in time to honor the acceptance. At maturity, the acceptance is presented for payment by its owner and the transaction is completed.

The cost of acceptance financing is the sum of the discount charged when the acceptance is discounted and the commission paid to the accepting bank. This cost may be paid by either of the commercial parties to the transaction, in accordance with the agreement made with the accepting bank.

Acceptances as an Investment

From the standpoint of security, a bankers' acceptance is an irrevocable primary obligation of the accepting bank, and a contingent obligation of the drawer and of any endorsers whose names appear upon it. The bank is protected by its customer's agreement to provide good funds by the time the acceptance matures and generally also by the pledge of documents such as invoices, bills of lading, independent warehouse or terminal receipts, trust receipts, and other papers evidencing ownership and insurance of the goods financed. In 69 years of usage in the United States, the bankers' acceptance has come through war and economic depression with no known principal loss to investors. Courts have held that the letter of credit agreement, from inception to conclusion, is based on the principle that the accepting bank holds the agreement not for its own benefit or that of its general creditors, but in trust for the holder of the acceptance. The landmark decision on this subject involved the failure of the Bank of the United States in New York in December 1930, with 403 acceptances outstanding.[2]

Acceptances with original maturities of 180 days or less and with 90 or fewer days remaining to maturity, which are owned by a member bank and which meet the other requirements of eligibility, are eligible collateral for borrowing from the Federal Reserve Banks.[3]

The gain or income realized on bankers' acceptances is subject to the U.S. income tax for American investors, but generally is exempt when owned by foreign investors.

---

2   Bank of the United States vs. Selzer, App. Div. 225,251 N.Y. Supp. 637 (1937).
3   Detailed criteria as to such eligibility may be found in the Summer 1981 issue of the Quarterly Review of the Federal Reserve Bank of New York.

Historical Background

On September 14, 1914, shortly after the passage of the Fed eral Reserve Act, the National City Bank of New York accepted the first draft in the amount of $27,361.90.[4] An early peak in the volume outstanding of $1,732 million was reached in 1929. From then until the middle of World War II, the volume shrank to a low of $117 million in 1943. In the postwar years, with the tremendous expansion of international trade, acceptance volume once again grew rapidly, with the highest outstandings reaching $82.0 billion in June of 1984. Since that time overall outstandings have decreased to their present level of $62.4 billion as of April 1988.

The Dealer Market

Shortly after the legislation provided by the Federal Reserve Act, the major banks encouraged the formation of acceptance dealers to provide a market for accepted drafts. The First Boston Corporation (then The First National Corporation, a wholly owned subsidiary of The First National Bank of Boston) was founded in 1918 and began dealing in acceptances and issuing letters of credit.

Bankers' acceptances are bought and sold at yields comparable to those on other actively traded money market instruments. The Federal Reserve is a frequent participant in the market on behalf of its foreign customers. Its earlier practice of buying acceptances for its own account was ended in 1977, and as of July 2, 1984, the Federal Reserve discontinued use of repurchase agreements on bankers' acceptances in its open market operations.

Acceptances are available in a wide variety of principal amounts. Since the acceptance dealers carry a stock of drafts purchased from the many prime commercial banks doing an international business, acceptances are usually available in principal amounts suitable for both large and small investments and with a wide variety of maturity dates.

Foreign Acceptances are U.S. dollar-denominated acceptances backed by the credit of foreign banks or agencies domiciled in the United States. Foreign acceptances have generally traded at a yield premium over acceptances issued by domestic banks. Historical spreads have ranged from a high of 100–125 basis points when the market was just getting established to the present yield spread of about five basis points, depending on market conditions. Many foreign banks of high

---

4   Bankers' Acceptance Volume and Rates in the Discount Money Markets (New York, American Acceptance Council, 1928), p.7.

quality, however, trade as well as or better than U.S. banks. Foreign bankers' acceptances are similar to domestic BAs in many respects. They face the same Federal Reserve eligibility requirements; usually have comparable maturity, settlement date, and delivery characteristics; have liquidity provided by an active secondary market; and have comparable safety, with no known principal loss to investors.

Foreign acceptances (primarily of Japanese banks) now account for more than half of the acceptances outstanding. Other foreign banks, realizing the advantages and profitability of the BA market, have also taken advantage of increased investor receptivity and have participated in this market. In addition to Japanese banks, French, English, German, Dutch, Swiss, Australian, and Canadian banks are now active, to varying degrees, in the foreign acceptance market.

Several primary dealers, including First Boston, are involved in the secondary trading of these foreign acceptances. The top 12 Japanese banks constitute what is called the "run" and all other foreign acceptances trade at varying spreads to the "run." As of April 1988, there were approximately $35 billion foreign BAs outstanding, including $31.6 billion Japanese acceptances.

Finance Bills, or working capital acceptances, are unlike the usual acceptances, as there is no underlying collateral. Rather, a draft to finance general business activity is accepted by a bank which assumes the obligation to make payment at maturity. Once widely available, working capital acceptances have diminished sharply since the Federal Reserve imposed reserve requirements in mid-1973 on bank liabilities under such arrangements. These acceptances are not acceptable for discount or purchase by the Federal Reserve but are backed by the accepting bank's unconditional obligation to pay the acceptance at maturity.

Investment Yields and Computations

Bankers' acceptances are quoted, bought and sold on a discount basis, as are Treasury bills.

Certificates of Deposit

Certificates of deposit, familiarly known as CDs, are negotiable certificates in denominations of $100,000 or more. They are issued by commercial banks and thrift institutions against funds deposited for specified periods of seven days or longer and earn specified rates of interest.

In early 1961, major New York commercial banks began to issue such interest-bearing negotiable certificates to domestic business corporations. Previously, only nonnegotiable certificates had been issued, but apparently were not actively solicited. Banks in other cities soon followed suit.

Negotiable certificates have developed into an important money market instrument. They give banks an opportunity to compete for corporate and other funds that in the past were invested in Treasury bills and other types of short-term marketable paper. They give corporations and others another money market instrument to invest in at competitive rates. CDs now bear rates of interest in line with money market rates at the time of issuance.

Major banks also issue variable-rate CDs with maturities of up to five years. The rate, which is adjusted every 30, 90, or 180 days, usually includes a fixed spread over or under the composite secondary market rate for major bank CDs, as compiled and published by the Federal Reserve Bank of New York. The federal funds, prime, and the London inter-bank rate are also sometimes used as benchmark rates.

Issuing banks may not purchase their own certificates of deposit, nor may issuers redeem their outstanding certificates prior to maturity, except under conditions which could be costly and inconvenient to certificate holders. Banks apparently will not lend funds against their own certificates, at least partly because in the event of default on the loan the bank might become the owner of the certificate, in effect redeeming it prior to maturity.

Unless otherwise agreed, certificates bought or sold in the secondary market are deliverable in New York on the business day following the date of the transaction. Payment is made in federal funds. CDs are issued in denominations of $100,000 to $1,000,000. The normal round-lot trading unit is $5,000,000. On CDs with maturities up to one year, interest is calculated on a 360-day basis and is paid at maturity.

A market in CDs is maintained by First Boston and other dealers at rates related to those on bankers' acceptances, commercial paper, Treasury bills, and other short-term money market instruments. Trading volume in domestic bank CDs by dealers reporting to the Federal Reserve Bank of New York averaged over $4 billion daily in 1987.

Most CDs are issued for terms of a year or less. The minimum maturity permitted is seven days and there is no limit on the maximum maturity banks are permitted to offer.

Term CDs are those issued with a maturity in excess of one year. They normally pay interest semiannually. Term CDs are often compared in value to corporate bonds. However, it is important to note that CD yields are computed on the basis of a 360-day year versus 365 days for bonds. As a result, CDs with the same quoted yield can actually return 10 to 15 basis points more than comparable bonds.

Deposit Notes

Deposit notes, also referred to as medium-term deposit notes or certificate of deposit (CD) notes, are medium-term obligations issued by domestic banks (not bank holding companies) and foreign banks via their U.S. branches. Deposit notes are a hybrid of traditional bank term CDs and intermediate-term corporate bonds. They are unsecured obligations ranking pari passu with all other unsecured and unsubordinated obligations of the issuing banks, including deposit obligations. Because deposit notes of foreign banks are issued by their U.S. branches, they are obligations of the bank, as well as the branch. The market for deposit notes is expanding. In 1986, $3.6 billion of deposit note programs were established, while in the first quarter of 1988, $3.1 billion were established.

Deposit notes may be issued in a regular periodic offering program where the bank may from time to time post and issue a small amount of deposit notes to specific maturities.

Deposit notes may also be offered daily. Offering levels are either quoted as a spread over Treasuries or floating-rate indices, or at an absolute rate.

A deposit note program provides the maximum flexibility in accessing all maturities from 18 months to 10 years. There are reserve requirements for maturities of 18 months and shorter. Deposit note programs allow issuers to take advantage of financing windows or reverse inquiry opportunities and offer a means to maximize cost-effective funding through derivative products (i.e., swaps, caps, futures and options). Deposit notes are exempt from registration with the Securities and Exchange Commission.

In addition to the traditional buyers of CDs such as money market funds, deposit notes are purchased by corporate bond buyers such as bank trust departments, insurance companies, investment advisers, corporations and pension funds. Certain Federal Home Loan Boards allow thrifts to purchase deposit notes for their liquidity portfolios.

Deposit note programs allow the investor to select daily from a wide range of credits, maturities and amounts, in either fixed rate or floating rate form, to fill targeted investment requirements for managed portfolios. Portfolio managers involved in rededication, in particular, find deposit note programs attractive because they represent assets that can be tailored to specific needs. First Boston makes an active secondary market for its clients' programs to provide investors with the liquidity they require.

Eurodollar CDs

Eurodollar CDs are negotiable dollar-denominated certificates of deposit issued by foreign (mainly London) branches of major American and foreign commercial banks. As of March 1988, outstandings were about $180 billion for branches of U.S. banks.

Eurodollar CDs were originally introduced in 1966 as a marketable alternative to Eurodollar time deposits. Eurodollar CDs have the advantage of a secondary market, which makes them more attractive to investors. The liquidity also allows banks to issue CDs at a rate slightly below the rates offered on time deposits of similar maturities. Initially, Eurodollar CDs grew rapidly due to the higher yields the London branches of U.S. banks were able to offer investors, as compared with their home offices whose rates were then restricted by Regulation Q. Regulation Q was abolished in the early 1970s, but somewhat higher rates are still available because reserve requirements are levied on domestic but not offshore CDs and because of a perceived political risk in the offshore origination.

Recent years have seen an expansion in the issuance of Eurodollar CDs by smaller U.S. banks, major Canadian institutions, the top "clearing banks" of the United Kingdom, and, in particular, the largest Japanese banks. The CDs of these issuers trade well in the secondary market but generally must offer a yield premium relative to the top U.S. banks. The secondary market for Japanese paper rivals the liquidity of the U.S. Eurodollar CD market.

Normally, Eurodollar CDs are delivered in London on the second business day following the transaction, with payment made in New York in clearinghouse funds. Delivery and payment are not simultaneous as with other money market instruments due to the time difference between London and New York. The separate transfer of the CDs and cash is accomplished through the use of "agreements of understanding" that guarantee the payment in New York following delivery earlier in the day in London.

Floating-Rate CDs (FRCDs) were first issued in 1977. Essentially, these are medium-term CDs with maturities most often ranging from 18 months plus one day to five years. They vary in size from $5,000,000 to over $100,000,000. Coupons are adjusted periodically according to a predetermined formula and generally carry a given premium over a chosen interest rate index. Coupons have been pegged to a one-, two-, three- or six-month London interbank offered rate (LIBOR); the cost of funds index; a three- or six-month Treasury bill rate; the prime rate; a one-, three- or six-month CD composite rate; a one-, two- or three-month commercial paper rate; and the daily or weekly federal funds rate. Interest may be paid monthly, quarterly or semiannually.

FRCDs can be issued by money center, regional, or foreign banks domiciled in the U.S. (Yankee banks) in either domestic or European markets. As a bank deposit, an FRCD is an obligation which is senior to holding company notes, and thereby offers investors greater credit protection. Both Moody's and S&P now rate the long-term and short-term deposits of the aforementioned banks. The secondary market liquidity is excellent.

Yankee CDs

Yankee CDs are U.S. dollar-denominated CDs issued by foreign banks domiciled in the United States. They have maturities of seven days or longer and earn specified rates of interest. Maturities of 18 months or less are subject to reserve requirements set by the Federal Reserve. Japanese, Canadian, British, German, and Dutch banks are active participants.

Interest on maturities of one year or less is usually paid at maturity. Term Yankee CDs, usually with maturities of two to five years, pay interest either annually or semiannually.

Computation of Proceeds

For CDs with original maturities of one year or less, interest is normally calculated for the actual number of days held, on a 360-day per year basis, and paid at maturity. The dollar price is computed as shown below.

Example: Find the dollar price on a $1,000,000, 8.00%, 180-day certificate sold 45 days before redemption date on a 7.75% basis.

(1) Compute gross proceeds on redemption date at issue rate.

A = (a) + (b)

   (a) Interest, 180 days at 8.00%

$$\$80{,}000 \times \frac{180}{360} \quad = \quad \$\ 40{,}000.00$$

   (b) Principal   1,000,000.00

      Gross proceeds at redemption   A = $1,040,000.00

(2) Compute accrued interest due seller at issue rate (B).

Interest for 135 days at 8.00% due seller

$$\$80{,}000 \times \frac{135}{360} \quad = B = \quad \$\ 30{,}000.00$$

(3) Compute Gross sales proceeds.

C = A + E

$$E = 1 + (7.75\% \times \frac{45}{360}) \quad = \quad 1.0096875$$

Gross sales proceeds

$$\frac{\$1{,}040{,}000.00}{1.0096875} \quad C = \quad \$1{,}030{,}021.67$$

(4) Compute principal dollar amount.
D = C – B

Gross sales proceeds less interest due seller

C = $1,030,021.67

B =   30,000.00

Principal dollar amount (per $ million)

D = $1,000,021.67

(5) Compute dollar price.
F=D ÷ 10,000

Dollar price (per $100)

F = $100.002167

For Fixed Rate Term CDs of over one year, calculating proceeds is somewhat more complex than for short-term CDs. However, once the concept of a repeated rediscounting of maturity proceeds is grasped, the mechanics are fairly simple.

The next example follows the usual convention in the United States of semiannual interest payments. In the Eurodollar CD market, interest payments are usually made annually on the anniversary date of the issue. Those calculations are the same as shown below, but whole years (365 or 366 days) must be substituted for the half-years used here.

Example: Find the net proceeds on a $1,000,000 CD with an original maturity of five years and a coupon of 8.00% which is sold at a yield of 7.75% after 120 days.

(1) First calculate the 10 semiannual interest payments:

(coupon/100) × (principal) × (number of days in coupon period/360).
Semiannual interest payments are:

Coupon period		
1 (182 days)		$40,444.44
2 (183 days)		40,666.67
3 (182 days)		40,444.44
4 (183 days)		40,666.67
5 (182 days)		40,444.44
6 (183 days)		40,666.67
7 (183 days—leap year)		40,666.67
8 (183 days)		40,666.67
9 (182 days)		40,444.44
10 (183 days)		40,666.67

Note: Semiannual coupon periods can vary from 181 to 184 days, depending on maturity and coupon dates.

(2) Maturity proceeds = principal + final interest payment =
$1,000,000 + $40,666.67 = $1,040,666.67

(3) Discount maturity proceeds as follows:

Coupon period 10 (183 days at 7.75%)

$$(\$1,040,666.67) \div \left(1 + \frac{7.75 \times 183}{100 \times 360}\right) = \$1,001,222.67$$

Coupon period 9 (182 days at 7.75%)

$$(\$1,001,222.67 + 40,444.44) \div \left(1 + \frac{7.75 \times 182}{100 \times 360}\right) = \$1,002,392.80$$

Coupon period 8 (183 days at 7.75%)

$$(\$1,002,392.80 + 40,666.67) \div \left(1 + \frac{7.75 \times 183}{100 \times 360}\right) = \$1,003,524.78$$

Coupon period 7 (183 days at 7.75%)

$$(\$1,003,524.78 + 40,666.67) \div \left(1 + \frac{7.75 \times 183}{100 \times 360}\right) = \$1,004,613.85$$

Coupon period 6 (183 days at 7.75%)

$$(\$1,004,613.85 + 40,666.67) \div \left(1 + \frac{7.75 \times 183}{100 \times 360}\right) = \$1,005,661.64$$

Coupon period 5 (182 days at 7.75%)

$$(\$1,005,661.64 + 40,444.44) \div \left(1 + \frac{7.75 \times 182}{100 \times 360}\right) = \$1,006,664.41$$

Coupon period 4 (183 days at 7.75%)

$$(\$1,006,664.41 + 40,666.67) \div \left(1 + \frac{7.75 \times 183}{100 \times 360}\right) = \$1,007,634.48$$

Coupon period 3 (182 days at 7.75%)

$$(\$1,007,634.48 + 40,444.44) \div \left(1 + \frac{7.75 \times 182}{100 \times 360}\right) = \$1,008,562.87$$

Coupon period 2 (183 days at 7.75%)

$$(\$1,008,562.87 + 40,666.67) \div \left(1 + \frac{7.75 \times 183}{100 \times 360}\right) = \$1,009,460.98$$

Discount for 62 days (182 days less 120 days held) of 1st coupon period at 7.75%.

$$(\$1,009,460.98 + 40,444.44) \div \left(1 + \frac{7.75 \times 62}{100 \times 360}\right) = \$1,036,076.67$$

Net proceeds = <u>$1,036,076.67</u>

For Floating Rate CDs (FRCDs). Trading is done on a dollar price rather than a yield to maturity basis.

To calculate the proceeds on a FRCD, the following information must be supplied:
a. The face value of the CD
b. The coupon for the present interest period
c. The number of days from last interest date to value date
d. Dollar price

Net proceeds can then be calculated using the following formula:

Net proceeds = proceeds + accrued interest

Proceeds = (a × d) ÷ 100

Accrued interest = (a × b × c) ÷ (360 × 100)

Example: A $1,000,000 FRCD originally issued for three years is bought with 15 months to run. Last interest date was 90 days prior to value date. Present coupon is 8.00%, and the purchase is at a dollar price of 99¾

$$\text{Proceeds} = \frac{\$1,000,000 \times 99.75}{100} = \$997,500.00$$

$$\text{Accrued interest} = \frac{\$1,000,000 \times 8.00 \times 90}{360 \times 100} = \$20,000.00$$

Net proceeds = $997,500.00 + $20,000.00 = <u>$1,017,500.00</u>

Commercial Paper

"Commercial paper" is the market name for the short-term unsecured promissory notes issued by various economic entities in the open market to finance certain short-term credit needs. The Securities Act of 1933 contains several provisions which exempt commercial paper from the registration requirements of the Securities and Exchange Commission. The most commonly used exemption applies to commercial paper sold with maturities not exceeding nine months, the proceeds of which are used to finance current transactions. Commercial paper ranks equally with the other unsecured debt of a borrower. Commercial paper having a maturity of not more than 90 days may be eligible collateral for borrowing from Federal Reserve Banks.

Presently some 1,350 entities issue commercial paper. These represent a variety of industrial companies, utilities, commercial bank holding companies, finance companies, insurance companies, savings and loan associations, and a growing number of foreign corporations and government bodies. Traditionally, commercial paper—the lowest-cost source of short-term dollars—has been used to fund seasonal working capital requirements. However, more and more issuers use commercial paper in new ways: to provide the floating-rate component of an interest rate swap, the dollar-based component of a currency swap, or bridge financing for an acquisition. The institutional market for commercial paper is open only to borrowers with substantial liquidity and strong credit standing.

Commercial paper is generally backed by unused bank credit lines to repay the notes in the event the issuer is unable to roll the paper over in the market at maturity. Virtually all paper issued through dealers is rated by at least one of the independent rating agencies such as Moody's Investors Service, Inc. or Standard & Poor's Corp. Buyers of commercial paper include business corporations, insurance companies, public entities, commercial bank trust departments, mutual funds, and pension funds.

The volume of commercial paper outstanding has expanded from $33 billion in December 1970 to approximately $353 billion in December 1987. Of the December 1987 outstandings, about $172 billion consisted of paper sold directly to investors, mainly by major finance companies and banks. The remainder, approximately $181 billion, consisted of paper sold through commercial paper dealers on behalf of a widely diversified group of issuers. First Boston is a major commercial paper dealer.

Commercial paper purchased from dealers such as First Boston is usually bought and sold on a discount basis, figured for the actual number of days to maturity on a 360-day basis, in the same manner as bankers' acceptances. Interest-bearing commercial paper is also available. Maturities range from one to 270 days. Yields on highest quality commercial paper are roughly equivalent to those available on bankers' acceptances and certificates of deposit of leading banks. This relationship can change temporarily due to technical factors or rapid market swings.

The minimum round-lot transaction is $100,000, although some issuers sell commercial paper in denominations as small as $25,000. The notes are normally issued in bearer form. Payment at maturity is effected by presentation to the bank designated as paying agent on the face of the note.

Most issuers of commercial paper have designated New York City banks as issuing/paying agents, and trading is customarily for New York delivery with settlement on the same day in federal funds. State and local governments issue tax-exempt short-term notes that resemble commercial paper. In most respects this paper is comparable to its taxable counterpart except for the exemption of interest from federal income taxes.

Funds Raised in Credit Markets

(In billions of dollars)

	Net Amount Raised				Year-end Level
	1984	*1985*	*1986*	*1987*	*1987*
Total	877.7	1,074.8	1,227.6	962.4	13,726.2
Corporate equities, market value	-65.7	-65.8	-71.7	-73.8	2,874.2
Investment company shares	29.3	85.7	163.3	64.5	478.0
Debt instruments	914.1	1,054.9	1,136.0	971.7	10,374.0
U.S. Government securities	273.8	324.2	393.5	311.5	2,927.0
Treasury issues	195.9	218.5	201.1	134.6	1,853.0
Savings bonds	3.0	5.3	13.6	7.8	101.1
Sponsored agency issues	30.4	20.6	15.2	29.9	300.9
Mortgage pool securities[1]	44.4	79.9	163.3	140.2	670.0
State and local obligations	50.4	136.4	30.8	31.3	725.2
Corporate bonds	86.1	126.1	192.9	193.7	1202.3
Foreign bonds	3.8	3.8	2.6	6.3	80.6
Open market paper	52.0	52.8	26.4	32.8	417.8
Commercial paper	48.3	62.1	32.2	26.8	352.9
Bankers' acceptances	3.7	-9.4	-5.9	6.0	64.8
U.S. Government loans	16.6	14.9	8.8	-4.6	193.9
Sponsored credit agency loans	16.0	11.8	19.2	28.0	170.3
Bank business loans	61.1	38.3	69.5	9.3	728.1
Consumer credit	90.4	94.6	65.8	30.1	753.1
Other loans	82.9	44.8	56.5	63.0	756.3
Mortgages	217.4	237.7	300.7	300.1	2,864.6
Residential	154.9	181.0	234.3	236.5	2,150.2
Commercial	63.5	62.6	74.7	69.7	623.7
Farm	-0.9	-6.0	-8.4	-6.1	90.7

Source: Federal Reserve Board, Flow of Funds Accounts.

[1]GNMA, FNMA, FHLMC, and FmHA pools. Excludes Federal Financial Bank holdings of pool securities.

Repurchase and Reverse Repurchase Agreements

A repurchase agreement consists of two simultaneous transactions. One is the purchase of securities (collateral) by an investor from a bank or dealer. The other is the commitment by the bank or dealer to repurchase the securities at the same price at some mutually agreed upon future date. The collateral used is most frequently Treasury, GNMA, or other agency securities, but may include any of the better-known money market instruments.

This dual transaction, which the market has dubbed a "repo" or simply an "RP" has developed into a meaningful money market instrument in its own right. It provides banks and dealers with an attractive alternative for financing positions, and it provides investors who want a short-term investment with a money market instrument that can be tailored to their exact maturity needs.

Early in their development, RPs were written mainly overnight or for very short terms. However, the market has now expanded so that RPs can be executed for maturities of between one day and one year (occasionally longer under special circumstances). The vast majority of RPs mature in three months or less. One-day transactions are called overnight RPs; longer transactions are called term RPs.

Participants in the long-term RP market include all major classes of private and government institutions who may have lendable collateral or excess investable funds. The long-term RP is frequently employed to increase interest return. For example, when the yield curve was favorable, customers were able to "reverse" Treasury or GNMA securities to a dealer and reinvest the proceeds in higher yielding CDs.

The RP rate is the rate of interest that the dealer pays the investor (lender) for the use of his funds. The RP typically trades at high yields relative to other money market instruments. Rates depend on the type of collateral. In general, the higher the credit quality and the easier the security is to deliver and hold (wireable versus physical, semiannual coupon versus monthly pay), the lower the RP rate. Rates also depend on whether the collateral is generic or special. Collateral becomes special when it is in high demand by government securities dealers who need to make deliveries to customers. The interest rate dealers are willing to accept when bidding on these issues can be several hundred basis points less than the rate for generic collateral.

The principal upon which interest is paid is based upon the price assigned to the collateral at the time of the transaction. The purchaser does not care what the market price of the security is, whether it goes up or down, or what coupon or maturity the security carries. The market risk of the collateral is completely borne by the seller. If market prices go down during the life of the RP so that the collateral is worth less than the principal amount of the trade, the purchaser is exposed should the seller default, file for bankruptcy, or be placed in receivership by the appropriate regulatory authority. The purchaser would require that the transaction be marked to market, either through a repricing (return of cash in excess of the now lower market value of the collateral) or through the delivery of additional collateral. The seller would have recourse to similar remedies, should market prices rise.

Customarily, collateral is priced at some discount from current market value in order to provide a margin of protection against price declines which might occur over the term of the RP. A typical margin would be between 1% and 3% of the trade principal, although "haircuts" required on reverse RP transactions may be substantially higher. If CDs are the collateral, they are usually priced at par.

There are several delivery alternatives for the RP collateral:

- Delivery: The seller delivers the securities to the purchaser versus the principal of the trade. At the maturity of the RP, the purchaser delivers the securities back versus trade principal and financing interest.

- Safekeeping: The seller holds the securities for the purchaser. The purchaser receives confirmations for the transaction, but the collateral is held in a segregated customer account by the seller.

- Third Party: Collateral is delivered to the purchaser's account at the seller's clearing bank. Since collateral moves within the bank, this arrangement has the operational advantages of safekeeping while still accomplishing delivery.

Securities dealers also often borrow securities they need to make deliveries. These loans are collateralized by other securities of equal value or cash. If the loan is collateralized by securities, the borrower pays the lender a fee. If collateralized by cash, the borrower receives a below market interest rate on the money. The fee or rate differential is determined by how special the security is (its relative availability), but is currently at least 30 basis points. Securities loans are generally done on an open basis (terminable at the option of the lender), but may have specific maturities.

The smallest customary amount of an RP is $1 million, and round lots are $25 million. As with other money market instruments, interest is calculated on a 360-day year, and transactions are settled in federal funds.

Reverse repurchase agreements, technically called matched sales-purchase agreements, are essentially the mirror image of RPs. In this instance, the investor is the owner of the collateral, and the bank or dealer is the lender of money. All other aspects remain similar to RP.

Short-Term Tax-Exempt Notes and "Commercial Paper"

Short-term tax-exempt notes are money market instruments that generally have maturities of less than one year. The bulk of these notes are obligations issued by states, municipalities, or other public agencies in anticipation of tax revenues or federal grants, or as interim financing prior to a bond sale. Interest paid on these securities is exempt from federal income tax. The notes are backed by the credit of the issuing body pursuant to borrowing authority granted by the voters.

The credit of the issuer is generally the sole guarantee. Increasingly, issuers are employing "credit enhancements" such as third party insurance and bank letters of credit. Tax-exempt notes sell at yields that depend on current money market and municipal market rates and the credit ratings of the issuer as assessed by the various rating agencies (Moody's, Standard & Poor's, or Fitch). The yield may be further affected by whether the securities are tax or revenue anticipation notes or bond anticipation notes (TANs, RANs, or BANs, respectively).

In the primary new issue market, notes vary in maturity from one month to the more common six-month and one-year maturities. Occasionally, longer maturities of up to several years are issued and may or may not be coupon bearing. During 1987, according to the Public Securities Association, a total of $18.3 billion of short-term obligations was sold.

The general obligation short-term notes of state and local governments are legal investments for commercial banks and most other classes of investors. Since state laws vary, they should be consulted for applicability in particular cases.

Tax-exempt "commercial paper" is becoming an increasingly important component of the short-term market. Like taxable paper, it provides both issuer and buyer with a highly flexible instrument that typically has maturities ranging from one to 60 days and may be "rolled" or renegotiated at maturity for a new period.

The proceeds from the sale of tax-exempt "commercial paper" are typically used for interim financing or to provide working capital during seasonal shortfalls in taxes or revenues. Tax-exempt paper is rated like other commercial paper and prices are competitive with other short-term notes.

Two other recently developed techniques for providing issuers with access to the short-term tax-exempt market are variable-rate demand notes and adjustable rate "put" bonds. These securities have been particularly attractive to tax-exempt money market mutual funds because of their frequent rate adjustments that guarantee current market rates of return, put options with notice of as little as one week or less, and superior credit quality resulting from various credit enhancements. Issuers have used the proceeds from the sale of such securities in place of conventional sources of short-term credit for bridging seasonal cash flow shortfalls, as well as for providing alternative permanent financing (at short-term rates) for public construction projects.

In most instances, short-term notes and "commercial paper" of states, municipalities or local agencies are also exempt from state and local income tax in the state of issuance, thus providing a multiple exemption to residents of those states. An exemption from all state income taxes also applies to notes of issuers in Puerto Rico, the Virgin Islands, Guam, and the various American Indian nations.

Short-term tax-exempt notes and "commercial paper" are both issued in fully negotiable bearer form. (The registration requirement that applies to tax-exempt obligations generally does not apply to obligations that have a maturity at issue of one year or less.) Denominations for notes usually range from $5,000 to $1,000,000 at the option of the underwriter or the issuer, while for paper the usual minimum denomination is $100,000. Principal and interest are paid at maturity (with the exception of maturities longer than one year, which may be coupon bearing) at the paying agency designated on the note—a bank or trust company selected by the initial underwriter or designated by the issuer. Transactions are usually in federal funds. Interest is generally computed on the basis of a 30-day month or 360-day year, but occasionally on the actual number of days in relation to 365 days. Initial delivery is normally on the date of issue for newly auctioned notes. In the secondary market, regular delivery is normally five days, but trading for same- or next-day delivery is quite common.

The Eurocurrency Market

A Eurocurrency deposit is created when a banking office in one country accepts a deposit denominated in the currency of another. The Eurocurrency deposit is then typically loaned or redeposited by the receiving bank (which may be a foreign branch of an American bank) through the mechanism of the Eurocurrency market. This market had its beginnings in the late 1950s. In December 1987, the Morgan Guaranty Trust Company estimated the annual volume of Eurocurrency credits was the equivalent of $112 billion. The part of the Eurocurrency market denominated in dollars is referred to as the Eurodollar market.

The principal instrument of the Eurocurrency market is the nonnegotiable time deposit ("Depo"). Other instruments include certificates of deposit, bankers' acceptances, letters of credit, commercial paper, and bank loans of various maturities. In the majority of cases, of course, the borrower is a bank receiving a time deposit rather than borrowing in the conventional sense.

A bank, corporation, political entity, etc., owning foreign currency in excess of working balances may seek to deposit these funds on a fixed-term basis, at the best rate available from those depositaries whose standing is acceptable to the lender. When mutually satisfactory terms are arranged, the borrower and the lender simply exchange written confirmations detailing the terms of the deposit and acknowledging the transfer of funds. The commonly accepted minimum deposit amount is one million currency units. No negotiable instrument is created, mainly because of legal obstacles to the issuance and clearance of negotiable instruments. Should the lender need short-term funds prior to the maturity of the deposit, he simply becomes a borrower for the required period by initiating another transaction in the Eurocurrency market. If the deposit is for a term of one year or less, interest is normally paid at maturity. Semiannual or annual, and occasionally quarterly, interest is paid on deposits of more than one year. The most frequently quoted rate at which these deposits are made among the leading international banks is the London interbank offered rate (LIBOR). The most common maturities available in the deposit market are one, two, three, six, and twelve months, plus the "short dates" used by banks to balance their positions. Short dates are deposits of fixed maturities such as two-, seven-, and occasionally 14-day "fix" and "over weekend"' or on a quasi-demand basis such as 48-hour "notice." Deposit rates are usually fixed, but on longer term deposits they may be floating; that is, the rate may be reset periodically at a fixed spread to a certain quoted interbank short-term rate.

The Eurocurrency market in no way resembles a central marketplace. In recent years, the integration of diverse capital markets has led to the development of active Eurocurrency markets in major cities all over the world. Transactions are negotiated by telex, cable, and telephone. Trading is normally done for settlement on the second business day following the trade date. The "short dates" are frequently traded for settlement on the same day. Same-day contracts are usually arranged by 12:00 noon London time with funds transferred by 3:20 p.m., or earlier in the case of other European money centers. Funds are transferred either directly through correspondent banks in the home country of the relevant currency or, according to the broker's instructions, against delivery of the required instrument. All terms of the transaction (amount, maturity, rate, currency, provisions for the payment of interest and principal, commission, etc.) are agreed upon at the time the trade is executed and are confirmed in writing by the broker.

Foreign Currency Hedged Investments
(Covered Interest Arbitrage)

Certain national and regional government securities, bank certificates of deposit, and other money market instruments can provide attractive fixed-rate short-term yields for multinational companies that choose to diversity investments outside their home currency. International currency "hedged paper" is readily available denominated in several foreign currencies, including the British pound, Canadian dollar, Deutsche mark, Japanese yen, and Swiss franc.

For an investor in foreign securities to obtain a known fixedrate short-term yield in his own currency, he must protect against the possibility that exchange rates may change prior to maturity. Such protection, or "hedging" is arranged by simultaneously purchasing a foreign security and establishing a currency hedge position in the forward market or the futures market.

The forward market is an extension of the Eurocurrency market described in the previous section. Forwards are traded through a worldwide interbank market where investors can reduce foreign exchange exposure by committing to convert a specified amount of currency at a set exchange rate on an agreed upon date in the future. Since all the terms of a forward market transaction are negotiated when the trade is executed, investors may establish a hedge which exactly matches the amount and maturity date of the foreign security.

The futures markets are confined to recognized exchanges which list standardized contracts through which investors agree to exchange a specific amount of currency on a set date in the future. Final settlement dates are limited to certain maturities, typically following a March, June, September, December schedule. Due to the standardized contract specifications established by the exchanges, the futures market provides somewhat less hedging flexibility than the forward market. Currency futures are traded in several major urban centers including Amsterdam, Chicago, London, Montreal, Singapore and Sydney.

In the following example of a foreign currency hedged investment, a forward contract—the oldest, most liquid, and most flexible currency hedging vehicle—is used to cover the foreign exchange risk.

On day one, a U.S. investor purchases a German 90-day security denominated in Deutsche marks (DM) at a yield (in Deutsche marks) of 3%. Assuming the investor buys DM 5,000,000 face value of securities, he must purchase a like amount of Deutsche marks to deliver against the bonds. To protect himself against adverse currency movements which could reduce the yield, the investor simultaneously contracts to sell Deutsche marks in the forward market.

Assume that the spot (two-day settlement) rate for Deutsche marks is 1.7220 per U.S. dollar. On the same day, the quoted three- month forward (90-day settlement) rate is 1.6900 Deutsche marks per U.S. dollar. The difference between the two rates (1.7220 less 1.6900) is a discount of 0.0320, called the "three-month forward swap."

The following example outlines the steps followed by a U.S. investor to hedge a 3% German security with a maturity of three months through the forward market.

Day 1: Investor buys DM5,000,000 spot
U.S. $ cost = DM face value ÷ spot
$$= 5,000,000 ÷ 1.7220$$
$$= \text{U.S. } \$2,903,600.46$$

Day 1: Investor contracts to sell total DM proceeds forward
DM proceeds = DM face value + interest

$$= 5,000,000 + (\text{face value} \times \text{rate} \times \frac{days}{365})$$

$$= 5,000,000 + (5,000,000 \times 0.03 \times \frac{90}{365})$$

$$= \text{DM } 5,036,986.30$$

U.S. $ proceeds = DM proceeds ÷ forward rate
$$= 5,036,986.30 ÷ 1.6990$$
$$= \$2,964,677.05$$

Day 90: Investor receives U.S. $2,964,677.05
In U.S. dollar terms, the hedged investment yields:

$$\frac{\$2,964,677.05 - \$2,903,600.46}{\$2,903,600.46} \times \frac{365}{90} = 8.53\%$$

Using the 360-day year U.S. money market convention, the hedged investment yield is:

$$8.53\% \times \frac{360}{365} = 8.41\%$$

On rare occasions, a discrepancy might emerge between foreign and domestic interest rates which provides the U.S. investor with a hedged investment yield that exceeds comparable returns from equivalent credits denominated in U.S. dollars. In these circumstances, the forward hedging strategy is called a "covered interest arbitrage." When international money markets function normally, such discrepancies are quickly bid away.

Money Market Futures and Options

Interest Rate Futures on money market instruments were introduced in January 1976 when contracts on three-month Treasury bills began trading at the International Monetary Market (IMM) of the Chicago Mercantile Exchange. The contract matures once each quarter and calls for delivery of $1 million face amount of 90-day Treasury bills. There are 12 contracts outstanding with the nearby contracts exhibiting more activity and liquidity than the deferred months. The bill contracts are quoted at an "index price" of 100 minus the discount yield; thus, a Treasury bill discount yield of 10.00% would be quoted on the IMM as 90.00. Price fluctuations occur in multiples of "0.01" or one basis point, with each "0.01" valued at $25.

The rapid success of bill futures combined with increased volatility in short-term interest rates prompted the IMM to structure contracts on other money market securities. As a result, 90-day bank CD futures started trading in July 1981, and 90-day Eurodollar time deposit futures started trading in December 1981. These new contracts contributed to the expansion of the futures markets such that by year-end 1987, money market futures accounted for approximately 23% of the total number of interest rate future contracts traded. Treasury bill futures captured 2% of the total contract volume, or 1.9 million contracts, and year-end open interest reached 18,752 contracts (at $1 million delivery obligation per contract, equivalent to $18.8 billion of Treasury bills). The Eurodollar time deposit contract has become the most liquid money market future, with total volume in 1987 of 20.4 million contracts (21% of total contract volume), and with year-end open interest reaching 292,326 contracts (representing $292.3 billion).

Interest rate futures on money market instruments are utilized by:

- investors with long positions in money market assets, to hedge against rising interest rates during the holding period;

- future borrowers of short-term funds, to hedge the issuance of their liabilities;

- investors, to hedge against having to roll over short-term investments at lower rates;

- speculators, to try to profit from anticipated changes in interest rates.

Options on Money Market Instruments made their debut on November 5, 1982, with the trading of options on three-month Treasury bills on the American Stock Exchange (AMEX). The Chicago Mercantile Exchange (CME) introduced options on the Treasury bill futures on April 10, 1986. The AMEX revamped its European-style option contract on physical Treasury bills in April 1986 to follow the pricing convention in Treasury bill futures. The greatest interest, however, has been in the options on Eurodollar time deposit futures, traded at the CME. One option represents the right to buy or sell one Eurodollar time deposit futures contract at the specified strike price. Strike prices are in increments of 0.25 of a point, or 25 basis points, of the futures contract. Thus strike prices will be 93.50, 93.75, 94.00, etc., bracketing the current futures price. Call buyers and put sellers have a long futures position, and call sellers and put buyers have a short futures position. Total volume in Eurodollar futures options topped 2.5 million contracts in 1987, with year-end open interest reaching 69,792 contracts (representing $69.8 billion).

First Boston is one of several dealers that currently offer over-the-counter (OTC) options on various money market securities. OTC options have the advantage of permitting investors to buy or write options with characteristics (strike prices, expiration dates, etc.) that more closely fit their financial needs.

The Government Securities Market

The Market Mechanism

Practically all trading in U.S. Government securities takes place in the over-the-counter market. Bond issues are listed on the New York Stock Exchange, but volume there is small. The over-the-counter market consists of a group of dealer firms, including First Boston, and several large banks that operate government bond departments. They deal directly with banks, insurance companies, corporations, brokers, and other large investors interested in the government securities market. Small investors have ready access to this market through their local banks, securities dealers, and brokers. A small group of government bond brokers serves to facilitate interdealer trading. Unlike the dealers, these brokers do not take positions themselves, but rather match the bids and offers placed with them by the dealer community. The best of these bids/offers are disseminated by the brokers to all dealers by means of a modern telecommunications network. As a result, the prevailing quotations from any dealer on a particular issue at a given time will be identical, or nearly so. The major government securities dealers are represented by the Primary Dealers Committee, Government and Federal Agency Securities Division of the Public Securities Association, which currently has a regular membership of 44 firms.

At present, normal domestic trading hours in the over-the-counter market are from 9 a.m. to 4 p.m., New York time. Trading often extends beyond these hours, however, when markets are active. In addition, active markets in London and Tokyo create a virtually around-the-clock market. Prices of government securities other than Treasury bills are normally quoted in terms of 32nds. Thus, a price quotation of 96-16, or 96.16, means 96 16/32. Occasionally, quotations are made in terms of 64ths, denoted "+". Thus, 96.16+ means 96 33/64. Treasury bills are quoted in terms of rate of bank discount securities at net prices. Dealers customarily buy and sell government securities at net prices; that is, no commission is added. A dealer's quotation, such as 93-5 bid, 93-7 asked, usually indicates that on full lots (usually 100 bonds—$100,000 face value—or more) the dealer will pay the bid price and will sell at the asked price. Service charges or price adjustments are made on small odd-lot transactions or transactions involving registered securities.

The difference between the bid and asked price is called the "spread." Variations in the spread between issues with different characteristics and/or maturities reflect the relative activity and market risk of holding the issues. The spread in the quotations on Treasury bills may be only $50 per million par value or even less.

On other short-term issues the spread may be 1/32 to 4/32s of a point ($312.50 to $1,250 per million), while on longer term or inactive issues it may be somewhat greater. The volume of market activity in the issue is a dominant factor in determining the width of the spreads.

Payment for and delivery of government securities normally takes place on the next full business day following the day of the transaction, except in instances where the dealer and the investor agree on settlement the same day—termed a "cash" transaction—or on some later day--termed a "delayed delivery" transaction. Accrued interest to the delivery date is added to the price of coupon obligations. Payment is normally made in federal funds. Odd-lot transactions are normally on a five-business-day settlement basis.

The Federal Reserve Bank of New York publishes daily composite closing quotations for government securities. It also reports consolidated statistics each week on the market activity of the primary dealers, showing volume, type of customer, positions, and financing.

Telegraphic Transfer of Government and Agency Securities. Telegraphic transfer facilities for all unmatured marketable bearer securities of the U.S. Treasury are available through the Federal Reserve Banks. The Federal Reserve Banks will transfer such securities for any purpose, including securities borrowed by primary dealers and collateral thereto. In addition to Treasury issues, agency securities that are eligible for custody in book-entry form are also eligible for telegraphic transfer (see below) through this nationwide communications network.

Telegraphic transfers are subject to certain limitations: in general, transfers of securities are not authorized on or after the date of maturity of an issue on or after the date on which securities are called for redemption and on which they cease to bear interest.

The fee for interdistrict transfer of securities of any one issue or series to be delivered to a single recipient is $2.25 and is payable at the time securities are presented for transfer.

Book-Entry and the Telecommunications Transfer System. All the large New York City banks, including those that handle the bulk of the transactions of the major government securities dealers, now clear most of their transactions with each other and with the Federal Reserve through the use of automated telecommunications and the "book-entry" custody system maintained by the Federal Reserve Bank of New York. These banks have deposited with the Federal Reserve Bank a major portion of their government and agency securities holdings, including securities held for the accounts of their customers or in a fiduciary capacity. Virtually all transfers for the account of the banks, as well as for the government securities dealers who are their clients, are now effected solely by bookkeeping entries. The system reduces the costs and risks of physical handling and speeds the completion of transactions.

Treasury bills are offered in book-entry form only. New issues of marketable Treasury bonds and notes have been entirely in book-entry form since mid-1986. Older issues remain available in definitive form as well.

Most of the major federal agencies have issued regulations requiring use of the book-entry procedure for issuance of their securities. To further assist the smooth functioning of the market, the Federal Reserve will lend securities from its own portfolio to primary dealers when needed to complete transactions on which there has been a "fail"—that is, when a security has not been delivered because it has been delayed in transit to the dealer. The usual charge for such loans of securities is at a rate of 1-1/2 %. The Federal Reserve requires the securities it lends to be fully collateralized by the borrowing dealer and, in addition, sets limits on the amount of an individual issue that a dealer may borrow. The Federal Reserve may charge an additional penalty if the securities are not returned to it within five business days.

Zero-Coupon Treasury Securities

Beginning in the 1970s, aggressive interpretations of federal tax law encouraged some dealers and investors to separate the component pieces of U.S. Treasury bonds and notes. The separation allowed the holder to sell the corpus, or principal payment, at a deep discount price of $0.05 to $0.10 on the dollar and claim a capital loss on the price of $0.05 to $0.10 on the dollar and claim a capital loss on the difference between the selling price of the corpus and the price paid for the whole bond. The income stream was still realized as regular income, but no tax was paid on the accretion until the securities were sold or had matured. Through this process, therefore, an investor could delay his tax liability and also be allowed a significant capital loss. Because of the significant loss of tax revenue, the Treasury by 1979 had asked the primary dealers to discourage this process. It eliminated the practice among the primary dealers, although it persisted among some smaller dealers and investors.

In 1982, the Congress, through the Tax Equity and Fiscal Responsibility Act (TEFRA), required the holders of zero-coupon and original issue discount securities to accrue a portion of the discount toward par each year, and to report this as yet unrealized accrual as taxable income. The tax status of coupon "stripping" was thus legally defined. Dealers consequently began again to separate coupon and principal payments, and an active secondary market developed for the component pieces.

TEFRA also mandated that as of January 1, 1983, all new U.S. Treasury issues would be available only in book-entry form. The process of stripping had depended on the availability of bearer bonds from which to physically separate the coupons; dealers now had to find a way to create separate principal and interest payments from registered bonds. They did so by introducing proprietary zero-coupon certificates. These were certificates of ownership of Treasury cash flows. Proprietary certificates differed from physical zeros in that a Treasury note or bond could be deposited with a custodian, who could then issue certificates against the coupon and principal cash flows. In practice, all Treasury issues could be stripped in this indirect manner.

While this system apparently solved the immediate problem of the diminishing supply of raw materials for stripping, it created a segmented market as dealers rushed to create proprietary certificates attributable to their own firm. These various brands of Treasury-based zero-coupon products were not interchangeable and therefore lacked the secondary market liquidity investors had come to expect in physical zeros. Furthermore, creation of the product slowed as dealers began to realize that a tremendous capital and trading commitment was required to maintain an active secondary market in a proprietary item.

In early 1984, First Boston and a group of other dealers who had been actively creating and trading physical strip securities developed a generic security. Treasury Receipts (TRs), the result of this effort, were first issued in January 1984 and were readily accepted by both the dealer and investor communities. By the end of 1984, over $50 billion face value of TRs had been created, and the average trading volume climbed to several hundred million dollars per day.

Treasury Zero-Coupon Products

Product Name	STRIPS	TRs	Physicals	Proprietary Receipts
	Separate Trading of Registered Interest and Principal of Securities.	Treasury Receipts		CATs, Cougars, ETRs, LIONs, STARs, TIGRs, ZEBRAs, etc.
Description	Generic, multiple market maker zero-coupon securities consisting of interest or principal on U.S. Treasury securities.	Generic, multiple market maker zero coupon securities representing interest or principal payments on U.S. Treasury securities.	Generic, multiple market maker zero coupon securities consisting of interest or principal payments on U.S. Treasury securities.	Proprietary, usually single market maker zero-coupon securities representing interest or principal payments on U.S. Treasury securities.
Unit Size	Interest and principal in $1,000 increments.	Interest payments denominated in multiples of the coupon on all issues where underlying Treasury is dated prior to August 1, 1984. On issues with underlying Treasury dated after this date, coupon certificates issued in $1,000 multiples. All principal certificates denominated in $1,000 units.	Interest payment denominated in multiples of the coupon on all issues. Principal payments always denominated in $1,000 units.	Principal and interest certificates usually denominated in $1,000 units.
Round Lot Size	$5,000,000	$5,000,000	$1,000,000 to $5,000,000	$1,000,000 to $5,000,000
Market Size	Over $90 billion nominal.	Over $51 billion nominal.	Over $45 billion nominal.	Combined, over $100 billion nominal.
Trading Spread	2–3 basis points.	10 basis points.	10 basis points.	10 basis points.
Delivery	Wire transfer versus federal funds through Federal Reserve book entry	Physical delivery of certificates versus federal funds.	Physical delivery of coupon or corpus versus federal funds.	Physical delivery of certificates versus federal funds.

The rapid development of this market and the large investor response once again drew the attention of the Treasury. This time, however, it approved of zeros because of indications that the demand for these securities was producing savings on government interest cost. After extensive study and consultation with the investment community, the Treasury announced that as of January 1985 all future note and bond issues with maturities of at least 10 years would be transferable in their component pieces on the Federal Reserve wire system, thereby creating a generic, book-entry Treasury zero. This product was named STRIPS (Separate Trading of Registered Interest and Principal of Securities).

The process of stripping bonds involves wiring Treasury bonds to the Federal Reserve Bank of New York and receiving generic coupon strips and a principal strip in return.

As of May 1987, the Treasury has allowed the reconstitution of stripped bonds. Generic coupon strips, in the proper face amount and maturities, are combined with the corresponding principal strip to reconstitute Treasury bonds. Since the program's inception, an average of two billion notes and bonds have been either stripped or reconstituted each month. With the enhanced ability of market participants to strip and reconstitute bonds, the liquidity and efficiency of the strip market has been vastly improved. Generic coupon strips generally trade on a two to three basis point market.

The liquidity of principal strips is dependent on the liquidity of the underlying bond. For very liquid bonds, the principal strip will trade in large size on a two basis point market.

Since the accretion of zeros is taxed annually as ordinary income, the principal investors in Treasury zeros are tax advantaged accounts such as domestic pension funds, insurance companies, and individual retirement accounts. Applications range from the matching of specific maturities to future liabilities to the use of long maturity zeros for adjusting portfolio volatility and convexity. Because of the elimination of reinvestment risk (a zero pays no interest until maturity and the rate of return is "locked in" at the time of purchase), zeros are frequently used to defease (in effect, guarantee the payment of) future liabilities. This can be either a simple cash flow match such as with a lottery payment or a guaranteed income contract, or a more complicated transaction such as a municipal bond defeasance or pension fund dedication. In contrast with this more passive role, longer maturity zeros with their low dollar price and high duration are often used to add volatility to actively managed portfolios. Intermediate zeros, with duration similar to Treasury notes and bonds, can be used as a substitute, generally at a higher yield, for coupon Treasury securities. Zeros of all maturities can be combined with high coupon Treasuries or other securities to create "synthetic" securities. These hybrids theoretically perform much like a current coupon Treasury, but can often be created at significantly higher yield and lower dollar price.

For income tax purposes, Treasury zeros are considered to be an original issue discount debt obligation. In general, the difference between the acquisition price and the maturing value is taxed as original issue discount. Treasury zeros are exempt from most forms of state and local taxation.

Federal Government Loan Asset Sales

Sales of federal agencies' loan assets, mandated by the Omnibus Budget Reconciliation Act of 1986 (OBRA), have been undertaken as a means of reducing the current federal deficit and enhancing the management of federal credit programs. The sales are designed to provide an incentive for federal agencies to improve loan origination and documentation so as to clarify the level of subsidy provided by the federal government in the related loan programs. The current guidelines for loan asset sales, prepared by the Federal Credit Policy Working Group and issued by the Office of Management and Budget, call for loan asset sales to be structured without future recourse or the right to make a claim against the federal government or its agencies in the event of borrower default. During fiscal 1987, loans with a face value of $7.9 billion were sold or prepaid by borrowers and yielded $5.5 billion in net receipts. The schedule for the 1988 fiscal year includes loan asset sales by the Department of Education, Farmers Home Community Program, Veterans Administration, and Departments of Interior and Housing and Urban Development. In the November 1987 Budget "Summit," President Reagan and Congress agreed to raise $5 billion in fiscal year 1988 and $3.5 billion in fiscal year 1989 through sales of loan assets.

Financial Futures Market

A futures contract is a standardized agreement to make or take delivery of a specified security or commodity at a specified price on a future date. Delivery and payment specifications are established by the exchange where the contract is traded. Financial futures are contracts to deliver or receive securities such as Treasury bonds, notes or bills, or foreign currencies. Some contracts, such as Eurodollar time deposit, municipal index, and stock index futures, are different in that they refer to an underlying index rather than a specific security. In the case of index futures, settlement is made by a cash payment based on the movement in the underlying index. The vast majority of financial futures commitments are never delivered; they are usually "closed" through offsetting transactions prior to the specified delivery date.

Comparison of Federal Loan Asset Sales

	FmHA Community Program	Department of Education	FmHA Rural Housing	Department of Education
Date of offering	September 2, 1987	September 21, 1987	September 23, 1987	May 3, 1988
Par amount of senior security	$1.8 billion	$127 million	$2.3 billion	$450.9 million
Type of loans	Loans to small local governments to finance water and sewer systems and other essential community facilities.	Loans to post-secondary educational institutions to build college and academic facilities.	Mortgage loans for low- and moderate-income rural residents.	Loans to post-secondary educational institutions to build college and academic facilities.
Principal amount of collateral	$2.3 billion	$237.2 million	$3.0 billion	$524.0 million
Collateral weighted avg. interest cost	5.30%	3.16%	8.63%	3.18%
Collateral weighted avg. remaining term to maturity	17.6 years	19.4 years	23.5 years	18.8 years
Financing structure	93% senior/7% subordinated multiclass sequential pay bonds. (Closer to 12% total subordination with reserve funds and residual cash flow.)	3 fixed-pay serial bonds/2 amortizing term bonds. 108% overcollateralized.	80% senior/20% subordinated pass-through securities election with REMIC.	Collateralized sequential pay bonds. 108% overcollateralization increases gradually to 125% during the life of the bonds.
Special features	Subordinated bonds rated A- by S&P sold 9/18/87.	Guaranteed investment contracts provided by FNMA used to eliminate prepayment risk; create synthetic corporate bond structure; serialization used to optimize positively sloped short end of the yield curve.	Bond insurance provided by American Loan Guaranty Assoc.; shifting interest structure used to eliminate reserve fund; four classes of senior cert. 11 subclasses; cross-support mechanism used to link all collateral classes together.	Certificates held by DOEd are subordinate to the Sequential Pay Bonds in order of payment; overcollateralization level increases over the course of the bonds' life since the bonds amortize faster than the collateral.
Ratings	Senior bonds Aaa/AAA	Aaa/AAA	Aaa/AAA	Aaa/AAA

Dealer Volume and Positions in Treasury and Agency Futures

(Daily averages; dollar value of contracts in millions of dollars)

| | Dealer Transactions | | | Dealer Positions | | |
| | Treasury Securities | | Agency | Treasury Securities | | Agency |
	Bills	Coupons	Securities	Bills	Coupons	Securities
1986						
Jan.	4,497	8,136	41	-14,663	3,966	-612
Feb.	5,423	9,140	2	-18,504	5,003	-313
Mar.	3,624	9,056	7	-27,539	5,293	-247
Apr.	4,397	8,372	6	-26,431	2,763	-82
May	4,308	7,776	44	-19,205	2,642	-70
June	2,912	7,202	17	-14,058	2,324	-95
July	2,196	5,276	13	-16,381	2,522	-67
Aug.	2,871	5,939	12	-16,246	2,427	-60
Sept.	3,056	7,784	4	-15,996	4,234	-64
Oct.	1,754	5,416	0	-15,845	3,424	-70
Nov.	2,801	6,374	21	-15,972	4,022	-82
Dec.	1,909	5,519	0	-16,170	3,359	-89
1987						
Jan.	2,879	7,029	0	-15,245	5,229	-92
Feb.	4,898	8,092	0	-13,476	6,669	-94
Mar.	3,577	6,891	9	-10,805	4,313	-98
Apr.	3,575	12,018	1	-5,004	3,936	-95
May	4,128	10,374	6	1,779	2,609	-98
June	2,810	8,001	13	-585	3,181	-100
July	2,091	6,821	6	916	6,194	-96
Aug.	2,786	8,953	10	-2,013	6,275	-95
Sept.	2,748	11,981	1	-200	7,295	-96
Oct.	4,056	11,462	8	2,492	8,809	-100
Nov.	2,774	8,489	2	1,158	9,170	-90
Dec.	2,342	7,364	5	450	8,179	-84

Source: Federal Reserve Bulletin.

Interest rate futures began trading in October 1975 when a GNMA futures contract was introduced on the Chicago Board of Trade (CBOT). The success of this contract prompted the CBOT and the International Monetary Market of the Chicago Mercantile Exchange (IMM) to introduce contracts on U.S. Treasury bonds, bills, notes, Eurodollar time deposits and municipal bonds. Currency futures, which predate interest rate futures, are traded on the IMM, while various stock index futures are traded on the Kansas City Board of Trade, the

New York Futures Exchange, the Chicago Mercantile Exchange, and the Chicago Board of Trade.

For the majority of futures contracts, there are up to eight deferred contract months. The nearby contracts exhibit more price movement and liquidity than the deferred months. When the yield curve is positively sloped, outright holdings of actual cash securities can be financed with positive carry. To compensate investors for foregoing this income and holding futures instead, prices for future delivery must be lower in the deferred months. By the same token, with a negatively sloped yield curve, the deferred prices will be higher.

The financial futures market enables investors in fixed income assets to transfer market risk inherent in long or short security positions to others who are willing to assume these risks. The act of reducing risk by taking a position in the futures market is referred to as hedging. Hedging through financial futures can be employed by:

- those intending to borrow in the future, to lock in a particular rate of interest and protect themselves from rising interest costs;

- holders of fixed-income securities, to offset declines in the value of their assets during periods when they expect interest rates to rise; and

- those intending to lend in the future, to lock in currently high interest rates if they expect rates to fall.

In contrast to hedgers, who use futures to reduce their risk, speculators and arbitrageurs are willing to assume risk with the expectation of profiting from perceived price anomalies.

The most common arbitrage technique is "spreading," which may be "intramarket" (purchasing a futures contract of one delivery month and selling another delivery month of the same contract) or "intermarket" (buying a contract on one commodity and selling a contract on a different commodity).

The need of large institutions and securities dealers to protect or hedge their investments in stocks, bonds, and other financial instruments has spurred extraordinary growth in financial futures trading volume. Daily dollar turnover in stock index futures exceeds that of cash trading on the New York Stock Exchange.

The financial futures market can look forward to continued expansion in the number and diversity of its participants. Recently, for example, the New York State Legislature liberalized the regulations on asset and liability hedging for life insurance companies. The new bill authorizes a twelvefold increase, up to 25%, in the portion of assets that may be hedged by life insurance companies. They will also be able to use over-the-counter options, caps, and floors, as well as exchange traded options.

The importance of stock index and bond futures for asset allocation strategies continues to grow. The Commodity Research Bureau (CRB) index of commodity futures prices has earned a following as a long-term leading indicator of inflation, and futures trading in the CRB index is becoming more popular. Spread trades like the TED (Treasury bill versus Eurodollar) and the MOB (municipal futures versus Treasury bond futures) also continue to attract investors.

To trade in the futures market, an investor is required to deposit an initial margin in the form of cash or Treasury bills which evidences the contract holder's ability to bear price risk. The initial margin is typically less than 5% of the face value of the position being held. Every day, the futures exchanges require that all price changes in every contract must be settled in cash. A futures holder can make or lose more than the original investment and therefore should be cognizant of the face amount traded and not merely the amount of initial margin that is required.

Major strides were taken during 1987 toward creation of a truly global futures market. First was the London International Financial Futures Exchange's (LIFFE) decision to switch its U.S. Treasury bond futures to the same delivery procedure used by the CBOT. In April the CBOT initiated a night trading session in Treasury bond and note futures and in options on the futures. This session coincides in timing with the Tokyo bond market and facilitates futures trading for Pacific Rim participants. The CBOT's night session has been successful, and longer trading hours can be expected. In volume terms, Marche a Terme des Instruments Financiers (MATIF) in Paris surpassed LIFFE and Sydney as the third largest futures exchange, behind Chicago and Tokyo.

Five-year Treasury futures (FYTR) were introduced by the Financial Instrument Exchange (FINEX), a division of the New York Cotton Exchange, to fill the gap on the yield curve between Eurodollar futures (based on three-month LIBOR) and Treasury note futures (based on seven- to ten-year Treasuries). Deliverable securities are limited to original-issue five-year Treasuries with at least four years and three months to maturity. This strict limitation forces the FYTR to mirror the price movements of the four-year sector to the benefit of hedgers since basis risk is minimized. The contract has been accepted by market participants as a viable hedge instrument.

The number of Eurodollar futures contracts traded on the Chicago Mercantile Exchange (CME) was expanded from eight to twelve. The four additional contracts provide market participants the opportunity to create synthetic instruments with a strip of Eurodollar futures as long as three years. It also enhances pricing efficiency in the interest rate swap markets and offers short-term investors hedging flexibility.

Average Daily Trading Volume in Treasury Bond Futures and Underlying Cash Bonds*
(In billions of dollars)

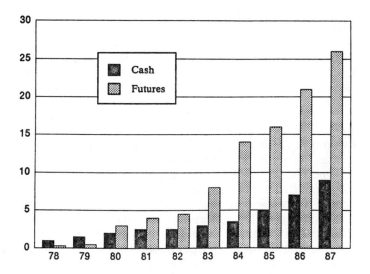

* Average daily cash trading volume, as reported by the Federal Reserve, divided by two (so as to count a purchase and sale only once).

Options Market

Options on fixed income securities began trading in the fourth quarter of 1982 when options on Treasury bond futures were first introduced. This product has been enormously successful. At present, options on Treasury bills and notes are traded on the American Stock Exchange, options on Treasury bonds on the Chicago Board Options Exchange (CBOE), and options on Treasury bond and Treasury note futures on the Chicago Board of Trade (CBOT). Options on Eurodollar futures are traded on the International Monetary Market of the Chicago Mercantile Exchange (IMM), and options on the five-year note futures (FYTR) contract, introduced in February 1988, are traded on the Financial Instrument Exchange (FINEX). Of the exchange-traded interest rate options, options on bond futures are by far the most active and liquid.

Unlike the stock options market in which initially only call options were traded, debt options have been available from the start as both puts and calls. A call option gives the buyer the right to purchase (exercise) from the seller a security or commodity for a fixed price (known as the exercise or strike price) at any time within a certain time period. This is known as an American-style option, whereas in a European-style option, exercise is allowed only at expiration. The buyer of a put option purchases the right to sell an underlying security to the seller of the option at a set price within a given time period. Call option buyers profit when prices on the underlying security rise, whereas the buyer of a put option profits when the price of the underlying security declines.

The sum of money which the purchaser of the option pays for the rights granted by the option is the option premium. The buyer of an option is known as the holder, while the seller of an option is often referred to as the writer. The option's expiration date is the last day on which the option can be exercised. If the option is not exercised by that date, then it ceases to exist. At worst, the buyer of an option can lose no more than the option premium. Purchasing a call option allows the investor to achieve gains as the market rises, but limits the loss to the option premium no matter how far the market declines. Conversely, the holder of a put option gains when prices fall (interest rates rise), but stands to lose only the option premium should prices advance. Thus, the investor may be able to increase the return on his portfolio and to hedge against interest rate risk. Furthermore, an investor can use fixed income options in a variety of complex combinations to manage and improve the risk, return, and volatility characteristics of a bond portfolio.

Fixed income options are employed by

- investors, to diminish portfolio risk, by purchasing options while investing their funds in relatively riskless short-term investments;

- those intending to borrow in the future, to lock in a ceiling on their financing costs, thereby protecting themselves from increases in interest rates; and

- holders of fixed-income securities, to hedge against adverse price movements or to lock in minimum returns without forfeiting the ability to benefit from a market rally.

Options on bond futures began trading on October 1, 1982. Each options contract calls for delivery of a single, $100,000 face value Treasury bond futures contract of a specified delivery month. The option expiration date is the last Friday in the month preceding the futures delivery month. Premiums are quoted in 64ths of a point, and

Dealer Volume and Positions in Treasury and Agency Forward Transactions
(Daily averages; in millions of dollars)

	Dealer Transactions		Dealer Positions	
	U.S. Govt. Securities	Agency Securities	U.S. Govt. Securities	Agency Securities
1986				
Jan.	2,592	6,655	-1,978	-12,167
Feb.	1,743	7,172	-928	-10,039
Mar.	1,287	8,148	-2,981	-12,151
Apr.	1,255	8,151	-1,888	-11,543
May	1,500	6,185	-1,985	-11,496
June	1,707	6,739	-2,363	-10,490
July	1,377	7,623	-3,046	-11,383
Aug.	2,907	7,785	-3,503	-9,906
Sept.	1,838	8,685	-3,769	-10,224
Oct.	1,731	8,450	-122	-11,322
Nov.	2,419	10,257	-781	-14,634
Dec.	2,066	9,933	-2,101	-17,058
1987				
Jan.	2,055	10,696	179	-16,646
Feb.	4,074	11,440	357	-16,383
Mar.	1,952	10,656	-2,151	-16,703
Apr.	2,760	15,961	-2,386	-15,767
May	2,841	11,951	-4,292	-20,339
June	1,869	9,875	-921	-19,241
July	819	9,854	-1,759	-20,187
Aug.	1,697	8,448	-1,873	-22,436
Sept.	788	8,292	-191	-21,797
Oct.	2,653	7,676	229	-22,780
Nov.	2,167	7,191	145	-18,489
Dec.	1,097	5,704	-1,641	-15,024

Source: Federal Reserve Bulletin.

strike prices are set at two-point intervals. Presently, there are three contract months that are traded, with the nearby contract exhibiting more liquidity than the deferred months.

The valuation of options requires at least five parameters: the term of the option, the exercise price, the value of the underlying security or commodity, the short-term rate of interest, and the volatility of the underlying commodity or security. The first two, the term of the option and the exercise price, are contractual features of the option, while the value of the underlying security and the short-term rate are easily observable from the market. It is the fifth parameter, the price volatility of the underlying security, that is difficult to measure accurately. Volatility refers to the tendency of the security to change in value over a given time frame. It is usually measured as the standard deviation in the expected annual rate of return from holding the security. Higher volatility is always associated with higher option premiums, whether the option is a put or call. The reason for this is that when the underlying security is more volatile, it is more probable for its value to fluctuate by large amounts, which will render option exercise profitable. An estimate of the volatility is often obtained by using past data. Another method for estimating volatility is to use the market's opinion. By taking the known market prices of options and their underlying securities and working backwards through an option-pricing formula, one can obtain the expected volatility that is implied by existing option premiums. Patterns in this "implied volatility," particularly in comparison to historical or actual volatility, are a commonly used indicator of market sentiment.

In an options transaction the buyer pays the premium in advance in cash, while the seller of an option is obligated to post margin in the form of cash or securities. The initial margin evidences the writer's ability to bear price risk. At the end of each trading session, each seller's position is marked to market to reflect gains or losses in the position. When the margin requirement exceeds the funds on deposit, the option writer is required to deposit additional funds or securities.

Futures and options users are continuing to find new applications for risk management. First Boston has developed sophisticated pricing models for variable-maturity securities, including adjustable rate mortgages (ARMs) and floating-rate collateralized mortgage obligations (FRCMO). Cap structures and prepayment risk make ARMs and FRCMOs subject to price risks that had previously been difficult to quantity. The latest models enable accurate hedging since they describe the price sensitivity of these securities to changes in yield levels. ARMs now represent over 50% of all new mortgage originations. The cap structure of ARM-backed securities is best hedged with options, which should increase their use as a risk management tool. Furthermore, development of option-adjusted pricing models for all mortgage and corporate securities enables construction of effective hedging strategies for entire portfolios of all corporate and mortgage-backed securities.

First Boston has been involved in the financial futures and options markets since their inception. First Boston professionals worldwide support hedging and arbitrage activities for customers. An extensive price database and wide array of fundamental and technical analyses are available to help in designing and executing specific strategies.

Price Volatility of Treasury Bond Futures*
(Daily, percent annualized)

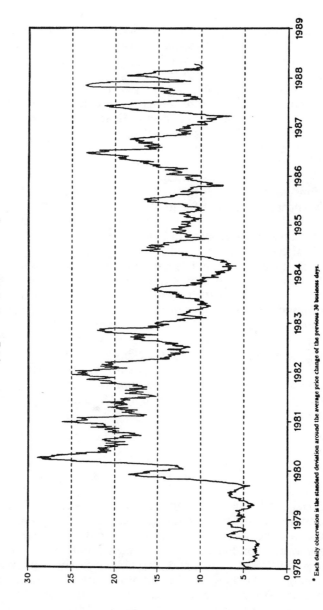

* Each daily observation is the standard deviation around the average price change of the previous 30 business days.

Interest Rate Swaps

An interest rate swap is an agreement between two parties to exchange payments that are based on specified interest rates and a notional amount. The exchange takes place over a specified period of time. Although swaps can take a variety of forms, typically one party pays fixed-rate and receives floating-rate payments, and the other party receives fixed and pays floating rate payments.

Interest rate swaps were created to take advantage of arbitrage opportunities in the various fixed- and floating-rate capital markets. Arbitrage opportunities exist because some markets react to change more rapidly than others, because credit perceptions differ from market to market, and because receptivity to specific debt structures differs from market to market. If, for instance, a corporation wants term floating rate funds but finds that the market for its fixed rate debt is comparatively cheaper than that for its floating rate debt, then it can issue a fixed rate bond and swap it into floating for an all-in cost lower than that for a floating rate bond or loan.

Financial engineering and structured transactions play an important role as investors and issuers use the swap market to transform existing cash flows on capital markets issues into more desirable cash flows. In the latter half of 1987 the most frequent example of such transformations was the generation of callable interest rate swaps (swaptions) using callable bond deals. Issuers found that they could sell the call provision in their bond deals by receiving fixed rates and paying floating rates to hedgers seeking to create fixed rate liabilities, but requiring flexibility regarding maturity. Deep discount and zero-coupon swap structures were also commonplace during 1987, driven primarily by the significant supply of Japanese equity warrants, Eurobonds, and associated asset swaps.

Nondollar Government Bonds

Financial market globalization has encouraged increased U.S. investor involvement in the nondollar bond markets. This represents the beginning of a trend, as the U.S. bond market now comprises less than half of the world bond market. The foreign bond markets have become more sophisticated, liquid, and accessible in recent years. Whether it be "Big Bang" in England or the establishment of a system of primary dealers in France, financial market liberalizations have advanced market- making capabilities and spurred innovations in all the major markets. Moreover, the global infrastructure developed by financial institutions facilitates foreign bond investing. Because of the increased

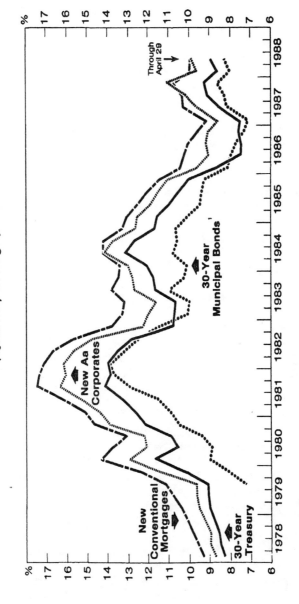

Long-Term Market Rates
(Quarterly averages)

New Aa Corporates

New Conventional Mortgages

30-Year Treasury

30-Year Municipal Bonds[1]

Through April 29

%
17
16
15
14
13
12
11
10
9
8
7
6

1978 1979 1980 1981 1982 1983 1984 1985 1986 1987 1988

Reproduced courtesy of the U.S. Treasury.
[1]The 30-year Bond Buyer Index was started September 21, 1979.

impact of these factors on the U.S. fixed-income market, U.S. investors now have an enhanced awareness of international developments.

Diverse investor groups account for the U.S. institutional participation in the foreign bond markets. The proliferation of global bond funds and unit trusts reflects the increased retail investor demand for international bonds. Public and private pension funds have diversified into nondollar investments, while total-return money managers have sought enhanced performance. High yield buyers have also been attracted to several sectors.

Investors have a wide choice of instruments within the various government bond markets. In Europe, Dutch and French securities provide an alternative to German bonds, while U.K. gilts represent another option. The Japanese bond market is the world's second largest. Many investors view the Canadian sector as a high-yielding alternative to the U.S. market, given the high correlation of these sectors and the relatively stable Canadian-U.S. currency relationship. The Australian and New Zealand sectors, too, have received new prominence in global portfolios.

Holders of the Public Debt

The distribution of ownership of the public debt has undergone large changes over the years. Investors are always adjusting their portfolios, reflecting not only variations in the funds they have available and the types of securities the Treasury is offering, but also each buyer's particular investment preferences, the attractiveness of alternative investments, and the legal or other constraints under which the buyer may be operating.

In general, financial institutions are sellers of government securities when business activity is strengthening and higher yielding loans and investments are readily available. They are buyers at times of slackening business activity and interest rates when, partly reflecting expansionary Federal Reserve policies, their inflow of funds exceeds normal investment outlets. Similarly, nonfinancial corporations tend to accumulate government securities when capital spending is low, and to "spend" these liquid assets when outlays on fixed capital and inventories expand. In recent years, individuals have become major buyers, both directly and through mutual funds. Foreign official and private financial institutions may also be major buyers, investing funds derived primarily from balance-of-payments surpluses. The Federal Reserve also is a sizable owner of marketable issues, largely as a result of its open market operations in its conduct of monetary policy. These operations are discussed in the next section. It should be noted that considerations of profit or loss do not enter into the Federal Reserve's decisions to buy or sell securities.

Government investment accounts comprise trust funds that by law are under the control of the Secretary of the Treasury or of the Treasurer of the United States and accounts under the control of certain U.S. Government agencies whose investments are handled through the facilities of the Treasury Department. These accounts also hold some marketable public debt, most of which was bought in the past when purchases would improve yield or help to cushion a market declining in price. Recently, however, they have not been actively acquiring marketable issues.

Federal Reserve Discount Rates
(Percent)

Date Effective	Discount Rate (New York)	Surcharge[1]	Date Effective	Discount Rate (New York)	Surcharge[1]
1979- July 20	10		1982- July 20	11½	
Aug. 17	10½		Aug. 2	11	
Sept. 19	11		Aug. 16	10½	
Oct. 8	12		Aug.27	10	
1980- Feb.15	13		Oct.12	9½	
Mar. 17		3	Nov. 22	9	
May 7		0	Dec. 15	8½	
May 30	12		1984- Apr. 9	9	
June 13	11		Nov. 21	8½	
July 28	10		Dec. 24	8	
Sept. 26	11		1985- May 20	7½	
1980- Nov. 17	12	2	1986- Mar. 7	7	
Dec. 5	13	3	Apr. 21	6½	
1981- May 5	14	4	July 11	6	
Sept. 22		3	Aug. 12	5½	
Oct. 12		2	1987- Sept. 4	6	
Nov. 2	13				
Nov. 17		0	In effect		
Dec. 4	12		March 31, 1988	6	

Source: Federal Reserve Bulletin.

[1]As of March 17, 1980, a surcharge was applied to institutions with deposits of $500 million or more that had short-term adjustment credit borrowings in successive weeks or in more than four weeks in a calendar quarter. As of October 1, 1981, the basis for application of a surcharge was changed from a calendar quarter to a moving 13-week period. The surcharge was eliminated on November 17, 1981.

Federal Reserve Open Market Operations

The execution of monetary policy through open market operations frequently brings the Federal Reserve into the government securities market. Purchases of securities by the Federal Reserve create bank reserves and provide the underpinning for monetary and credit expansion. Sales of securities by the central bank absorb bank reserves and reduce the potential for monetary expansion. The Federal Reserve may enter the market to purchase or sell securities outright, as well as through repurchase agreements and so-called "reverse repurchase" agreements (formally designated as "matched sale-purchase agreements"). In repurchase or reverse repurchase transactions, the Federal Reserve buys or sells securities under agreements that call for automatic reversal of the operation within a specified number of days (at most 15, but more generally only two or three). These agreements are in effect loans between the Federal Reserve and the dealers. The effective interest rate is set by an auction technique whereby dealers bid for or offer funds in competition with one another.

Over longer periods, the Federal Reserve is normally a large buyer of securities. This is to create the bank reserves needed to offset the loss of reserves resulting from increases in the public's holdings of currency, as well as to provide the reserve base to support growth in the quantity of deposits.

The Federal Reserve added $20.6 billion of government securities to its outright holdings in 1986 and $21.3 billion in 1987. Net purchases of coupon issues were $1.5 billion in 1986 and $17.4 billion in 1987. Treasury bill holdings increased by $19.1 billion in 1986 and $3.9 billion in 1987.

Since September 1971, the Federal Reserve has also engaged in open market operations in the securities of federal agencies and government-sponsored enterprises. Authorization for such transactions was given by law in 1966, but until September 1971 was used only for repurchase agreements. Under guidelines established by the Federal Reserve, its market purchases or sales of issues maturing in five years or less are limited to those of which at least $300 million is outstanding, while for longer term issues the cutoff is $200 million. Holdings of agency securities were reduced by $0.4 billion in 1986 and a further $0.3 billion in 1987. The gross volume of Federal Reserve transactions is much larger than the net acquisitions because, for seasonal or other reasons, the Federal Reserve may be both a seller and buyer of Treasury bills.

Total volume in bills and other Treasury securities through the market for the Federal Reserve's own account was $26.6 billion in 1986 and $44.0 billion in 1987. These figures do not include enormous additional transactions on behalf of foreign monetary authorities, the Treasury, and others, nor redemptions of Treasury bills and repurchase or reverse repurchase agreements.

Reserve Balances of Depository Institutions at Federal Reserve Banks and Related Items
(Year-end; in millions of dollars)

	1980	1983	1984	1985	1986	1987
Factors providing reserves						
U.S. Gov't. securities[1]	131,368	161,213	169,627	191,248	221,459	231,420
Discounts & advances	1,809	918	3,577	3,060	1,565	3,815
Float	4,467	1,563	833	988	1,261	811
Other assets[2]	11,257	13,384	16,965	20,020	22,493	20,855
Gold stock	11,160	11,121	11,096	11,090	11,064	11,078
Treasury currency outstanding	13,838	13,786	16,418	17,052	17,567	18,177
Factors absorbing reserves						
Currency in circulation	137,244	170,005	183,796	197,465	211,995	230,213
Treasury cash holdings	437	463	513	550	427	446
Treasury deposits with Federal Reserve Banks	3,062	3,661	5,316	9,351	7,588	5,313
Other deposits	1,028	1,036	1,120	1,521	1,204	1,271
Required clearing balances	—	1,013	1,126	1,490	1,812	1,687
Other Federal Reserve accounts	4,671	5,394	5,952	6,622	6,088	7,129
Reserve balances of depository institutions[3]						
Federal Reserve Banks	27,277	22,305	22,171	27,928	38,659	37,055
Currency and coin	18,482	20,912	22,129	23,612	24,729	26,960
Total reserves[4]	41,054	40,140	41,832	48,950	61,417	62,160
Required reserves	40,558	39,182	40,625	47,644	59,369	61,354
Excess reserves	496	958	1,207	1,307	2,048	806
Federal Reserve Bank security holdings						
Total	131,368	161,213	169,627	191,248	221,459	231,420
Held outright:						
Treasury bills	43,688	65,810	71,035	85,425	103,775	107,691
Treasury notes	58,718	63,934	65,237	67,647	68,126	82,973
Treasury bonds	16,893	20,814	22,951	24,726	25,724	28,242
Agency securities	8,739	8,645	8,389	8,227	7,829	7,553
Held under repurchase agreement	3,330	2,010	2,015	5,223	16,005	4,961

Source: Federal Reserve Bulletin.

[1]Also includes federal agency obligations, eligible acceptances, and securities held under repurchase agreements.

[2]Includes Federal Reserve assets not elsewhere classified and SDR certificates.

[3]Daily averages; last reserve period of the year.

[4]Includes reserve balances and vault cash used to satisfy reserve requirements.

Appendix 3

Categories of Glossary Entries

This appendix sorts Glossary entries by category. It is designed to help those readers who want to focus on a particular area of the market. Categories are chosen by breadth and importance to the fixed income market.

Categories

1) Accounting and Credit Analysis
2) Banking System
3) Bond Mathematics
4) Corporate Bonds
5) Derivative Products (Futures, Options, Swaps)
6) Economics
7) Equity and Equity-Related Securities
8) Floating Rate Securities
9) International Securities
10) Mortgage-Related Securities
11) Municipal Securities
12) Portfolio Management
13) Preferred Stock
14) Securities Law
15) Trading (Secondary Market)
16) Underwriting (Primary Market)
17) U.S. Government and Agency Securities

1) Accounting and Credit Analysis

Aboriginal Cost
Acid Test Ratio
Accelerated Cost Recovery System (ACRS)
Accelerated Depreciation
Accountancy
Accounting
Accounting Cycle
Accounting Equation
Accounting Period
Account Payable
Account Receivable
Accounts Receivable Turnover
Accrual
Accrual Accounting
Accrued Depreciation
Accumulated Depreciation
Acid Test Ratio
Actual Cost
Actuarial
Actuarial Interest as Scheduled
Actuarial Rate
Actuary
Additional Paid-In Capital
Adequate Disclosure
Adjusted Basis
Adverse Opinion
All-Capital Earnings Rate
All Financial Resources
Allocate
Amortization
Antidilution
Asset
Asset Depreciation Range
Asset Turnover Ratio
Assumed Bond
At Risk
Balance
Balance Sheet
Balance Sheet Equation
Bank Grade
Bank Quality
Basic Accounting Equation
Basis

Credit
Cross Default
Current Assets
Current Liabilities
Current Ratio
Daily Accretion
Debit
Debt Capital
Debt/Equity Ratio
Default
Default Risk
Defeasance
Defensive Interval
Depletion
Depreciation
Derived Book Value
Disclosure
Double Declining Balance (DDB)
Double Entry
Downgrade
Duality
Earned Income
Earned Surplus
Earnings
Earnings Before Interest and Taxes (EBIT)
Earnings per Share
Earnings Yield
Economic Life
Expense
Extraordinary Item
Favorable Variance
Financial Accounting
Financial Accounting Standards Board (FASB)
Financial Distress
Financial Statement
First-In First-Out
Fiscal Year
Fitch Investors Service, Inc.
Fixed Assets
Fixed Charge Coverage
Fixed Charges
Fixed Charges Earned Coverage Ratio
Fixed Liability
Flow Through Accounting
Form 8K

Form 10K
Form 10Q
Free Cash Flow
Full Faith and Credit
Fully Diluted
Fundamental Accounting Equation
Funded Ratio
Funds Flow
Funds From Operations
Gilt Edged
Going Concern Assumption
Grade
High-Grade Bond
Historical Cost
Idiosyncratic Return
Impairment of Capital
Income
Income Statement
Incremental Capital-Output Ratio
Intangible Asset
Interest Coverage
Interest Coverage Ratio
Interim Statement
In the Black
In the Red
Invested Capital
Investment Grade
Last-In First-Out (LIFO)
Letter of Credit
Leverage
Leveraged Corporation
Leverage Ratio
Liability
Limitation on Liens
Liquidation
Liquidity Ratio
Liquidity Trap
Long-Term Debt Ratio
Long-Term Debt to Long-Term Capital
Managerial Accounting
Maintenance and Replacement Fund
Margin of Profit
Margin of Profit Ratio
Market Multiple
Matching

Modified Cash Basis
Monetary Items
Money Bonds
Moody's
Natural Business Year
Net Assets
Net Asset Value (NAV)
Net Capital Formation
Net Cash Flow
Net Current Assets
Net Current Asset Value
Net Debt
Net Earnings
Net Income
Net Operating Loss (NOL)
Net Quick Assets
Net Tangible Assets to Long-Term Debt
Net Tangible Assets to Total Debt
Net Worth
Noncurrent Assets
Non-Recurring
Normalized Accounting
Not Related
Off-Balance Sheet Financing
Operating Cash Flow to Current Liabilities
Operating Income
Operating Profit Margin
Operating Ratio
Opinion
Original Cost
Other Income
Owners' Equity
Paid in Arrears
Paid-In Capital
Paid-In Surplus
Pennsylvania Bond
Preferred Stock Ratio
Price-Earnings Ratio
Price-Sales Ratio (PSR)
Primary Earnings per Share
Profitability Ratio
Profit and Loss Statement
Profit Margin Ratio
Profits
Pro Forma Statement

Purchase Acquisition Method
Qualified Opinion
Qualitative Analysis
Quality
Quality Spread
Quantitative Analysis
Quick Asset Ratio
Quick Assets
Quick Ratio
Rate Base/Phase In
Rating
Ratio Analysis
Receivable
Recognize
Regulatory Accounting Principles
Reserve
Reserve for Depreciation
Retained Earnings
Return on Assets (ROA)
Return on Equity (ROE)
Return on Permanent Capital
Revenue
Shareholders' Equity
Split Rating
Standard & Poor's (S&P)
Statement of Cash Flows
Statement of Changes in Financial Position (SCFP)
Stockholders' Equity
Stock-Value Ratio
Straight Line
Subsequent Event
Sum-of-the-Years' Digits
Surplus
T Account
Tax Basis
Tax Deferred
Term Cost Method
Times Fixed Charges
Total Debt to Capital
Total Liabilities to Tangible Worth
Undistributed Earnings
Unearned Income
Upgrade
Useful Life
Wasting

Window Dressing
Working Capital

2) Banking System

Actual Reserves
African Development Bank
Agent Bank
American Depositary Receipt (ADR)
Bank
Bank Call
Bank Check
Bank Deposit Note
Bankers' Acceptance (BA)
Bank for Cooperatives
Bank Guarantee Letter
Banking Act
Bank Note
Bank of England (B of E)
Bank of Japan (BOJ)
Bank Rate
Bank Reserves
Bank Risk
Bank Wire
Base Rate
Bill Pass
Blanket Bills
Board of Governors of the Federal Reserve System
Borrowed Reserves
Borrower Limit
Brassage
British Clearer
Building Society
Call Loan
Call Money
Call Rate
Capitalization Rate
Central Bank
Clearing Bank
Clearing Day
Clearing House Bank
Clearing House Funds
Clearing House Interbank Payments System
Commercial Bank
Committed Facility
Consortium Bank
Correspondent Bank
Cost of Funds

Coupon Pass
Current Account
Customer Repo
Daylight Overdraft
Demand Deposits
Demand Loan
Depository
Depository Trust Company
Development Bank
Discount Rate
Discount Window
Draft
Drain
Drawdown
Dual Banking System
Easy
Edge Act
Edge Act Corporation
Edge Bank
Eligible
Equity Commitment note
Equity Contract note
Excess Reserves
Eximbank
Exit Bond
Export-Import Bank
FDIC
Fed
Fed Action Time
Federal Deposit Insurance Corporation (FDIC)
Federal Farm Credit Bank
Federal Farm Credit System
Federal Financing Bank (FFB)
Federal Funds
Federal Funds Rate
Federal Home Loan Bank Board (FHLBB)
Federal Home Loan Banks (FHLB)
Federal Home Loan Bank System
Federal Intermediate Credit Bank
Federal Land Bank
Federal Reserve Act
Federal Reserve Bank
Federal Reserve Board
Federal Reserve Float
Federal Reserve Open Market Committee (FOMC)

Federal Reserve Open Market Operations
Federal Reserve System
Federal Savings and Loan Insurance Corporation (FSLIC)
Fed Wire
Financing Corporation (FICO)
Fiscal Agent
Float
Fractional Reserve System
Free Reserves
FSLIC
Go-Around
High-Powered Money
Interbank Rates
International Bank for Reconstruction and Development (IBRD)
Lender of Last Resort
Letter of Credit (LOC)
LIMEAN
Line of Credit
Loaned Up
London Interbank Bid Rate
London Interbank Offered Rate
Mandatory Convertible Bond
Matched Sales
Member Bank
Merchant Bank
Monetary Base
Monetary Policy
Monetized Gold
Monetizing the Debt
Money
Money Center Bank
Moral Suasion
Multiplier
National Bank
Near Money
Negative Free Reserves
Negative Gap
Negotiated Order of Withdrawal
Net Bank Position
Net Borrowed Reserve
New Money
New York Interbank Offered Rate
Non-Bank bank
Nonrecourse Commodity Loan
Official Discount Rate

Open Market Committee
Open Market Operations
Paying Agent
Primary Capital
Prime Bank
Prime Rate
Principal Paying Agent
Purchase Agent
Quantitative Controls
Reference Bank
Regional Bank
Reintermediation
Repurchase Agreement
Reserve Assets
Reserve Bank of Australia
Reserve Ratio
Reserve Requirements
Retail Repo
Retention Requirements
Run
Savings and Loan (S&L)
Savings Certificate
Selective Controls
Snugging
Special Depository
Spread Banking
Super Regional Bank
Syndicated Loan
System Repo
Term Fed Funds
Thrift
Tight
Till Money
Time Deposit
Total Reserves
Transfer Agent
TT&L Account
Unrestricted
Vault Cash
Vneshtorgbank
Warehousing
Window
World Bank

3) Bond Mathematics

Accounting Rate of Return
Accretion
Accrual Rate
Accrued Interest
Accumulated Interest
Actual Return
Actuarial Rate
Actuarial Yield
Actuary
Adjusted Basis
Adjusted Duration
After-Tax Yield
AIBD Yield
Annual Equivalent
Annualize
Annually Compounded Yield
Annual Percentage Rate (APR)
Annual Return
Arbitrage Pricing Theory (APT)
Arithmetic Mean
Arithmetic Return
Ascending Yield Curve
Assumed Rate of Return
Average Life
Average Yield
Balance-of-Term Yield
Bank Basis
Base Market Value
Basis
Basis Book
Basis Point
Basis Price
Beta
Big Figure
Binomial Option Pricing
Black-Scholes
Body
Bond Basis
Bond Days
Bond Equivalent Yield (BEY)
Bond Price Quotation
Bond Ratio
Bond Reinvestment Equivalent (BRE)

Bond Years
Book Yield
Breakeven Analysis
Breakeven Exchange Rate
Breakeven Point
Breakeven Reinvestment Rate
Breakeven Yield
Canadian Interest Cost
Capitalization Rate
Capitalized Interest
Capital Market Line
Clean
Clear Price
Compound Accreted Value
Compound Interest
Concavity
Convexity
Corporate Bond Equivalent (CBE) Yield
Corporation Settlement
Corporate Tax Equivalent Yield
Coupon
Coupon Payment Period
Coupon Rate
Covariance
Coverage
Cumulative Rate of Return
Current Coupon
Current Call Ratio
Current Maturity
Current Yield
Daily Accretion
Dated Date
Descending Yield Curve
Dime
Dirty
Discount
Discount Basis
Discounted Cash Flows
Discounting
Discount Yield
Dispersion
Dividend Yield
Dollar Duration
Dollar Price
Dollar Return

Implicit Interest Factor
Implied Forward Rate
Implied Volatility
Implied Yield
Income Yield
Interest
Interest Assumption
Interest Rate
Interest Yield
Interest Yield Equivalent (IYE)
Internal Rate of Return (IRR)
Inverted
Jawboning
Life-to-Call
Life-to-Put
Liquidity Preference
Liquidity Premium
Liquidity Theory
Long Coupon
Macaulay Duration
Market Segmentation Hypothesis
Maturity Premium
Maturity Value
Mean Return
Middle Price
Modern Portfolio Theory
Modified Duration
Money Market Basis
Money Yield
Moving Average
Negative Convexity
Negative Duration
Negatively Sloped
Negative Yield
Negative Yield Curve
Net
Net Present Value
Net Yield
Nickel
Nominal Interest Rate
Nominal Yield
Normal Yield Curve
Option-Adjusted Convexity
Option-Adjusted Duration
Option-Adjusted Spread

Option-Adjusted Yield
Ordinary Interest
Original Issue Discount
Parallel Shift
Par Compression
Parity Price
Par Value
Par Yield Curve
Pip
Plus
Point
Premium
Present Value (PV)
Price Yield Curve
Principal Value
Rate of Return
Ratio
Realizable Tail
Realized Compound Yield
Realized Return
Realized Yield
Real Rate of Return
Real Yield
Reinvestment Rate
Required Rate of Return
Return
Risk
Risk Free Return
Risk Premium
Rolling Yield
Rollover Yield
Rule of 69
Rule of 72
Rule of 78
Scenario Analysis
Second Generation Duration
Sensitivity
Short Coupon
Simple Interest
Simple Yield to Maturity
Spot Rate
Spot Rate Curve
Spread
Spread Duration
Spread for Life (SFL)

Standard Deviation
Standstill Return
Steenth
Stochastic Duration
Stripped Price
Systematic Risk
Taxable Equivalent Yield (TEY)
Term Structure
Term Structure Hypothesis
Total Return
Trade Weighting
True Interest Cost (TIC)
Unmodified Duration
Unsystematic Return
Unsystematic Risk
Value of an 01
Variance
Volatility
Weighted Average
Weighting the Trade
Yield
Yield Basis
Yield Curve
Yield Premium
Yield Spread
Yield to Adjusted Minimum Maturity
Yield to Average Life
Yield to Call
Yield to Crash
Yield to Equivalent Life
Yield to Maturity (YTM)
Yield to Operative Date
Yield to Put
Yield to Worst

4) Corporate Bonds

Acquisition
Active
Advance Refunding
Affiliated Corporation
Alien Corporation
Annual Report
Any-Interest-Date Call
Assumed Bond
Balloon
Bear Hug
Black Knight
Bond Ratio
Bootstrap
Building Society
Buying Ahead
Call
Call Deferment
Call Protection
Callable
Callable Bond
Called Away
Call Schedule
Call Yield Premium
Canadian Sinking Fund
Capability Margin
Cash Call
Cash Index
Cash Sinking Fund
Change of Control Bond
Channel Sinking Fund
Clean
Corporate Bond
Corporate Bond Equivalent Yield
Corporate Settlement
Corporate Tax Equivalent Yield
Crown Jewel
Cumulative Sinking Fund
Curing
Cushion Bond
Dawn Raid
Debenture
Default Risk
Defensive Corporation

Downstream
Drawing
Embedded Option Value
Event Risk
Ex Redemption
Fair Rate of Return
Fallen Angel
First Call Date
Golden Parachute
Greenmail
Guaranteed Bond
Guaranteed Sinking Fund
Hell or High Water Obligation
High Yield Bond
Indorsed Bond
Industrial Bond
Intercorporate Debt
Intermediate
Invested Sinking Fund
January Effect
Joint Bonds
Junk Bond
Killer Bee
Leakage
Leverage Buyout (LBO)
Lobster Trap
Maintenance and Replacement Fund (M&R)
Mandatory Redemption
Medium-Term
Moody's
Mortgage Cash Flow Obligation (MCF)
Non-Cumulative Sinking Fund
Not Rated (NR)
Optional Redemption
Option to Double
Pac Man
Par Bond
Poison Pill
Poison Put
Prerefunding
Property Additions Sinking Fund
Pro Rata Sinking Fund
Public Utility Holding Company Act
Putable
Raider

5) Derivative Products (Futures, Options, Swaps)

Abandon
Actuals
Against Actuals
Aggregate Exercise Price
Alligator Spread
American Option
Anticipatory Hedge
Assay
Assign
Assignment
At the Money (ATM)
Automatic Exercise
Back Bond
Back Contract
Back Month
Backspread
Backwardation
Basis
Basis Net of Carry (BNOC)
Basis Order
Basis Risk
Basis Swap
Basis Trading
Basket Delivery
Basket Option
Bear Spread
Black-Scholes
Board Broker (BB)
Box Spread
Bull Spread
Butterfly Spread
Buying/Selling the Basis
Buying the Basis
Buying the Spread
Buy on Close
Buy on Opening
Buywrite
Calendar Spread
Call
Call Market
Call Option Deutsche Marks (CODM)
Cap
Capping

Credit Spread
Cross Hedge
Crush Spread
Current Delivery
Daily Price Limit
Debit Spread
Deep in the Money
Deep out of the Money
Deferred Contract
Deferred Futures
Deliverable
Delivery
Delivery Date
Delivery Factor
Delivery Mechanism
Delivery Month
Delivery Notice
Delivery Price
Delta
Delta Hedge
Demand Certificate
Depository Receipt
Derivative
Diagonal Spread
Direct Hedge
Disclosure Document
Discount Market
Down-and-Out Option
Dressed
Early Exercise
Equivalent Contracts
Escrow Receipt
European Option
Exchange for Physicals
Exchange-Traded Option
Exercise
Exercise Limit
Exercise Notice
Exercise Price
Expiration Cycle
Expiration Date
Ex-Pit
Extrinsic Value
Factor Slippage
Farther In

Farther Out
Fast Market
Fighter (FYTR)
Financial Futures
First Notice Day
Fixed Deliverable Option
Floating-Floating
Floor
Foreign Currency Options Principal (FCOP)
Forward
Forward Exchange Rate
Forward Fed Funds
Forward Market
Forward Points
Free on Board (FOB)
Front Contract
Front Month
Front Running
Future
Futures Commission Merchant (FCM)
Futures Contract
Futures Delivery
Futures Market
Gamma
Gingy
GNMA Standby
Guaranteed Coupon
Hedge
Hedge Period
Hedge Ratio
Horizontal Spread
Imperfect Hedge
Implied Forward Rate
Implied Repo Rate
Implied Volatility
Index Option
Interest Rate Futures
Interest Rate Swap
Intermarket Spread Swap
In the Money
Intrinsic Value
Inverted Market
Invoice Amount
JAJO
Jelly Roll Spread

Kansas City Board of Trade (KBOT)
Kappa
Lambda
Lapsed
Last Trading Day
Leg
Limit
Limited Risk
Liquidation
Liquidity Market
Local
Lock Limit
London International Financial Futures Exchange (LIFFE)
Long Hedge
Long Leg
Long Straddle
Long the Basis
Look-Back Option
Macro-Hedge
Mae West Spread
Marking
Married Put
Micro Hedge
Mortgage Swap
MJSD
Multiply-Traded Options
Municipal Over Bond (MOB) Spread
Naked
Natural Spread
Near the Money
Nearby
Net Arbitrage Profit
Net Writer
Neutral
Neutral Hedge
Neutral Spread
Normal Market
Notional Amount
Offset
On the Money
Open Interest
Opening Purchase
Opening Rotation
Opening Sale
Option

Rho
Right
Roll Down
Roll Forward
Rolling Curve
Rolling Forward the Hedge
Roll Up
Round Turn
Scale Order
Seller's Option
Series
Shadow Market
Shipping Certificate
Short Hedge
Short Leg
Short Straddle
Short the Basis
Short the Board
Side by Side
Simple Option
Specific Option
Spot
Spot Month
Spot Price
Spot Rate
Spread
Spreading
Spread Option
Spread Order
Spread Position
Stale Date
Stepped Call
Stock Index Future
Straddle
Strangle
Strap
Strike Price
Strip
Switch Order
Synthetic
Synthetic Call
Synthetic Long
Synthetic Position
Synthetic Put
Synthetic Short

Take Delivery
Theoretical Time Value
Theoretical Value
Theta
Time Spread
Time Value
Trading Against the Box
Trading Limit
Triple Witching Hour
Two-Fer
Uncovered
Underlying Security
Unit
Variable Deliverable Option
Vertical Call Bear Spread
Vertical Call Bull Spread
Vertical Put Bear Spread
Vertical Put Bull Spread
Vertical Spread
Volatility Spread
Warehouse Receipt
Wasting
Writer

6) Economics

Abatement
Ability-to-Pay
Abstinence Theory
Accelerationist theory
Acceleration Principal
Accelerator
Accomodative
Ad Valorem Tax
Aggregate Demand
Aggregate Supply
Agio Theory
Apportioned Tax
Appropriation
Arbitrage Pricing Theory
Astronomical Theory of Business Cycles
Babson Break
Backward Bending Supply Curve
Balance of Payments
Balance of Trade
Bancor
Barometer
Barrel
Base Period
Basic Accounting Equation
Benefit Received
Beggar-Thy-Neighbor
Beige Book
Blast Furnace Barometer
Boom
Bottleneck inflation
Bretton Woods
Bubble
Budget Deficit
Budget Sequester
Burden
Business Cycle
Business Sector
Bust
Capacity
Capacity Utilization Rate
Capillarity
Capital
Capital Account

Defensive Corporation
Deficit
Deficit Financing
Deficit Spending
Deflation
Degressive Tax
Demand
Demand Elasticity
Demand-Pull Inflation
Demonitization
Depletion
Deregulation
Devaluation
Diffusion
Dirty Float
Discretionary Consumer Spending
Disinflation
Disintermediation
Dismal Science
Disposable Income
Dole
Domestic Production
Downturn
Duesenberry Effect
Durable Goods
Duty
Earned Income
Easy
Econometrics
Economic Growth Rate
Economic Indicator
Economic Liberalism
Economic Resources
Efficient
Elastic Demand
Elastic Supply
Elasticity
Emolument
Endogenous Theory of Business Cycles
Engel's Law
Equilibrium
Even Keel
Exogenous
Expansion
Expansive

Nominal Interest
Nonhuman Resources
Normal Unemployment
Okun's Law
Oligopoly
Oligopsony
Orthodox School
Overheating
Paradox of Thrift
Parallel Importation
Pareto's Law
Perfect Elasticity
Perfect Inelasticity
Peril Point
Permanent Income
Personal Income
Phillips Curve
Physiocrat
Presidential Effect
Price Elasticity
Pro-Cyclical
Producer Goods
Producer Price Index (PPI)
Progressive Tax
Protectionism
Public Choice
Public Debt
Public Goods
Purchasing Power Parity (PPP)
Purchasing Power Risk
Quantitative Controls
Quantity Theory of Money
Random Walk
Rational Expectations
Reaganomics
Real Economic Growth Rate
Real GNP
Real Income
Real Interest Rate
Recession
Recessionary Gap
Recovery
Reflation
Regressive Tax
Restrictive

Retail Price Index (RPI)
Revulsion
Say's Law
Seasonal
Seasonally Adjusted Statistics
Sector
Sectoral Inflation
Selective Controls
Sellers' Inflation
Sentiment Indicator
Slippage
Social Goods
Stagflation
Stagnation
Sterilization
Stimulative
Structural Unemployment
Supply Elasticity
Supply Side Economics
Technical Condition
Term Structure Hypothesis
Total Output
Total Spending
Trade Balance
Trade Deficit
Trade Surplus
Transfer Payment
Unemployment Rate
Utility Theory of Value
Velocity
Velocity Ratio
Wage-Price Spiral
Wealth Effect
Wholesale Price Index (WPI)

7) Equity and Equity-Related Securities

Acceleration Feature
Adjustable Rate Convertible Note (ARCN)
Antidilution Clause
Antidilutive
Arbitrage Short Sale
Attached
Authorized Capital Stock
Babson Break
Back Bond
Bearer Participation Certificate
Big Board
Black Friday
Blue Chip
Blue Monday
Bond Value
Bourse
Breakeven Time
Broken
Busted Convertible
Call Price
Call Protective Warrant
Capital Stock
Cash Dividend
Chart Analysis
Chartist
Classical Security Analysis
Classic Warrant
Closely Held
Common Stock
Common Stock Warrant
Contingent Claim
Conversion Date
Conversion Parity
Conversion Premium
Conversion Price
Conversion Ratio
Conversion Value
Convertible
Convertible Arbitrage
Convertible Bond
Cram Down Paper
Cum
Cum Warrant

Cumulative Voting
Curb Exchange
Curb Stock
Currency Warrant
Cutting a Melon
Cyclical Stock
Debenture with Warrants
Declare
Delayed Convertible
Derived Book Value
Dilution
Dividend
Dividend Capture
Dividend Discount Model
Dividend Payout Ratio
Dividend Reinvestment
Dividend Scrip
Dividend Yield
Double Taxation
Dow Jones
Dow Jones Industrial Average
Dow Jones Transportation Average
Dow Jones Utility Average
Dual Option (Du-Op)
Earnings Yield
Equity
Equity Financing
Equity-Linked Security
Ex-All
Exchangeable
Exchange Ratio
Ex-Date
Ex-Dividend
Ex-Dividend Date
Exercise Content
Exercise Premium
Extra Dividend
Extraordinary Dividend
Ex-Warrants
Floor
Floor Broker
Forced Conversion
Fractional
Full Cover
Fully Diluted

Fundamental Analysis
Going Public
Greenmail
Growth Stock
Half-Stock
Harmless Income Warrant
Harmless Warrant
Head and Shoulders
Host Bond
Income Warrant
Index Arbitrage
Interested
Income Stock
Investment Letter Stock
Irish Dividend
Kicker
Limited Liability
Listing
Lobster Trap
Market Analysis
Market Content
Minority Interest
Mirror Warrant
Money Back Warrant
Naked
Naked Warrant
Nine Bond Rule
No Par
Optional Dividend
Option Warrant
Ordinary Shares
Package Trading
Paper Barrel
Parity
Passed Dividend
Penny Stock
Premium Convertible
Program Trading
Property Dividend
Proxy
Proxy Statement
Put Harmless Warrant
Put Warrant
Qualitative Analysis
Quantitative Analysis

Raider
Rate-to-Triple
Record Date
Reverse Hedge
Reverse Stock Split
Right
Risk Arbitrage
Scrip
Seat
Specialist
Statutory Voting
Stock
Stock Ahead
Stock Clearing Corporation
Stock Dividend
Stock Exchange
Stock Index Arbitrage
Stock Index Future
Stock Jobbing
Stock Repurchase
Stock Split
Stock-Value Ratio
Stockholder of Record
Straight Debt Value
Street
Stripped Yield
Support Level
Sweetener
Technical Analysis
Toehold
Treasury Stock
Trigger Price
Unissued
Unit
Unlisted
Unpaid Dividend
Usable
Wall Street
Warrant
Watered Stock
Wedding Warrant
Widow and Orphan
Window Warrant
Working Control
Z

8) Floating Rate Securities

Adjustment Frequency
Agent Bank
Bull Floating Rate Note
Cap
Capped Floating Rate Note
Catch-Up Floater
Collar
Collateralized Floating Rate Note
Convertible Floating Rate Note
Coupon Spread
Current Coupon
Delayed Cap Floating Rate Note
Discounted Margin
Double Drop-Lock Security
Drop Lock
Effective Margin
Effective Spread
FBC Yield
Fixing
Floater
Floating Rate Certificate of Deposit (FRCD)
Floating Rate CMO
Floating Rate REMIC
Floating Rate Interest
Floating Rate Note (FRN)
Floor
Grantor Underwritten Note
High-Low Floater
Index
Interest Rate Cap
Inverse Floater
Leveraged Floater
London Interbank Offered Rate
Lower Floater
Margin
Mini-Max Bond
Minimum Rate
Neutral Price
Payment Basis
Payment Delay
Payment Frequency
Perpetual
Quoted Margin

Reset Frequency
Reset Margin
Reverse Floater
Reverse Super Floater
Rollover Price
Simple Margin
Spread
Spread for Life (SFL)
Spread-to-Maturity
Step Down Floating Rate Note
Step Up Floating Rate Note
Stub Period
Subordinated Variable Rate Notes
Super Floater
Trigger Rate
Yield Curve Note
Yield to Maturity for Floating Rate Securities
YTM Spread

9) International Securities

Absolute Rate
Agent Bank
Agreement Among Managers
American Depositary Receipt
Association of International Bond Dealers
Auslandobligation
Aussie Bond
Back-to-Back Loan
Bancor
Bank of England
Bank of Japan
Basket
Bearer Depositary Receipt
Benchmark Issue
Bid Deadline
Breakeven Exchange Rate
British Clearer
Bulldog Bond
Bundbahnpost Bond
Bundesbank
Bundeskassenobligation(en)
Bundesobligation(en)
Capital Debenture
CEDEL
Centrale de Livraison de Valeurs Mobilieres
Clean Float
Clearing System
Covered Interest Arbitrage
Crossrate
Currency Basket
Currency-Linked Bond
Currency of Denomination
Currency Swap
Currency Warrant
Daimyo
Development Bank
Dirty Float
Discount Currency
Discounted Investment in Negotiated Government
  Obligations (DINGO)
Discount House
Dollar Bloc
Double Dated

Down Under
Dual Currency Bond
Duet Bonds
Eurobond
Euro Certificate of Deposit
Euroclear
Eurocommercial Paper
Eurocurrency
Eurodollar
Eurodollar CD
Euro Floater
Euro Issue
Euromarket
Euronote
Euronote Facility
European Currency Unit (ECU)
European Depository Receipt
European Monetary System (EMS)
European Unit of Account (EUA)
Eurosecurity
Exchange Rate
FIMEAN
Fixed Dates
Floating Eurodollar Repackaged Assets of the Republic of
  Italy (FERARI)
Flowback
Foreign Bond
Foreign Currency Bond
Foreign Exchange Market
Foreign Interest Payment Securities (FIPS)
Foreign Targeted Note
Forex-Linked Bond
Forward Forward Contract
Forward Points
Forward Rate
Frankfurt Interbank Bid Rate
Frankfurt Interbank Offered Rate
Geisha Bond
Gensaki
Gilt
Global Note Facility
Go-Shugi
Government Broker
Granny
Grey Market

Hang Seng Index
Index Linked Bond
Interest Rate Differential
International Bank for Reconstruction and Development (IBRD)
International Commodities Clearing House (ICCH)
International Monetary Fund (IMF)
International Primary Markets Association
International Securities Regulatory Organization
Itaku Gansaki
Jobber
Kaffirs
Kangaroo Bond
Kassenobligation(en)
Kassenvereine
Kiwi Bond
Kommunalobligation(en)
Lender's Option—Borrower's Option
LIMEAN
Local Authority Bond
Lock-Up Period
Lombard Rate
London Interbank Bid Rate
London Interbank Offered Rate
Multicurrency Clause
Multi-Option Financing Facility
Neutral Period
New York Interbank Offered Rate
Nikkei
Non-Underwritten Euronote
Old Lady of Threadneedle Street
Over-the-Bridge
Pfandbrief(e)
Premium Currency
Revolving Underwriting Facility
Samurai Bond
Schuldscheindarlehen
Shibosai Bond
Shogun Bond
Short-Term Note Issuance Facility
Singapore Interbank Offered Rate
Special Drawing Right
Spot Rate
Standard Basket
Standby Facility
Stock

Sushi Bond
Tap
Tengoku/Jigoku Bond
World Bank
Yankee Bond
Yen CD
Yen Government Bond

10) Mortgage-Related Securities

Absolute Prepayment Rate
A/B Structure
Accelerated Remittance Cycle (ARC)
Acccleration Clause
Acceleration Feature
Accounting Current Yield
Accretion Bond
Accretion Determination Date
Accrual Bond
Accrual Date
Accrual Factor
Accrual Rate
Actual Delay
Adjustable Rate Index
Adjustable Rate Mortgage
Adjustment Frequency
After Acquired Clause
Alternative Mortgage Instrument (AMI)
Amortization
Annual Percentage Rate
Ascending Rate Bond
Asset Backed Security
Assumable
Assumption
Average Life
Balloon
Balloon Interest
Balloon Payment
Beamer (BMIR)
Biweekly Mortgage
Bond Value
Builder Bond
Builder Buydown Loan
Builder Operative Loan
Burnout
Buydown
Calamity Call
California VRM
Canadian Rollover
Cash Flow Bond
Cash Flow Uncertainty
Cash Flow Yield
Cash Immediate Market

Cash Program
Catch-up Floater
Chattel Mortgage
Class
Cleanup Call
Closing
Closing Date
CMO Equity
Collateral
Collateralized
Collateralized Depository Receipt (CDR)
Collateralized Mortgage Obligation (CMO)
Collateral Mortgage Bond (CMB)
Collateral Value
Collateral Value Cap
Collection Account
Concurrent Pay
Conditional Prepayment Rate (CPR)
Conduit
Conforming Loan
Connie Mac
Consistency
Consolidated Mortgage Bond
Constant Maturity Treasury (CMT)
Constant Percent Prepayment (CPP)
Construction Loan
Controlled Amortization Bond (CAB)
Conventional Loan
Conventional Mortgage-Backed Security (CMBS)
Convertible
Corporate Bond Equivalent
Cost of Funds
Coupon
Coupon Rate
Credit Card Asset Backed Security
Cumulative Prepayment Experience
Current Coupon
Current Coupon Spread
Current Maturity
Custom Pool
Cut-Off Date
Dated Date
Debt Service
Debt Service Fund
Decrement Table

Graduated Payment Mortgage Reserve Fund
Gross Coupon
Gross Margin
Growing Equity Mortgage (GEM)
Guaranteed Mortgage Certificate (GMC)
Guarantor Program
Half-PAC
Honest-to-God (HTG) Yield
Independent
Index
Index Duration
Initial Rate
Interest Only (IO)
Interest Only Period
Interest Rate Shock
Interim Experience
Jumbo
Level Debt Service
Level Payment Mortgage
Life-of-Loan Cap
Loan-to-Value
Lockout
Low-Start Mortgage
Master Servicer
Midget
Mobile Homes
Modified
Mortgage
Mortgage-Backed Security (MBS)
Mortgage Banker
Mortgage Bond
Mortgage Cash Flow Obligation
Mortgage Certificate
Mortgage Insurance
Mortgage Pipeline
Mortgage Pool
Mortgage REIT
Mortgage Servicing
Mortgagee
Mortgagor
Motorcycles
Multifamily
Multiple Pool
Multiple Servicing
Negative Amortization

Negative Amortization Cap
Negative Convexity
Net Coupon
Net Margin
Non-Amortization Period
Non-Conforming Loan
Non-Gnome
Non-Recourse
Nuisance Call
Open-End
Open Mortgage
Option-Adjusted Duration
Option-Adjusted Spread
Option-Adjusted Yield
Optional Redemption
Original Principal
Originator
Overcollateralization
Owner Trust
Pair Off
Parallel Pay
Par Cap
Par Compression
Participation
Participation Certificate (PC)
Pass-Through
Pass-Through Rate
Pass-Through Yield
Paydown
Paying Agent
Payment Cap
Payment Date
Payment Delay
Payment in Advance
Payment in Arrears
Payment Shock
Payout Event
Pay-Through Bond
Periodic Rate Caps
Permitted Investments
Pipeline
Plan III GPM
Planned Amortization Class (PAC)
Planned Redemption Obligation (PRO)
Points

Pool
Pool Factor
Pool Insurance
Prepaid Life
Prepayment
Prepayment Experience
Prepayment Model
Prepayment Reserve Fund
Prepayment Risk
Prepayment Table
Pricing Date
Pricing Speed
Principal
Principal Only (PO)
Prior Lien
Private Mortgage Insurance (PMI)
Private Pass-Through
Production Rate
Prohibited Transaction
Project Loan
PSA Standard Prepayment Model
Qualified Mortgage
Qualified Real Estate Investment
Qualified Replacement Mortgage
Qualified Reserve Fund
Rate Cap
Rate Change
Real Estate Investment Trust
Real Estate Mortgage Investment Conduit (REMIC)
Real Property
Recast
Record Date
Reduction Option Loan
Refinancing
Relocation Mortgage
Remaining Term
REMIC
Renegotiated Rate Mortgage (RRM)
Required Net Yield (RNY)
Reserve Fund
Residual
Reverse Annuity Mortgage (RAM)
Reverse Floater
Revolver
Revolving Period

Risk-Controlled Arbitrage
Rocket Bond
Rollover Mortgage (ROM)
Sandwich Bond
Scheduled Redemption Obligation (SRO) Class
Seasonality
Seasoned
Securitization
Semi-PAC
Senior/Subordinated Pass-Through
Series
Servicing
Servicing Fee
Shared Appreciation Mortgage (SAM)
Short WAM
Single Family
Single Monthly Mortality (SMM)
Slow Pay
Special Purpose Vehicle
Special Redemption
Spike
Spread Duration
Standard Prepayment Assumption (SPA)
Standby Commitment
Stated Delay
Stated Maturity
Straight Pass-Through
Strip
Swap PC
Tangible
Targeted Amortization Class (TAC)
Teaser
Traditional Mortgage
Tranche
Twelve-Year Life
Underlying Security
Variable Rate Mortgage (VRM)
Veterans Administration (VA)
Vintage
Warehousing
Weighted Average Coupon (WAC)
Weighted Average Maturity (WAM)
Weighted Average Remaining Maturity (WARM)
Whole Loan
Whole Pool

Whole Pool Test
Wrap-Around Mortgage
Yield Maintenance
Z Bond
Z Factor

11) Municipal Securities

Acceptance Ratio
Accumulation Account
Additional Bonds Test
Advance Refunding
Agency Cross
American Municipal Bond Assurance Corporation (AMBAC)
Arbitrage Bond
Assessed Valuation
Bid Form
Blue List
Bond Anticipation Note (BAN)
Bond Buyer Municipal Bond Index
Bonded Debt
Bond Investors Guaranty Insurance Company (BIGI)
Capital Appreciation Bond (CAB)
Capitalized Interest
Conduit Financing
Construction Loan Note
Debt Limit
Debt Service Reserve Fund
Direct Debt
Dollar Bond
Double-Barrelled Bond
Double Exempt
Eastern Account
Eleven Bond Index
Equivalent Taxable Yield (ETY)
Ex-Legal
Feasibility Study
Financial Guaranty Insurance Company (FGIC)
Floating Debt
Funded Debt
General Obligation Bond (GO)
Governmental Accounting Standards Board (GASB)
Government Finance Officers Association (GFOA)
Grant Anticipation Note
Gross Revenue Pledge
Group Net Order
Guerilla Group
Industrial Development Bond
Industrial Development Bond Insurance (IDBI)
Industrial Revenue Bond
Insured Bonds

Legal Opinion
Level Debt Service
Limited Tax Bond
Member Order
Moody's Investment Grade (MIG)
Moral Obligation Bond
Municipal Bond
Municipal Bond Insurance
Municipal Bond Insurance Association (MBIA)
Municipal Investment Trust
Municipal Over Bond (MOB) Spread
Municipal Note
Municipal Securities Rulemaking Board (MSRB)
Munifacts
National Association of Bond Lawyers (NABL)
Net Interest Cost (NIC)
Net Revenue Pledge
New Housing Authority Bonds
Non-Litigation Certificate
Notice of Sale
Official Notice of Sale
Official Statement
Overlapping Debt
Per Capita Debt
Placement Ratio
Pledged Revenues
Presale Order
Private Activity Bond
Project Note
Protective Covenant
Public Housing Authority Bonds
Rate Covenant
Revenue Anticipation Note (RAN)
Revenue Bond
Revenue Bond Index
Self-Supporting
Shelf Offering
Special Assessment Bond
Special Tax Bond
State and Local Government Series
Taxable Equivalent Yield
Tax Anticipation Note (TAN)
Tax-Exempt Bond
Ten Percent Rule
Term Bond

12) Portfolio Management

Accounting Current Yield
Accumulation
Accumulation Account
Active Management
Aggressive Portfolio
Alpha
Arbitrage
Arbitrage Pricing Theory (APT)
Asset/Liability Management
Average Down
Average Up
Balanced Company
Balanced Fund
Balanced Manager
Barbell
Basket
Basket Trading
Bearding
Bottom-Up Manager
Cash Flow Buyer
Cash Flow Matching
Closed-End
Closet Indexer
Combination Matching
Common Trust Fund
Constant Dollar (C$)
Contingent Immunization
Convexity
Core Holding
Core Management
Covered Industry Investing
Dedication
Defeasance
Defensive Portfolio
Dispersion
Diversifiable Risk
Diversification
Dollar Cost Averaging
Dollar Duration
Dual Purpose Fund
Dumbbell
Duration Matching
Duration-Weighted Trade

13) Preferred Stock

Accrued Dividend
Adjustable Rate Preferred Stock
Applicable Percentage
Arrearage
Asset Backed Preferred Stock
Auction
Basis
Beneficial Owner
Callable Preferred Stock
Collar
Comparable
Convertible Adjustable Preferred Stock
Convertible Preferred Stock
Cumulative
Cumulative Preferred
Current Yield
Debenture Stock
Declaration Date
Depository Preferred
Dividend
Dividend Period
Dividends Received Deduction
Dutch Auction
Ex-Dividend Date
Existing Holder
Extraordinary Dividend
Fixed Charges
Flat
Good Standing
Implied Dividend Rate
Life Spread
Market Price Adjustment Ratio
Net Earnings
New Money Preferred
Non Cumulative
Non-Participating Preferred Stock
Old Money Preferred
PAR Preferred
Participating Preferred
Par Value
Passed Dividend
Pay Date
Pay-in-Kind (PIK)

Perpetual
Potential Holder
Preference Stock
Preferred Stock
Prior Preferred
Purchase Fund
Record Date
Reference Rate
Remarketed Preferred
Seasoned Private
Share Adjusted Broker Remarketed Equity Shares (SABRES)
Short-Term Auction Rate (STAR) Preferred Stock
Single Point Adjustable Rate Preferred
Stripped Price
Variable Term Preferred (VTP)

14) Securities Law

Accredited Investor
Adequate Consideration
Adequate Disclosure
Adjusted Trade
Advertisement
Affiliated Person
Arbitration
Arm's Length
Articles of Incorporation
Assignment
Associated Person
At-Risk Rule
Authentication
Backup Withholding
Bankruptcy
BD Form
Bear Raid
Bedbug
Beneficial Owner
Blue Sky
Blue-Skying
Bond Counsel
Bond Power
Breakpoint Sales
Bucketing
Bucket Shop
Business Conduct Committee (BCC)
Buy-In
Bylaws
Capping
Caveat Emptor
Caveat Venditor
C&D
Certificate of Incorporation
Chapter 11
Charter
Chinese Wall
Churning
Commingling
Commission Give-Up
Control Person
Control Stock
Convenience Shelf

Cooked Books
Corporate Resolution
Corporation
Covenant
Creeping Tender Offer
Crossed Trade
Cross-Trading
Customer Agreement
Daisy Chain
Defalcation
Defeasance
Deficiency Judgment
Deficiency Letter
Deficit Reduction Act
Delist
Deregulation
Disclaimer
District Business Conduct Committee (DBCC)
Domicile
Due Diligence
Economic Defeasance
Effective
Employees Retirement Income Security Act (ERISA)
Erroneous Report Rule
Escheat
Exempt Securities
Exhibit A
Federal Reserve Act
Fictitious Credit
Fidelity Bond
Final Prospectus
Financial and Operations Principal (FINOP)
Five Hundred Dollar Rule
Five Percent Policy
Form 3
Form 4
Form 8K
Form 10K
Form 10Q
Form S-1
Free Credit Balance
Freeriding
Front Running
Frozen
Full Disclosure

Fully Registered
Gather in the Stops
Glass-Steagall Act
Going Ahead
Government in the Sunshine Law
Guarantee
Guaranteed
Gun Jumping
Haircut
Hedge Clause
Holder of Record
Holding
House Call
House Rules
Hypothecation
Indenture
Indenture Supplement
Initial Margin
Inside Information
Insider
Intra-State Offering
Investment Act of 1940
Investment Letter Stock
Keep Well Agreement
Kiting
Know Your Customer
Lapping
Launder
Legality
Legal Defeasance
Legal List
Legal Tender
Letter of Notification
Letter Security
Lien
Loan Value
Maintenance Call
Maintenance Margin
Maloney Act of 1938
Manipulation
Margin
Margin Account
Margin Agreement
Margin Call
Margin Equity

Margin Security
Matched Orders
Material
Minus Tick
Misappropriation
National Association of Securities Dealers (NASD)
Negative Covenants
Negative Pledge Clause
Net Capital Requirement
Nine Bond Rule
Nominal Owner
Nominative Security
Nominee
Non-Affiliated Persons
Non-Exempt Security
Non-Marketable Debt
Non-Refundable
Novation
Nuisance Call
Nuisance Lawsuit
Offer
Offer for Sale
Offshore
Overtrading
Painting the Tape
Papilsky
Pari Passu Clause
Parking
Pegging
Person
Ponzi
Position Limit
Power of Attorney
Preliminary Official Statement
Preliminary Prospectus
Presale Order
Prescribed Period
Private Placement
Prohibited Transaction
Prospectus
Prospectus Supplement
Protective Covenant
Prudent Man Rule
Public Utility Holding Company Act
Purchaser Representative

Purpose Statement
Qualified Legal Opinion
Quiet Period
Receivership
Reciprocal Immunity
Recision
Reclamation
Registered in Legal Form
Registration Statement
Regulation A
Regulation D
Regulation G
Regulation M
Regulation Q
Regulation T
Regulation U
Regulation Z
Rehypothecation
Resolution
Restricted
Restrictive Covenant
Retention Requirement
Risk Disclosure Statement
Rule 3b-3
Rule 10a-1
Rule 10b-2
Rule 10b-4
Rule 10b-5
Rule 10b-6
Rule 10b-7
Rule 10b-10
Rule 10b-13
Rule 10b-16
Rule 12b-1
Rule 13d
Rule 13e
Rule 15c2-1
Rule 15c3-1
Rule 15c3-2
Rule 15c3-3
Rule 19b-3
Rule 144
Rule 237
Rule 254
Rule 396

Rule 405
Rule 415
Rule 425A
Rule 433
Rules of Fair Practice
Running Ahead
Safe Harbor
Sale
Schedule 13D
Secondary Private Placement
Securities Act of 1933
Securities and Exchange Commission (SEC)
Securities Exchange Act of 1934
Securities Investors Protection Act (SIPA)
Segregation
Seller's Market
Self-Regulatory Organization (SRO)
Shelf Registration
Short Swing Rule
Short Tender
Sovereign Immunity
Special Miscellaneous Account (SMA)
Sunshine Law
Tape Dancing
Tax Equity and Fiscal Responsibility Act of 1982 (TEFRA)
T Call
Trading Authorization
Trust Indenture
Trust Indenture Act of 1939
Ultra Vires
Undermargined
Uniform Gifts to Minors Act (UGMA)
Uniform Practice Code
Unrestricted
Usury
Validation
Variation Margin
Waiting Period
Wash Sale
Wash Sale Rule
Williams Act
Wooden Ticket

15) Trading (Secondary Market)

Above the Market
Accumulation Area
Accumulator
Acquisition Date
Across the Board
Acting in Concert
Active
Active Bond Crowd
Active Box
Affirmation
After Market
Against the Box
Aged Fail
Agency Trade
Air Pocket
All or Any Part (AOAP)
Alternative Order
And Interest
Anomaly Switch
Applied Proceeds Swap
Arbitrage
Asked
At Best
At or Better
At the Close Order
At the Market
At the Open Order
Auction Market
Available Information
Average Down
Average Equity
Average Up
Away
Away from the Market
Axe
Backing Away
Back Up
Bad Delivery
Balance Order
Bear
Bearish
Bear Market
Bear Raid

Bid
Bid-Asked Spread
Bidding Up
Bid Only
Bid Wanted (BW)
Bid Will Improve (BWI)
Bid Without
Blind Broker
Block
Block Positioner
Block Trade
Board Broker (BB)
Board Order
Book Entry
Book Entry Securities
Bottom Fisher
Break
Breakout
Breakout Level
Broad Market
Broker's Transaction
Bulge
Bull
Bullish
Bull Market
Bunching
Buy Bullish News
Buyer's Market
Buying Climax
Buying the Yield Curve
Buy on Close
Buy on Opening
Buyout
Buy Stop
Buy the Book
Cabinet Crowd
Cabinet Security
Cancel
Can Crowd
Cap Order
Cash Flow Buyer
Cash on Delivery
Churning
Clean
Clean on the Print

Clear
Clearing House
Clearing System
Close
Close Up
Closing a Market
Closing Price
Closing Range
Closing Sale
Come Back
Coming to Me
Comparison Ticket
Compensation Bid
Compo
Confirmation
Confirmation Note
Congestion Area
Constructive
Contingent Bargain
Contingent Order
Continuity
Contracyclical Trading
Contra-Party
Corner
Correction
Crossed Market
Cross-Trading
Cuff Quote
Day Order
Day Trading
Deal
Dealer Market
Deep Bid/Offer
Direct Placement Memorandum
Discretionary Order
Do Not Reduce (DNR)
Doubling Up
Dump
Elect
Exit Value
Exchange
Faded
Fail
Fair Market Value
Fast

Matrix Trading
Miss the Market
Most Active List
Narrowing the Spread
Natural
Negotiated Market
Net Arbitrage Profit
Nominal Quotation
Not Held
Numbers Only
Odd Lot
Odd Lot Theory
Off Board
Off-Floor
Off to Off
Offer
Offer Wanted
One-Decision Issue
One-Man Picture
One-Sided Market
On the Hook Order
Open
Open Order
Open Outcry
Opening
Opening Range
Open Up
Order
Out Firm
Over the Counter
Overbought
Overnight Position
Oversold
Overvalued
Pay-Up
Percentage Order
Pick-Up
Picture
Piece
Profit Taking
Program Trading
Rally
Range
Round Lot
Scale Order

Scalper
Scalping
Seasoned
Second Market
Secondary Transaction
Selling Short
Selling Short Against the Box
SLD Last Sale
Stop Order
Stopped Out
Strong
Subject
Sunshine Trading
Suspended
Tax Selling
Thin
Third Market
Throwaway
Top
Trade
Trade Date
Trading on the Wind
Trading Over the Curve
Trading Through the Curve
Transaction
Trigger
Undercut
Weak
With or Without

16) Underwriting (Primary Market)

Absorbed
Account
Advances Option
Agreement Among Underwriters
Aladdin Bond
All-In Cost
All or None (AON)
Allotment
Announcement Date
Assimilation
Authentication
Award
Backstop
Best Effort
Bidding Syndicate
Black Market Bond
Blowout
Bond Administration Agreement
Book
Book-Running
Borrower
Bought Deal
Bracket
Break
Breaking the Syndicate
Calendar
Cancel
Circle
Closed
Closing
Closing Date
Co-Lead Manager
Co-Manager
Competitive Bid
Concession
Conduit
Convenience Shelf
Conversion Issue
Cooling-Off Period
Cost of Issuance
Cover
Cover Bid
Dated Date

Date of Record
Dealer Pot
Dealer's Reallowance
Debt Financing
Delayed Delivery
Demand
Designation
Distribution
Distributor
Divided Account
Due Diligence Meeting
Eastern Account
Equity Financing
Firm Commitment
Fixed Price
Floatation
Freeriding
Free to Trade
Fully Distributed
Global Bond
Going Public
Governing Law
Green Shoe
Gross Spread
Hot Issue
Hung Deal
Initial Public Offering (IPO)
Institutional Pot
In Syndicate
Invitation Telex
Involuntary Underwriter
Issue Bid
Issue Date
Issue Price
Issuing and Paying Agent
Joint and Several
Launch Date
Lead Manager
Less the Reallowance
Lock-Out Period
Management Group
Manager
Manager's Fee
Market Out Clause
Mezzanine

Negotiated Offering
New Issue
Note Issuance Facility
Offer for Sale
Offering Circular
Offering Date
Offering Memorandum
Offering Scale
Open
Originator
Out the Window
Overallotment
Overbanked
Overbooked
Overhang
Oversubscribed
Partly Paid
Payment Date
Payout Ratio
Pegging
Pipeline
Place
Placing Memorandum
Pot
Pot Protection
Praecipuum
Preliminary Prospectus
Prepaid Syndicate Expense (PPSE)
Presold
Price Talk
Primary Market
Primary Offering
Primary Underwriter
Primary Underwriting Commitment
Private Placement
Private Placement Memorandum
Proceeds
Protection
Public Offering
Purchase Fund
Reallowance
Red Herring
Reoffer
Reopening
Retention

Voluntary Underwriter
Waiting Period
Western Account
Wide Open
Withholding

17) U.S. Government and Agency Securities

Accelerated Remittance Cycle (ARC)
Add-Ons
Agency
Agency for International Development (AID)
Auction
Bill
Bill Strip
Bo Derek
Bond Authority
Butterfly
Carter Bonds
Cash Management Bill
Cash Settlement
Competitive Auction
Competitive Bid
Constant Maturity Treasury (CMT)
Corpus TR
Coupon Issue
Coupon Market
Coupon Stripping
Coupon TR
Crowding Out
Current Income Bonds
Debt Ceiling
Debt Limit
Dirt Bonds
Dutch Auction
Farmer Mac
Federal Agricultural Mortgage Corporation
Federal Home Loan Mortgage Corporation
Federal National Mortgage Association
FHLMC
Financial Assistance Corporation (FAC)
Financing Corporation (FICO)
Flower Bonds
FNMA
Foreign Targeted Note
Full Faith and Credit
GNMA
Go-Around
Good Trader
Government National Mortgage Association
Governments

Government Trust Certificate (GTC)
Govies
Granny
James Bond
Junior Refunding
Long Coupon
Mini-Refunding
New Housing Authority Bonds
Non-Competitive Auction
Non-Competitive Bid
Non-Marketable Debt
Nonrecourse Commodity Loan
Off-the-Run
On-the-Run
Paydown
Physical Strip
Primary Dealer
Primary Distribution
Public Debt
Public Housing Authority (PHA) Bonds
Reconstitution
Refunding
Reopening
Risk Free Return
Riskless
Roll
Savings Bond
Second Liberty Bond Act
Separately Traded Registered Interest and Principal Security
   (STRIPS)
Series E
Series EE
Series HH
Small Business Administration (SBA)
Spot Rate
State and Local Government Series (SLGS)
Stop
Stop-Out Price
Tail
Tax Anticipation Bill (TAB)
Tennessee Valley Authority (TVA)
Term Bond
To the Buck
Treasury Bill
Treasury Bond

Appendix 4

Abbreviations and Acronyms

General

AAU—Agreement Among Underwriters

ABC—Accrual Bond CMO

ABS—1) Asset Backed Security 2) Absolute Prepayment Rate

ACE—American Commodities Exchange

ACH—Automated Clearinghouse

ACQ—Acquisition

ACRS—Accelerated Cost Recovery System

ACU—Asian Currency Units

A/D—Advances versus Declines

ADB—1) Asian Development Bank 2) Adjusted Debit Balance

ADR—American Depository Receipt

AfDB—African Development Bank. *See* World Bank

AFUDC—Allowance for Funds Used During Construction

AGY—Agency

AI—Accrued Interest

AIBD—Association of International Bond Dealers

AID—1) Any Interest Date 2) Agency for International Development

AL—Average Life

AMBAC—American Municipal Bond Assurance Corporation

AMEX—American Stock Exchange

AMI—Alternative Mortgage Instrument

AMOS—Amex Options Switching System

AMPS—Auction-Market Preferred Stock

AOAP—All or Any Part

AON—All or None

APR—Annual Percentage Rate

APT—Arbitrage Pricing Theory

ARB—1) Ascending Rate Bond 2) Arbitrager

ARBL—Assets Repriced Before Liabilities

ARC—Accelerated Remittance Cycle

ARCN—Adjustable Rate Convertible Note

ARM—Adjustable Rate Mortgage

ARP—Adjustable Rate Preferred Stock

ASCA—All Subsequent Coupons Attached

ASE—American Stock Exchange

AVG—Average

BA—Bankers' Acceptance

BAN—Bond Anticipation Note

BASIC—Banking and Securities Industry Committee

BB—Board Broker

BCC—Business Conduct Committee

Bd—Bond

BDR—Bearer Depository Receipt

B of E—Bank of England

BG—Bank Guaranteed

BIGI—Bond Investors Guaranty Insurance Company

BIS—Bank for International Settlements

BO DEREKS—11 3/4s of 2/15/10

BLS—Bureau of Labor Statistics

BMIR—Below Market Interest Rate

BNOC—Basis Net of Carry

BOJ—Bank of Japan

BOLO—Borrower's Option—Lender's Option

BOM—Branch Office Manager

BOP—Balance of Payments

BOT—1) Bought 2) Balance of Trade 3) Board of Trustees

BP—Basis Point(s)

BPC—Bearer Participation Certificate

BRE—Bond Reinvestment Equivalent

BSE—Boston Stock Exchange

BSPRA—Builder/Sponsor Profit and Risk Allowance

BW—Bid Wanted

BWI—Bid Will Improve

C$—1) Constant Dollar 2) Canadian Dollar

CAB—1) Capital Appreciation Bond 2) Controlled Amortization Bond

CAML—Certainly Affordable Mortgage Loan

CAMPS—Cumulative Auction-Market Preferred Stock

CAP—Convertible Adjustable Preferred

CAPM—Capital Asset Pricing Model

CARPS—Controlled (or Collateralized) Adjustable Rate Preferred Stock

CATS—Certificates of Accrual on Treasury Securities

CAV—Compound Accreted Value

CBE—Corporate Bond Equivalent

CBO—Certificate of Beneficial Ownership

CBOE—Chicago Board of Options Exchange

CBOT—Chicago Board of Trade

CCABS—Credit Card Asset Backed Security

CD—1) Certificate of Deposit 2) Certificate Delivery

C&D—1) Cease and Desist 2) Construction and Development

CDR—Collateralized Depository Receipt

CEA—Commodity Exchange Authority

CEDEL—Centrale de Livraison de Valeurs Mobilieres

CENTURIES—7 7/8s of 2/15/00-95

CEO—Chief Executive Officer

CFO—1) Cancel Former Order 2) Chief Financial Officer

CFTC—Commodity Futures Trading Commission

CHIPS—Clearing House Interbank Payments System

CHOC—Currency Hedge Option Combination

CIC—Canadian Interest Cost

CIF—1) Cost, Insurance, Freight 2) Corporate Income Fund

CLN—Construction Loan Note

CMB—Collateral Mortgage Bond

CMBR—Commercial Mortgage-Backed Receipt

CMBS—Conventional Mortgage-Backed Security

CME—Chicago Mercantile Exchange

CMO—Collateralized Mortgage Obligation

CMT—Constant Maturity Treasury

CMTA—Clearing Member Trade Agreement

CMV—Current Market Value

CODM—Call Option Deutsche Marks

COF—Cost of Funds

COLA—Cost of Living Adjustment

COMEX—Commodity Exchange

Connie Mac—Conventional Mortgage Pass-Through Security

CONV—Convertible

COOP—Bank for Cooperatives

COT—Competitive Options Trader

COUP—Coupon

CP—Commercial Paper

CPI—Consumer Price Index

CPN—Coupon

CPO—Commodity Pool Operator

CPP—Conditional Percent Prepayment

CPR—Constant Prepayment Rate

Cr—Credit

CRB—Commodities Research Bureau

CREF—Commingled Real Estate Fund

CROP—Compliance Registered Options Principal

CS—Common Stock

CT—Certificate

CTA—Commodity Trading Advisor

CTE—Corporate Tax Equivalent

CTF—Certificate

CTM—Coming to Me

CUB—Corporate bond index to corporate bond spread

CUBES—Coupon Under Book-Entry Safekeeping

CUSIP—Committee on Uniform Securities Identification Procedures

CV—Convertible

CVB—Customs Value Basis

CVT—Convertible

D₁—Duration

D₂—Modified Duration

DAC—Delivery Against Cash

DARTS—Dutch Auction-Rate Transferable Securities

D&B—Dun & Bradstreet

DBA—Doing Business As

DBCC—District Business Conduct Committee

DBO—Delivery Balance Order

DC-10s—10s of 5/15/10-05

DCF—Discounted Cash Flow

DD—Delayed Delivery

DDB—Double Declining Balance

DDM—Dividend Discount Model

DDN—Documented Discount Note

Deb—Debenture

DELY—Delivery

DF—Balance Sheet Liabilities

DINGO—Discounted Investment in Negotiated Government Obligations

DIRT BONDS—Farmers Home Administration

DISCO—Discount

DIST—Distribution

DJIA—Dow Jones Industrial Average

DK—Don't Know

DM—1) Deutsche Mark 2) Discounted Margin

DN—Don't Know

DNE—Discretion Not Exercised

DNR—Do Not Reduce

DOT—Designated Order Turnaround

DPN—Deferred Purchase Note

Dr—Debit

DRD—Dividends Received Deduction

DRT—Disregard Tape

DTC—Depository Trust Company

Du-Op—Dual Option

DVP—Delivery Versus Payment

EBIT—Earnings Before Interest and Taxes

EBY—Equivalent Bond Yield

ECP—Eurocommercial Paper

ECSC—European Coal & Steel Community

ECU—European Currency Unit

EDR—European Depository Receipt

EDS—Enter Day Stop Order

EEC—European Economic Community

EFFAS—European Federation of Financial Analyst Societies

EFTA—European Free Trade Association

EIB—European Investment Bank

EMCF—European Monetary Cooperation Fund

EMS—European Monetary System

EOM—1) End of Month 2) Early Ownership Mortgage

EOS—Enter Open Stop Order

ERISA—Employees Retirement Income Securities Act

ESOP—Employee Stock Ownership Plan

ETC—Equipment Trust Certificate

ETM—Escrowed to Maturity

ETR—Estimated Total Return

ETY—Equivalent Taxable Yield

EUA—European Unit of Account

F—Foreign

FAC—Financial Assistance Corporation

Fannie Mae—Federal National Mortgage Association

Farmer Mac—Federal Agricultural Mortgage Corporation

FASB—Financial Accounting Standards Board

FBC—First Boston Corporation

FC—1) Final Confirmation 2) First Call Date 3) First Coupon Date

FCM—Futures Commission Merchant

FCOP—Foreign Currency Options Principal

FCO—Foreign Currency Option

FDIC—Federal Deposit Insurance Corporation

FED—Federal Reserve Board

Fed Wire—Federal Reserve Wire Network

FERARI—Floating Eurodollar Repackaged Assets of the Republic of Italy

FF—1) Federal Funds 2) French Franc

FFB—Federal Financing Bank

FGIC—Financial Guaranty Insurance Company

FHA—Federal Housing Administration

FHLB—Federal Home Loan Banks

FHLBB—Federal Home Loan Bank Board

FHLMC—Federal Home Loan Mortgage Corporation

FIBID—Frankfort Interbank Bid Rate

FIBOR—Frankfurt Interbank Offered Rate

FIC—Federal Intermediate Credit Bank

FICO—Financing Corporation

FIFO—First-In First-Out

FIMEAN—The mean between FIBOR and FIBID

FIN—Finance

FINOP—Financial and Operations Principal

FIVER—Five-year Treasury note futures contract

FIPS—Foreign Interest Payment Securities

FLB—Federal Land Banks

FLIP—Flexible Loan Insurance Program Mortgage

FMB—First Mortgage Bonds

FmHA—Farmers Home Administration

FNMA—Federal National Mortgage Association

FOB—1) The First Boston Corporation 2) Free on Board

FOK—Fill or Kill

FOMC—Federal Reserve Open Market Committee

FOTRA—Free of Tax to Residents Abroad

FRB—Federal Reserve Bank

FRCD—Floating Rate Certificate of Deposit

FRCMO—Floating Rate Collateralized Mortgage Obligation

Freddie Mac—Federal Home Loan Mortgage Corporation

FRN—Floating Rate Note

FSA—Financial Security Assurance

FSC—Foreign Sales Corporation

FSF—First Sinking Fund Date

FSLIC—Federal Savings and Loan Insuran e Corporation

FTD—Fail to Deliver

FTN—Foreign Targeted Note

FTR—Fail to Receive

FY—Fiscal Year

FYI—For Your Information

FYTR—Five-year Treasury note futures contract

GAAP—Generally Accepted Accounting Principles

GAN—Grant Anticipation Note

GASB—Governmental Accounting Standards Board

GAY NINETIES—3 1/2s of 2/15/90

GDP—Gross Domestic Product

GEM—Growing Equity Mortgage

GFOA—Government Finance Officers Association

GG—Government Guaranteed

GIC—1) Guaranteed Investment Contract 2) Government Insurance Corporation

Ginnie Mae—Government National Mortgage Association

GMC—Guaranteed Mortgage Certificate

GNMA—Government National Mortgage Association

GNP—Gross National Product

GO—General Obligation

GOV—Government

GPARM—Graduated Payment Adjustable Rate Mortgage

GPM—Graduated Payment Mortgage

GSA—General Services Administration

GSE—Government-Sponsored Enterprise

GTC—1) Good 'til Cancelled 2) Government Trust Certificate

GTD—Guaranteed Bond

GUN—Grantor Underwritten Note

GVT—Government

GYP'EMS—GNMA Graduated Payment Mortgage Securities

HAP—Housing Assistance Payment

HFA—Housing Finance Authority

HITS—High Income Trust Securities

HOME LOAN—Federal Home Loan Bank

HTG—Honest to God (Yield)

HTG CBE—Honest to God Corporate Bond Equivalent

HUD—Department of Housing and Urban Development

HUMPS—3 1/4s of 6/15/83-78

IA—Investment Advisor

IADB—Inter-American Development Bank

IASC—International Accounting Standards Committee

IB—Interbank

IBRD—International Bank for Reconstruction and Development

ICCH—International Commodities Clearing House

ID—Institutional Delivery

IDB—Industrial Development Bond

IDBI—Industrial Development Bond Insurance

IET—Interest Equalization Tax

IFC—International Finance Corporation

IMF—International Monetary Fund

IMM—International Monetary Market (at the Chicago Mercantile Exchange)

IND—Industrial

INDU—Industrial

IO—Interest Only

IOC—Immediate or Cancel

IOM—Index and Option Market

IPMA—International Primary Markets Association

IPO—Initial Public Offering

IRA—Individual Retirement Account

IRB—Industrial Revenue Bond

IRR—Internal Rate of Return

ISDA—International Swap Dealers Association

ISFD—Indexed Sinking Fund Debenture

ISO—Incentive Stock Option

ISRO—International Securities Regulatory Organization

ITC—Investment Tax Credit

ITM—In the Money

ITS—Intermarket Trading System

IVA—Inventory Valuation Adjustment

IYE—Interest Yield Equivalent

JAJO—January, April, July, October option expiration cycle

JAMES BOND—7 5/8s of 2/15/07

JDR—Japanese Depository Receipt

JEEPS—GNMA Graduated Payment Mortgage Securities

JT—Joint Tenants

JTWROS—Joint Tenants With Right of Survivorship

KCBT—Kansas City Board of Trade

KIM—Keep in Mind

LAND BANK—Federal Land Bank

LBO—Leveraged Buyout

LDC—Less Developed Country

LIBID—London Interbank Bid Rate

LIBOR—London Interbank Offered Rate

LIFFE—London International Financial Futures Exchange

LIFO—Last-In First-Out

LIMEAN—The mean of LIBOR and LIBID

LME—London Metal Exchange

LOBO—Lender's Option—Borrower's Option

LOC—Letter of Credit

LOI—Letter of Intent

LOIS—Limit Order Information System

LSE—London Stock Exchange

LTL—Less than full Truck Load

LTV—Loan to Value

M—1) Thousands (10M = 10,000) 2) Money Supply 3) Eligible for margin purchases

MARP—Maturing Adjustable Rate Preferred

MAT—Maturity

MBA—Mortgage Bankers Association

MBB—Mortgage-Backed Bond

MBIA—Municipal Bond Insurance Association

MBS—Mortgage Backed Security

MCC—Mortgage Credit Certificate

MCF—Mortgage Cash Flow Obligation

MERC—Chicago Mercantile Exchange

MEW—Measure of Economic Welfare

MF—Multifamily

MFOA—Municipal Finance Officers Association

MFP—Matched Funding Program

MI—Mortgage Issuer

MIDANET—Mortgage Information Direct Access Network

MIF—Market Inventory Fund

MIG—Moody's Investment Grade

MIP—1) Mortgage Insurance Premium 2) Monthly Investment Plan

MIT—1) Market if Touched 2) Municipal Investment Trust

MMC—Money Market Certificate

MMDA—Money Market Deposit Account

MN—Master Note

MOB—Municipals Over Bonds (municipal to Treasury bond spread)

MOF—Ministry of Finance (of Japan)

MOFF—Multiple-Option Financing Facility

MOTORCYCLES—Guaranteed Mortgage Certificates

MPT—Modern Portfolio Theory

M&R—Maintenance and Replacement

MRB—Mortgage Revenue Bond

MRS—Mortgage-Related Security

MSRB—Municipal Securities Rulemaking Board

MSVR—Mandatory Security Valuation Reserve

MTG—Mortgage

MTN—Medium Term Note

Muni—Municipal

NABL—National Association of Bond Lawyers

NAPM—National Association of Purchasing Management

NASD—National Association of Securities Dealers

NASDAQ—National Association of Securities Dealers Automated Quotations

NAV—Net Asset Value

NC—Non-Callable

NCC—National Clearing Corporation

NFA—National Futures Association

NH—Not Held

NIB—Nordic Investment Bank

NIBOR—New York Interbank Offered Rate

NIC—1) Newly Industrialized Country 2) Net Interest Cost

NICKELS—8 1/4s of 5/15/05-00

NIDS—National Institutional Delivery System

NIF—Note Issuance Facility

NIT—New Investment Technology

NOB—Notes Over Bonds (Treasury note-bond yield spread)

NOL—Net Operating Loss

NOO—Non-Owner Occupied

NOW—Negotiable Order of Withdrawal

NR—Not Rated

NYFE—New York Futures Exchange

NYSE—New York Stock Exchange

OARS—Opening Automated Report Service

OB—Or Better

OBO—Order Book Official

OCC—Options Clearing Corporation

OCO—One Cancels Other

OECD—Organization for Economic Cooperation and Development

OID—Original Issue Discount

OIP—Original Issue Premium

OMC—Open Market Committee

O&O—Own and Offer

OPD—Opening Delayed

OPEC—Organization of Petroleum Exporting Countries

OPM—1) Other People's Money 2) Option Pricing Model

OPRA—Options Price Reporting Authority

OSS—Order Support System

OTC—Over the Counter

OTM—Out of the Money

OW—Offer Wanted

P—Put Option

PAC—Planned Amortization Class

PACE—Philadelphia Automated Communication and Execution

P and L—Profit and Loss

PAR—Price Adjusted Rate

PBGC—Pension Benefit Guaranty Corporation

PBW—Philadelphia-Baltimore-Washington Exchange

PC—Participation Certificate

PCR—Pollution Control Revenue Bond

P/E—Price/Earnings Ratio

PENNY'S—8s of 8/15/01-96

PER—Post Execution Reporting

PFD—Preferred

PHA—Public Housing Authority

PIG—Passive-Income Generator

PIK—Pay in Kind

PITI—Principal, Interest, Taxes, and Insurance

PLC—Public Limited Company

PMI—Private Mortgage Insurance

PN—Project Note

PO—Principal Only

POS—Preliminary Official Statement

PPI—Producer Price Index

PPM—Private Placement Memorandum

PPP—Purchasing Power Parity

PPSE—Prepaid Syndicate Expense

PRO—Planned Redemption Obligation

PSA—Public Securities Association

PSBR—Public Sector Borrowing Requirement

PSR—Price-Sales Ratio

PT—Point

PUD—Planned Unit Development

PUF—Prime Underwriting Facility

PV—1) Present Value 2) Par Value

PX—Price

Q—Bankrupt

QT—Questioned Trade

Q-TIP—Qualified Terminable Interest Property
RAM—Reverse Annuity Mortgage
RAN—Revenue Anticipation Note
RAP—Regulatory Accounting Principles
RBO—Receive Balance Order
REIT—Real Estate Investment Trust
REMIC—Real Estate Mortgage Investment Conduit
REO—Real Estate Owned
RFC—Regulated Futures Contract
RNY—Required Net Yield
ROA—Return on Assets
ROE—Return on Equity
ROI—Return on Investment
ROM—Rollover Mortgage
ROP—Registered Options Principal
RP—Repurchase Agreement
RPI—Retail Price Index
RR—1) Reinvestment Rate 2) Registered Representative
RRM—Renegotiated Rate Mortgage
RTD—Rated
RUF—Revolving Underwriting Facility
RVP—Receipt Versus Payment
RW—Regular Way
S—Shares
SABRES—Share Adjusted Broker Remarketed Equity Securities
Sally Mae—Student Loan Marketing Association
SAM—Shared Appreciation Mortgage
SAPR—Seasonally Adjusted Prepayment Rate
SBA—Small Business Administration
SCC—Stock Clearing Corporation
SCFP—Statement of Changes in Financial Position
SDR—Special Drawing Rights
SEC—Securities and Exchange Commission

SECO—Securities and Exchange Commission Organization

SEP—Simplified Employee Pension Plan

SF—1) Sinking Fund 2) Single-Family

SFL—Spread for Life

SIA—Securities Industry Association

SIAC—Securities Industry Automation Corporation

SIB—Securities and Investment Board

SIBOR—Singapore Interbank Offered Rate

SIPA—Securities Investors Protection Act of 1970

SJ—Subject

SK—Safekeeping

S&L—Savings and Loan

SLD—Sold

SLGS—State and Local Government Series Bonds

SLMA—Student Loan Marketing Association

SLOB—Secured Lease Obligation Bond

SM—Simple Margin

SMA—Special Miscellaneous Account

SMBS—Stripped Mortgage-Backed Securities

SMM—Single Monthly Mortality

SMMEA—Secondary Mortgage Market Enhancement Act

SN—Serial Note

SNIF—Short-Term Note Issuance Facility

SOB—Special Obligation Bond

SOES—Small Order Execution System

SOP—1) Statement of Policy 2) Standard Operating Procedures

SOREX—Special Order Routing and Execution System

SOYD—Sum of the Years' Digits

S&P—Standard and Poor's

SPA—1) Standard Prepayment Assumption 2) Special Premium Annuity

SPDA—Single Premium Deferred Annuity

SRO—1) Self Regulatory Organization 2) Scheduled Redemption Obligation

SROP—Senior Registered Option Principal

STAR—Short-Term Auction Rate (Preferred Stock)

STG—Sterling

STIF—Short-Term Investment Funds

STREMIC—Securitized Real Estate Mortgage Investment Conduit

STRIPS—Separately Traded Registered Interest and Principal Security

SUB—1) Subsidiary 2) Subject 3) Subordinated

T—Treasury

TAA—Tactical Asset Allocation

TAB—Tax Anticipation Bill

TAC—Targeted Amortization Class

TAGSS—Triple-A Guaranteed Secondary Securities

TAN—Tax Anticipation Note

TBA—To Be Announced

TED—Treasury Bill to Euro-Dollar Spread

TEFRA—Tax Equity and Fiscal Responsibility Act of 1982

TEL—Telephone

TENR—Tax-Exempt Note Rate

TFTV—Total Financing-to-Value

THDA—Tennessee Housing Development Agency

TIC—1) True Interest Cost 2) Tenants in Common

TIGR—Treasury Investment Growth Receipt

TIL—Truth in Lending

TIN—Tax Identification Number

TLTV—Total Loan-to-Value

TR—Treasury Receipt

TSY—Treasury

TTV—Trading to Total Volume

TVA—Tennessee Valley Authority

UGMA—Uniform Gifts to Minors Act

UIT—Unit Investment Trust

UPB—Unpaid Balance

UR—Under Review

USGG—United States Government-Guaranteed

USM—Unlisted Securities Market

UT—Unlimited Tax Bond

UTIL—Utility

VA—Veterans Administration

VDN—Variable Duration Note

VRM—Variable Rate Mortgage

VTP—Variable Term Preferred

WABO—We Are Buyers Of

WAC—Weighted Average Coupon

WAL—Weighted Average Life

WAM—Weighted Average Maturity

WARM—Weighted Average Remaining Maturity

WART—Weighted Average Remaining Term

WASO—We Are Sellers Of

WAVER—Weighted Average Expected Return

WB—We Bid

WBF—We Bid Firm

WBR—We Buy Retail

WBS—We Bid Subject

WD—When Distributed

WPPSS—Washington Public Power Supply System

WI—When Issued

WO—We Offer

WOF—We Offer Firm

WOR—We Offer Retail

WOS—We Offer Subject

WOW—With Or Without

WPI—Wholesale Price Index

WROS—With Rights of Survivorship

WSJ—Wall Street Journal

WT—Warrant

WW—With Warrants

X—1) Without interest 2) Ex-Dividend

XCH—Ex-Clearing House

XD—Ex-Dividend

XR—Ex-Rights

XW—Ex-Warrants

YLD—Yield

YTAL—Yield to Average Life

YTC—Yield to Call

YTM—Yield to Maturity

YTOD—Yield to Operative Date

YTP—Yield to Put

UTILITIES

APPLE—Appalachian Power

ARKIE—Arkansas Power & Light

ARKLOUIE—Arkansas Louisiana Gas (or ARKLA)

BAMA—Alabama Power

BEE GEE—Baltimore Gas & Electric

BELL CAN—Bell Telephone of Canada

BLIP—Bell Telephone of Pennsylvania

BUG—Brooklyn Union Gas

CEE WEE—Commonwealth Edison

CHES POT—Chesapeake & Potomac Telephone of Maryland, Virginia, etc.

CIL—Central Illinois Light

CIP—Central Illinois Public Service

CINCY BELL—Cincinnati Bell Telephone

COC—Columbus & Southern Ohio Electric

CON ED—Consolidated Edison (or EDISON)

CON NAT—Consolidated Natural Gas

CPL—Carolina Power & Light

CSM—Consumers Power

CVX—Cleveland Electric Illumination

DEWAP—Department of Water and Power of Los Angeles

DUKE—Duke Power

FLIPPER—FPL Group, Inc. (formerly Florida Power & Light Co.)

FPC—Florida Power Corporation

HANGNAIL—Houston Natural Gas Corporation (HNG)

IBT—Illinois Bell Telephone

IGLOO—Iowa Illinois Gas & Electric

JENNY TEL—General Telephone of California, Midwest, Northeast, etc.

JYP—Jersey Central Power & Light (or GYPPER)

LILCO—Long Island Lighting

LOLLYPOP—Louisiana Power & Light

MA BELL—American Telephone & Telegraph

MASS ELEC—Massachusetts Electric

MET ED—Metropolitan Edison

MICH BELL—Michigan Bell Telephone

MICH CON GAS—Michigan Consolidated Gas

MICH WISH—Michigan Wisconsin Pipeline

MON DAK—Montana Dakota Utilities

NET—New England Telephone & Telegraph

NIP—Northern Illinois Power

NIPPER—Northern Indiana Public Service

NMK—Niagara Mohawk Power

NO NAT—Northern Natural Gas

NOPPER—New Orleans Public Service

OBT—Ohio Bell Telephone

OKIE—Oklahoma Gas & Electric

PAC GAS—Pacific Gas & Electric (or PCG)

PAC TEL—Pacific Telephone & Telegraph

PEGGY—Public Service Electric & Gas (of New Jersey)

PHILLY ELEC—Philadelphia Electric

PIN—Public Service of Indiana

PP&L—Pennsylvania Power & Light

PSR—Public Service of Colorado

SERI—Systems Energy Resource, Inc.

SNET—Southern New England Telephone

SO BELL—Southern California Edison

SWEP—Southwestern Public Service

TEDDY—Toledo Edison

TEL STRIPS—American Telephone & Telegraph 8 3/4s of 5/15/00 ex-warrants

TRANSCO—Transcontinental Pipeline

VEPCO—Virginia Electric & Power

WHISKEY TEL—Wisconsin Telephone

WIGGLEY—Washington Gas Light (WGL)

ZIPPER—Arizona Public Service

Industrials and Rails

ALCAN—Aluminum Company of Canada

ARCO—Atlantic Richfield (or RICHFIELD)

ATCH—Atchison, Topeka & Santa Fe

BAG—Union Camp

BARE ASS—Boeing (BA)

BENNY—Beneficial Finance

BESSY—Bethlehem Steel (BS)

BIG BLUE—International Business Machines (IBM)

BIG STEEL—United States Steel (USX)

BISCUIT—National Biscuit

B&O—Baltimore & Ohio Railroad

BOA—Bank of America

BUNNY—Playboy Enterprises, Inc.

CALIFORNIA—Standard Oil of California (or CAL)

CAN—American Can

CANPAC—Canadian Pacific Railway

CARBIDE—Union Carbide

CASH REGISTER—National Cash Register

CAT—Caterpillar Tractor

COTTON BELT—St. Louis Southwestern Railway

CRAZY MARY—Community Psychiatric Centers (CMX)

DAIRY—National Dairy Products

DEADHEAD—Dayton Hudson (DH)

DECK—Digital Equipment (DEC)

EYE BEEM—International Business Machines (IBM)

FAMILY—Family Finance

FIRE TIRE—Firestone

GE—General Electric

GEE-MAC—General Motors Acceptance Corporation

JENNY TEL—General Telephone and Electronics

HARVESTER—International Harvester

HOUSEHOLD—Household Finance

INDIANA—Standard Oil of Indiana

IOL—Interstate Oil Pipeline

KNOCKOUT—Coca-Cola (KO)

L&N—Louisville & Nashville Railroad

LOUSY LOUIE—Louisiana Land & Exploration (LLX)

MAD DOG—McDonnell Douglas (MD)

MONKEY—Montgomery Ward

MONKEY CREDIT—Montgomery Ward Credit

MOP—Missouri Pacific Railroad

MOTOR—General Motors (GM)

OATS—Quaker Oats

PENNY—J.C. Penney

PIE IN THE SKY—Piedmont Aviation (PIE)

PROCTER—Procter & Gamble (or P&G)

PUSSY—Pillsbury (PSY)

RADIO—R.C.A.

REBECCA—Republic Steel

RUBBER—United States Rubber

SEARS—Sears, Roebuck & Co.

SLOB—Schlumberger (SLB)

SO-PAC—Southern Pacific

STANDING ROOM ONLY—Southland Royalty (SRO)

TANK—Union Tank Car

TEX-PAC—Texas & Pacific Railway

TI—Texas Instruments

TOBACCO—American Tobacco

TRAP—SOHIO BP Pipeline

TRIPLE MARY—Minnesota Mining & Manufacturing (MMM)

T-WAY—Trans World Airlines

UKELELE—Union Carbide (UK)

UP—Union Pacific Railroad

WET MARY—Western Maryland Railroad

WEYER—Weyerhaeuser

WICKY—Warner Communications (WCI)

YELLOW BELLY—Youngstown Sheet & Tube

Bond Market Etymology

English has a teeming vocabulary, most of which has roots in other languages. The German satirist Kurt Tucholsky said much the same thing in a slightly exaggerated and hostile way: "English is both a simple and difficult language. It has no grammar, and the vocabulary consists entirely of foreign words—which are mispronounced."

Our foreign heritage is particularly noticeable in the bond market. This appendix lists the foreign origins of over 150 common bond market terms. The word "etymology" is from two Greek words meaning true account. For millenia etymology belonged to the realms of guesswork and folklore, producing mistaken and sometimes humorous results. For example, the Greek word for heaven was thought to consist of several smaller words meaning "from looking at things above"; "Rome" was thought to come from the name of one of its founders (Romulus); "pontiff" was thought to come from *pons* (bridge) plus *fex* (maker) instead of the linguistically correct *pontifex* (priest); and "testicles" was thought to come from the Latin word for witness (*testes*), the testicles being a witness to one's virility. Plato makes fun of searching for word origins as an amateur pursuit in the dialogue *Cratylus*. Despite Plato's authority, however, etymology continued to be a favorite pastime among literate Romans, and the medieval authors Cassiodorus and Isidore of Seville wrote etymologies. The modern discipline, using phonetic laws and philology, produces more accurate results.

Abatement—From a Latin word meaning to beat down.

Accrue—From a Latin word meaning to grow.

Ad Valorem—From the Latin for according to value.

Agency—From a Greek word meaning to do or to drive.

Amortize—From two Latin words meaning toward death.

Arbitrage—From a Latin word meaning to give judgment, or to act as umpire.

Asset—From a Latin word meaning enough. The Anglo-French legal term that derived from the Latin meant having enough property to pay debts.

Assumable—From a Latin word meaning to take or to adopt.

Auction—From a Latin word meaning to increase.

Audit—From a Latin word meaning to hear.

Ax (to Grind)—This phrase comes from Charles Miner's story "Who'll Turn the Grindstone," published in 1811. In the story, a man with a dull ax flatters a boy and inveigles him into turning his father's grindstone while he sharpens his ax. Thus the phrase came to mean having something to do, and getting someone else to do it.

Bank—From a Germanic, and later an Italian, word meaning a money exchanger's table. The word mountebank comes from the Italian for climb on a bench, which is exactly what quacks and vendors did to attract customers.

Bankrupt—From the Germanic word for money exchanger's table plus the Latin word meaning broken. A bankrupt man was metaphorically broken. Taken literally, a bankrupt man had his bench (i.e., money table) broken.

Billion—French for million to the second power. In England this derivation is taken literally (billion = 10^{12}). In America, billion = 10^9.

Blackmail—The ancient Scottish word for rent is mail. If paid in silver, it was called white mail; if paid in cattle or grain, it was called black mail. Tribute money (in the form of cattle and grain) paid to outlaws became known as blackmail.

Black Monday—The day after Easter, and the anniversary of several English disasters: the massacre of 500 English by the Irish in Dublin in 1209; large losses sustained by the Black Prince, Edward, Prince of Wales, while invading France in 1357; and losses sustained by Edward III during the siege of Paris in 1360.

Blue Chip—This synonym for gilt-edged, or high quality investment comes from the game of poker, in which the blue chip is the most valuable (followed by the red and white chips).

Blue Sky—Laws designed to protect the public from securities fraud. So-called because of a reported statement by a Kansas legislator on the enactment day of the first state securities law in the early 1900s: "Now Kansas citizens will have more of a basis for making investment decisions than merely by the shade of blue sky."

Bogey—This word probably comes from a Welsh root meaning a threat, an object of terror, or something that causes annoyance.

Borrow—From an Anglo-Saxon word meaning to protect or to give a pledge.

Bourse—From a Greek word meaning bull's hide. The Phoenician Pygmalion, nephew of the biblical Queen Jezebel, was the king of Tyre. When Pygmalion murdered Sychaeus for his wealth, Sychaeus' widow fled to North Africa. Her name was Dido, whose tribulations are recorded in Vergil's *Aeneid*. Dido is credited with founding Carthage by the following ruse. Having made a deal with the local inhabitants to buy as much land as could be contained by a bull's hide, she cut the hide into thin strips and laid the boundaries of Carthage (north of Tunis). The area measured out was called Byrsa (hide). Dido's followers built three walls around the Byrsa, which contained a citadel and a shelter for three hundred elephants and four thousand horses. Descendants of these beasts later crossed the Alps with another famous Carthaginian, Hannibal, to attack the Romans. The word Byrsa became the Latin word for sack, the English purse, and the French word for stock exchange.

Broker—From a Latin word meaning a pointed stick. A broker originally broached wine, or pierced holes in a wine casket with a spike.

Buck—From the English buckskin, a popular frontier unit of trade. Not the same buck as in "pass the buck" or "the buck stops here," which is from the buckhorn knife. Passing the buck at a poker game meant pointing the knife to the next dealer.

Budget—From a fifteenth-century French word for purse.

Bull and Bear—As market slang, these words were originally used as verbs, in the sense of causing prices to rise and fall, respectively. For example, a writer in the *Chicago Times* of 4 June 1881 speculates that "If we succeed in bulling silver we shall also succeed in bearing gold to the same extent." Although the origins of the slang use of bull and bear are not known with certainty, it is probable that they derive from animal combat tactics: a bull tends to throw its opponent up with its horns, while a bear more cautiously tends to throw its opponent down. Observation of these tactics was commonplace because of bullbaiting and bearbaiting, popular public spectacles from the twelfth to the nineteenth centuries, in which a bull or a bear was tethered to a stake and forced to fight with specially trained dogs. It was common at these spectacles to see bulls toss dogs upward and bears throw dogs downward. In a nineteenth-century variation on the American frontier, a chained bull was matched against a grizzly bear in a battle to the death.

Instances of similar contests appear in ancient cultures. A Roman mosaic (Mosaic of the Dar Buc Ammera from Zliten) from the second century A.D. pictures a naked gladiator trying to separate a bull tied to a chained bear. Not surprisingly, the bear is pawing the bull's head downward while the bull, just as ferociously, tries to thrust the bear upward with its horns. Several centuries earlier an Etruscan artist cast a burial urn on which several men lead a bull toward a chained bear, presumably to engage in combat.

"Bear" may also derive from an eighteenth-century proverb from the London exchange about "selling a bearskin" (before the bear was caught). The proverb defines bearish market strategy: selling what one doesn't own in the hope of buying it at a lower price. Speculators in London's Exchange Alley were called bearskin jobbers. The term became popular after the South Sea Bubble burst in 1720, making fortunes for speculators who sold South Sea Company stock short. "Bear skin" is still English slang for stock. Brokers who went bankrupt were called lame ducks (unkind spectators watched them waddle out of the Alley).

Business—From an Anglo-Saxon word meaning busy or anxious.

Calendar—From a Greek word meaning to proclaim or summon. The Latin word that derives from the Greek means the first day of each month, on which interest was due, and then the book in which a money changer kept records.

Capital—From a Latin word meaning belonging to the head. The word came to mean cattle, which was literally live stock, or a means of exchange.

Cash—From a Latin word meaning chest, in which ready money was kept.

Charter—From an Egyptian word meaning papyrus, on which contracts were written.

Churn—From a Middle English word for a vessel for making butter.

Class—From a Latin word meaning a constitutional division of the Roman people. The Latin word came to mean army or fleet. The Greek root of the Latin word meant a breaking (into parts).

Client—From a Greek word meaning to hear. A client is one who listens.

Coin—From a Latin word meaning wedge, because coins were stamped by means of a wedge.

Collateral—From two Latin words meaning side by side.

Commingle—Commingle has roots in two languages. A Latin prefix and an English stem together mean to mix.

Commodity—From a Latin word meaning convenient.

Conduit—From an Old French word for canal.

Conglomerate—From two Latin words meaning to form into a ball or globe.

Consortium—From two Latin words meaning a lot or a share in common.

Contango—Probably from a Spanish word meaning to repress, curb, or contain.

Convertible—From a Latin word meaning to turn.

Convexity—From two Latin words meaning to bring together, or to unite by an arch. The graph of a security's convexity usually is in the form of an arch.

Corporation—From a Latin word meaning body.

Corpus—From a Latin word meaning body.

Coupon—From a Greek word meaning a blow on the ear, presumably hard enough to knock it off. It came to mean cut or a piece cut off, and a series of conjoined certificates that were to be clipped.

Covenant—From a Latin word meaning to come together, or to assemble, which came to mean to come together in the sense of to agree.

Credit—From a Latin word meaning to entrust or to loan.

Currency—From a Latin word meaning to run, which later meant to flow.

Custodian—From a Greek word meaning to hide. The Latin term meant to guard.

Cyclical—From a Greek word meaning circle.

Data—From a Latin word meaning things given.

Deal—From an Anglo-Saxon word meaning to divide and share (as in to deal cards).

Debenture—Latin for they are due. Latin receipts began with the words *debentur mihi* (they are due to me).

Defalcation—From a Latin word meaning to cut with a sickle.

Default—From two Latin words meaning a failing.

Defeasance—From two Latin words meaning to undo, which in Old French came to mean to render [a deed] null and void.

Deliver—From two Latin words meaning to set free.

Deposit—From a Latin word meaning to put aside.

Depreciate—From two Latin words meaning to go down in price.

Diligence—From a Greek word meaning to choose. The Latin word meant not only to choose but also to love.

Dime—From a Latin word meaning one-tenth.

Dispersion—From a Latin word meaning to scatter.

Dividend—From a Latin word meaning to divide.

Dollar—From the Germanic word for valley. Silver was discovered near Prague, in the valley of the town of Joachim, in 1516. The Count of Schlick, who owned the land, minted his own coins, imprinted with the face of St. Joachim. The coin was called *Joachimsthaler,* meaning "of the valley of Joachim," which contracted to *thaler,* which became the English dollar.

Dynamic—From a Greek word meaning power.

Economics—From two Greek words meaning household laws.

Electric—From the Greek word for amber (*electron*), with which the Greeks discovered static electricity in the seventh century B.C.

Eleemosynary—From a Greek word meaning compassion, or alms.

Emolument—From a Latin word meaning a miller's toll.

Entrepreneur—From an Old French word meaning to undertake.

Escrow—From an old Germanic word meaning scroll, on which deeds were written.

Exchequer—The English term for the government department in charge of public revenue comes from "chequers board," because accounting calculations in the twelfth century in England were made on a square table that resembled one. The word for checkers comes from the ancient Persian word for chess as well as the game's most important piece, the king (*shah*). The Arabs took the Persian game to Spain in the middle ages, where the word became *xaque.* It then became *eschec* in Old French and *chek* in Middle English. Checkmate means the king is dead.

Farm—From the Latin word for fixed or settled. The English word originally meant annual rent; a farmer collected the rent. In the sixteenth century, the term came to mean the land that was rented.

Federal—From a Latin word meaning treaty, covenant, or league.

Fee—From a Middle English word meaning property or cattle.

Fidelity—From a Latin word meaning faith.

Fiduciary—From a Latin word meaning trust.

Finance—From a Latin word meaning a settled payment or to pay a fine or tax. In Old French the word came to mean gift, and in Middle English it meant money supply.

Foreign—From a Latin word meaning out of doors. *See* Economics.

Forward—From a Middle English word meaning promise.

Franc—From the French word for Frenchman. When John II minted a new coin in the fourteenth century (he needed to debase the currency in order to raise enough money to pay the English for his ransom), he had the Latin phrase *Johannes Dei gracia Francorum rex* (John, by the grace of God, King of the Franks) and an image of himself on horseback imprinted on it. The coin became known as *franc a cheval* (a Franc with a horse), and simply as franc. The name originally comes from the Roman name for a Germanic tribe—the Franci. After they won their independence from a weakened Roman Empire, the word frank came to mean free.

Fund—From a Latin word meaning piece of land.

Fundamentals—From a Latin word meaning foundation, or bottom.

Gilt—From a Germanic word meaning to cover with gold. The original gilt certificates had gold edges (now the certificates are green).

Gnome—From a Greek word meaning to know or an opinion.

Government—From a Greek word meaning to steer a ship.

Governor—From a Greek word meaning helmsman.

Green Shoe—Provision so called because it was used first for an equity offering of the Green Shoe Company.

Guarantee—From a Germanic root meaning warrant. The Old High German *w* became *w*, then *gu*, and finally *g* in Old French. In Old French, guarantee and warrant are the same word.

Host—From a Latin word meaning someone who takes strangers into his home.

Hybrid—From a Greek word meaning sow or hog.

Hypothecate—From two Greek words meaning to place beneath, or an under-prop. It came to mean to pledge, or to mortgage, in the sense that the pledged property remained with the debtor until default.

Immunize—From two Latin words meaning exempt from public or military service.

Income—From two English words meaning an influx, an arrival, or a coming in.

Indenture—From two Latin words meaning in teeth, which became an Old French word meaning to indent. Indentures originally were cut with indented, or serrated, edges. Each party to the contract kept an indented portion of the contract, which was needed to put the entire contract back together.

Inflation—From two Latin words meaning to blow into.

Interest—From a Latin word meaning to be lost.

Inventory—From the Latin word meaning to find.

Invest—From a Latin word meaning to clothe.

Judgment—From two Latin words meaning to point out what is law.

Junk—From an Old French word meaning old rope.

Launder—From a Latin word meaning things to be washed. Ironically, in finance, as in politics, launder has become a dirty word.

Liability—From a Latin word meaning to bind.

Manipulation—From two Latin words meaning to fill the hand.

Margin—From a Latin word meaning a brink or a border.

Market—From a Latin word meaning to buy.

Maturity—From a Latin word meaning ripe.

Million—An Old Italian word meaning a great thousand. Latin for million was too bulky (*deciens centena milia,* meaning ten hundred thousand).

Money—Carthaginian term that became the Latin epithet for Juno, because her temple in Rome housed the mint. Romans appealed to the goddess Juno for help in battle. In appreciation for her help, they dedicated a temple to her in the forum, giving it the name Moneta—the advisor. Silver coins, first produced in this temple in 269 B.C., were called moneta, to distinguish them from earlier copper coins. Our words money, monetary, and mint all come from the Roman Moneta.

Monopoly—From two Greek words meaning sole barterer.

Mortgage—From two Latin words meaning dead pledge. The Church in the middle ages loaned money to nobles, secured by a pledge of land. The loan was a live pledge if the revenue contributed to repayment of principal. The loan was a dead pledge if the debt was not reduced by the payments. Thus mortgages, in the original sense of the term, could not be paid down.

By the seventeenth century there was another interpretation of the origin of the word: the pledge (property) was dead to the borrower if he missed a payment, and dead to the lender if the borrower made the payments. In the words of the famous English jurist Sir Edward Coke, "It seemeth that the cause why it is called mortgage is, for that it is doubtful whether the Feoffor will pay at the day limited such summe or not, & if he doth not pay, then the Land which is put in pledge upon condition for the payment of the money, is taken from him for euer, and so dead to him upon condition &c. And if he doth pay the money, then the pledge is dead as to the Tenant, &c."

Municipal—From a Latin word meaning a free citizen, that is, one who takes public office.

Negotiate—From two Latin words meaning not having leisure.

Nickel—From an old Teutonic word for demon. German copper miners before the mid-eighteeth century were fooled by an ore that looked like copper when they excavated it but turned out to be worthless. They thought a demon entered the copper ore and transformed it into what they called *kupfernickel* (copper demon). When nickel was first isolated from copper in 1751, it was named after the miners' demon.

Obligation—From a Latin word meaning to bind.

Option—From a Latin word meaning a chosen one, referring to Roman soldiers who handled administrative matters.

Origination—From a Latin word meaning to rise. Orient, the place where the sun rises, has the same root.

Orthodox—From two Greek words meaning right opinion.

Ounce—A Roman unit of currency was a pound of copper (*as*), which was divided into twelve *unciae*, which became the English ounce and inch. Ten ounces of copper (ten *asses*) was called a *denarius*, which became the Spanish *dinero*. The first letter of the Latin *denarius* was used by the British to abbreviate penny.

Panic—From a Greek word for the god Pan.

Par—From a Latin word meaning equal.

Pari Passu—Latin words meaning with equal step, or side by side.

Pecuniary—From a Latin word meaning flock. In many ancient states, including Sumeria, Babylonia, Egypt, and early Greece and Rome, cattle were the standard of value.

Penny—Perhaps from the eighth-century B.C. Mercian king Penda, who first minted pennies. For the British abbreviation for penny, *see* Ounce.

Pension—From a Latin word meaning to weigh out or pay.

Peruvian Bond—Slang for a worthless security, so called because National City Bank president Charles E. Mitchell pushed two ill-fated Peruvian bond issues in 1928 and 1929.

Pound—The sign for pound sterling stands for libra, Latin for pound, which came from a Greek word for a pound (twelve ounce) silver coin minted in Sicily. Libra, originally the pair of scales still used as a sign of the zodiac, was also the root of the Italian lira.

Position—From a Latin word meaning to put in place.

Preferred—From two Latin words meaning to bear before, or to have priority.

Principal—From two Latin words meaning first head, which became one Latin word meaning chief or prince.

Prospectus—From two Latin words meaning to look before.

Quality—From a Latin word meaning "of what kind?"

Random—From an Old French word meaning to run or haphazard.

Rank—From a Germanic root meaning circle or ring, originally referring to a line of soldiers.

Redemption—From a Latin word meaning to buy back.

Red Herring—So called because the disclaimer is printed in red. The term may derive from English fox hunting. To train dogs to follow scent, hunters would drag a red (cured) herring over the ground. A red herring came to be known as something that put one on (or off) the right track.

Rent—From a Latin word meaning to render. In Old French *rentes* is an annual income on an annuity. A French *rentier* received income from *rentes*.

Revenue—Latin for that which is returned to one.

Risk—From a Latin word meaning to cut back. A Spanish word derived from the Latin root means a steep, abrupt rock, or a rock that has been sheared or cut off (this kind of rock being a danger to sailors).

Salary—From a Latin word meaning salt. Salary was originally money given to Roman soldiers for salt.

Scalper—Scalp has several linguistic roots, which have in common the concept of an outer covering. The Scandinavian root means skin of the head, the medieval Dutch and the Old French roots mean shell, the Middle Swedish and Icelandic roots mean sheath, and a Danish root means husk. Latin and Germanic verbs with similar roots mean to cut or peel off. Hence a scalpel is a surgical instrument used for precise cutting. A scalper, in a different context, takes something off the top.

Scrip—From a Scandinavian word meaning scrap or wallet.

Secular—From a Latin word meaning generation, or belonging to the age.

Security—From two Latin words meaning free from care.

Speculator—From a Latin word meaning to look at. A related Latin word means to behold from a watch tower. Perhaps from the Etruscan *haruspex*, a reader of entrails.

Sterilize—From a Greek word meaning a barren cow.

Stochastic—From a Greek word meaning to aim, or to guess at. Mathematicians on Wall Street use stochastic methods with problems involving a random variable and probability.

Stock—A financial term borrowed from animal husbandry. Cattle, in ancient times a unit of currency, were live stock. Adam Smith, well aware of the origins of finance and trading, called gold and silver dead stock. For other terms with similar bovine origins, *see* Bourse, Capital, Fee, Pecuniary, Sterilize, and Watered Stock.

Supply—From two Latin words meaning to fill up.

Swap—From a Middle English word meaning to strike. It was used in the sense of swapping off someone's head as well as swapping hands to seal a bargain.

Syndicate—From two Greek words meaning with justice.

Synthetic—From two Greek words meaning to put together. A synthetic transaction is created by, among other things, putting securities and risk management tools together.

Tariff—From the Arabic word for inventory. By coincidence, the Arabic town at the tip of the Rock of Gibraltar, from which Moorish pirates sailed to exact tribute from ships passing through the straights, was Tarifa.

Tax—From a Latin word meaning to touch.

Technicals—From a Greek word meaning art, or belonging to the arts.

Thrift—From an Icelandic word meaning to clutch or seize.

Tranche—From an Old French word meaning a slice.

Treasury—From a Greek root meaning to lay up (hoard) or to put. From the same root are thesaurus (a hoard of knowledge) and apothecary (keeper of a hoard of goods). The Latin *tresuiri* was a three-man board directing the Roman mint, established 269 B.C.

Underwriter—Originally a Greek citizen who guaranteed a state debt.

Undigested—Term coined by J. P. Morgan to refer to unbought securities.

Vintage—From two Latin words meaning to gather grapes, which came to mean the year of a particular harvest.

Volatility—From a Latin word meaning to fly.

Volume—From the Latin word for scroll. The Latin word for rolling (what a reader does to a scroll) was *volvo*; the scroll was called *volumen*, or the thing that is rolled. When books replaced scrolls, they were called volumes. Volume ultimately acquired the meaning of anything large.

Wall Street—So called because of the wall of brush and mud built along the street (originally a dirt path), shortly after the Dutch founded New York as a trading post in 1609. The wall, later fortified with a wooden fence, was intended to keep cows from wandering out and Indians from wandering in.

Warrant—Possibly from a Germanic word for man, that is, someone who offered himself as a surety.

Watered Stock—This term has its origins not in foreign languages but in a kind of manipulation. Cattlemen used to feed their cattle (stock) salt in order to make them drink large quantities of water. The cattle then appeared heavier, and were therefore more valuable, in the marketplace. The most famous case involves Daniel Drew, who in his early days as a cattle drover cheated butcher Heinrich Astor, brother of John Jacob Astor.

Wealth—From an Anglo-Saxon word plus suffix meaning a condition or state of well being.

Yield—From a Teutonic word meaning to pay.